Course	Personal Selling
Course Number	**MKT 301**
	Dominic Nucera
	La Salle University

http://create.mheducation.com

ISBN-10: 1121465730   ISBN-13: 9781121465732

Contents

Credits

chapter **1**

SELLING AND SALESPEOPLE

SOME QUESTIONS ANSWERED IN THIS CHAPTER ARE

- What is selling?
- Why should you learn about selling even if you do not plan to be a salesperson?
- What is the role of personal selling in a firm?
- What are the different types of salespeople?
- What are the rewards of a selling career?

PROFILE

PROFILE I have always been a people person and someone that enjoys a challenge. My name is Lauren Bearden, and I am a 2009 graduate of the Northern Illinois University Sales Program. I began my college career at Northern not knowing what field of study I wanted to pursue, but after meeting with the career services team, it became apparent that my true fit would be the college of business. From that point it was an easy decision that marketing should be my field of study—I'm outgoing and love working with people and learning about new products.

In my first marketing class I learned about the Professional Selling Program at Northern. It is a selective entry program and one of the top sales programs in the country. My parents had always said I would be good in sales, so I thought I would give it a shot. Also, as a competitive person, the idea of getting into a top program posed a task that I was up to.

In order to enter the program, I had to not only interview, but also conduct a role play trying to sell a textbook to the head of our sales program, Dr. Dan Weilbaker. Sitting in front of Dr. Weilbaker was my first experience selling ever, and I have to admit I was so nervous I let out a string of "word vomit" (as Dr. Weilbaker calls it) during my presentation. I was on my agenda and didn't give my "client" the opportunity to tell me the key information I needed to hear to get the sale. While I couldn't close the deal in that role play, getting through it was my first step in learning how to get in front of customers and ask the right questions—and not do all of the talking!

Throughout college I worked as an intern at the Career Services office, where I learned the importance of networking and put the skills I learned to use with the recruiters who came through our doors. While I was fortunate to be surrounded by career information and job search skills on a daily basis throughout college, it was really my extracurricular activities that gave me an edge when it came time to interview. Completing internships and being actively involved in several organizations and professional groups demonstrated the leadership, organization skills, and drive it would take to be a successful team player in a sales organization. Differentiating yourself—whether in an interview, or a cold call, is what gets you noticed and gets your foot in the door. Doing your research, staying up to date on your clients' industries, and going the extra mile amounts to big payoffs.

By job searching and reaching out to recruiters and contacts I had built in my years working at the career services office, I earned a position at AT&T, the largest telecommunications provider in the country and a *Fortune* 10 company, where I was placed in an extensive six-month mobility training program.

As an account executive in the AT&T Business Sales Leadership Program, I learned the ins and outs of the products I would be selling, how to sell strategically, and what it would take to close business. It was an intense program, but having a strong knowledge of the products and services I would be selling made it easier to show value to my customers in the field.

After training I transitioned into the acquisition segment of the AT&T Premier Client Group. This segment focuses on gaining new business, and required momentum right out of the gates. I was attracted to the opportunity that the position presented because it focuses on hunting for new business. This means active prospecting and meeting with new potential customers. Without a doubt, establishing a career in sales takes a great amount of time, energy, and long days, but the hard work and activity are what lays the foundation for future sales and success—and let's not forget about the money!

In my new role as a corporate account executive, I meet with businesses, learn the business processes, and find ways mobility can improve those processes. Building trust is the key to earning the right to act as a consultant to clients, which brings value and differentiates a salesperson among the competition.

Because I sell to all different market verticals, I am able to meet and work with a variety of people every day. One day I could be conducting a meeting in a high-power executive office, and the next I could be out in a hard hat touring the manufacturing plant of a company. The change and diversity of each day make me excited about my career and keep me challenged. Being able to meet with so many new people is my favorite part of selling—it

sure beats being behind a desk and computer all day! The relationships and contacts you make selling will carry into your professional life no matter what route you take with your career.

Without a doubt, sales offers the freedom, recognition, and financial benefits that few other roles can offer. I hope you find sales as rewarding as I do.

See our Web site at:
www.att.com

WHY LEARN ABOUT PERSONAL SELLING?

What's the first thing that pops into your mind when you hear the phrase "personal selling"? Do you conjure up images of fast-talking, nonlistening, pushy guys who won't take no for an answer? Does the cartoon in Exhibit 1.1 resonate with your idea of a seller? Maybe your definition would be something like this: "Personal selling is the craft of persuading people to buy what they do not want and do not need for more than it is worth."[1] If so, it's not all that surprising because that is exactly how television and the movies have represented salespeople for over 100 years.

If that is your view of selling, we encourage you to read and study this book carefully. You're going to learn things about selling that you never knew before.

Exhibit 1.1

"People like sincerity - learn to fake that and you've got it made."

© Business Cartoons by UK Cartoonist Morris/Visual Humour

Let's start with a more accurate definition of a professional salesperson, which is quite different from the one just mentioned. **Personal selling** is a person-to-person business activity in which a salesperson uncovers and satisfies the needs of a buyer to the mutual, long-term benefit of both parties. This definition stresses that selling is more than making a sale and getting an order. Selling involves helping customers identify problems, offering information about potential solutions, and providing after-sale service to ensure long-term satisfaction. The phrase often used to describe this is **customer-centric**, which means making the customer the center of everything the salesperson does.[2] Quite a bit different from the image of the seller in the cartoon, isn't it?

The days of salespeople dragging around briefcases overstuffed with brochures and knocking on every door they can find to drum up interest in their companies' products are waning. Buyers simply don't tolerate such salespeople. Buying firms today compete in global markets, using sophisticated communication, transportation, and management information systems. And these sophisticated buyers are demanding **24/7 service** (which means they expect a selling firm to be available for them 24 hours a day, 7 days a week). Today's professional salespeople coordinate the resources of their companies to help customers solve complex problems. They use e-mail and Web conferencing to communicate with customers and support staff around the world; exchange information from their firms' computers with their own laptop computers so they can know more about their prospects and customers; and develop client-specific multimedia presentations to illustrate the benefits of their firms' products and services. In all of this, the seller's goal is to add **value**, which is the total benefit that the seller's products and services provide to the buyer. When describing this to prospects, the seller often refers to the collection of buyer-specific benefits as the **customer value proposition**.[3] Jeff Lehman, author of *The Sales Manager's Mentor*, would suggest that the nucleus of the salesperson's life is the value proposition, because without the value proposition, there is no real and meaningful presentation.[4] As you can read in "From the Buyer's Seat 1.1," buyers want long-term relationships that result in increased value for their firms. Customer value propositions are discussed more fully in Chapter 9.

EVERYONE SELLS

This text discusses personal selling as a business activity undertaken by salespeople. But keep in mind that the principles of selling are useful to everyone, not just people with the title of salesperson. Developing mutually beneficial, long-term relationships is vital to all of us. In fact, the author team has taught the principles in this book to many groups of nonsalespeople. Let's look at some examples of how nonsalespeople sell ideas.

As a college student, you might use selling techniques when asking another student to go out on a date or to ask a professor to let you enroll in a course that is closed out. When you near graduation, you will certainly confront a very important sales job: selling yourself to an employer.

To get a job after graduation, you will go through the same steps used in the sales process (discussed in Part 2, Chapters 6 through 14). First you will identify some potential employers (customers). On the basis of an analysis of each employer's needs, you will develop a presentation (as well as answers to questions you might encounter) to demonstrate your ability to satisfy those needs. During the interview you will listen to what the recruiter says, ask and answer questions, and perhaps alter your presentation based on the new information you receive

From the BUYER'S SEAT

WHAT I WISH SALESPEOPLE WHO CALLED ON ME KNEW

By Lt. N.C. McCahill, U.S. Navy

I'm a procurement officer for the U.S. Navy. What's my wish list of things I'd tell new salespeople? Here we go.

Almost on a daily basis I have salespeople who ask me the frustrating, and almost illegal, question, "So, how does our bid look compared to others you've gotten?" Don't ask. Just bid the best you can and don't worry about the others.

I want to establish a long-term agreement and honest relationship with my suppliers. But the first meeting with some sellers is almost like a first date. They're trying to put their best face forward. Don't. I need honest answers and I need to know what you can and can't do. I'll find out eventually anyway, so why play the game of trying to impress me beyond what you can deliver?

I don't like sellers who just stop by to say, "Hi!" I'm guessing they are doing so just so they can count my call on their call sheets and impress their managers. It doesn't impress me. If you don't have a reason to stop by, then don't! My time is valuable.

Salespeople need to have patience. I'm not going to change the way I do things overnight. If something is working, I'm not looking to change. If I do change, it's going to take me a long time. Accept that.

Low price does not equal low cost. There's generally a reason for a higher price, which is higher quality, and I'm willing to pay for it. Don't try to sell me your cheapest model.

I am a professional buyer and know exactly what salespeople are trained to do and to say. I know all the "tricks" they might try to use on me, and I get pretty upset when I see them playing games with me, as though I was too dumb to catch on to their game.

One thing that really burns me up is the way suppliers try to take all of my money. What do I mean? We're in the public sector and everything is budget driven. When I tell a salesperson the budget we have to work with, they usually spend it all. For example, I had to procure services to have a new parking garage built. I told the various sellers that our budget was $10 million. You guessed it, all the bids came in at that amount. They knew what our budget was, and decided to bid for all of the money we had. It's not a lot different from a used car salesman, who knows you have $6,000 to spend and makes sure to take all of your $6,000.

One thing I love is when a seller tells me, "Sorry, I don't have what you need. But my competitor does. Here's their contact information..." That impresses the socks off of me! It builds trust and a long-term relationship. I really get tired of salespeople who stop by and say, "Let me buy you lunch." I'm not allowed to accept meals, and even if I was, I don't want to be beholden to buy from you just because you bought me a $25 meal one day. I know you want to sell deeper to me, but I don't like to get too comfortable with one supplier. I keep my eyes open in the market and test to see if other companies have a better product. I actually like to have several suppliers working for me: approved suppliers are those who can make what we need, and preferred suppliers are those we prefer to give most of our business to. That way, if my preferred supplier can't handle an order, I already have a relationship with other approved suppliers. So don't be surprised if I don't give you 100% of my business.

Don't tell me how bad your competition is. I've had sales reps ask who we were currently using and then proceed to tell me how bad that supplier was. I don't want to hear what your competitor can or can't do, I want to hear what you can do. Besides, it's an insult to my intelligence to point that out. I may already be aware of the problems, and that is part of the reason I am willing to talk to you.

Source: Lt. N.C. McCahill, U.S. Navy, personal correspondence; names changed to protect confidentiality; used with permission.

during the interview. At some point you might negotiate with the employer over starting salary or other issues. Eventually you will try to secure a commitment from the employer to hire you. This process is selling at a very personal level. Chapter 17 reviews the steps you need to undertake to get a sales job.

Nonsalespeople in business use selling principles all the time. Engineers convince managers to support their R&D projects; industrial relations executives use selling approaches when negotiating with unions; and aspiring management trainees sell themselves to associates, superiors, and subordinates to get raises and promotions.

It's not just businesspeople who practice the art of selling. Presidents encourage politicians in Congress to support certain programs; charities solicit contributions and volunteers to run organizations; scientists try to convince foundations and government agencies to fund research; and doctors try to get their patients to adopt more healthful lifestyles. People skilled at selling value, influencing others, and developing long-term relationships are usually leaders in our society.

CREATING VALUE: THE ROLE OF SALESPEOPLE IN BUSINESS

Firms exist only when their products and services are sold. And salespeople sell by creating value for their customers. It takes skill for salespeople to uncover exactly what a customer is looking for and how a potential product or service could add such value. Because this is so critical, this topic is covered in great detail in many chapters in this book.

Firms have many options in how they can approach customers as they add value, and the various methods are sometimes called **go-to-market strategies.** Strategies include selling through the Internet, field sales representatives, business partners, resellers, manufacturer agents, franchises, telemarketers, and others. Selling firms determine which strategy to use for each customer based on such factors as the estimated value of the customer over the lifetime of the relationship, often called **customer lifetime value.**[5] (Because this concept is so important, it is more fully discussed in Chapter 14.) Organizations whose go-to-market strategies rely heavily on salespeople are called **sales force–intensive organizations.** Naturally some firms use several strategies at the same time, and this is called **multichannel strategy.** For example, Motorola uses the Internet for very small customers, telemarketers for midsized customers, and a field sales force for large, important customers.

Another way to view the role of salespeople in business is to realize that they are one element in the firms' marketing communications program, as Exhibit 1.2

Exhibit 1.2
Communication
Methods

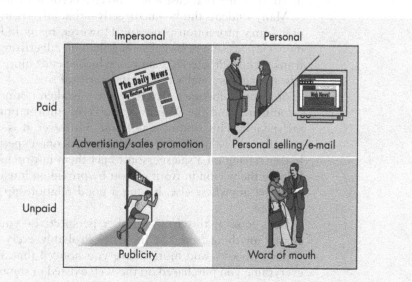

indicates.[6] Advertising uses impersonal mass media such as newspapers and TV to give information to customers, while sales promotions offer incentives to customers to purchase products during a specific period. Salespeople provide paid personal communication to customers, whereas publicity is communication through significant unpaid presentations about the firm (usually a news story). Finally, communication also occurs at no cost through word of mouth (communication among buyers about the selling firm).

Each of the communication methods in Exhibit 1.2 has strengths and weaknesses. For example, firms have more control when using paid versus unpaid methods. However, because publicity and word of mouth are communicated by independent sources, their information is usually perceived as more credible than information from paid communication sources. When using advertising, Internet sites, and sales promotions, companies can determine the message's exact content and the time of its delivery. They have less control over the communication delivered by salespeople and have very little control over the content or timing of publicity and word-of-mouth communication. Personal selling comes out on top in flexibility because salespeople can talk with each customer, discover the customer's specific needs, and develop unique presentations for that customer. Not surprisingly, personal selling is the most costly method of communication. The average cost of a sales call can be 10,000 times more expensive than exposing that single customer to a newspaper, radio, or TV ad.

Because each communication vehicle in Exhibit 1.2 has strengths and weaknesses, firms often use **integrated marketing communications,** which are communication programs that coordinate the use of various vehicles to maximize the total impact of the programs on customers.

For example, when Stouffer's introduced its new Spa Cuisine Classics, dinners that were inspired by chefs from wellness spas across the country, it used integrated marketing communications. Salespeople called on supermarkets and wholesale clubs. Advertising was created to generate awareness in consumers' minds. Coupons were offered to consumers to create interest and spur more rapid sales. Taste tests in stores were offered to build excitement and word of mouth. Publicity was generated that focused on the dinners' balance of great taste combined with the nutrition of whole grains. Although using salespeople in this example was an expensive part of the communication mix, it was important to do so to ensure that customers' precise needs were met.

Many students think—incorrectly—that advertising is the most important part of a firm's promotion program. However, many industrial companies place far more emphasis on personal selling than on advertising. Even in consumer product firms such as Procter & Gamble, which spends more than $8 billion annually on advertising, personal selling plays a critical role.

Students sometimes also have the mistaken notion that the growing world of e-commerce and the Web as a source of information are causing the demise of salespeople. This simply is not true. However, it is critical that the salesperson actually add value in this new reality. As one expert notes, "Companies are no longer relying on a salesperson to get them information . . . if you aren't directly helping the person in front of you by providing intelligence and insight that they can't get anywhere else, having a good relationship isn't going to get you sales anymore."[7]

Let's look at this from another perspective—your own life. Have you purchased anything from the Internet? Probably every student has—travel, music, clothing, books, and more. Have you noticed that, other than Internet services, everything you purchased on the Web existed in some form before the Web? Why, then, has the Web become such a ubiquitous place for commerce? Simple. The

Internet makes products and services available the way the consumer wants to buy them. Those who sell via the Web gain competitive advantage by selling the way the buyers (or at least some buyers in some situations) want to buy.

The reality for salespeople is that if they want to sell effectively, they have to recognize that the buyer has needs that are met not only by the product but also by the selling process itself. These needs include time, shopping costs such as gas if they drive around, and others. Part of the salesperson's responsibility is to sell the way the buyer wants to buy.

In general, sellers sell to make a profit. Why do buyers buy? Typically a student will say, "To satisfy a need or a want," and that is a good basic answer. More helpful is to recognize that buyers also buy to make a profit. But they calculate profit differently. A seller's profit is selling price minus cost of goods sold and selling costs. A buyer's profit, or value, is the benefit received minus the selling price and costs and hassles of buying, or time and effort as noted in this equation:

$$\text{Value} = \text{Benefits received} - (\text{Selling price} + \text{Time and effort to purchase})$$

For example, when someone buys a product from a salesperson, the buyer's profit may be higher than that obtained by buying on the Internet due to the benefits received (expert knowledge in determining the appropriate product to purchase, assistance with installation, resolution of concerns, creation of new offerings based on the buyer's specific needs, and so forth).

WHAT DO SALESPEOPLE DO?

The activities of salespeople depend on the type of selling job they choose. The responsibilities of salespeople selling financial services for General Electric differ greatly from those of salespeople selling pharmaceuticals for Merck or paper products for James River. Salespeople often have multiple roles to play, including client relationship manager, account team manager, vendor and channel manager, and information provider for their firms.[8] Studies have shown that when a salesperson's role encompasses more than simply the selling function, the seller's firm has more overall value.[9]

Sales reps help with installations to ensure proper use.

CLIENT RELATIONSHIP MANAGER

Sales jobs involve prospecting for new customers, making sales presentations, demonstrating products, negotiating price and delivery terms, writing orders, and increasing sales to existing customers. But these sales-generating activities (discussed in Chapters 6 through 14) are only part of the job. Although the numbers would vary greatly depending on the type of sales job, one study found that salespeople spend less than 35 percent of their time on-site in face-to-face meetings with customers and prospects (for world-class firms that percentage rises to 40 percent, whereas for poorly performing firms the percentage drops to just 20 percent).[10] The rest of salespeople's time is spent in meetings, working with support people in their companies (internal selling), traveling, waiting for a sales interview, doing paperwork, and servicing customers.

Rather than buying from the lowest-cost suppliers, many buyers now are building competitive advantages by developing and maintaining close, cooperative relationships with a select set of suppliers, and salespeople play a key role in these relationships.[11] When salespeople fail in maintaining these relationships, the results are catastrophic. Research indicates that buyers worldwide are deserting firms they used to do business with in record numbers when their expectations are not met. For example, two-thirds of consumers surveyed cited poor service as the reason they left a provider in the last 12 months.[12]

The salesperson's job does not end when the customer places an order. Sales representatives must make sure customers get the benefits they expect from the product. Thus salespeople work with other company employees to ensure that deliveries are made on time, equipment is properly installed, operators are trained to use the equipment, and questions or complaints are resolved quickly. Progressive selling firms like Standard Register and Johnson & Johnson's Ortho-Clinical Diagnostics are beginning to implement **six sigma selling programs,** which are designed to reduce errors introduced by the selling system to practically zero. Chapter 14 provides more insights on developing ongoing relationships through customer service.

ACCOUNT TEAM MANAGER

Salespeople also coordinate the activities within their firms to solve customer problems.[13] Many sales situations call for team selling, and at least one study shows that salespeople who attempt to go it alone (sometimes called being "lone wolves") perform poorly, have lower job satisfaction, and have higher turnover intentions.[14] An example of team selling occurred when Dick Holder, president of Reynolds Metal Company, spent five years "selling" Campbell Soup Company on using aluminum cans for its tomato juice products. He coordinated a team of graphic designers, marketing people, and engineers that educated and convinced Campbell to use a packaging material it had never used before. Approaches for improving efficiency by working closely with other functional units in the firm are fully discussed in Chapter 16.

VENDOR AND CHANNEL MANAGER

Sometimes it is necessary to interact with other partners and vendors to meet a customer's needs, and salespeople are often the key managers of these many relationships. For example, if a customer buys a new jet from Boeing, with features that will be added by a third-party vendor, the salesperson will need to coordinate the efforts of the vendor with Boeing. Glenn Price, who sells life and disability insurance with Northwestern Mutual, realizes the importance of working with channel partners. "Today the financial services industry is very complex, as are the needs of my clients, and I can't be all things to all people. I can, however, create a team of specialists. For areas outside of my expertise, all I have to do is identify which specialists are needed and bring them in. This approach allows me to operate at maximum efficiency while providing the highest level of expertise and service to my clients."[15] "Sales Technology 1.1" describes how one company uses technology to keep all members in the channel well informed.

INFORMATION PROVIDER TO THEIR FIRM

Salespeople are the eyes and ears of the company in the marketplace. For example, when Bob Meyer, a salesperson at Ballard Medical Products, was demonstrating a medical device, a surgeon commented that he could not tell whether the device was working properly because the tube was opaque. Meyer relayed this information to the vice president of engineering, and the product was redesigned, substituting a clear tube for the opaque tube.

To truly have effective impact on their organization, salespeople need to be skillful at disseminating the knowledge they have acquired from customers to other

MAKE IT EASY FOR YOUR CUSTOMERS TO TRACK INFORMATION

Enterprise is one of the largest and most successful rental car companies in the world. It has achieved that status due to hard work and creative use of technology to keep all of its customers in the loop. Although some readers may have rented a car from Enterprise and witnessed firsthand how Enterprise uses the Web and e-mail to keep consumers updated, some may not know how Enterprise works with corporate customers.

Enterprise has strong ties with insurance companies and works hard to ensure the absolute best level of service possible in the industry. It has created a Web-based application called ARMS that allows insurance companies to easily keep track of car rentals. The ARMS automotive application connects thousands of body shops all across the United States to the Enterprise software system. With these systems, Enterprise can quickly and easily discover the status of customer repairs and can even have updates sent electronically to the business customer (in this case, the insurance company that is providing a rental car while a consumer's damaged car is being repaired). The result is no more telephone tag, trying to find out the status of the repairs and whether the rental car is going to be needed longer. This helps the insurance company as well as the consumer who is getting the car repairs. For example, if the repair is taking longer than was anticipated, ARMS can automatically notify the insurance company requesting a longer rental period for the consumer. Not surprisingly, insurance companies love this system, and the new technology has helped Enterprise get a bigger piece of the rental business for car repairs.

Sources: Enterprise.com; Kirk Kazanjian, *Exceeding Customer Expectations* (New York: Current Doubleday Books, 2007).

Salespeople share important market information with their boss and others in the firm.

people in their companies.[16] In their reporting activities, salespeople provide information to their firms about expenses, calls made, future calls scheduled, sales forecasts, competitor activities, business conditions, and unsatisfied customer needs. It's not surprising, therefore, that the vice presidents of finance and manufacturing in most firms, for example, care greatly about the work and information provided by salespeople. Much of this information is now transmitted electronically to the company, its salespeople, and its customers and is contained in a **customer relationship management (CRM)** system.[17] For example, each night salespeople at Curtin Matheson Scientific, a distributor of clinical and laboratory supplies in Baton Rouge, Louisiana, enter call report information and download all the ordering and shipping information for their customers from the company mainframe to their laptop computers. Chapter 16 discusses the relationship between salespeople and their companies in great detail.[18]

TYPES OF SALESPEOPLE

Almost everyone is familiar with people who sell products and services to consumers in retail outlets. Behind these retail salespeople is an army of salespeople working for commercial firms. Consider an iPod or MP3 player you might purchase in a store. To make the player, the manufacturer bought processed material, such as plastic and electronic components, from various salespeople. In addition, it purchased capital equipment from other salespeople to mold the plastic, assemble the components, and test the player. Finally, the player manufacturer bought services such as an employment agency to hire people and an accounting firm to audit the company's financial statements. The manufacturer's salespeople then sold the players to a wholesaler. The wholesaler purchased transportation services and warehouse space from other salespeople. Then the wholesaler's salespeople sold the players to a retailer.

SELLING AND DISTRIBUTION CHANNELS

As the MP3 player example shows, salespeople work for different types of firms and call on different types of customers. These differences in sales positions come from the many roles salespeople play in a firm's distribution channel. A **distribution channel** is a set of people and organizations responsible for the flow of products and services from the producer to the ultimate user. Exhibit 1.3 shows the principal types of distribution channels used for business-to-business and consumer products and the varied roles salespeople play.

Business-to-Business Channels

The two main channels for producers and providers of business-to-business, or industrial, products and services are (1) direct sales to a business customer and (2) sales through distributors. In the direct channel, salespeople working for the manufacturer call directly on other manufacturers. For example, Nucor salespeople sell steel directly to automobile manufacturers, Dow Chemical salespeople sell plastics directly to toy manufacturers, and Nielsen salespeople sell marketing research services directly to business customers.

In the distributor channel the manufacturer employs salespeople to sell to distributors. These salespeople are referred to as **trade salespeople** because they sell to firms that resell the products (that is, they sell to the trade) rather than using them within the firm. Distributor salespeople sell products made by a number of manufacturers to businesses. For example, some Intel salespeople sell microprocessors to distributors such as Arrow Electronics, and Arrow salespeople then resell the microprocessors and other electronic components to customers such as HP.

Many firms use more than one channel of distribution and thus employ several types of salespeople. For example, Dow Chemical has trade salespeople who call on distributors as well as direct salespeople who call on large companies.

Sales Jobs and the Distribution Channel

In the second business-to-business channel (see Exhibit 1.3), a missionary salesperson is employed. **Missionary salespeople** work for a manufacturer and promote the manufacturer's products to other firms. However, those firms buy the products from distributors or other manufacturers, not directly from the salesperson's firm. For example, sales representatives at Driltech, a manufacturer of mining equipment, call on mine owners to promote their products. The mines, however, place orders for drills with the local Driltech distributor rather than with Driltech directly. Normally missionary and local distributor salespeople work together to build relationships with customers.

Frequently missionary salespeople call on people who influence a buying decision but do not actually place the order. For example, Du Pont sales representatives call on Liz Claiborne and other clothing designers to encourage them to design garments made with Teflon, and Merck sales representatives call on physicians to encourage them to prescribe Merck pharmaceutical products.

Consumer Channels

The remaining channels shown in Exhibit 1.3 are used by producers and providers of consumer products and services. The third channel shows a firm,

Exhibit 1.3
Sales Jobs and the
Distribution Channel

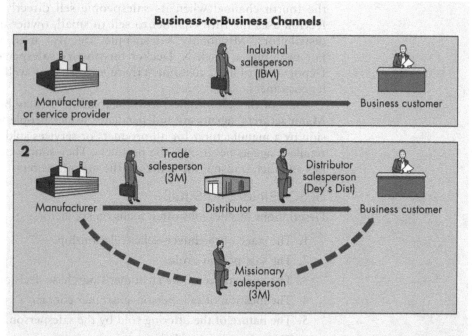

Business-to-Business Channels

1 Manufacturer or service provider ——— Industrial salesperson (IBM) ——— Business customer

2 Manufacturer ——— Trade salesperson (3M) ——— Distributor ——— Distributor salesperson (Dey's Dist) ——— Business customer — Missionary salesperson (3M)

Consumer Channels

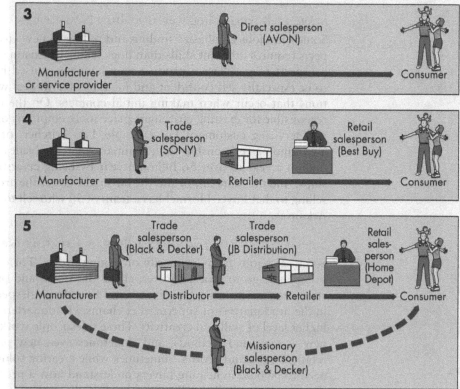

3 Manufacturer or service provider ——— Direct salesperson (AVON) ——— Consumer

4 Manufacturer ——— Trade salesperson (SONY) ——— Retailer ——— Retail salesperson (Best Buy) ——— Consumer

5 Manufacturer ——— Trade salesperson (Black & Decker) ——— Distributor ——— Trade salesperson (JB Distribution) ——— Retailer ——— Retail salesperson (Home Depot) ——— Consumer — Missionary salesperson (Black & Decker)

Note: Representative company names listed under each salesperson in this exhibit merely indicate the types of companies which are represented in that group.

such as State Farm Insurance, whose salespeople sell insurance directly to consumers. The fourth and fifth channels show manufacturers that employ trade salespeople to sell to either retailers or distributors. For example, Revlon uses the fourth channel when its salespeople sell directly to Walmart. However, Revlon uses the fifth channel to sell to small, owner-operated stores through distributors. Missionary salespeople are also used in consumer channels. For example, a Black & Decker missionary salesperson may go to a Home Depot store to meet customers there and see how well Home Depot is serving its customers.

Some of the salespeople shown in Exhibit 1.3 may be manufacturers' agents. **Manufacturers' agents** are independent businesspeople who are paid a commission by a manufacturer for all products or services sold. Unlike distributors and retailers, agents never own the products. They simply perform the selling activities and then transmit the orders to the manufacturers.

DESCRIBING SALES JOBS

Descriptions of sales jobs often focus on six factors:

1. The stage of the buyer–seller relationship.
2. The salesperson's role.
3. The importance of the customer's purchase decision.
4. The location of salesperson–customer contact.
5. The nature of the offering sold by the salesperson.
6. The salesperson's role in securing customer commitment.

Stage of Buyer–Seller Relationship: New or Continuing

Some sales jobs emphasize finding and selling to new customers. Selling to prospects requires different skills than does selling to existing customers. To convince prospects to purchase a product they have never used before, salespeople need to be especially self-confident and must be able to deal with the inevitable rejections that occur when making initial contacts. On the other hand, salespeople responsible for existing customers place more emphasis on building relationships and servicing customers. For example, Lou Pritchett of Procter & Gamble, in a continuing relationship with Walmart, increased sales to Walmart from $400 million a year to over $6 billion a year by being creative and building partnerships. And the more important the buyer, the larger the group of sellers engaged in selling to that buyer. Hormel has a team of 50 who sell to Walmart in Bentonville, Arkansas.

Salesperson's Role: Taking Orders or Creating New Solutions

Some sales jobs focus primarily on taking orders. For example, most Frito-Lay salespeople go to grocery stores, check the stock, and prepare an order for the store manager to sign. However, some Frito-Lay salespeople sell only to buyers in the headquarters of supermarket chains. Headquarters selling requires a much higher level of skill and creativity. These salespeople work with buyers to develop new systems and methods, and sometimes even new products, to increase the retailer's sales and profits. Sometimes while creating solutions, a salesperson will need to be bold in helping buyers understand how a product or service can meet their needs, as "Building Partnerships 1.1" illustrates.

Importance of the Purchase to the Customer

Consumers and businesses make many purchase decisions each year. Some decisions are important to them, such as purchasing a building or a business telephone system. Others are less crucial, such as buying candy or cleaning supplies. Sales

BUILDING Partnerships   1.1

I'M SORRY BUT I DISAGREE; YOU SHOULD HIRE THIS PERSON...

I work for a company that matches jobs with entry-level job candidates. A big part of my job consists of soliciting businesses that might have job openings, and then once I actually gain that account I retain it and become their main point of contact for job candidates. Obviously we build strong relationships with companies, and they really feel comfortable trusting us and our opinions on candidates.

A difficulty arises when I need to push a company to make a move on a candidate that they may not feel would be a good fit for their organization, but in my opinion the candidate is a great fit. Recently I was working with this corporate account, and I have a wonderful friendship and strong working relationship with the hiring manager. She decided she was going to pass on (not hire) one of our top candidates. I thought the candidate was a great fit, and obviously I wanted to place the candidate and make the money. But how could I encourage the hiring manager to see that she was making the wrong decision without being pushy and overbearing? How could I show her the value in the candidate and explain why she should reconsider hiring her? What would you do?

I do a number of things in this kind of situation. First, I ask questions about their needs to make sure we're on the same page, and then ask the hiring manager why she thinks the candidate doesn't meet those needs. Sometimes I ask the hiring manager to give my candidate another job interview. Maybe it was just a bad day for the job candidate or the hiring manager. Finally, I occasionally ask the hiring manager to test the candidate out: Put them through the paces of the actual job itself, if possible. For example, put the candidate on the phone to see if he can in fact make cold calls. Testing the actual skills can often show that a candidate does have the needed qualifications, even though she didn't interview well.

Above all, I maintain the relationship and realize that all of my candidates won't get hired. But I do try my best to create a win–win–win situation where the hiring manager, the candidate, and my company all win in the end.

Source: Personal correspondence with Heather Carr, Career Professionals; used with permission.

jobs involving important decisions for customers differ greatly from sales jobs involving minor decisions. Consider a company that needs a computer-controlled drill press. Buying the drill press is a big decision. The drill press sales representative needs to be knowledgeable about the customer's needs and the features of drill presses. The salesperson will have to interact with a number of people involved in the purchase decision.

Even though many sales jobs do not involve building long-term partnerships, we stress the concept of developing partnering relationships throughout this textbook because the roles of salespeople in many companies are evolving toward a partnering orientation. As you'll see in Chapter 16, partnering orientations are important within one's own organization as well as with customers. Further, salespeople are called on to build partnerships with some accounts and other types of relationships with other accounts. The partnering orientation does not prevent salespeople from developing other types of relationships; rather, people who are good partners are likely to also be good at other types of relationships. Understanding partnerships is critical to understanding the professional selling process, as will become apparent as the book unfolds.

Location of Salesperson–Customer Contact: Field or Inside Sales

Field salespeople spend considerable time in the customer's place of business, communicating with the customer face-to-face. **Inside salespeople** work at their

Field salespeople go directly to the customer's place of business.

employer's location and typically communicate with customers by telephone or letter.

Field selling typically is more demanding than inside selling because the former entails more intense interactions with customers. Field salespeople are more involved in problem solving with customers, whereas inside salespeople often respond to customer-initiated requests.

thinking **it** through   Which do you think you would prefer, an inside sales job or a field sales job? What makes one more attractive to you than the other?

The Nature of the Offering Sold by the Salesperson: Products or Services

The type of benefits provided by products and services affects the nature of the sales job. Products such as chemicals and trucks typically have tangible benefits: Customers can objectively measure a chemical's purity and a truck's payload. The benefits of services, such as business insurance or investment opportunities, are more intangible: Customers cannot easily see how the insurance company handles claims or objectively measure the riskiness of an investment.

Intangible benefits are harder to sell than tangible benefits because it is difficult to demonstrate intangible benefits to customers. It is much easier to show a customer the payload of a truck than the benefits of carrying insurance.

The Salesperson's Role in Securing Customer Commitment: Information or Placing an Order

Sales jobs differ by the types of commitments sought and the manner in which they are obtained. For example, the Du Pont missionary salesperson might encourage a clothing designer to use Du Pont Teflon fibers. The salesperson might ask the designer to consider using the fiber but does not undertake the more difficult task of asking the designer to place an order. If the designer decides to use Teflon fabric in a dress, the actual order for nylon will be secured by the fabric manufacturer salesperson, not the Du Pont salesperson.

THE SALES JOBS CONTINUUM

Exhibit 1.4 uses the factors just discussed to illustrate the continuum of sales jobs in terms of creativity. Sales jobs described by the responses in the far right column require salespeople to go into the field, call on new customers who make important buying decisions, promote products or services with intangible benefits, and seek purchase commitments. These types of sales jobs require the most creativity and skill and, consequently, offer the highest pay.

The next section examines the responsibilities of specific types of salespeople in more detail.

EXAMPLES OF SALES JOBS

The following are brief examples of several of the thousands of sales jobs that exist today. As you read each example, notice the vast differences in the type of compensation, the number of accounts, the length of an average sales call, the length of the order cycle, the need to prospect, and so forth. All are based on real

Exhibit 1.4
Creativity Level of
Sales Jobs

Factors in Sales Jobs	Lower Creativity	Higher Creativity
1. Stage of the customer-firm relationship	Existing customer	New customer
2. The salesperson's role	Order taking	Creating new solutions
3. Importance of the customer's purchase decision	Low	High
4. Location of salesperson-customer contact	Inside company	Field customer
5. Nature of the offering sold by the salesperson	Products	Services
6. Salesperson's role in securing customer commitment	Limited role	Significant role

salespeople and the sales jobs they got when they first graduated from college. As you read the examples, think about which would be more attractive to you personally.

Chris is a salesperson for IBM Large Systems, selling mainframe computers to organizations. She has five clients, provided to her by her company, and does no prospecting for new accounts. She is paid a straight salary and travels by plane three to five days each week. Each visit to an account is roughly three hours long. For the first three years she had no sales. In her third year she made the largest sale in the company's history.

Lauree works for Standard Register selling business forms and document management solutions. She has 200 clients and does a good bit of searching for new accounts. She is paid salary plus commission and gets orders essentially every single day, with no overnight travel. Each visit lasts about 45 minutes.

Scott works for Pfizer, a pharmaceutical company, calling on 100 doctors to tell them about his company's drugs. He is paid a salary plus a year-end bonus, and as a missionary salesperson never gets an actual order from a doctor (the patients buy the Pfizer drugs). He does no overnight travel and never searches for new accounts, and each call is about five minutes long.

Jim sells Makita power tools and serves 75 dealers. He is paid a salary plus commission and does very limited searching for new accounts. He gets orders every day and has little overnight travel. Each call is about 30 minutes long.

Jeff works for Hormel, selling refrigerated meat products as well as pantry products like canned chili, and has about 100 accounts. He does no searching for new accounts and is paid a salary plus a year-end bonus. Each call lasts about 10 minutes, and he has no overnight travel.

Niki works for MetLife, selling life, auto, homeowners, long-term care, and disability insurance as well as investments (IRAs, mutual funds, annuities, and so forth). She has 250 clients, has no overnight travel, and is paid straight salary. She does a good bit of searching for new accounts, and here average first in-person sales call to a new account lasts about 30 minutes.

The next section reviews some of the skills required to be effective in the sales positions just discussed.

CHARACTERISTICS OF SUCCESSFUL SALESPEOPLE

The market is full of books and articles discussing why some people are successful in selling and others are not.[19] Yet no one has identified the profile of the "perfect" salesperson because sales jobs are so different, as the examples just provided illustrated. In addition, each customer is unique. However, the following traits are generally associated with successful salespeople.

SELF-MOTIVATED

Most salespeople work in the field without direct supervision. Under these conditions they may be tempted to get up late, take long lunch breaks, and stop work early. But successful salespeople are self-starters who do not need the fear inspired by a glaring supervisor to get them going in the morning or to keep them working hard all day. Furthermore, successful salespeople are motivated to learn, and they work at improving their skills by analyzing their performance and using their mistakes as learning opportunities.

DEPENDABILITY AND TRUSTWORTHINESS

This book focuses on business-to-business selling situations in which the customer and salesperson often have a continuing relationship. Such salespeople are interested not only in what the customers will buy this time but also in getting orders in the years to come. Customers develop long-term relationships only with salespeople who are dependable and trustworthy.[20] When salespeople say the equipment will perform in a certain way, they had better make sure the equipment performs that way! If it doesn't, the customer will not rely on them again. And dependability and trustworthiness can't just be a false front: Salespeople who are genuine and come across as authentic are better-performing salespeople.

thinking **it** through

Take a minute and think about yourself. How dependable are you right now? Can people count on you to do what you say you will do? Or do they have to look you up and remind you of your promises? You don't start developing dependability when you graduate from college; it is something you should be working on right now. What can you do to start improving your dependability?

ethics

ETHICAL SALES BEHAVIOR

Honesty and integrity are critical for developing effective relationships. Over the long run, customers will find out who can be trusted and who cannot. Good ethics are good business.[21] Ethical sales behavior is such an important topic that much of Chapter 2 is devoted to it.

CUSTOMER AND PRODUCT KNOWLEDGE

Effective salespeople need to know how businesses make purchase decisions and how individuals evaluate product alternatives. In addition, effective salespeople need product knowledge—how their products work and how the products' features are related to the benefits customers are seeking. Chapter 3 reviews the buying process, and Chapter 5 discusses product knowledge.

ANALYTICAL SKILLS AND THE ABILITY TO USE
INFORMATION TECHNOLOGY

Salespeople need to know how to analyze data and situations and use the Internet, databases, and software to effectively sell in today's marketplace.[22] Information technology will be discussed in every chapter in this book, and the use of analytical tools will be covered in Chapter 9 and other chapters.

COMMUNICATION SKILLS

The key to building strong long-term relationships is to be responsive to a customer's needs. To do that, the salesperson needs to be a good communicator. But talking is not enough; the salesperson must also listen to what the customer says, ask questions that uncover problems and needs, and pay attention to the responses.

To compete in world markets, salespeople need to learn how to communicate in international markets. For example, business is conducted differently in Europe than in the United States. In the United States business transactions generally proceed at a rapid pace, whereas Europeans take more time reaching decisions. European customers place more emphasis on the rapport developed with a salesperson, whereas U.S. firms look more at the size and reputation of the salesperson's company. Because Europeans want to do business with salespeople they like and trust, the latter devote a lot of time to building close personal relationships with customers. Chapter 4 is devoted to developing communication skills, with considerable emphasis on communicating in other cultures.

FLEXIBILITY AND AGILITY

The successful salesperson realizes that the same sales approach does not work with all customers; it must be adapted to each selling situation. The salesperson must be sensitive to what is happening, and agile enough to make those adaptations during the sales presentation. Again, it is this flexibility that causes companies to spend so much money on personal selling instead of just advertising, which can't be tailored as easily or quickly to each individual.

CREATIVITY

Creativity is the trait of having imagination and inventiveness and using them to come up with new solutions and ideas. Sometimes it takes creativity to get an appointment with a prospect. It takes creativity to develop presentation that the buyer will long remember. It takes creativity to solve a sticky installation problem after the product is sold.

CONFIDENCE AND OPTIMISM

Successful salespeople tend to be confident about themselves, their company, and their products. They optimistically believe that their efforts will lead to success. Don't confuse confidence, however, with wishful thinking. According to research, truly confident people are willing to work hard to achieve their goals. They are open to criticism, seek advice from others, and learn from their mistakes. They expect good things to happen, but they take personal responsibility for their fate. People who lack confidence, according to these same studies, are not honest about their own limits, react defensively when criticized, and set unrealistic goals.

Salespeople need emotional intelligence to be able to recognize customers' emotions.

EMOTIONAL INTELLIGENCE

Emotional intelligence is the ability to effectively understand and regulate one's own emotions, and to read and respond to the emotions of others, and this is an important trait for salespeople.[23] Emotional intelligence has four aspects: (1) knowing one's own feelings and emotions as they are experienced, (2) controlling one's emotions to avoid acting impulsively, (3) recognizing customers' emotions (called *empathy*), and (4) using one's emotions to interact effectively with customers.[24] One well-known source identifies the following as evidences of emotional maturity: "the ability to deal constructively with reality, the capacity to adapt to change, a relative freedom from symptoms that are produced by tensions and anxieties, the capacity to find more satisfaction in giving than receiving, the capacity to relate to other people in a consistent manner with mutual satisfaction and helpfulness, the capacity to direct one's instinctive hostile energy into creative and constructive outlets, and the capacity to love."[25] A recent study of over 6,000 people from a wide spectrum of industries found that good decision makers consistently score high in emotional intelligence.[26] Bad decisions result from a lack of emotional intelligence, so it is not surprising that emotional immaturity plays a large role in many employee terminations. What are some good first steps in improving your emotional maturity? Learn to identify and understand your own emotions as they arise, and recognize the fact that it is often in your best interest to step away from emotional situations and become more reflective.[27] We discuss aspects of emotional intelligence as they relate to adaptive selling and effective verbal and nonverbal intelligence in Chapters 4 and 5.

ARE SALESPEOPLE BORN OR MADE?

On the basis of the preceding discussion, you can see that most of the skills required to be a successful salesperson can be learned. People can learn to work hard, plan their time, and adapt their sales approach to their customers' needs. In fact, companies show their faith in their ability to teach sales skills by spending billions of dollars each year on training programs. The next section discusses the rewards you can realize if you develop the skills required for sales success.

REWARDS IN SELLING

Personal selling offers interesting and rewarding career opportunities. More than 8 million people in the United States currently work in sales positions, and the number of sales positions is growing. In fact, based on a study of nearly 37,000 employers in 27 countries, the demand for salespeople is greater than the supply.[28] Exhibit 1.5 provides a breakdown of employment by the type of sales job.

Exhibit 1.5
Employment in Sales Positions

Type of Sales Job	Employed in 2008	Projected Employed for 2018	Average Earnings in 2008
Retail salesperson	4,500,000	+8%	$9.86/hour
Manufacturers' and wholesale sales reps	2,000,000	+7%	$70,200
Insurance sales agents	434,000	+12%	$45,430
Securities, commodities, and financial sales agents	317,200	+9%	$68,680
Real estate agents and brokers	517,800	+14%	$40,150
Sales engineers	78,000	+9%	$83,100
Advertising sales agents	166,800	+7%	$43,800
Travel agents	105,300	−1%	$30,570
Totals	8,119,100		

Source: *Occupational Outlook Handbook*, 2010–2011 edition, U.S. Department of Labor, Bureau of Labor Statistics.

INDEPENDENCE AND RESPONSIBILITY

Many people do not want to spend long hours behind a desk, doing the same thing every day. They prefer to be outside, moving around, meeting people, and working on various problems. Selling ideally suits people with these interests. The typical salesperson interacts with dozens of people daily. Most of these contacts involve challenging new experiences.

Selling also offers unusual freedom and flexibility. It is not a nine-to-five job. Most salespeople decide how to spend their time; they do not have to report in. They have the freedom to determine what they do during a day, to decide which customers to call on and when to do paperwork. Long hours may be required on some days, and other days may bring fewer demands.

Because of this freedom, salespeople are like independent entrepreneurs. They have a territory to manage and few restrictions on how to do it. They are responsible for the sales and profits the territory generates. Thus their success or failure rests largely on their own skills and efforts.

FINANCIAL REWARDS

ethics

Salespeople tend to earn more money the longer they sell, as Exhibit 1.6 clearly indicates. Occasionally the top salespeople in a firm will even earn more than the sales executives in that firm. The average amount earned by salespeople depends somewhat on the annual revenues of the firm: For firms with revenues of less than $1 million, the average salesperson earns $99,058, while for companies earning from $1 to $10 billion, the average is $199,590.[29]

The financial rewards of selling depend on the level of skill and sophistication needed to do the job. For example, salespeople who sell to businesses typically are paid more than retail salespeople. Exhibit 1.5 shows the average compensation for salespeople in various jobs.

Exhibit 1.6
Average Annual Compensation for Salespeople by Years of Sales/Marketing Experience

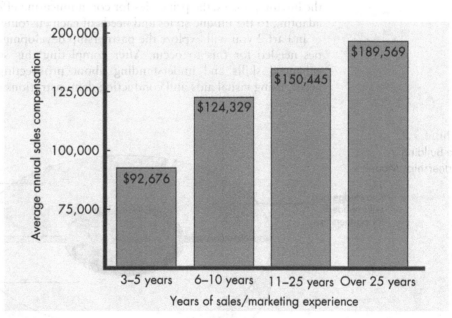

Source: Rebecca Aronauer, "Trends," *Sales and Marketing Management Magazine* 159, no. 4 (May 2007), pp. 38–39.

This young manager learned the ropes as a salesperson before moving into product management at his firm.

MANAGEMENT OPPORTUNITIES

Selling jobs provide a firm base for launching a business career. For example, Mark Alvarez started his sales career in the Medical Systems Division at General Electric (GE) selling diagnostic imaging equipment to hospitals in central Illinois. Over the years he held positions in the firm that included district and regional sales manager and product manager; at one point he had responsibility for all Medical Systems Division business in Latin America. Sixteen years later, he was in corporate marketing and was responsible for managing the relationships between GE's 39 divisions and key customers in the southeastern United States. These include such accounts as Federal Express, Disney, and Home Depot. Some of his businesses do more than $500 million worth of business with GE annually. His entry-level job in selling provided great experience for his current assignment. As another example, both the chairman and the CEO/president of Federated Insurance, like many of their counterparts in business, started their careers as salespeople.

THE BUILDING PARTNERSHIPS MODEL

This book is divided into three parts, as illustrated in Exhibit 1.7.

The knowledge and skills needed for successful partnerships are covered in Part 1. You will learn about the legal and ethical responsibilities of salespeople, the buying process, the principles for communicating effectively, and methods for adapting to the unique styles and needs of each customer.

In Part 2 you will explore the partnership development process and the activities needed for this to occur. After completing this section, you should have enhanced skills and understanding about prospecting, planning, discovering needs, using visual aids and conducting demonstrations effectively, responding to

Exhibit 1.7
The Building
Partnerships Model

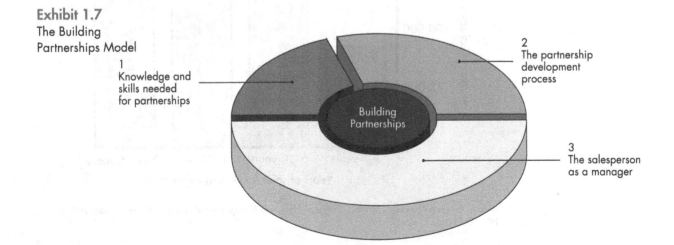

1
Knowledge and
skills needed
for partnerships

2
The partnership
development
process

3
The salesperson
as a manager

objections, obtaining commitment, formally negotiating, and providing excellent after-sale service.

Finally, Part 3 discusses the role of the salesperson as a manager. You'll learn how you can improve your effectiveness as a salesperson by managing your time and territory and by managing the relationships within your own company. This section also discusses ways to manage your career.

SELLING YOURSELF

The "Selling Yourself" sections of this book are designed to help you see the connections of the chapter material with all aspects of your life right now. Of course we're all different, with different interests and activities, so some of the examples might better fit you than others. But read them all, and try to make a connection with something in your life. Selling is something you do all the time, and the ideas found in this book can help you now, not just after you graduate!

Let's say you belong to a campus club or organization that is doing a little fund-raising. You find some product or service to sell, or come up with something to raffle off. Then you set up a booth outside the bookstore and staff the booth with your friendliest and maybe most attractive club members. Sound familiar? What happens? A bunch of people won't stop at your booth, no matter how much you try to coax them. Some stop, but don't buy. Why is this happening?

Simple. You're not meeting their needs. In other words, if a student gives you cash, your club's needs are certainly getting met (you are gaining needed revenue), but the student giving the money might not be getting any of her needs met. Remember that the definition of personal selling says that both parties have their needs met, not just one party!

The solution? Discover the real wants and needs of your fellow college students (your customers, those who are going to buy from you) and then sell on that basis. Make sure the product or service or raffle is something the college students really want or need, not just something you think they might need. Do some research to find this out. If you are the one to discover that information, pass it on to your officers (that's being an information provider to your group, which is something that salespeople do, too).

And why not assign a missionary salesperson to hang around the booth? That person, who would be someone with great emotional intelligence, can approach some people who didn't stop at your booth and politely ask "Why not?" but not try to sell them anything. The missionary salesperson can also ask those who did buy "Why?" and "How is the product working out?" and pass that information back to the club's officers. Changes can be made right away to the offering or the way the offering is publicized and sold. Or it can be changed the next time your club tries to do fund-raising.

Happy selling!

SUMMARY

You should study personal selling because we all use selling techniques. If you want to work in business, you need to know about selling because salespeople play a vital role in business activities. Finally, you might become a salesperson. Selling jobs are inherently interesting because of the variety of people encountered and activities undertaken. In addition, selling offers opportunities for financial rewards and promotions.

Salespeople engage in a wide range of activities, including providing information about products and services to customers and employees within their firms.

Most of us are not aware of many of these activities because the salespeople we meet most frequently work in retail stores. However, the most exciting, rewarding, and challenging sales positions involve building partnerships: long-term, win–win relationships with customers.

The specific duties and responsibilities of salespeople depend on the type of selling position. But most salespeople engage in various tasks in addition to influencing customers. These tasks include managing customer relations, serving as the account team manager for their firm, managing the relationships with vendor and channel members, and providing information to their firm.

Sales jobs can be classified by the roles salespeople and their firms play in the channel of distribution. The nature of the selling job is affected by whom salespeople work for and whether they sell to manufacturers, distributors, or retailers. Other factors affecting the nature of selling jobs are the customer's relationship to the salesperson's firm, the salesperson's duties, the importance of the buying decision to the customer, where the selling occurs, the tangibility of the benefits considered by the customer, and the degree to which the salesperson seeks a commitment from customers.

Research on the characteristics of effective salespeople indicates that many different personality types can be successful in sales. However, successful salespeople do share some common characteristics. They are self-motivated, dependable, ethical, knowledgeable, good communicators, flexible, creative, confident, and emotionally intelligent; have good analytical skills; and aren't afraid of technology.

KEY TERMS

creativity 19
customer-centric 5
customer lifetime value (CLV) 7
customer relationship management (CRM) 11
customer value proposition 5
distribution channel 12
emotional intelligence 19
field salespeople 15
go-to-market strategies 7
inside salespeople 15

integrated marketing communications 8
manufacturers' agents 14
missionary salespeople 12
multichannel strategy 7
personal selling 5
sales force–intensive organization 7
six sigma selling programs 10
trade salespeople 12
24/7 service 5
value 5

ETHICS PROBLEMS

1. Many buyers are now demanding 24/7 response (24 hours a day, 7 days a week) from their suppliers. What impact do you think that would have on a salesperson's personal life?

2. The chapter says that selling jobs can be a great way to get your foot in the door at an employer. Let's say you really want to be in product development, not sales, yet the position that is being offered at the company is in sales. You hope that after doing the sales job for six months to a year you'll get promoted to the product development job. Should you be honest and tell the interviewer (the sales manager) that now? Or should you act as though you want to be a career salesperson?

QUESTIONS AND PROBLEMS

1. There are many different go-to-market strategies. For which of the following products and services do you think a sales force–intensive strategy would probably not be used? Why? Make any assumptions needed, and list your assumptions in your answer.
   a. Tennis racquets.
   b. Home air conditioning maintenance service.
   c. Shredding service for sensitive documents.
   d. Solar-powered compactor garbage cans for city use on city streets (the specially designed cans actually compact the garbage that is thrown into the can four times a time, using energy from the sun, reducing the number of times the can needs to be emptied).

2. In "Building Partnerships 1.1" you read about how Ms. Carr politely disagrees with her customer if she thinks the customer is making a decision that is not in the customer's best interests.
   a. What could be some positive outcomes of such salesperson behavior?
   b. What could be some negative outcomes of such salesperson behavior?

3. Comment on each of the following statements:
   a. Salespeople rip people off.
   b. Salespeople are born, not made.
   c. Selling is just a big bag of tricks.
   d. A salesperson should never take no for an answer.
   e. A good salesperson can sell anything to anybody.

4. Fay Roberson has been working as a receptionist at her father's business for two years since graduating from college. She is considering taking a selling job with a pharmaceutical company. The job involves calling on doctors and explaining the benefits of the firm's products. What are the similarities and differences between her receptionist job and the selling job she is considering?

5. Benjamin Chapman worked his way through college by selling home theater systems at Best Buy. He has done well on the job and is one of the top salespeople in the home electronics department. Last week Safety Harness Inc. offered him a job selling seat belt kits to school bus manufacturers. Explain the differences between selling in a consumer electronics store and the Safety Harness Inc. sales job.

6. Poll at least five students who are not taking your selling course (and who, better yet, are outside the business school or program). What are their opinions about salespeople? How accurate are their opinions based on what you've read in this chapter?

7. Think about what you want in your first job out of college. Based on what you know so far from this chapter, how well does selling match your desires in a job?

8. According to the text, some sales jobs involve taking orders instead of creating new solutions. Why would anyone want a job that involves only taking orders?

9. "Sales Technology 1.1" described the use of Enterprise's ARMS system. How could having the ARMS system help an Enterprise salesperson sell to a new insurance company?

10. Assume you are a sales manager and you need to recruit someone for the following sales positions. For each position, list the qualities you would want in the recruit:
    a. Salesperson selling Web design services to small businesses.
    b. Salesperson calling on college bookstores, selling university logo backpacks.
    c. Used car salesperson.
    d. Salesperson selling janitorial services to a county courthouse.

CASE PROBLEMS

case 1.1

Tropical Landscaping, Inc.

Jenna Jones has been the owner and general manager of Tropical Landscaping for the last five years, having bought the business from the entrepreneur and landscape architect who started it 25 years earlier. Tropical is a full-service lawn care company that caters to the business sector, not the consumer sector. They are experts in designing, irrigation, and maintenance of landscapes and have a strong reputation for fast, efficient, and reasonably priced services.

When Jenna purchased the company there were three full-time salespeople who called on businesses in the region. One quit right after she arrived, and Floyd, a knowledgeable landscaper with good connections in the business community, was hired as a replacement. Floyd has been a real asset to the firm, building business in the commercial landscape design area.

Jenna thought everything was going smoothly until yesterday, when Chad, another salesperson, dropped a bombshell. He turned in his notice. Chad indicated he was going to work for a local competitor who was paying him about 25 percent more than Jenna.

Jenna sat in her office, mulling over the situation and half-heartedly working on the job description for Chad's position, when one of her most trusted administrative assistants, Katie, walked in. After they chatted for a few minutes, the following conversation ensued:

Katie: So why do you need a salesperson anyway? Why not just use advertising?

Jenna: We have to have a salesperson, Katie. I mean, there's always been three salespeople in our office.

Katie: But I'm asking you to think outside the dots, Jenna. Why do we need them? They cost the company a lot of money that we could save by just relying on advertising. Besides, Tropical Landscaping is already well-known in this region. There's no need for salespeople. Tropical Landscaping sells itself.

The conversation continued in this vein for a few minutes; then Katie left to work on some invoice disputes. Jenna sat there, thinking about what Katie said. Who knows? Maybe Katie had a good idea.

Questions

1. What impact would dropping one or more salespeople have on Tropical Landscaping? You might want to review the section titled "What Do Salespeople Do?" as you answer this question.
2. If you were Jenna, what would you do? Why?

case 1.2

Mountain Valley Spring Water

Kyle Welborn is a salesperson for Roehl Trucking. For the past three or four months he has tried to get in to see Steve Hayes, a transportation specialist at Mountain Valley Spring Water Company. Mountain Valley is an award-winning water bottler that has been in business since 1871. Its water has been served in the White House by a number of presidents, as well as in the Senate, and many celebrities have endorsed the products.

Kyle knows that Mountain Valley uses the services of a number of trucking companies, and he would like Steve to consider adding Roehl as one of its transportation suppliers. Roehl has a three-part vision statement: To be recognized by our customers as the nation's premier provider of truckload services, to be a high-energy, high-performance team, and to be the safest carrier on the road—emphasizing and expecting safe behaviors from everyone. With that vision the company has grown to be one of the largest and most profitable trucking companies in the United States.

Kyle has never actually been able to talk to Steve, not even for a few seconds. His voice mail is all he has ever gotten when making phone calls to Steve. Visits in person have resulted in Steve's secretary just taking Kyle's card and telling him that Steve will call if he is interested. Kyle is now under pressure from his sales manager because Kyle has placed Mountain Valley on his prospect list for the last three months and has nothing to show for all his efforts.

Sources: www.mountainvalleyspring.com, www.roehl.net.

Questions

1. One of the skills that salespeople should possess is creativity. Come up with three creative and totally ethical methods Kyle can use to get Steve's attention.
2. Assume Kyle does get Steve's attention with one of the methods you've described, and Steve is willing to speak with Kyle on the phone the next time he is called. What should Kyle plan on saying, assuming he has just two or three minutes of phone time?

ROLE PLAY CASE

At the end of each chapter, beginning just below this paragraph, you'll find a short role play exercise that focuses on the product NetSuite. NetSuite is a leading contact management software package. Contact management software is a form of software designed to help salespeople increase their productivity by helping them keep track of the customers they call. In addition to a calendar that tells them when to call on an account, the software can track account information concerning what has been bought, when it was bought, the decision-making process, and even personal information about each person in the account. In addition, sales managers can generate reports automatically when reps upload information to the company network. Reps don't have to type as many reports as they would otherwise, such as sales forecasts and call reports. Further, the system can tie into the company's ordering system, which helps save the salesperson paperwork time.

You can learn more about NetSuite from its Web page: www.netsuite.com.

Congratulations, you've just graduated from college! Unfortunately you focused so much on your studies that you have not interviewed for any jobs. You moved back home, but you keep in touch with the school's Career Services Center, where you saw a job posting for NetSuite. Apparently it is some sort of software for salespeople. You've not had any serious interviews, so you thought you'd sign up. Today is your interview. Be yourself; interview honestly as if you were truly talking with NetSuite. To help you prepare for this job interview role play, you may want to take some time to find out about NetSuite by visiting www.netsuite.com for more information.

To the instructor: Additional information needed to complete the role play is available in the Instructor's Manual.

ADDITIONAL REFERENCES

Batislam, Emine Persentili, Meltem Denizel, and Alpay Filiztekin. "Empirical Validation and Comparison of Models for Customer Base Analysis." *International Journal of Research in Marketing* 24, no. 3 (September 2007), pp. 201–9.

Belonax Jr., Joseph J., Stephen J. Newell, and Richard E. Plank. "The Role of Purchase Importance on Buyer Perceptions of the Trust and Expertise Components of Supplier and Salesperson Credibility in Business-to-Business Relationships." *Journal of Personal Selling & Sales Management* 27, no. 3 (Summer 2007), pp. 247–58.

Bradberry, Travis. *Emotional Intelligence* 2.0. TalentSmart: Har/Dig En edition, 2009.

"Continuous Customer Dialogues: Strategies for Growth and Loyalty in Multi-Channel Customer-Oriented Organizations." *CRM Magazine* 12, no. 6 (2008), p. S5.

Crowder, Martin, David J. Hand, and Wojtek Krzanowski. "On Optimal Intervention for Customer Lifetime Value." *European Journal of Operational Research* 183 no. 3 (December 16, 2007), pp. 1550–59.

"Customer Analytics: Becoming Customer-Centric." *CRM Magazine* 11, no. 9 (September 2007), pp. 1–3.

"Determining 'CLV' Can Lead to Making Magical Marketing Decisions: Ask the Expert" (interview). *B to B* 92, no. 6 (May 7, 2007), p. 18.

Fox, Jeffrey J. *How to Be a Fierce Competitor: What Winning Companies and Great Managers Do in Tough Times.* Jossey-Bass, 2010.

Gaffney, John. "The Myth of Customer Loyalty." *1 to 1 Magazine,* March 2007, pp. 18–22.

Grayson, Kent, Devon Johnson, and Der-Fa Robert Chen. "Is Firm Trust Essential in a Trusted Environment? How Trust in the Business Context Influences Customers." *Journal of Marketing Research* 45, no. 2 (2008).

Green Jr., Kenneth, W. R. Anthony Inman, and Gene Brown. "Just-in-Time Selling Construct: Definition and Measurement." *Industrial Marketing Management* 37, no. 2 (April 2008), pp. 131–42.

Guenzi, Paolo, and Gabriele Troilo. "The Joint Contribution of Marketing and Sales to the Creation of Superior Customer Value." *Journal of Business Research* 60, no. 2 (February 2007), pp. 98–107.

Heilman, T. "Implementing 'Extreme' Customer Service." *Evaluation Engineering* 48, no. 11 (November 2009), pp. 14–19.

Hoff, Garth. "Customer-Centric Availability Evaluations in Revenue Management Applications." *Journal of Revenue & Pricing Management* 7, no. 1 (2008), pp. 40–51.

Homburg, Christian, Ove Jensen, and Harley Krohmer. "Configurations of Marketing and Sales: A Taxonomy." *Journal of Marketing* 72, no. 2 (2008), pp. 133–54.

Hosford, Christopher. "Measuring for the Long Haul: Customer Lifetime Value Metrics Give Marketers a Long View of How to Spend." *B to B* 92, no. 6 (May 7, 2007), p. 18.

Jaramillo, Fernando, Douglas B. Grisaffe, Lawrence B. Chonko, and James A. Roberts. "Examining the Impact of Servant Leadership on Salesperson's Turnover Intention." *Journal of Personal Selling & Sales Management* 29, no. 4 (Fall 2009), pp. 351–66.

Krasnikov, Alexander, Satish Jayachandran, and V. Kumar. "The Impact of Customer Relationship Management Implementation on Cost and Profit Efficiencies: Evidence from the U.S. Commercial Banking Industry." *Journal of Marketing* 73, no. 6 (2009), pp. 61–76.

Kumar, V., and Bharath Rajan. "Nurturing the Right Customers: By Measuring and Improving Customer Lifetime Value, You'll Be Able to Grow Your Most Profitable Customers." *Strategic Finance* 91, no. 3 (2009), pp. 27–33.

Kumar, V., Rajkumar Venkatesan, and Werner Reinartz. "Performance Implications of Adopting a Customer-Focused Sales Campaign." *Journal of Marketing* 72, no. 5 (2008), pp. 50–68.

Lee, Nancy. "It's All about the Customer: Commercial Perspectives on Customer-Centric Marketing and Managing the Customer Relationship." *Social Marketing Quarterly* 3, no. 3 (September 2007), pp. 12–16.

McArdle, Kevin. "Competing on Value: How to Get Your Unique Value Recognized and Rewarded by Customers." *Precision Manufacturing,* May–June 2007, 20.

McKee, Judy. *The Sales Survival Guide: Your Powerful Interactive Guide to Sales Success and Financial Freedom.* AuthorHouse, 2009.

Miao, C. Fred, and Kenneth R. Evans. "The Impact of Salesperson Motivation on Role Perceptions and Job Performance: A Cognitive and Affective Perspective." *Journal of Personal Selling & Sales Management* 27, no. 1 (Winter 2007), pp. 89–101.

Musico, C. "They Aim to Please." *CRM Magazine* 12, no. 12 (December 2008), pp. 36–41.

Pettijohn, Charles E., Linda S. Pettijohn, and A.J. Taylor. "Does Salesperson Perception of the Importance of Sales Skills Improve Sales Performance, Customer Orientation, Job Satisfaction, and Organizational Commitment, and Reduce Turnover?" *Journal of Personal Selling & Sales Management* 27, no. 1 (Winter 2007), pp. 75–88.

Piercy, Nigel F. "Strategic Relationships between Boundary-Spanning Functions: Aligning Customer Relationship Management with Supplier Relationship Management." *Industrial Marketing Management* 38, no. 8 (November 2009), pp. 857–64.

Poujol, F. Juliet, and John F. Tanner, "The Impact of Contests on Salespeople's Customer Orientation: An Application of Tournament Theory," *Journal of Personal Selling and Sales Management* 30, no. 1 (Winter 2010), pp. 33–46.

Rich, David. "Create Your Own Upturn: A Shift from Managing Volume to Managing Relationships." *CRM Magazine* 13, no. 10 (2009), pp.14–15.

Rouzies, Dominique, et al. "Determinants of Pay Levels and Structures in Sales Organizations." *Journal of Marketing* 73, no. 6 (2009).

Rust, Roland T., Christine Moorman, and Gaurav Bhalla. "Rethinking Marketing." *Harvard Business Review* 88, no. 1 (2010), pp. 94–101.

Schieffer, Robert, and Eric Leininger. "Customers at the Core." *Marketing Management* 17, no. 1 (January–February 2008), pp. 30–37.

Schoder, Detlef. "The Flaw in Customer Lifetime Value." *Harvard Business Review* 85, no. 12 (December 2007), p. 26.

Sebor, J. "Gets Serious." *CRM Magazine* 12, no. 2 (February 2008), pp. 22–26.

Smith, J. Brock, and Mark Colgate. "Customer Value Creation: A Practical Framework." *Journal of Marketing Theory & Practice* 15, no. 1 (Winter 2007), pp. 7–23.

Taulli, T. "Three Steps to a Sound Business Model." *BusinessWeek Online* 19 (March 2, 2009).

Temkin, Bruce. "7 Keys to Customer Experience: Big-Picture Advice for How to Improve the Customer Experience over the Next Year." *CRM Magazine* 13, no. 12 (2009), p. 12.

Thomson, D. "Essential No. 2: Redefine Your Market." *BusinessWeek Online* 17 (November 16, 2009).

Thomson, D. "No. 1: The Breakthrough Value Proposition." *BusinessWeek Online* 7 (November 9, 2009).

Uncles, M. "Know Thy Changing Consumer." *Journal of Direct, Data and Digital Marketing Practice* 10, no. 1 (2008), pp. 84–85.

Knowledge and Skill Requirements

1

PART

chapter **2**

ETHICAL AND LEGAL ISSUES IN SELLING

SOME QUESTIONS ANSWERED IN THIS CHAPTER ARE

- Why do salespeople need to develop their own codes of ethics?
- Which ethical responsibilities do salespeople have toward themselves, their firms, and their customers?
- Do ethics get in the way of being a successful salesperson?
- What guidelines should salespeople consider when confronting situations involving an ethical issue?
- Which laws apply to personal selling?

PROFILE

> *"Doing the right thing is not an option, but an obligation."*
>
> *Patricia Gietl, HP*

PROFILE Ethics and legal compliance are critical components of the selling process. As a leader in HP public sector sales, I'm responsible not only for developing technical solutions for our customers, but also for ensuring that we work within the required ethical and legal parameters for any given deal. Rules for public sector business can be different from those in the private sector. Further, what is considered unethical in one country may be a common custom in another. As employees of a global company working with a wide range of customers, we must always be cognizant of the rules of the business environment in which we're engaged.

At HP, we share values that include a passion for customers, trust and respect for individuals, and uncompromising integrity. These values have become inherent in our corporate culture and guide our innovation, creation, and sales and marketing behavior. As our CEO, Mark Hurd, states, "Innovation and trust are at the core of the HP brand." All employees are expected to live by these values in all business encounters.

HP employees are required to take training courses every year to keep us current on the "Standards of Business Conduct" (SBC). The corporate training and documentation cover company policies and guidelines for dealing with ethical and legal issues, such as fair competition, gifts, false claims and statements, conflicts of interest, workplace harassment, and handling of sensitive information. All HP employees who deal with public sector customers are required to take additional specialized training to help recognize the unique requirements of the U.S. public sector, and most importantly to know how to comply and, if needed, identify and contact the correct HP source for advice. A key underlying message in all communication is "Doing the right thing is not an option, but an obligation." Violation of the SBC or company policies by employees could result in disciplinary action, up to and including termination of employment.

How we conduct business impacts everyone with whom we interact, including customers, partners, coworkers, competitors, and family members. We've all heard or seen on the news those instances of individuals and organizations who are being prosecuted for unscrupulous and illegal business practices. While not all misconduct is newsworthy, any infraction can have significant impact on us individually and on our business. For example, if we provide false information or make false claims about our products or services, we could not only lose the trust of our customers and partners, but could face criminal charges. This situation could impose unnecessary litigation costs to the corporation, and could result in short- and long-term loss of revenue if customers decide to take their business elsewhere. The ramifications can also take a financial and emotional toll on our family members.

In the public sector, constituting or even creating an appearance of impropriety can be the basis for governmental inquiries or the loss of our ability to conduct government business. Violation could result in civil and or criminal fines or penalties up to and including imprisonment, termination, debarment, and severe financial damages.

One of the important parts of the sales cycle is to work the sales plan and develop/strengthen the customer relationship. While working with the U.S. public sector customer, HP employees need to be extra careful of our policy around gifts, gratuities, bribes, and kickbacks. It clearly prohibits us from offering, giving, soliciting, or receiving any gift or other thing of value in exchange for favorable treatment or advantage, or for the purpose of obtaining, or attempting to influence the award of a contract or subcontract. Some common examples of gifts are money, tickets to sporting/entertainment events, travel, lodging, training, meals/drinks (includes working lunches), and so on. Some examples of things that may not qualify as gifts include modest refreshments (certain state/local entities may consider modest refreshments), greeting cards, plaques, certificates, benefits (such as discounts) that are also available to the public or to all government employees, rewards and prizes for contests or events that are open to the public, or anything for which the government employee pays market value.

> As a hypothetical example: An HP salesperson, Mark, develops a professional relationship with Ted, a U.S. Department of Defense contracting officer who used to be in charge of a major HP contract. Although Ted is no longer directly responsible for any contracts held by HP, the two have kept in touch and grew their friendship. Mark wants to invite Ted to a major sporting event as a guest. At HP, we consider this to be an inappropriate action because although Mark and Ted may have developed a friendship over the years, Mark's interactions with Ted have been in the context of business and professional activities, and would not be seen as being "based on a personal relationship."

U.S. government agencies usually issue a request for proposal (RFP) to solicit responses/proposals from vendors. While assembling the solutioning team (HP employees, subcontractors, and partners) that will work on preparing a response to the RFP, we must ensure that there is no organizational conflict of interest (OCI) or personal conflict of interest in play. An OCI exists if a company offering to do work with a public sector entity has an unfair competitive advantage or has other interests that may impair its objectivity or ability to perform satisfactorily. At HP we must follow any applicable government requirements—plus we impose some extra requirements of our own.

The personal conflict of interest and OCI apply to HP employees, subcontractors, and partners. Violations may result in disqualification from current or future U.S. public sector business opportunities. For example, if any entity on the HP team has been hired by the government to write the specifications to be included in a competitive RFP for a computer system, HP may be precluded from bidding in the procurement.

As part of the response we usually develop a business model, technical solution, and cost/price proposal. While developing the proposal response, the HP solutioning team needs to be aware of the two chief sources of potential liability for U.S. government contractors—the False Statements Act and the False Claims Act. These statutes impose civil or even criminal penalties on contractors who provide false or misleading information to the government in connection with a government contract.

Thus the solutioning team may never knowingly make a false statement or submit a false claim to the government. This would include the submission of inaccurate or misleading information in support of prices offered by HP to the government, the submission of improper invoices, or inaccurate or misleading representations or certifications, either to a government representative or a prime contractor when the end user is the government.

> For example, in some cases the government may request "cost or pricing data"—that is, information about the company's actual costs of doing business. Additionally, proof of certain certifications is requested to ensure compliance with various socio-economic requirements such as equal opportunity laws. Certifications may also be used to ensure that the bidder is a responsible government contractor. (For example, HP may be asked to certify that it has not been debarred from government contracting or had a contract terminated for default.). In all these cases it is essential that this information be accurately represented to the government in order to avoid claims of "defective pricing."

If HP is selected as a finalist, the government may request a best and final offer, which initiates the contract negotiation process. The procurement integrity rules in HP's SBC ensure employee compliance with the U.S. Procurement Integrity Act. Under this act, government officials may not disclose, and HP employees may not knowingly obtain, source selection information (such as bid prices prior to public opening, evaluations, rankings, and the like) and contractor bid or proposal information (cost or pricing data, any information marked as proprietary, labor rates, and so on) in connection with a pending procurement. The Procurement Integrity Act does not apply to any information that has been publicly disclosed.

> For example, during the solutioning or contract negotiations, the HP Team may not obtain nonpublic information by illegal activities involving industrial espionage or by asking a competitor's current or former employees, partners, or contractors to violate their obligations regarding the competitor's confidential data.

Whether public or private sector, you must think about your code of ethics in any business interaction. Your best interest requires you to become familiar with the policies and processes, as well as the resources that are available to you, should you find yourself in a questionable business situation. Developing and maintaining the trust of your colleagues, customers, and partners is critical to your success as a salesperson, as well as the success of your business. By making ethical decisions, you and your organization will earn respect in the industry and consequently improve your bottom line.

**Visit our Web site at
www.hp.com.**

ETHICS AND PERSONAL SELLING

February 16, 2010: On the front page of *The Wall Street Journal* are four articles, two of which deal with business people acting unethically and probably illegally. One article focuses on a man who sold dreams of moving to America to Dutch dairy farmers, bilking them of millions. The other article centers on a plan to convince terminally ill individuals to purchase an investment product that pays the seller on the death of the patient. In return, the patient receives an upfront fee.[1] If all you ever saw about salespeople was that front page, you'd conclude that salespeople are all crooks. The reality, though, is that most sales transactions are aboveboard and free of ethical questions. These two stories are news precisely because such behavior is rare.

Ethics are the principles governing the behavior of an individual or a group. These principles establish appropriate behavior indicating what is right and wrong. Defining the term is easy, but determining what the principles are is difficult. What one person thinks is right another may consider wrong. For example, 58 percent of sales managers in one poll report believing that sales contests between salespeople do not generate unethical behavior—such as asking customers to take unwanted orders and then returning the merchandise after the contest is over—but 42 percent do believe that unethical behaviors are a consequence of sales contests.[2] So the feelings and experiences of sales managers are mixed when it comes to a commonly accepted practice.

What is ethical can vary from country to country and from industry to industry. For example, offering bribes to overcome bureaucratic roadblocks may be an accepted practice in Middle Eastern countries but is considered unethical, and illegal, in the United States. Further, while prevailing religions may influence ethics beliefs and practices, regional differences can occur. Egypt and Turkey, for example, are both populated almost entirely by Muslims; yet in Egypt, the courteousness of the salesperson is an important indicator of ethical practices. Not so in Turkey, which is more like the United States in not placing so much emphasis on courtesy; rather, actual customer service is preferred.[3]

An ethical principle can change over time. For example, some years ago doctors and lawyers who advertised their services were considered unethical. Today such advertising is accepted as common practice. Similarly, providing free pens and other gifts to doctors was once considered standard business practice; now a growing number of doctors consider the practice unethical and have even banned some companies from their offices or medical centers.[4]

THE EVOLUTION OF SELLING

The selling function has been a part of humankind since the beginning, perhaps when one person traded meat for berries. With the arrival of the Industrial Revolution in the 1800s, companies began to make more goods more cheaply. Even so, demand outstripped supply, and for many companies, the key issue in selling was to make people aware of the product and what it could do. Forward-thinking companies such as NCR and Singer Sewing Machines hired salespeople, called

Exhibit 2.1
The Evolution of
Personal Selling

	Production	Sales	Marketing	Partnering
Time Period	Before 1930	1930 to 1960	1960 to 1990	After 1990
Objective	Making sales	Making sales	Satisfying customer needs	Building relationships
Orientation	Short-term seller needs	Short-term seller needs	Short-term customer needs	Long-term customer and seller needs
Role of Salesperson	Provider	Persuader	Problem solver	Value creator
Activities of Salespeople	Taking orders, delivering goods	Aggressively convincing buyers to buy products	Matching available offerings to buyer needs	Creating new alternatives, matching buyer needs with seller capabilities

drummers or peddlers, and sent them across the country to sell. Then the companies brought the most effective salespeople back into the company office and wrote down their sales pitches. These **canned sales pitches** were distributed to all salespeople, who were expected to follow the scripts every time without deviation.

Since that time things have changed greatly. The nature of business evolved, necessarily changing how people sell. Exhibit 2.1 illustrates how the role of the salesperson has evolved from taking orders through persuading customers to building partnerships.[5]

As Exhibit 2.1 shows, the orientations of salespeople emerged in different periods. However, all these selling orientations still exist in business today. For example, inbound telephone salespeople working for retailers like Lands' End and Spiegel are providers with a production orientation. They answer a toll-free number and simply take orders. Many outbound telephone, real estate, and insurance salespeople are persuaders with a sales orientation. Partnering-oriented selling is becoming more common as companies make strategic choices about the type of selling best suited to their situation, but recent research indicates that even within partnerships, there are times when the buyer needs to hear persuasive messages that might be scripted.[6]

Even so, the move from a production orientation to a partnering orientation has affected the ethical perspective of the sales profession. The marketing orientation has created a customer-focused perspective that increases awareness of the buyer's needs. This customer awareness naturally leads to a less selfish seller and increases the importance of ethics. Further, the partnering orientation of the current period means long-term relationships are the norm. Salespeople who are less than ethical get caught in long-term relationships. The era of the peddler who can leave town and dupe the citizens of the next town is over.

ETHICS AND PARTNERING RELATIONSHIPS

Ethical principles are particularly important in personal selling. Most businesses try to develop long-term, mutually beneficial relationships with their customers. Salespeople are the official representatives of their companies, responsible for

2.1

From the BUYER'S SEAT

THE IMPORTANCE OF ETHICS IN THE SUPPLY CHAIN: GRANITE CONSTRUCTION

By Rick Carlysle, Granite Construction

I have worked for Granite Construction for over 20 years, during which time we've grown from $300 million to about $3 billion in annual revenue. We are a civil projects construction company building major projects like airports, highways, transit systems, and the like. I started in Texas as an engineer but moved to the corporate office in California, then New York City where I am now the regional contracts administrator. I've been involved in negotiating contracts with our subcontractors for the past 14 years.

Granite established a code of ethics a long time ago. Our company has been around since 1922, and we developed that code of ethics very early on. You can find it on our Web site; we share it with our customers and our subcontractors and with our vendors. In Granite, there is no gray area—we know what the expectations are. We're one of the prime contractors, and people want to work with us because they know our ethics. It (the code of ethics) is the basis for how we work.

Dealings with other companies have been better in New York City than I thought they would be. Contractors in New York may not have the greatest image, but I've not had any under-the-table dealings and not seen anything funny. But that's likely to be as much due to our reputation; and when you have a reputation for being honest and ethical, you attract like-minded companies.

If we have four bidders for a $10m electrical package and they are all within say $1m, we talk to the low bidder so that we know we're not being low-balled. If he is missing something, we need to put in plugs to fill the gap. We don't shop the bid. We don't tell subs, "You gotta do better than that," or (wink wink), "You gotta get down to such and such number." We ask for the best bid to begin with and we work with that. Once we've won a job, I work through the negotiations with the sub on issues such as payment terms, insurance, default, retainage and bonding, and so on. During the negotiations you formulate a good relationship with the sub, and you can tell at that point if there are any questionable issues or ethics. And if there are, we address them then.

One of our projects can last from one to four years, or even longer. We have to have subs we can rely on to do the right thing. The owner of the project (the state, or airport, or other agency) has to live with us, too. Ethics and fairness really come into play regarding change orders. Envision an owner that wants to add to the project and wants a price. We have to go back to subs, ask for prices, then put it together and go back to the owner. Then it is negotiated. We need this to be a positive experience, a win–win. We are a publicly traded company, and we are open on our books with the owner. We want a fair markup and overhead. Once you've established a reputation and people believe in it and in you, then our subs know it and our customers know it, and they all want to work with us.

Our reputation is really important. Building this reputation has taken a long time, but only one mess-up can tear it down. Therefore, when it comes to ethics, we operate as if there are no second chances.

Source: Contributed by Rick Carlysle, regional contracts administrator, Granite Construction.

developing and maintaining these relationships, which are built on trust. Partnerships between buyers and sellers cannot develop when salespeople behave unethically or illegally.[7] Further, research shows that trust deteriorates rapidly even in well-established relationships if integrity becomes questionable.[8]

Legal principles guide business transactions. The issues governing buying and selling are typically straightforward when the transaction is simple and the purchase is a one-time deal. The terms and conditions can be well defined and easily written into a traditional contract. In longer-term relationships, though, legal principles cannot cover all behaviors between buyer and seller.

Ethical principles become increasingly important as firms move toward longer-term relationships. Many issues cannot be reduced to contractual terms. For example, a salesperson might make a concession for a buyer with a special problem, anticipating that the buyer will reciprocate on future orders. Yet there is no legal obligation for the buyer to do so; this type of give-and-take is exactly why trust is such an important part of relationships. Because of the high levels of investment and uncertainty, the parties in these relationships cannot accurately assess the potential benefits—the size of the pie—accruing from strategic investments in the relationships or the contributions of each party in producing those benefits. Thus the parties in a longer-term relationship have to trust one another to divide the pie fairly. Further, many business settings require that the pie be divided amongst several suppliers or subcontractors, as well as with the customer. "From the Buyer's Seat 2.1" illustrates how important ethics are in the broader supply chain.

A basic principle of ethical selling is that the customer remains free to make a choice. **Manipulation** eliminates or reduces the buyer's choice unfairly. Salespeople can persuade; but with **persuasion,** one may influence the buyer's decision, but the decision remains the buyer's. Manipulation is unethical; persuasion is not. Keep that difference in mind as you read the rest of this chapter.

Here are some examples of difficult situations that salespeople face:

- Should you give an expensive Christmas gift to your biggest customer?
- If a buyer tells you it is common practice to pay off purchasing agents to get orders in his or her country, should you do it?
- Is it acceptable to use a high-pressure sales approach when you know your product is the best for the customer's needs?
- Is it okay to *not* share information about your product that could cost you a sale?
- Should you attempt to sell a product to a customer if you know a better product exists for that application?
- If you know about the poor performance features of a competing product, should you tell the customer about them?
- How do you handle a customer who has been lied to about your product by one of your competitors?

thinking **it** through   How would you respond to the situations in the preceding list? Why? How do you think your friends and your family would respond?

FACTORS INFLUENCING THE ETHICAL BEHAVIOR OF SALESPEOPLE

Exhibit 2.2 illustrates the factors that affect the ethical behavior of salespeople. The personal needs of salespeople, the needs of their companies and customers, company policies, the values of significant others, and the salesperson's personal code of ethics affect ethical choices.[9]

Personal, Company, and Customer Needs

Exhibit 2.3 shows how the personal needs of salespeople can conflict with needs of their firms and their customers. Both the salesperson's company and its customers want to make profits. But sometimes these objectives are conflicting. For example, should a salesperson tell a customer about problems his or her firm is having with a new product? Concealing this information might help make a sale,

Exhibit 2.2
Factors Affecting Ethical Behavior of Salespeople

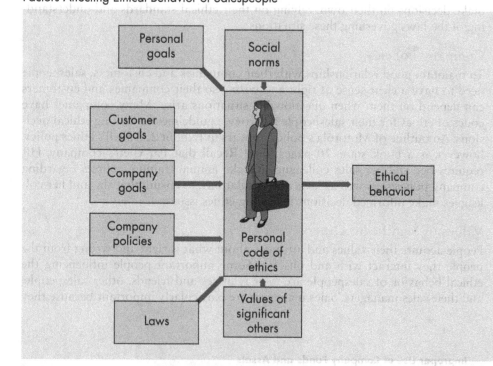

Exhibit 2.3
Conflicting Objectives

Company Objectives	Salesperson Objectives	Customer Objectives
Increase profits	Increase compensation	Increase profits
Increase sales	Receive recognition	Solve problems, satisfy needs
Reduce sales costs	Satisfy customers	Reduce costs
Build long-term customer relationships	Build long-term customer relationships	Build relationships with suppliers
Avoid legal trouble	Maintain personal code of ethics	Avoid legal trouble

increase the company's profits, and enhance the salesperson's chances of getting a promotion and a bonus; but doing so could also decrease the customer's profits when the product does not perform adequately.

Companies need to make sales, and that need can drive some unethical behavior. One salesperson was recently asked by his boss to bid on a project that required all of the work to be done locally. Yet he knew that his company planned to have some of the work done in India. The CEO's justification was that the company needed the business, and the customer was going to get a better price. The sales rep decided to not bid the job and told the CEO that he didn't. Fortunately for him, the CEO did not get upset.

Resolving serious ethical problems is difficult, but companies that resolve ethical issues well experience many benefits. Research shows that a positive ethical climate is related to job satisfaction, commitment to the organization, and intention to stay among salespeople—especially better-performing salespeople.[10] Organizations that have a positive ethical climate also have salespeople more committed to meeting the organization's goals.

Ethical conflicts often are not covered by company policies and procedures, and managers may not be available to provide advice. Thus salespeople must make decisions on their own, relying on their ethical standards and understanding of the laws governing these situations.

Company Policies

To maintain good relationships with their companies and customers, salespeople need to have a clear sense of right and wrong so their companies and customers can depend on them when questionable situations arise. Many companies have codes of ethics for their salespeople to provide guidelines in making ethical decisions. An outline of Motorola's policy appears in Exhibit 2.4. Shell's ethics policy, however, is a book some 20 pages long! Recall that Pat Gietl's company, HP, requires her and her sales colleagues to take annual training courses regarding company policies, as well as laws and regulations, to ensure that she and her colleagues make informed decisions regarding ethics issues.

Values of Significant Others

People acquire their values and attitudes about what is right and wrong from the people they interact with and observe. Some important people influencing the ethical behavior of salespeople are their relatives and friends, other salespeople, and their sales managers. Sales managers are particularly important because they

Exhibit 2.4
Ethics Policy for
Motorola Salespeople

Improper Use of Company Funds and Assets

The funds and assets of Motorola may not be used for influential gifts, illegal payments of any kind, or political contributions, whether legal or illegal.

The funds and assets of Motorola must be properly and accurately recorded on the books and records of Motorola.

Motorola shall not enter into, with dealers, distributors, agents, or consultants, any agreements that are not in compliance with U.S. laws and the laws of any other country that may be involved, or that provide for the payment of a commission or fee that is not commensurate with the services to be rendered.

Customer/Supplier/Government Relationships

Motorola will respect the confidence of its customers. Motorola will respect the laws, customs, and traditions of each country in which it operates but, in so doing, will not engage in any act or course of conduct that may violate U.S. laws or its business ethics. Employees of Motorola shall not accept payments, gifts, gratuities, or favors from customers or suppliers.

Conflict of Interest

A Motorola employee shall not be a supplier or a competitor of Motorola or be employed by a competitor, supplier, or customer of Motorola. A Motorola employee shall not engage in any activity where the skill and knowledge developed while in the employment of Motorola is transferred or applied to such activity in a way that results in a negative impact on the present or prospective business interest of Motorola.

A Motorola employee shall not have any relationship with any other business enterprise that might affect the employee's independence of judgment in transactions between Motorola and the other business enterprise.

A Motorola employee may not have any interest in any supplier or customer of Motorola that could compromise the employee's loyalty to Motorola.

Compliance with the Code of Conduct is a condition of employment. We urge you to read the complete code.

Should any questions remain, you are encouraged to consult your Motorola law department. In the world of business, your understanding and cooperation are essential. As in all things, Motorola cannot operate to the highest standards without you.

Source: Company document. Used with permission.

establish the ethical climate in their organization through the salespeople they hire, the ethical training they provide for their salespeople, and the degree to which they enforce ethical standards.[11]

Some people hesitate to pursue a sales career because they think selling will force them to compromise their principles.[12] Research, though, suggests otherwise. One series of studies finds that salespeople are less prone to unethical behaviors like exaggeration than are politicians, preachers, and even professors![13] No matter the industry, research finds that ethical behavior leads to higher customer satisfaction, trust, loyalty, and repeat purchases. As one of our former students now selling commercial real estate told us, "Unethical reps are run out of our industry." Good ethics are good business, and sales managers and salespeople know that.

Laws

In this chapter we examine ethical and legal issues in personal selling. *Laws* dictate which activities society has deemed to be clearly wrong—the activities for which salespeople and their companies will be punished. Some of these laws are reviewed later in the chapter. However, most sales situations are not covered by laws. Salespeople have to rely on their own codes of ethics and/or their firms' and industries' codes of ethics to determine the right thing to do.

A Personal Code of Ethics

Long before salespeople go to work they develop a sense of what is right and wrong—a standard of conduct—from family and friends. Although salespeople should abide by their own codes of ethics, they may be tempted to avoid difficult ethical choices by developing "logical" reasons for unethical conduct. For example, a salesperson may use the following rationalizations:

- All salespeople behave "this way" (unethically) in this situation.
- No one will be hurt by this behavior.
- This behavior is the lesser of two evils.
- This conduct is the price one has to pay for being in business.

Salespeople who use such reasoning want to avoid feeling responsible for their behavior and being bound by ethical considerations. Even though the pressure to make sales may tempt some salespeople to be unethical and act against their internal standards, maintaining an ethical self-image is important. Compromising ethical standards to achieve short-term gains can have adverse long-term effects. When salespeople violate their own principles, they lose self-respect and confidence in their abilities. They may begin to think that the only way they can make sales is to be dishonest or unethical, a downward spiral that can have significant negative effects.

Short-term compromises also make long-term customer relationships more difficult to form. As discussed earlier, customers who have been treated unethically will be reluctant to deal with those salespeople again. Also, they may relate these experiences to business associates in other companies.

Exhibit 2.5 lists some questions you can ask yourself to determine whether a sales behavior or activity is unethical. The questions emphasize that ethical behavior is determined by widely accepted views of what is right and wrong. Thus you should engage only in activities about which you would be proud to tell your family, friends, employer, and customers.

Your firm can strongly affect the ethical choices you will have to make. What if your manager asks you to engage in activity you consider unethical? There are

Exhibit 2.5
Checklist for Making
Ethical Decisions

1. Would I be embarrassed if a customer found out about this behavior?
2. Would my supervisor disapprove of this behavior?
3. Would most salespeople feel that this behavior is unusual?
4. Am I about to do this because I think I can get away with it?
5. Would I be upset if a salesperson did this to me?
6. Would my family or friends think less of me if I told them about engaging in this sales activity?
7. Am I concerned about the possible consequences of this behavior?
8. Would I be upset if this behavior or activity were publicized in a newspaper article?
9. Would society be worse off if everyone engaged in this behavior or activity?

If the answer to any of these questions is yes, the behavior or activity is probably unethical and you should not do it.

a number of choices you can make that are discussed in greater detail in Chapter 16, when we focus on relationships with your manager. From a personal perspective, however, here are three of those choices:

1. *Ignore your personal values, and do what your company asks you to do.* Self-respect suffers when you have to compromise principles to please an employer. If you take this path, you will probably feel guilty and quickly become dissatisfied with yourself and your job.

2. *Take a stand, and tell your employer what you think.* Try to influence the decisions and policies of your company and supervisors.

3. *Refuse to compromise your principles.* Taking this path may mean you will get fired or be forced to quit. Long-term benefits, though, can accrue as customers find that you are trustworthy.

You should not take a job with a company whose products, policies, and conduct conflict with your standards. Before taking a sales job, investigate the company's procedures and selling approach to see whether they conflict with your personal ethical standards. The issues concerning the relationship between salespeople and their companies are discussed in more detail in Chapter 16, and methods for evaluating companies are presented in Chapter 17.

SELLING ETHICS AND RELATIONSHIPS

The core principle at work in considering ethics in professional selling is that of fairness. The buyer has the right to make the purchase decision with equal and fair access to the information needed to make the decision; further, all competitors should have fair access to the sales opportunity. Keeping information from the customer or misrepresenting information is not fair because it does not allow the customer to make an informed decision. Kickbacks, bribes, and other unethical activities are unfair to both the customer's organization and to competitors. Those types of activities do not allow fair access to the sales opportunity. These and other situations can confront salespeople in their relationships with their customers, competitors, and colleagues (other salespeople).

RELATIONSHIPS WITH CUSTOMERS

The most common areas of ethical concern involving customers include using deception; offering gifts, bribes, and entertainment; divulging confidential information and rights to privacy; and backdoor selling.

Deception

Deliberately presenting inaccurate information, or lying, to a customer is illegal. Further, misleading customers by telling half-truths or withholding important information can also lead to legal consequences, but is more often a matter of ethics. Some salespeople believe it is the customer's responsibility to uncover potential product problems. These salespeople answer questions, perhaps incompletely, and don't offer information that might make a sale more difficult. For example, a salesperson selling life insurance may fail to mention that the policy won't pay off under certain circumstances.

Customers expect salespeople to be enthusiastic about their firm and its products and recognize that this enthusiasm can result in a certain amount of exaggeration as part of the persuasion process. Customers also expect salespeople to emphasize the positive aspects of their products and spend little time talking about the negative aspects. But practicing **deception** by withholding information or telling lies is clearly manipulative and therefore unethical. Such salespeople take advantage of the trust customers place in them. When buyers uncover these deceptions, they will be reluctant to trust such salespeople in the future. Not only that, but sophisticated buyers recognize such deceptions and assume the worst anyway.[14]

Salespeople who fail to provide customers with complete information about products lose an opportunity to develop trust. Trust is created through many actions, such as keeping all promises, especially the small promises like calling back when you say you will. In "Building Partnerships 2.1" we develop this concept of trust more completely.

Bribes, Gifts, and Entertainment

Bribes and kickbacks may be illegal. **Bribes** are payments made to buyers to influence their purchase decisions, whereas **kickbacks** are payments made to buyers based on the amount of orders placed. A purchasing agent personally benefits from bribes and kickbacks, but these payments typically have negative consequences for the purchasing agent's firm because the product's performance is not considered in buying decisions.

Entertaining clients is an accepted business practice in most industries, and this is an acceptable way to build relationships as long as the entertainment is not too lavish.

Taking customers to lunch is a commonly accepted business practice. Most salespeople take customers to lunch occasionally or frequently, and in many instances salespeople use this time to get to know the buyer better rather than pitch business. However, some companies take customers to sporting events, to play golf, or even on overnight trips to the company's plant or headquarters. In some cases these trips can become quite lavish; the pharmaceutical industry, for example, came under close governmental regulation for questionable practices regarding exotic and expensive trips for doctors who prescribe certain medications.

Determining which gifts and entertainment activities are acceptable and which are not brings up ethical issues. To avoid these issues, many U.S. companies have policies that forbid employees to accept gifts (more than pencils or coffee cups) or entertainment from suppliers. These firms require that all gifts sent to the employee's home or office be returned. IBM does not allow any gifts, even coffee cups; Walmart, the largest retailer in the world, makes no allowance for entertainment

BUILDING Partnerships

BUILDING TRUST BUILDS PARTNERSHIPS

"Anyone working with Jessica Ni can be confident that she will overdeliver on whatever you requested, no matter how impossible the request may be," says client Jordan Levinson. "It's comforting to know there are still people out there who truly care about your brand and what you're trying to do for it. The industry at large could learn a lot from the little things Jessica does right day in and day out." With compliments like that coming from customers, it is no wonder that Jessica Ni was named Salesperson of the Year by an industry association. Jessica is a sales representative for *The Atlantic*, a monthly magazine, and works with advertisers to see that they get the most for their advertising dollars.

What Levinson is describing is a person that can be trusted. Trust, to buyers, means that the salesperson can be counted on to deliver what is needed. And when building partnerships, trust is the most important ingredient.

Randy Garutti, managing partner in charge of all purchasing for Shake Shack, a chain of hamburger restaurants in the New York City area, agrees. When asked what he looks for in a supplier, "trust" is the first word out of his mouth. Before price and before service, he wants someone he can trust. "If we run out of products,

they will put whatever we need in their car and drive it to us."

Levinson and Garutti both point out the importance of being able to count on someone to deliver. But there's also an aspect of empathy, or caring for the buyer, that seems to be important. These buyers want someone who will work for them, knowing that things don't always go as planned but that the salesperson is there to make it right. Research shows that ethical behavior builds trust. Further, buyers have difficulty separating trust in a company from trust in the salesperson, but it is clear that unethical behavior depletes trust. And without trust, there is no business opportunity—at least not with buyers like Levinson and Garutti.

Sources: The Levinson quote is from "Salesperson of the Year," *MIN Online*, http://www.minonline.com/best_sellers/Salesperson-of-the-Year-Manager-Level-Single-Title-With-Circ-Between-100K-500K-Jessica-Ni-Midwest-Integrated-Account-Manager-The-Atlantic_11207.html, accessed February 18, 2010. The Garutti quote is from Caroline Perkins, "Trust Is the Key Trait for Sales Reps, Says USHG's Garutti," *Nation's Restaurant News* 43, no. 39 (October 19, 2009), p. 18; the research cited is Mei-Fang Chen and Liang-Hung Mau, "The Impacts of Ethical Sales Behaviour on Customer Loyalty in the Life Insurance Industry," *The Service Industries Journal* 29 (2009), pp. 1–21.

because all contact between buyers and vendors can occur only at business meetings at Walmart's or the vendor's headquarters. On the other hand, many companies have no policy on receiving gifts or entertainment. Some unethical employees will accept and even solicit gifts, even though their company has a policy against such practices.

To develop a productive, long-term relationship, salespeople need to avoid embarrassing customers by asking them to engage in activities they might see as unethical. If a salesperson wants to give a gift out of friendship or invite a customer to lunch to develop a better business relationship, she or he should phrase the offer so the customer can easily refuse it. For example, a salesperson with a large industrial firm might have this conversation with a customer:

SALESPERSON: John, we have worked well together over the last five years, and I would like to give you something to show my appreciation. Would that be OK?

BUYER: That's very nice of you, but what are you thinking of giving me?

SALESPERSON: Well, I want to give you a Mont Blanc pen. I really enjoy using my pen, and I thought you might like one also. Is that OK?

BUYER: I would appreciate that gift. Thank you.

Buyers typically are sensitive about receiving expensive gifts, according to Shirley Hunter, account manager for Teradata. "It's like getting five dozen roses after a first date. It's embarrassing if anyone finds out, and you have to wonder what's the catch?"[15] Some industries used promotional items frequently; but in pharmaceutical sales, government regulations have increasingly forbidden the use of gifts because no one wants the choice of a prescription to be influenced by a salesperson's gift to a doctor. Some guidelines for gift giving are as follows:

- Check your motives for giving the gift. The gift should be given to foster a mutually beneficial, long-term relationship, not to obligate or pay off the customer for placing an order.
- Make sure the customer views the gift as a symbol of your appreciation and respect with no strings attached. Never give customers the impression that you are attempting to buy their business with a gift.
- Make sure the gift does not violate the customer's or your firm's policies.
- The safest gifts are inexpensive business items imprinted with the salesperson's company's name or logo.

Even when customers encourage and accept gifts, lavish gifts and entertainment are both unethical and bad business. Treating a customer to a three-day fishing trip is no substitute for effective selling. Sales won this way are usually short-lived. Salespeople who offer expensive gifts to get orders may be blackmailed into continually providing these gifts to obtain orders in the future. Customers who can be bribed are likely to switch their business when presented with better offers.

Special Treatment

Some customers try to take advantage of their status to get special treatment from salespeople. For example, a buyer asks a salesperson to make a weekly check on the performance of equipment even after the customer's employees have been thoroughly trained in the operation and maintenance of the equipment. Providing this extra service may upset other customers who do not get the special attention. In addition, the special service can reduce the salesperson's productivity. Salespeople should be diplomatic but careful about undertaking requests to provide unusual services.

Confidential Information

During sales calls salespeople often encounter confidential company information such as new products under development, costs, and production schedules. Offering information about a customer's competitor in exchange for an order is unethical. Many times, though, the request is not that obvious. For example, a customer asks how well your product is selling and you reply, "Great!" The customer then asks, "Well, how is it doing at HEB?" If the customer is told how many cases are sold at HEB, then HEB's right to confidentiality was violated. We discuss legal issues around privacy later in this chapter, but there are ethical issues regarding confidentiality that are not always covered by law.

Long-term relationships can develop only when customers trust salespeople to maintain confidentiality. By disclosing confidential information, a salesperson will get a reputation for being untrustworthy. Even the customer who solicited the confidential information will not trust the salesperson, who will then be denied access to information needed to make an effective sales presentation.

Backdoor Selling

Sometimes purchasing agents require that all contacts with the prospect's employees be made through them because they want to be fully informed about and control the buying process. The purchasing agent insists that salespeople get his or her approval before meeting with other people involved in the purchase decision. This policy can make it difficult for a new supplier to get business from a customer using a competitor's products.

Salespeople engage in **backdoor selling** when they ignore the purchasing agent's policy, go around his or her back, and contact other people directly involved in the purchasing decision. Backdoor selling can be risky and unethical. If the purchasing agent finds out, the salesperson may never be able to get an order. To avoid these potential problems, the salesperson needs to convince the purchasing agent of the benefits to be gained by direct contact with other people in the customer's firm.

Jason Evans, MD, wrote a letter to the pharmaceutical salespeople who called on him, and he posted it in several conspicuous places in his office building. This letter specifies his expectations for acceptable selling tactics; a few of his points are listed in Exhibit 2.6. He reports that many salespeople commented that they appreciated knowing his expectations for their behavior, and from his perspective, interactions with salespeople have improved. Yet salespeople we've interviewed find the list too restrictive. Whether fair or too restrictive, Evans's letter has caught on and can now be found in many doctors' offices.

Sneaking in the back door to sell behind the purchasing agent's back directly to a user in the buying company is considered unethical and can get a company blacklisted, unable to sell to that buyer again.

Research on buyers in general suggests additional behaviors that they think are unethical or inappropriate. Exhibit 2.7 summarizes that research. The research suggests that buyers will go out of their way to avoid salespeople who engage in these practices.[16]

RELATIONSHIPS WITH THE SALESPERSON'S COMPANY

Because salespeople's activities in the field cannot be closely monitored, their employers trust them to act in the company's best interests. Professional salespeople do not abuse this trust. They put the interests of their companies above self-interest. Taking

Exhibit 2.6
One Doctor's Request for Ethical Behavior

DO: Tell me why your drug is exceptional using the STEPS approach: *safety, tolerability, efficacy, price,* and *simplicity.*

DON'T: Say negative things about your competitors or their drugs.

DON'T: Tell me what and how much another physician in the area uses your drug.

DON'T: Invite me to dinner.

DO: Arrange for specialists to come to our office during lunch so I can pick their brains.

DON'T: Offer me pens, notepads, or any other "freebies" with your drug's name on it. The cost is in your company's budget, which raises the price you charge my patients.

Source: Adapted from Jason Evans, "Establishing Rules of the Road for Pharmaceutical Representatives," *Family Practice Management,* March 2005, pp. 10–11.

Exhibit 2.7
Buyers' View of
Unethical Sales
Behaviors

- Exaggerates benefits of product.
- Passes the blame for something he or she did to someone else.
- Lies about product availability.
- Misrepresents guarantees.
- Lies about competition.
- Sells products that people do not need.
- Makes oral promises that are not legally binding.
- Is not interested in customer needs.
- Answers questions even when he or she does not know the correct answer.
- Sells hazardous products.

Source: Adapted from William Bearden, Thomas Ingram, and Raymond LaForge, *Marketing: Principles and Perspectives* (New York: McGraw-Hill/Irwin, 2004).

this perspective may require them to make short-term sacrifices to achieve long-term benefits for their companies and themselves. Some problem areas in the salesperson–company relationship involve expense accounts, reporting work time information and activities, and switching jobs. "Sales Technology 2.1" illustrates some problems salespeople may have with use of the company computer.

Expense Accounts

Many companies provide their salespeople with cars and reimburse them for travel and entertainment expenses. Developing a reimbursement policy that prevents salespeople from cheating and still allows them the flexibility they need to cover their territories and entertain customers is almost impossible. Moreover, a lack of tight control can tempt salespeople to use their expense accounts to increase their income.

To do their jobs well, salespeople need to incur expenses. However, using their expense accounts to offset what they consider to be inadequate compensation is unethical. A salesperson who cannot live within the company compensation plan and expense policies has two ethical alternatives: (1) persuade the company to change its compensation plan or expense policy or (2) find another job. Salespeople are given expense accounts to cover legitimate expenses such as for travel. Act as though you are spending your own money; an expense account does not mean you should stay in the most luxurious hotel in town.

Reporting Work Time Information and Activities

Employers expect their salespeople to work full-time. Salespeople on salary are stealing from their employers when they waste time on coffee breaks, long lunches, or unauthorized days off. Even salespeople paid by commission cheat their companies by not working full-time. Their incomes and company profits both decrease when salespeople take time off. In "Sales Technology 2.1" we take a light-hearted look at the reality of technology and the ever-increasing ability of companies to ensure accurate reporting and full use of company time.

To monitor work activities, many companies ask their salespeople to provide daily call reports. Most salespeople dislike this clerical task. Some provide false information, including calls they never made. Giving inaccurate information or bending the truth is clearly unethical. A failure to get an appointment with a customer is not a sales call. Providing a brief glimpse of a product is not a demonstration.

SALES Technology

2.1

THE BIG BROTHER EFFECT OF TECHNOLOGY

Orwell's frightening tale of totalitarian government control, *1984*, introduced the term "Big Brother," the notion that someone is looking over your shoulder and tracking your every movement in order to control your activities. Key to Big Brother in the Orwell novel was the use of technology, unavailable when the novel was written but maybe close to being available now.

Sneaking out to the golf course? Busted by the company-issued cell phone! GPS technology in the phone can be used to identify where a salesperson is.

Waiting until the end of the month to create your reports? Busted! The software notes when you entered the data, and the sales manager assumes the data are, at best, a little fuzzy and perhaps not all that accurate. Or at worst the manager assumes the calls weren't made, and now someone is looking for a new job.

Spending work time on Facebook? Busted! But Facebook can be a real business tool, with its IM feature used between colleagues at work, and the social network aspects used for identifying prospects (finding friends) or sending a message. Just don't put this on your wall: "Work sucks! Three more days to the weekend!"

Sending risqué photos and jokes via e-mail? Busted again! Some companies closely monitor e-mail. While stories abound of salespeople accidentally copying customers on e-mail messages that make fun of those same customers, more recently companies have cracked down on using work computers for personal activities. And it's not worth the possibility of getting fired to share jokes or pictures that some might think are funny but others think are sexual harassment.

Many salespeople complain of not being able to get away from work. Carrying a company-issued Blackberry or iPhone leads to answering e-mail and customer calls 24/7. Couple that around-the-clock availability with the facts that even though only 52 percent of salespeople reached quota last year, 85 percent of companies increased quotas further this year. and the pressure is on to stay connected. Add to that the ability to track a salesperson's activity on the Web, e-mail, or even the phone, and it can feel like Big Brother is watching every move. When every move is the right move, though, it's no problem.

Source for survey data: Jim Dickie, "Avoid the Disaster of 2009," *CRM Magazine*, February 2010, p. 10.

Switching Jobs

When salespeople decide to change jobs, they have an ethical responsibility to their employers. The company often makes a considerable investment in training salespeople and then gives them confidential information about new products and programs. Over time, salespeople use this training and information to build strong relationships with their customers.

A salesperson may have good reasons to switch jobs. However, if a salesperson goes to work for a competitor, she or he should not say negative things about the past employer. Also, disclosing confidential information about the former employer's business is improper. The ethical approach to leaving a job includes the following:

- *Give ample notice.* If you leave a job during a busy time and with inadequate notice, your employer may suffer significant lost sales opportunities. Do not be surprised, though, if you are escorted out that day. Many companies are concerned about the loss of information by, as well as lack of productivity of, someone who has turned in notice, so the policy may be that you are turned out that day.

- *Offer assistance during the transition phase.* Help your replacement learn about your customers and territory, if given the opportunity.

- *Don't burn your bridges.* Don't say things in anger that may come back to haunt you. Remember that you may want to return to the company or ask the company for a reference in the future. You may even find that the people you worked with move to a company you want to work for or sell to!
- *Don't take anything with you that belongs to the company.* That includes all your records and notes on companies you called on, even if you are going to a noncompeting company. In many states, customer records are considered **trade secrets,** or information owned by the company by which the company gains a competitive advantage. Trade secrets are protected by law, so if you take customer records with you, you could face a civil lawsuit.

RELATIONSHIPS WITH COLLEAGUES

To be effective, salespeople need to work together with other salespeople. Unethical behavior by salespeople toward their coworkers, such as engaging in sexual harassment and taking advantage of colleagues, can weaken company morale and harm the company's reputation.

Sexual Harassment

Sexual harassment includes unwelcome sexual advances, requests for sexual favors, jokes or graffiti, posting sexually explicit material on bulletin boards or cubicle walls, and physical conduct. Harassment is not confined to requests for sexual favors in exchange for job considerations such as a raise or promotion; creating a hostile work environment can be considered sexual harassment. Some actions that are considered sexual harassment are engaging in suggestive behavior, treating people differently because they are male or female, making lewd sexual comments and gestures, jokes that have sexual content shared by e-mail, showing obscene photographs, alleging that an employee got rewards by engaging in sexual acts, and spreading rumors about a person's sexual conduct.

Customers as well as coworkers can sexually harass salespeople. Salespeople are particularly vulnerable to harassment from important customers who may seek sexual favors in exchange for their business. Following are some suggestions for dealing with sexual harassment from customers:

- Don't become so dependent on one customer that you would consider compromising your principles to retain the customer's business. Develop a large base of customers and prospects to minimize the importance of one customer—a good idea for a lot of reasons.
- Tell the harasser in person or write a letter stating that the behavior is offensive, is unacceptable, and must be stopped. Clearly indicate that you are in control and will not be passive.
- Use the sexual harassment policies of your firm and your customer's firm to resolve problems. These policies typically state the procedure for filing a complaint, the person responsible for investigating the complaint, the time frame for completing the investigation, and the means by which the parties will be informed about the resolution.

Recent research indicates that sexual harassment is rare; one study found only an average of 1.3 cases per year per company in all areas of the company, not just sales.[17] That study also found that companies are much more worried about making sure their employees have a safe environment in which to work than any fear of lawsuits; in other words, executives want to make sure their people have a good environment in which to work because it is the right thing to do, not because they may get sued if they fail to do so.

Taking Advantage of Other Salespeople

Salespeople can behave unethically when they are too aggressive in pursuing their own goals at the expense of their colleagues. For example, it is unethical to steal potential customers from other salespeople. Colleagues usually discover such unethical behavior and return the lack of support. If the company has policies protecting customers or territories, such behavior can lead to immediate termination.

RELATIONSHIPS WITH COMPETITORS

Making false claims about competitors' products or sabotaging their efforts is clearly unethical and often illegal. For example, a salesperson who rearranges the display of a competitor's products in a customer's store to make it less appealing is being unethical. This type of behavior can backfire. When customers detect these practices, the reputations of the salespeople and their companies may be permanently damaged.

Another questionable tactic is criticizing a competitor's products or policies. Although you may be tempted to say negative things about a competitor, this approach usually does not work. Customers will assume you are biased toward your own company and its products and discount negative comments you make about the competition. Some customers may even be offended. If they have bought the competitor's products in the past, they may regard these comments as a criticism of their judgment.

LEGAL ISSUES

Society has determined that some activities are clearly unethical and has created a legal system to prevent people from engaging in these activities. Salespeople who violate these laws can cause serious problems for themselves and their companies—problems more serious than being considered unethical by a buyer. By engaging in illegal activities, salespeople expose themselves and their firms to costly legal fees and millions of dollars in fines.

The activities of salespeople in the United States are affected by three forms of law: statutory, administrative, and common. **Statutory law** is based on legislation passed either by state legislatures or by Congress. The main statutory laws governing salespeople are the Uniform Commercial Code and antitrust laws. **Administrative laws** are established by local, state, or federal regulatory agencies. The Federal Trade Commission is the most active agency in developing administrative laws affecting salespeople. However, the Securities and Exchange Commission regulates stockbrokers, and the Food and Drug Administration regulates pharmaceutical salespeople. Finally, **common law** grows out of court decisions. Precedents set by these decisions fill in the gaps where no laws exist.

This section discusses current laws affecting salespeople, but every year important new laws are developed and court decisions rendered. Thus you should contact your firm for advice when a potential legal issue arises.

UNIFORM COMMERCIAL CODE

The **Uniform Commercial Code (UCC)** is the legal guide to commercial practice in the United States. The UCC defines a number of terms related to salespeople.

Agency

A person who acts in place of his or her company is an **agent**. Authorized agents of a company have the authority to legally obligate their firm in a business transaction. This authorization to represent the company does not have to be in writing. Thus, as a salesperson, your statements and actions can legally bind your company and have significant financial impact.

Sale

The UCC defines a **sale** as "the transfer of title to goods by the seller to the buyer for a consideration known as price." A sale differs from a **contract to sell.** Any time a salesperson makes an offer and receives an unqualified acceptance, a contract exists. A sale is made when the contract is completed and title passes from the seller to the buyer.

The UCC also distinguishes between an offer and an invitation to negotiate. A sales presentation is usually considered to be an **invitation to negotiate.** An **offer** takes place when the salesperson quotes specific terms. The offer specifically states what the seller promises to deliver and what it expects from the buyer.

This buyer is inspecting a shipment of flowers. Because the flowers were shipped FOB destination, the buyer is not responsible for the merchandise until it shows up at the buyer's warehouse. The buyer can even turn down the sale now if the flowers are not up to standard.

If the buyer accepts these terms, the parties will have established a binding contract.

Salespeople are agents when they have the authority to make offers. However, most salespeople are not agents because they have the power only to solicit written offers from buyers. These written offers, called **orders,** become contracts when they are signed by an authorized representative in the salesperson's company. Sometimes these orders contain clauses stating that the firm is not obligated by its salesperson's statements. However, the buyer usually can have the contract nullified and may even sue for damages if salespeople make misleading statements, even though they are not official agents.

Title and Risk of Loss

If the contract terms specify **free on board (FOB) destination,** the seller has title until the goods are received at the destination. In this case any loss or damage incurred during transportation is the responsibility of the seller. The buyer assumes this responsibility and risk if contract terms call for **FOB factory.** The UCC also defines when titles transfer for goods shipped cash on delivery (COD) and for goods sold on consignment. Understanding the terms of the sale and who has title can be useful in resolving complaints about damaged merchandise.

thinking it through   If a salesperson is not an agent, then what is the salesperson? Does not being an agent change the salesperson's obligations to the company in any way? Or to the customer?

Oral versus Written Agreements

In most cases oral agreements between a salesperson and a customer are just as binding as written agreements. Normally, written agreements are required for sales over $500. Salespeople may be the legal representatives of their firms and thus must be careful when signing written agreements.

Obligations and Performance

When the salesperson and the customer agree on the terms of a contract, both firms must perform according to those terms in "good faith," which means they have to try to fulfill the contract. In addition, both parties must perform according to commonly accepted industry practices. Even if salespeople overstate the performance of their products, their firms have to provide the stated performance and meet the terms of the contract.

Warranties

A **warranty** is an assurance by the seller that the products will perform as represented. Sometimes a warranty is called a *guarantee*. The UCC distinguishes between two types of warranties: expressed and implied. An **expressed warranty** is an oral or a written statement by the seller. An **implied warranty** is not actually stated but is still an obligation defined by law. For example, products sold using an oral or a written description (the buyer never sees the products) carry an implied warranty that the products are of average quality. However, if the buyer inspects the product before placing an order, the implied warranty applies only to any performance aspects that the inspection would not have uncovered. Typically an implied warranty also guarantees that the product can be used in the manner stated by the seller.

Problems with warranties often arise when the sale is to a reseller (a distributor or retailer). The ultimate user—the reseller's customer—may complain about a product to the reseller. The reseller, in turn, tries to shift the responsibility to the manufacturer. Salespeople often have to investigate and resolve these issues.

MISREPRESENTATION OR SALES PUFFERY

In their enthusiasm salespeople may exaggerate the performance of products and even make false statements to get an order. Over time, common and administrative laws have defined the difference between illegal misrepresentation and sales puffery. Not all statements salespeople make have legal consequences. However, misrepresentation, even if legal, can destroy a business relationship and may involve salespeople and their firms in lawsuits.

Glowing descriptions such as "Our service can't be beat" are considered to be opinions or **sales puffery**. Customers cannot reasonably rely on these statements. Following are some examples of puffery:

- This is a top-notch product.
- This product will last a lifetime.
- Our school bus chassis has been designed to provide the utmost safety and reliability for carrying the nation's most precious cargo—schoolchildren.
- The most complete line of reliable, economical gas heating appliances.

However, statements about the inherent capabilities of products or services, such as "Our system will reduce your inventory by 40 percent," may be treated as statements of fact and warranties. Here are examples of such statements found to be legally binding:

- Mechanically, this oil rig is a 9 on a scale of 10.
- Feel free to prescribe this drug to your patients, doctor. It's nonaddicting.
- This equipment will keep up with any other machine you are using and will work well with your other machines.

Rich Kraus owned a company providing document shredding services using special trucks that contain high-speed shredders. When purchasing a new truck, he looked to another small company. The salesperson was the owner's son, and his pride came through as he gave a demo and rattled off the capabilities of the equipment. Compared to Kraus's current model, this shredder was 40 percent faster and had 30 percent more capacity for storing shredded material, so he placed an order for the $250,000 truck.

Unfortunately he quickly realized the truck was capable of holding only 60 percent of the paper that the salesperson said it could. When the problem was discussed with the engineer, he admitted that the salesperson had provided incorrect information. However, he didn't want to correct the owner's son in front of a prospective customer. He added that the salesperson was a good honest person and that his enthusiasm probably just got the best of him.

Only after threatening legal action did Kraus get his money back and order a truck from his original vendor. Since then, Kraus sold his company to a larger company that purchases an average of 50 trucks per year, all from Kraus's original vendor.

As Kraus says, "Since that time we have had dozens of associates in the industry ask us about our experience with this company. It's hard to fathom how many orders it lost as a result." Risking the reputation of the company for even a single unit just wasn't worth it.[18]

The **False Claims Act**, or Lincoln Law, was passed in 1863 during the Civil War to encourage citizens to press claims against vendors that fraudulently sold to the U.S. government (all states now have their own version, too). During the war, defense contractors were selling all manner of products (including mules) that could not live up to the claims made by the salespeople. As a result, the government was losing money and the war. This law enabled a person bringing a claim of fraud to share in the proceeds if the contractor was found guilty and damages are assessed. Although this law is well over 100 years old, as you read in the opening profile, today's businesspeople like Pat Gietl at HP still have to ensure that their claims are accurate, especially when selling to the government.

U.S. salespeople need to be aware of both U.S. laws and laws in the host country when selling internationally. All countries have laws regulating marketing and selling activities. In Canada all claims and statements made in advertisements and sales presentations about comparisons with competitive products must pass the **credulous person standard.** This standard means the company and the salesperson have to pay damages if a reasonable person could misunderstand a statement. Thus a statement like "This is the strongest axle in Canada" might be considered puffery in the United States but be viewed as misleading in Canada unless the firm had absolute evidence that the axle was stronger than any other axle sold in Canada.

To avoid legal and ethical problems with misrepresentation, you should try to educate customers thoroughly before concluding a sale. You should tell the customer as much about the specific performance of the product as possible. Unless your firm has test results concerning the product's performance, you should avoid offering an opinion about the product's specific benefits for the customer's application. If you don't have the answer to a customer's question, don't guess. Say that you don't know the answer and will get back to the customer with the information.

ILLEGAL BUSINESS PRACTICES

The Sherman Antitrust Act of 1890, the Clayton Act of 1914, the Federal Trade Commission Act of 1914, and the Robinson-Patman Act of 1934 prohibit unfair business practices that may reduce competition. The courts used these laws to create common law that defines the illegal business practices discussed in this section.

Business Defamation

Business defamation occurs when a salesperson makes unfair or untrue statements to customers about a competitor, its products, or its salespeople. These statements are illegal when they damage the competitor's reputation or the reputation of its salespeople.

Following are some examples of false statements made about competitors that have been found to be illegal:

- Company X broke the law when it offered you a free case of toilet paper with every 12 cases you buy.
- Company X is going bankrupt.
- You shouldn't do business with Company X. Mr. Jones, the CEO, is really incompetent and dishonest.

You should avoid making negative comments about a competitor, its salespeople, or its products unless you have proof to support the statements.

Reciprocity

Reciprocity is a special relationship in which two companies agree to buy products from each other. For example, a manufacturer of computers agrees to use microprocessors from a component manufacturer if the component manufacturer agrees to buy its computers. Such interrelationships can lead to greater trust and cooperation between the firms. However, reciprocity agreements are illegal if one company forces another company to join the agreement. Reciprocity is legal only when both parties consent to the agreement willingly.

Tying Agreements

In a **tying agreement** a buyer is required to purchase one product in order to get another product. For example, a customer who wants to buy a copy machine is required to buy paper from the same company, or a distributor that wants to stock one product must stock the manufacturer's entire product line. Because they reduce competition, tying agreements typically are illegal. They are legal only when the seller can show that the products must be used together—that is, that one product will not function properly unless the other product is used with it.

Tying agreements are also legal when a company's reputation depends on the proper functioning of equipment. Thus a firm can be required to buy a service contract for equipment it purchases, although the customer need not buy the contract from the manufacturer.

A tying agreement, which requires someone to buy one product in order to get another, is illegal. For example, if the maker of this copier required customers to buy only its paper, that would be an illegal tying agreement.

Conspiracy and Collusion

An agreement between competitors before customers are contacted is a **conspiracy**, whereas **collusion** refers to competitors working together while the customer is making a purchase decision. For example, competitors are conspiring when they get together and divide up a territory so that only one competitor will call on each prospect. Collusion occurs when competitors agree to charge the same price for equipment that a prospect is considering. These examples of collusion and conspiracy are illegal because they reduce competition.

Interference with Competitors

Salespeople may illegally interfere with competitors by

- Trying to get a customer to break a contract with a competitor.
- Tampering with a competitor's product.
- Confusing a competitor's market research by buying merchandise from stores.

Restrictions on Resellers

Numerous laws govern the relationship between manufacturers and resellers—wholesalers and retailers. At one time it was illegal for companies to establish a minimum price below which their distributors or retailers could not resell their products. Today this practice, called **resale price maintenance,** is legal in some situations.

Manufacturers do not have to sell their products to any reseller that wants to buy them. Sellers can use their judgment to select resellers if they announce their selection criteria in advance. One sales practice considered unfair is providing special incentives to get a reseller's salespeople to push products. For example, salespeople for a cosmetics company may give a department store's cosmetics salespeople prizes based on sales of the company's product. These special incentives, called **spiffs** (or **push money**), are legal only if the reseller knows and approves of the incentive and it is offered to all the reseller's salespeople. *Spiff* stands for "special promotion incentive fund" and dates back to a time when there was more selling by retail salespeople. Even if they are legal, though, not everyone agrees that spiffs are ethical.[19]

Price Discrimination

The Robinson-Patman Act became law because independent wholesalers and retailers wanted additional protection from the aggressive marketing tactics of large chain stores. Principally, the act forbids price discrimination in interstate commerce. Robinson-Patman applies only to interstate commerce, but most states have passed similar laws to govern sales transactions between buyers and sellers within the same state.

Court decisions related to the Robinson-Patman Act define **price discrimination** as a seller giving *unjustified* special prices, discounts, or services to some customers and not to others. To justify a special price or discount, the seller must prove that it results from (1) differences in the cost of manufacture, sale, or delivery; (2) differences in the quality or nature of the product delivered; or (3) an attempt to meet prices offered by competitors in a market. Different prices can be charged, however, if the cost of doing business is different or if a customer negotiates more effectively. For example, a customer who buys in large volume can be charged a lower price if the manufacturing and shipping charges for higher-volume orders are lower than they are for smaller orders.

Using spiffs to promote one product over another, such as one brand of oven, is legal, but research shows consumers believe the practice to be unethical.

In general, firms also may not offer special allowances to one reseller unless those allowances are made available to competing resellers. Because most resellers compete in limited geographic areas, firms frequently offer allowances in specific regions of the country. However, recent Supreme Court decisions allow some leeway in offering discounts to resellers who are engaged in competitive bids. These discounts do not necessarily have to be offered uniformly to all resellers for all customers, but can be selectively offered to meet specific competitive situations. In one case a Volvo truck dealer sued Volvo, citing discounts given to other Volvo dealers in situations where the dealers were all bidding on the same customer's contract. The Supreme Court ruled that these instances did not violate the law because they were negotiated individually to meet bids from non-Volvo providers.

Privacy Laws

Privacy laws limit the amount of information that a firm can obtain about a consumer and specify how that information can be used or shared. The Gramm-Leach-Bliley Act, passed in 1999, requires written notification of customers regarding privacy policies. Note that the law does not discriminate in how the information was obtained. In other words, the law is the same for a customer who fills out a credit application or a customer who responds to questions from a salesperson. Although this law applies primarily to financial institutions, a second phase of the act became law in 2003, broadening its application. Further, any company that publishes a privacy policy is expected, by regulation of the Federal Trade Commission, to follow that policy and is liable to prosecution if it uses customer information inappropriately.

European Union law is even more stringent than U.S. law. The application of privacy applies to many more settings, and transfer of information is forbidden in nearly all circumstances. Further, the law can apply to information that could be shared among non-EU subsidiaries, which means that in some instances an account manager in Europe cannot share information with an American colleague.

Do-Not-Call Law

The federal Do-Not-Call Registry originally took effect in 2003 and was strengthened in 2007, and limits the conditions under which anyone on the registry may be telephoned at home or on a cell phone. A salesperson, for example, cannot call the number of someone on the registry if the person is not already a customer. This registry was set up by the Federal Trade Commission (FTC) under its ability to set rules for commerce, and is an administrative law. However, the FTC can levy fines against companies and individuals that violate the rules, as some companies have already learned. The rules do not apply to business phones.

INTERNATIONAL ETHICAL AND LEGAL ISSUES

Ethical and legal issues are complex for selling in international markets. Value judgments and laws vary widely across cultures and countries. Behavior that is commonly accepted as proper in one country can be completely unacceptable in another country. For example, a small payment to expedite the loading of a truck is considered a cost of doing business in some Middle Eastern countries but may be viewed as a bribe in the United States.

Many countries make a clear distinction between payments for lubrication and payments for subordination. **Lubrication** involves small sums of money or gifts, typically made to low-ranking managers or government officials, in countries where these payments are not illegal. The lubrication payments are made to get the official or manager to do the job more rapidly—to process an order more quickly or to provide a copy of a request for a proposal. For example, Halliburton, the company hired to rebuild Iraq, says, "Sometimes the company [Halliburton] may be required to make facilitating or expediting payments to a low-level government employee or employee in some other countries than the United States to expedite or secure the routine governmental action. . . . Such facilitating payments may not be illegal. . . . Accordingly, facilitating payments must be strictly controlled, and every effort must be made to eliminate or minimize such payments."[20] The policy goes on to say that any such payments must have advance authorization from the company's legal department so there will be no question whether the payment is lubrication or subordination. **Subordination** involves paying larger sums of money to higher-ranking officials to get them to do something that is illegal or to ignore an illegal act. Even in countries where bribery is common, subordination is considered unethical.[21]

RESOLVING CULTURAL DIFFERENCES

What do you do when the ethical standards in a country differ from the standards in your country? This is an old question. Cultural relativism and ethical imperialism are two extreme answers to this question. **Cultural relativism** is the view that no culture's ethics are superior. If the people in Indonesia tolerate bribery, their attitude toward bribery is no better or worse than that of people in Singapore who refuse to give or accept bribes. When in Rome, do as the Romans do. But is it right for a European pharmaceutical company to pay a Nigerian company to dispose of the pharmaceutical company's highly toxic waste near Nigerian residential neighborhoods, even though Nigeria has no rules against toxic waste disposal?

On the other hand, **ethical imperialism** is the view that ethical standards in one's home country should be applied to one's behavior across the world. This view suggests, for example, that Saudi Arabian salespeople working for a U.S. firm should go through the same sexual harassment training U.S. salespeople do, even though the strict conventions governing relationships between men and women in Saudi Arabia make the training meaningless and potentially embarrassing.

Adopting one of these extreme positions is probably not the best approach. To guide your behavior in dealing with cultural differences, you need to distinguish between what is merely a cultural difference and what is clearly wrong. You must not only respect core human values that should apply in all business situations but also respect local traditions and use the cultural background to help you decide what is right and what is wrong. For example, exchanging expensive gifts is common in Japanese business relationships, although it may be considered unethical in Western cultures. Most Western firms operating in Japan now accept this practice as an appropriate local tradition.

Research indicates that salespeople, particularly those who operate in foreign cultures, need significant corporate support and guidance in handling cultural ethical differences. Even a high level of personal morality may not prevent an individual from violating a law in a sales context, so it is imperative that companies establish specific standards of conduct, provide ethical training, and monitor behavior to enforce standards as uniformly as possible around the globe.[22]

LEGAL ISSUES

Regardless of the country in which U.S. salespeople sell, they are subject to U.S. laws that prohibit participating in unauthorized boycotts, trading with enemies of the United States, or engaging in activities that adversely affect the U.S. economy. The **Foreign Corrupt Practices Act** makes it illegal for U.S. companies to pay bribes to foreign officials; however, an amendment to the act permits small lubrication payments when they are customary in a culture. Violations of the law can result in sizable fines for company managers, employees, and agents who knowingly participate in or authorize the payment of such bribes. Recently 22 people were arrested at a conference for arms industry executives when they allegedly attempted to bribe a senior government minister in an African country. Included among those arrested was a vice president for sales with Smith & Wesson. Note that the individuals were charged with violating the law, while their companies were not indicted.[23] Siemens, a company indicted under the FCPA, paid a fine of over $1.6 billion, as well as the cost of over 100 attorneys and 1,300 forensic accountants.[24] One method companies can use to protect themselves, in the event an employee does violate the law, is to include the FCPA in the company's code of ethics. If the company takes specific steps, such as mentioning the law in company policy, the government's assumption is that the employee acted on his or her own and is individually responsible.[25]

The U.S. laws concerning bribery are much more restrictive than laws in other countries. For example, in Italy and Germany bribes made outside the countries are clearly defined as legal and tax-deductible.

SELLING YOURSELF

Most college students do not give much thought to their reputations, at least in terms of a professional reputation. Yet your actions in class and around campus add up to a professional reputation in the sense that faculty form an opinion that is shared with recruiters and others who make important decisions. For example, faculty recommendations may be necessary for scholarships, membership in prestigious organizations, and, of course, jobs. Professors and instructors base their recommendations not only on what they observe, but also on what they hear.

Carrying your weight in group projects, contributing your share in study groups, and doing your own work are actions that exhibit more than a professional work ethic; they also show your integrity. Other small things, like coming to class and leaving your cell phone silent in your backpack during class, can also contribute to a professor's estimation of a student's overall professional demeanor.

Of course, obvious actions such as claiming illness without any documentation, cheating on an exam (or even giving the appearance of cheating), or collaborating too closely with another student on an independent exercise can damage your credibility. Students may believe they can get away with such actions in classes not in their major and still get good faculty recommendations, but in reality reputation is much bigger than that. Although not every faculty member will learn a student's complete reputation, most of us learn enough from our colleagues and our students to know whom to recommend and whom to avoid.

Start working on your professional reputation now. Whether or not you decide to create one intentionally, you are building that reputation anyway.

SUMMARY

This chapter discussed the legal and ethical responsibilities of salespeople. These responsibilities are particularly important in personal selling because salespeople may face conflicts between their personal standards and the standards of their firms and customers. However, the evolution of selling has raised ethical standards and expectations; building long-term relationships with customers doesn't allow for unethical behavior.

Salespeople's ethical standards determine how they conduct relationships with their customers, employers, and competitors. Ethical issues in relations with customers involve the use of entertainment and gifts and the disclosure of confidential information. Ethical issues in relations with employers involve expenses and job changes. Finally, salespeople must be careful in how they talk about competitors and treat competitive products.

Many companies have ethical standards that describe the behavior expected of their salespeople. In evaluating potential employers, salespeople should consider these standards.

Salespeople also encounter many situations not covered by company statements and therefore must develop personal standards of right and wrong. Without personal standards, salespeople will lose their self-respect and the respect of their company and customers. Good ethics are good business. Over the long run, salespeople with a strong sense of ethics will be more successful than salespeople who compromise their own and society's ethics for short-term gain.

Statutory laws (such as the Uniform Commercial Code) and administrative laws (such as Federal Trade Commission rulings) guide the activities of salespeople in the United States. Selling in international markets is complex because of cultural differences in ethical judgments and laws that relate to sales activities in various countries.

KEY TERMS

QUESTIONS AND PROBLEMS

1. There are certainly many ethical and legal issues in selling, as this chapter demonstrates. Do you think there are more ethical and legal issues in selling than other jobs, such as accounting, finance, retail store management, or the like? Which issues raised in the chapter are likely to be present, no matter the job, and which are likely to be specific to sales jobs?

2. Rick Carlysle of Granite Construction says he doesn't run into ethical challenges when dealing with salespeople. What is it about Granite that would prevent a seller from acting unethically? How important is reputation in his business? Whose reputation is more important in influencing ethical behavior?

3. For centuries the guideline for business transactions was the Latin term *caveat emptor* (let the buyer beware). This principle suggests that the seller is not responsible for the buyer's welfare. Is this principle still appropriate in modern business transactions? Why or why not? How has the evolution of selling influenced ethics in professional selling?

4. You are calling on an account when the customer asks how the lawsuit is going. "What lawsuit?" you reply. Your competitor, it seems, has been saying that you are within a week of declaring bankruptcy because a former customer is suing. How do you respond to the customer? What other action should you take?

5. Some professors believe that ethics cannot be taught; only laws need to be taught. Do you agree? Why or why not? What do you think Pat Gietl's (in the opening profile) answer would be to this question? Why? Would her answer differ from that of someone who sells to other businesses?

6. Your customer asks you what you think of a competitor's product. You know from experience with other customers that it is unreliable and breaks down frequently. Further, given this particular customer's needs, you expect that this issue would be an even bigger problem if the customer chose this product. How do you respond? Be specific about what you would say.

7. Your company has a contact management software system in which you enter all the information you can about your customers. The company wants to partner with another firm in marketing products. Your company wants to give your database to the other firm so the other firm can create marketing pieces and e-mail them to your clients. Is this legal? Is it ethical? Why or why not?

8. Review Dr. Evans's list of requests for salespeople (Exhibit 2.6).
   a. What principle seems to underlie all his requests?
   b. He requests that salespeople not ask what he prescribes or why—he feels that this is collecting marketing information and debating his choices. In addition, he requests that salespeople not ask him to prescribe their drug—he'll make that decision on a case-by-case basis when appropriate. These are two standard practices in selling: finding out what customers' current products are and asking for the order. Why would he consider these bothersome practices? Should his request be honored in all situations with all customers? Why or why not?

9. For each of the following situations, evaluate the salesperson's action and indicate what you think the appropriate action would be:
   a. In an electronics store, salespeople are offered an extra $50 for each sale of HDTV models that are being closed out. The manufacturer is offering the extra spiff, and management is fully aware of it. Salespeople, though, are encouraged to not mention either the spiff or the fact that these are closeout models.
   b. A customer asks if you can remove a safety feature because it slows down the operators of the equipment.
   c. The custom of the trade is that competitive firms submit bids based on specifications provided by the buyer; then the buyer places an order with the firm offering the lowest bid. After a salesperson submits a bid, the purchasing agent calls him and indicates that the bid is too high; the lowest bid so far is almost 8 percent lower than that. The buyer asks the salesperson to submit another bid at a price at least 10 percent lower.
   d. A few months after joining a company, you learn about a credit card that gives you a 20 percent cash refund on meals at certain restaurants. You get the card and start taking

clients to restaurants offering the rebate, pocketing the rebate.

e. A customer gives a salesperson a suggestion for a new service. The salesperson does not turn in the idea to her company, even though the company's policy manual states that all customer ideas should be submitted with the monthly expense report. Instead the salesperson quits her job and starts her own business using the customer's suggestion.

CASE PROBLEMS

case **2.1**

E-Town

Marty Selig was looking over his financial statement for E-Town, his small chain of electronics stores. Marty's company sells electronics such as HDTVs, but where he really distinguishes his company from big box discounters like Best Buy and Walmart is in service. His best opportunities to provide value and make money are for services such as installing home theaters. But a tight economy has buyers either downsizing their purchases or not buying at all, and Marty is worried about whether his business will make it.

A knock at the door interrupted his thoughts. "Hey, Marty!" exclaimed Amanda Duron as she entered his office and sat down. "We've just come out with a limited offer, something that we have very few units for, and we're targeting value-added resellers like E-Town." Amanda represented a lesser-known Korean brand of televisions and other electronics. "What we'd like to do is consolidate all of our remaining inventory on this year's models into stores like yours, then offer a 30% rebate to you. You can use it as a spiff for your reps, a sales price for customers, or a combination of the two. And we won't consolidate these models into any store here in San Antonio except E-Towns. What do you say?"

"Why the big rebate? Are these closeouts?" he asked.

"Yes, they are. With this big rebate, I can't help you with advertising costs, but you can offset advertising costs by charging full price and keeping the rebate. Or, as I said, offer your sales staff a spiff."

"How many do I have to take?"

"I worked out a plan that is 50 units per store, and based on your past sales with us, I've already got a matrix for allocating the various models to each store. Can I count on you for this promotion? I'd rather it be E-Town than Circuit Country!" she said, mentioning one of Marty's toughest competitors.

Marty considered her offer. The brand she represented had good picture quality but was known, at least among dealers, for needing more service. The cost for installation was also a bit higher in home theater applications because of the way the cabling had to be done, but more service and higher installation costs would mean more revenue for Marty.

Marty decided to take Amanda up on her offer. He marked the TVs down 10 percent, offered the salespeople a 10 percent spiff (ranging from $50 to $350), and applied the final 10 percent to local advertising costs. As he walked through one of his stores, he overheard a salesperson say about one of Amanda's TVs, "This TV is every bit as good as that one (pointing to a different brand), but this sale price makes it the best choice for you."

Questions

1. If you were Marty, how would you have spent the 30 percent rebate? Are there any ethical issues in the choices he made?

2. Should Marty step in and clarify what the salesperson is talking about? Or let the rep handle the customer?

3. Many retail store clerks work on straight commission and may get spiffs for selling certain products. Should this information be publicly available—perhaps posted somewhere in the store? Why or why not?

case 2.2

DuBois Polymers

DuBois Polymers manufactures and distributes chemicals in the northwest United States and western Canada. Usually the company sells to a distributor, which sells to the customer that uses the chemicals. Mitch Thompson is Betsy Briles's biggest customer. His business, which distributes chemicals in British Columbia and Washington State, represents nearly 15 percent of Betsy's annual sales. Recently Betsy acquired a new account in the same area, Crago Chemicals, which has the potential to be just as large. Her most recent meeting with Mitch, though, went like this:

"Look, Crago Chemicals underbid us on the Canuck contract by 10 percent. You must be offering them a better price than us, and I want to know why," said Mitch.

Betsy knew that Crago bid that job with no profit in order to expand into Vancouver and that the price she quoted them was actually 5 percent more than Mitch's. "Mitch, I'm not giving them a better price—they don't buy as much as you do from us, so I can't."

"Huh. You'll have to do better than that. You know that the Farley contract is coming up, and it is going to be big. I want to know what they intend to do about it."

"Mitch, if I told you their pricing strategy, as if I knew it, why would you ever trust me with your information?"

"C'mon. I'm your biggest customer. We have to stick together."

"Well, I don't know their strategy."

"Try to find out. And while you're at it, I think I can get the Hudson Pulp and Paper account away from National if you'll give me just a 5 percent discount on those products."

Betsy knew she was as low as she could go pricing-wise. But if she gave him a few barrels a month free and marked it down as a sample, then she would effectively lower the price and get away with it. And National was not one of her accounts—if Mitch won the Hudson account, she would see another $100,000 in revenue per month.

Questions

1. What should she do about the Farley situation? Should she try to find out if Canuck plans to bid on the Farley contract and, if so, what its strategy is?
2. What should she do about the Hudson account?
3. Describe her relationship with Mitch. Where should she go with this account in the future?

ROLE PLAY CASE

(Note: If you've not completed the Role Play Case in Chapter 1, you should review it before starting this role play.) Weaver Medical is a national distributor of medical equipment. You are calling on Ms. Weaver, and everything seems to be going well. M&F has 48 salespeople, managed by six sales managers who report to Ms. Weaver. Currently they e-mail sales call reports to their managers at the end of each week, and sales are forecast for the following week. Weaver uses these forecasts to manage inventory, but always orders less than forecast because salespeople are overly optimistic. Sales are also lower than she would prefer, and she thinks with better knowledge of what is happening in each account, she could help salespeople perform better.

It's time to ask for the order. You should summarize how NetSuite lets the manager summarize the sales team's activities daily. Salespeople no longer have to e-mail their reports; they simply have to log into NetSuite and enter the day's activities. Not only will NetSuite give the managers a forecast daily, but it will also summarize each rep's performance by level of the sales process. The manager can then use that information to pinpoint how to improve each rep's performance. Once you've summarized, ask for an order of 55 units. Each buyer will be given a sheet with information about how to respond.

ADDITIONAL REFERENCES

Bellizi, Joseph A. "Honoring Accounts of Top Sales Performers and Poor Sales Performers Who Have Engaged in Unethical Selling Behavior." *Journal of Global Business Issues* 2, no. 2, pp. 207–15.

Bristow, Dennis N., Rajesh Gulati, Douglas Amyx, and Jennifer Slack. "An Empirical Look at Professional Selling from a Student Perspective." *Journal of Education for Business* 81, no. 5 (2006), pp. 242–49.

Cadogan, John Nick Lee, Anssi Tarkiainen, and Sanna Sundqvist. "Sales Manager and Sales Team Determinants of Salesperson Ethical Behavior." *European Journal of Marketing* 43, no. 7/8 (2009), pp. 907–22.

Calderaro, Fabio, and Anne T. Coughlan. "Spiffed-Up Channels: The Role of Spiffs in Hierarchical Selling Organizations." *Marketing Science* 26, no. 1 (2007), pp. 31–52.

Hansen, John D., and Robert J. Riggle. "Ethical Salesperson Behavior in Sales Relationships." *Journal of Personal Selling & Sales Management* 29, no. 2 (2009), pp. 151–66.

Hoivik, Heidi von Weltzien. "East Meets West: Tacit Messages about Business Ethics in Stories Told by Chinese Managers." *Journal of Business Ethics* 74, no. 4 (2007), pp. 457–69.

Mantel, Susan P. "Choice or Perception: How Affect Influences Ethical Choices among Salespeople." *Journal of Personal Selling & Sales Management* 25, no. 1 (2005), pp. 43–57.

Nevins, Jennifer L., William O. Bearden, and Bruce Money. "Ethical Values and Long-Term Orientation." *Journal of Business Ethics* 71, no. 3 (2007), pp. 261–74.

Pettijohn, Charles, Linda Pettijohn, and A.J. Taylor. "Salesperson Perceptions of Ethical Behaviors: Their Influence on Job Satisfaction and Turnover Intentions." *Journal of Business Ethics* 78, no. 4 (2008), pp. 547–57.

Román, Sergio, and José Luis Munuera. "Determinants and Consequences of Ethical Behaviour: An Empirical Study of Salespeople." *European Journal of Marketing* 39, no. 5–6 (2005), pp. 473–496.

Sangtani, Vinita, and John Andy Wood. "The Impact of Stigma: Negative Stereotypes of Salespeople." *Journal of Selling and Major Account Management* 7, no. 4, pp. 38–52.

Schwepker Jr., Charles H., and David J. Good. "Sales Management's Influence on Employment and Training in Developing an Ethical Sales Force." *Journal of Personal Selling & Sales Management* 27, no. 4 (2007), pp. 325–39.

Schwepker Jr., Charles H., and Michael D. Hartline. "Managing the Ethical Climate of Customer-Contact Service Employees." *Journal of Service Research* 7, no. 4 (2007), pp. 377–97.

Valentine, Sean, and Tim Barnett. "Perceived Organizational Ethics and the Ethical Decisions of Sales and Marketing Personnel." *Journal of Personal Selling & Sales Management* 27, no. 4 (2007), pp. 373–389.

Weeks, William A., Terry W. Loe, Lawrence B. Chonko, Carlos Ruy Martinez, and Kirk Wakefield. "Cognitive Moral Development and the Impact of Perceived Ethical Climate on the Search for Sales Force Excellence: A Cross-Cultural Study." *Journal of Personal Selling & Sales Management* 26 (Summer 2006), pp. 205–24.

Zhuang, Guijun, and Alex Tsang. "A Study of Ethically Problematic Selling: Methods in China with a Broader Concept of Gray Marketing." *Journal of Business Ethics* 79, no. 1–2 (2008), pp. 85–101.

chapter **3**

BUYING BEHAVIOR AND THE BUYING PROCESS

SOME QUESTIONS ANSWERED IN THIS CHAPTER ARE

- What are the different types of customers?
- How do organizations make purchase decisions?
- Which factors do organizations consider when they evaluate products and services?
- Who is involved in the buying decision?
- What should salespeople do in the different types of buying situations?
- Which changes are occurring in organizational buying, and how will these changes affect salespeople?

PROFILE

"I look at the buying process it takes, the many buying decisions involved, and I'm fascinated. First, the process is quite complex. . . . Second, the buying process is multifaceted. . . . It is important to understand your buyers in order to execute a successful plan."

Jenna Weber, Hormel

PROFILE I started my career with Hormel Foods as a meat products marketing intern for a summer. As an intern, I learned about the marketing side of the business. Most importantly, I got a taste of how our product managers run multiple projects simultaneously while interacting with almost every department in our company, from accounting to logistics to the sales field. Not only are marketing managers responsible for creating products that the end consumer will like, but they need to keep in mind the retailers (Walmart, Kroger, SUPERVALU, and so on). After the conclusion of my internship, I finished my last semester and received my marketing degree from the University of Wisconsin–Eau Claire. From there, I trained as a sales representative at our Kansas City location. This role taught me about the consumer products industry, Hormel Foods, and our competitors at the store level. In seven months, I gained a brief understanding of consumers at the retail level and how promotions are executed. After training, I was promoted to an account in the East.

My understanding of how a product got from raw materials to the grocery store, and from my cart to my house, was very limited prior to working at Hormel Foods. I had never really thought about it. Now, I look at the process it takes, the many buying decisions involved, and I'm fascinated. First, the process is quite complex. Raw materials are manufactured in a plant to create pepperoni. That pepperoni is sent from a Hormel warehouse to a warehouse for a grocery chain. The pepperoni then gets sent on a truck from the warehouse to the retail store where it is placed on the shelf and ready for sale. Second, the buying process is multifaceted—which I didn't expect. There are multiple decisions that are made between the plant and your home. The corporate buyer from a grocery chain decides to purchase our pepperoni, and then the manager of the pepperoni category at the store level decides where to carry it. Now, you (the consumer) walk into the store, stand in front of the pepperoni set,

and decide which brand to take home. The corporate buyer and category manager are just as important as the end consumer. If the corporate buyer or the category manager doesn't purchase HORMEL® pepperoni, then customers of that store don't even have the option to buy our brand. My role is to give the consumer every opportunity to purchase Hormel products by getting the products on the shelf and supporting the products through promotions.

I currently work with a regional retail customer that has over 100 stores in the Northeast. Pepperoni is just one category out of 23 that I manage at my retail account. I must sell products, promotions, and strategies for each one of my categories. However, the most difficult part of my job is dealing with different buyers. Some categories have the same buyer. For example, HORMEL® chili, DINTY MOORE® beef stew, and SPAM® are all purchased by the same grocery buyer. But there are five different buyers overall, and each buyer has a different style. For example, my meat buyer is very relationship oriented and appreciates that I bring him donuts and coffee. We talk about his children, his plans for the weekend, and of course the business. He doesn't like long presentations with data-filled pages. He just wants to know, "Will this item sell?" He is easy to deal with, especially on promotions that are run annually (such as hams during the holidays).

Another buyer is the complete opposite. He wants to know every detail of the item, including pages of analytical data that support the success of the product. He takes longer to make a decision and needs data to prove his choice. This can be good and bad. For example, we were running a bacon promotion, and I argued with my meat buyer that one truckload wasn't enough. It didn't matter to him that I had past history of similar promotions that proved he needed more; he simply refused. Conversely, for a large promotion in grocery, I used multiple analytical tools to prove the volume my grocery buyer needed. By showing him the facts, I successfully sold him three truckloads of displays. As you can see, it's important to understand your buyer's personality and the most effective way to connect with him or her.

The end consumer is also very important in the buying process. While I do not sell to consumers directly, they play a key role in my decision making. When planning a promotion, does it make the most sense to present a deal at 2/$4 or at $1.99? In making that choice, I have to decide which price point seems like the best deal to my end user. For an item that a customer may already buy multiples of, such as CHI-CHI'S® salsa, 2/$4 makes the most sense. However, most people won't purchase more than one 38-ounce DINTY MOORE® beef stew, so that item is better left at a single price point. Along with deciding price, I also have to choose which products are items that should be displayed. Most of Hormel's products are impulse items, but it is up to the retailer if they are worthy of an end-cap or aisle display. My job is to ensure that Hormel products are highly visible to our end user, thus encouraging increased sales.

Whether it is the corporate buyer or the end consumer, the purchasing process is very complex. It is important to understand your buyers and your consumers in order to execute a successful plan. Hormel is committed to helping all of its employees understand these processes and providing them with the tools to be successful.

Visit our Web site at www.hormelfoods.com.

TYPES OF CUSTOMERS

Business is full of a wide variety of customers, including producers, resellers, government agencies, institutions, and consumers. Each of these customer types has different needs and uses a different process to buy products and services. In many situations salespeople will have only one type of customer, but in other territories they may have many different types of customers. Thus salespeople may need to use different approaches when selling to different types of customers.

PRODUCERS

Producers buy products and services to manufacture and sell their products and services to customers. Buyers working for producers are involved in two types of buying situations: buying products that will be included in the products the company is manufacturing or buying products and services to support the manufacturing operation.

OEM PURCHASERS

Buyers for **original equipment manufacturers (OEMs)** purchase goods (components, subassemblies, raw and processed materials) to use in making their products. For example, when one of Jenna Weber's (profiled at the start of this chapter) distributors sells pizza toppings to a restaurant, that it is an OEM purchase. The pizza topping is a processed material used in making the restaurant's product, pizza. Another example of an OEM buyer would be Dell. Dell is an OEM purchaser. It may use Intel processors in its computers, but Dell is the OEM. Sometimes, though, Dell sells computers to other OEM manufacturers. For example, when you use a kiosk at the airport to print your boarding pass, the computer inside it is a Dell, but the kiosk is put together and sold by someone else.

Salespeople selling OEM products need to demonstrate that their products help their customers produce products that will offer superior value. For example, Tim Pavlovich, OEM salesperson for Dell, says that one reason why Dell gets contracts like the kiosk contract is because Dell has a nationwide service team already in place and can fix the computers anywhere in the world.

Most OEM products are bought in large quantities on an annual contract. The purchasing department negotiates the contract with the supplier; however, engineering and production departments play a major role in the purchase decision. Engineers evaluate the products and may prepare specifications for a custom design. The production department works with the supplier to make sure the OEM products are delivered "just in time."

OEM customers are building long-term relationships with a limited number of OEM suppliers. Thus relationship building with more than one department in a customer firm is particularly important when selling OEM products.

END USERS

When producers buy goods and services to support their own production and operations, they are acting as **end users.** End-user buying situations include the purchase of capital equipment; maintenance, repair, and overhaul (MRO) supplies; and services. **Capital equipment** items are major purchases, such as mainframe computers and machine tools that the producer uses for a number of years. **MRO supplies** include paper towels and replacement parts for machinery. **Services** include Internet and telephone connections, employment agencies, consultants, and transportation.

Because capital equipment purchases typically require major financial commitments, capital equipment salespeople need to work with a number of people involved in the purchase decision, including high-level corporate executives. These salespeople need to demonstrate the reliability of their products and their support services because an equipment failure can shut down the producer's operation. Capital equipment buying often focuses on lifetime operating cost rather than the initial purchase price because the equipment is used over a long period. Thus capital equipment salespeople need to present the financial implications as well as the operating features and benefits of their products.

MRO supplies and services are typically a minor expense and therefore are usually less important to businesses than are many other items. Purchasing agents typically oversee MRO buying decisions. Because they often do not want to spend the time to evaluate all suppliers, they tend to purchase from vendors who have performed well in the past, creating functional relationships.

Although the cost of MRO supplies is typically low, availability can be critical. For example, the failure of a $10 motor in an industrial robot can shut down an entire assembly line. Some professional services, such as accounting, advertising, and consulting, also are important to the company and may be purchased in a manner similar to capital equipment purchases.

RESELLERS

Resellers buy finished products or services with the intention to resell them to businesses and consumers. Hormel sells precooked meats, such as pepperoni for pizza toppings, to resellers—distributors who then sell to restaurants. Other examples of resellers include McKesson Corporation, a wholesaler that buys health care products from manufacturers and resells those products to drugstores; Brazos Valley Equipment, a dealer for John Deere, selling tractors, harvesters, combines, and other agricultural implements to farmers; and Dealer's Electric, selling lighting, conduit, and other electrical components to electricians and contractors. All these are resellers, and they buy for similar reasons.

Resellers consider three elements when making decisions about which products to sell: profit margin, turnover, and effort. Resellers want to maximize their return on investment (ROI), which is a function of **profit margin** or how much they make on each sale, **turnover** or how quickly a product will sell, and how much effort it takes to sell the product. Buyers for resellers often simplify their decisions by a focus on either profit margin or turnover, but all resellers are interested in putting together an assortment of products that will yield the greatest overall ROI.

Salespeople work with resellers to help them build their ROI. Not only do salespeople help resellers choose which products to sell, but they also train resellers on how to sell and service products, build point-of-purchase displays and promotions, and may also help resellers with developing advertising and marketing campaigns to boost sales. For example, with increasing competition between grocery chains, retailers are asking suppliers to create excitement and generate traffic in stores.

"Retailers' expectations for our products' performance continue to escalate. Price is important but not the only thing retailers are demanding," Eddy Patterson, of Stubb's Legendary Kitchen, said. "We need to look at innovative ways that not only help sell our products and create brand awareness but also ways to contribute to the success of our customers, the retailers who sell our products." For example, Stubb's Bar-B-Q has sold its line of barbecue sauces and marinades in supermarkets and has created a loyal following. Stubb's recently entered a license agreement for Stubb's All Natural Charcoal Briquettes and a Stubb's cookbook. By entering a licensing agreement with third-party manufacturers, Stubb's created complementary items to build its brand awareness. Stubb's has developed not only another revenue source for the company but also exposure for the brand in areas beyond current supermarket retailers. This creates a win for the retailers, a win for Stubb's Bar-B-Q, and a win for the licensing manufacturers.[1]

Patterson then took the cross-licensed products and created in-store promotions to help retailers sell the products. "We also gained incredible merchandising opportunities within our core stores by cross-promoting the newly developed items. Many of our supermarket retailers bought the Stubb's cookbooks and had stands next to the sauce displaying both items. We expect our charcoal to have the same effect from our retailers by creating lobby displays promoting the sauce and charcoal as a nice tie-in."

Stubb's partners with grocers to cross-promote the full line of Stubb's products with in-store displays, building sales for both Stubb's and the retailer.

Note that the same customer can act as an OEM manufacturer, an end user, and a reseller. For example, Dell Computer makes OEM buying decisions when it purchases microprocessors for its computers, acts as an end user when it buys materials handling equipment for its warehouse, and functions as a reseller when it buys software to resell to its computer customers when they place orders.

GOVERNMENT AGENCIES

The largest customers for goods and services in the United States are federal, state, and local governments, which collectively purchase goods and services valued at more than $1 trillion annually. Not counting defense spending, the federal government purchases the equivalent of 14 percent of the country's entire gross domestic product, making it the largest customer in the world.[2] Government buyers typically develop detailed specifications for a product and then invite qualified suppliers to submit bids. A contract is awarded to the lowest bidder. The government has also developed procedures for small purchases without a bid, streamlining the process and reducing costs.

Effective selling to government agencies requires a thorough knowledge of their unique procurement procedures and rules. Salespeople also need to know about projected needs so they can influence the development of the buying specifications. For example, Harris Corporation worked for six years with the Federal Aviation Administration and finally won a $1.7 billion contract to modernize air traffic communication systems.

Some resources available to salespeople working with the federal and state governments are

- Guidelines for selling to the government published by the U.S. Government Printing Office.
- The *Commerce Business Daily*, which contains all invitations for bids issued by the federal government.
- The National Association of State Purchasing Officials in Washington, D.C., which publishes information for all 50 states, including the availability of vendor guides, registration fees, and how to get on bidder lists.
- The Procurement Automated Source System (PASS), the Small Business Administration database with information about more than 900 federal purchasing agents and prime contractors working on federal contracts.
- FedBizOpps.gov, a Web site listing all business opportunities greater than $25,000. Keep in mind, though, that 90 percent of federal purchasing opportunities are less than $25,000.[3]

Many international salespeople are selling to government agencies, even though private companies may be the biggest buyers of these products and services in the United States. For example, Alcatel-Lucent, a French company that manufactures telephone equipment, sells not only to private companies such as Verizon and AT&T in the United States but also to the post, telephone, and telegraph (PTT) government agencies in many countries in Europe, Asia, and Africa.

Selling to foreign governments is challenging. The percentage of domestic product (countries may require that a certain percentage of the product be manufactured or assembled locally) and exchange rates (the values of local currencies in U.S. dollars) are as important as the characteristics of the product. Different economic and political systems, cultures, and languages also can make international selling difficult.

INSTITUTIONS

Another important customer group consists of public and private institutions such as churches, hospitals, and colleges. Often these institutions have purchasing rules and procedures that are as complex and rigid as those used by government agencies.

Packaged goods manufacturers, such as Stubbs and Hormel, sell to both resellers (supermarkets) and institutional customers (restaurants and hospitals). These customers have different needs and buying processes.

CONSUMERS

Consumers purchase products and services for use by themselves or by their families. A lot of salespeople sell insurance, automobiles, clothing, and real estate to consumers. However, college graduates often take sales jobs that involve selling to business enterprises, government agencies, or institutions. Thus the examples in this text focus on these selling situations, and this chapter discusses organizational rather than consumer buying behavior.

In the next section we contrast the buying processes of consumers and organizations. Then we describe the buying process that organizations use in more detail, including the steps in the process, who influences the decisions, and how salespeople can influence the decisions.

ORGANIZATIONAL BUYING AND SELLING

Salespeople who sell to consumers and salespeople who call on organizations have very different jobs. Because the organizational buying process typically is more complex than the consumer buying process, selling to organizations often requires more skills and is more challenging than selling to consumers. Relationships, too, can differ because of the size of the organizations involved.

COMPLEXITY OF THE ORGANIZATIONAL BUYING PROCESS

The typical organizational purchase is much larger and more complex than the typical consumer purchase. Organizations use highly trained, knowledgeable purchasing agents to make these decisions. Many other people in organizations are involved in purchase decisions, including engineers, production managers, business analysts, and senior executives.

Organizational buying decisions often involve extensive evaluations and negotiations over time. The average time required to complete a purchase is five months, and during that period salespeople need to make many calls to gather and provide information.

Ashley Anderson, salesperson for "The Ranch" country-western radio station in the Dallas–Fort Worth area, worked for over a year with one account before getting the sale. The account is an eye surgeon promoting his Lasik surgery practice. Ashley worked with his PR agency and him, calling at least twice a month on one or both. "I think three factors finally won him over," says Ashley. "First, over the course of the year, I built a strong relationship with him and he began to trust me. Second, I was able to show him that advertising with us would reach a market no one else was going after. And third, I leveraged a free month of advertising to create an urgency to make a decision." Two years later he still advertises with "The Ranch."

The complexity of organizational purchase decisions means salespeople must be able to work effectively with a wide range of people working for their customer and their company. For example, when selling a new additive to a food processor such as Nabisco, an International Flavors and Fragrances salesperson may interact with advertising, product development, legal, production, quality control, and customer service people at Nabisco. The salesperson needs to know the technical and economic benefits of the additive to Nabisco and the benefits to consumers.

In addition, the salesperson coordinates all areas of his or her own firm to assist in making the sale. The salesperson works with research and development to provide data on consumer taste tests, with production to meet the customer's delivery requirements, and with finance to set the purchasing terms. (Working effectively within the salesperson's organization is discussed in more detail in Chapter 16.)

The complexity of organizational selling is increasing as more customers become global businesses. For example, Deere and Company has a special unit to coordinate worldwide purchases. The unit evaluates potential suppliers across the globe for each of its product lines and manufacturing facilities. Further, the company wants to standardize products made in different plants. A harvester made in Ottumwa, Iowa, should have the same belt as the same model harvester made at Arc-les-Gray, France. Thus a salesperson selling belts to Deere must work with the special corporate buying unit as well as with the employees at each

If you want to sell a part such as a belt for a John Deere harvester made in Ottumwa, Iowa, then you must be able to sell and service this plant in Arc-les-Gray, France, too.

manufacturing location around the world.[4] There's no doubt that global competitiveness is a key factor increasing the complexity of organizational buying, but global sourcing is also a key factor for achieving a sustainable competitive advantage.[5]

DERIVED VERSUS DIRECT DEMAND

Salespeople selling to consumers typically can focus on individual consumer or family needs. Organizational selling often requires salespeople to know about the customer's customers. Sales to OEMs and resellers are based on derived demand rather than direct demand. **Derived demand** means that purchases made by these customers ultimately depend on the demand for their products—either other organizations or consumers. For example, Apple's iPad has not only increased sales for touch screens made by Wintek and computer chips made by Samsung; the demand for the equipment that makes touch screens and computer chips has also been affected.[6]

HOW DO ORGANIZATIONS MAKE BUYING DECISIONS?

To effectively sell to organizations, salespeople need to understand how organizations make buying decisions. This section discusses the steps in the organizational buying process, the different types of buying decisions, and the people involved in making the decisions.[7]

STEPS IN THE BUYING PROCESS

Exhibit 3.1 shows the eight steps in an organizational buying process.

Exhibit 3.1
Steps in the
Organizational Buying
Process

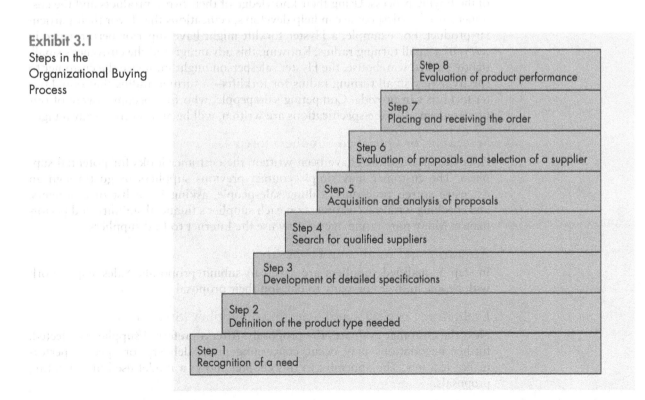

Step 8
Evaluation of product performance

Step 7
Placing and receiving the order

Step 6
Evaluation of proposals and selection of a supplier

Step 5
Acquisition and analysis of proposals

Step 4
Search for qualified suppliers

Step 3
Development of detailed specifications

Step 2
Definition of the product type needed

Step 1
Recognition of a need

Recognizing a Need or a Problem (Step 1)

The buying process starts when someone realizes a problem exists. Employees in the customer's firm or outside salespeople can trigger this recognition. For example, a supermarket cashier might discover that the optical scanner is making mistakes in reading bar code labels. Salespeople often trigger the buying process by demonstrating how their products can improve the efficiency of the customer's operation.

Defining the Type of Product Needed (Step 2)

After identifying a problem, organization members develop a general approach to solving it. For example, a production manager who concludes that the factory is not running efficiently recognizes a problem, but this insight may not lead to a purchase decision. The manager may think the inefficiency is caused by poor supervision or unskilled workers.

However, a production equipment salesperson might work with the manager to analyze the situation and show how efficiency could be improved by purchasing some automated assembly equipment. Thus the problem solution is defined in terms of purchasing a product or service—the automated assembly equipment needed—and the buying process moves to step 3. If the decision to continue requires senior management participation, research suggests that these executives will approve the manager's request to consider the purchase, then leave it up the manager to cover the next few steps before stepping back in when a final decision is made.[8]

Developing Product Specifications (Step 3)

In step 3 the specifications for the product needed to solve the problem are prepared. Potential suppliers will use these specifications to develop proposals. The buyers will use them to objectively evaluate the proposals.

Steps 2 and 3 offer great opportunities for salespeople to influence the outcome of the buying process. Using their knowledge of their firm's products and the customer's needs, salespeople can help develop specifications that favor their particular product. For example, a Hyster forklift might have superior performance in terms of a small turning radius. Knowing this advantage and the customer's small, tightly packed warehouse, the Hyster salesperson might influence the customer to specify a very small turning radius for forklifts—a turning radius that only Hyster forklifts can provide. Competing salespeople, who first become aware of this procurement after the specifications are written, will be at a severe disadvantage.

Searching for Qualified Suppliers (Step 4)

After the specifications have been written, the customer looks for potential suppliers. The customer may simply contact previous suppliers or go through an extensive search procedure: calling salespeople, asking for a list of customers, and checking with the customers on each supplier's financial stability and performance. Many purchasing agents now use the Internet to find suppliers.

Acquiring and Analyzing Proposals (Step 5)

In step 5 qualified suppliers are asked to submit proposals. Salespeople work with people in their company to develop their proposal.

Evaluating Proposals and Selecting a Supplier (Step 6)

Next the customer evaluates the proposals. After a preferred supplier is selected, further negotiations may occur concerning price, delivery, or specific performance features. The appendix to this chapter shows a model used in evaluating proposals.

Placing an Order and Receiving the Product (Step 7)

In step 7 an order is placed with the selected supplier. The order goes to the supplier, who acknowledges receipt and commits to a delivery date. After the product is shipped, the buying firm inspects the received goods and then pays the supplier for the product. During this step salespeople need to make sure the paperwork is correct and their firm knows what has to be done to satisfy the customer's requirements.

Evaluating Product Performance (Step 8)

In the final step of the purchasing process, the product's performance is evaluated. The evaluation may be a formal or informal assessment made by people involved in the buying process.

Salespeople play an important role in this step. They need to work with the users to make sure the product performs well. In addition, salespeople need to work with purchasing agents to ensure that they are satisfied with the communications and delivery.

This after-sale support ensures that the salesperson's product will get a positive evaluation and that he or she will be considered a qualified supplier in future procurement. This step is critical to establishing successful long-term relationships. (Building relationships through after-sale support is discussed in more detail in Chapter 14.)

CREEPING COMMITMENT

Creeping commitment means a customer becomes increasingly committed to a particular course of action while going through the steps in the buying process. As decisions are made at each step, the range of alternatives narrows; the customer becomes more and more committed to a specific course of action and even to a specific vendor. Thus it is vital that salespeople be involved in the initial steps so they will have an opportunity to participate in the final steps.

In instances involving purchasing components or materials as part of new product development, buyers are more interested in early involvement by possible vendors than when buying other types of products. Called *early procurement involvement* or *early supplier involvement,* this strategy has potential suppliers participate in the actual design process for a new product. BASF, the giant German chemical company, engages in early vendor involvement to ensure that the proper levels and quality of supply are available.[9] Other companies use supplier involvement to aid in designing a more effective new product.[10] Whatever the reason, each design decision represents a creeping commitment to a final set of decisions that are difficult to undo.

thinking **it** through

What steps did you go through in making the choice to attend this university? How can you relate your decision-making process to the eight steps in the organizational buying process? Did any decisions you made early in the process affect decisions you made later in the process? What roles did your family and friends play in the decision process?

TYPES OF ORGANIZATIONAL BUYING DECISIONS

Many purchase decisions are made without going through all the steps just described. For example, a Frito-Lay salesperson may check the supply of his or her products in a supermarket, write a purchase order to restock the shelves, and present it to the store manager. After recognizing the problem of low stock, the manager simply signs the order (step 6) without going through any of the other steps. However, if the Frito-Lay salesperson wanted the manager to devote more shelf space to Frito-Lay snacks, the manager might go through all eight steps in making and evaluating this decision.

Exhibit 3.2 describes three types of buying decisions—new tasks, modified rebuys, and straight rebuys[11]—along with the strategies salespeople need to use in each situation. In this exhibit the "in" company is the seller that has provided the product or service to the company in the past, and the "out" company is the seller that is not or has not been a supplier to the customer.

NEW TASKS

When a customer purchases a product or service for the first time, a **new-task** situation occurs. Most purchase decisions involving capital equipment or the initial purchase of OEM products are new tasks.

Because the customer has not made the purchase decision recently, the company's knowledge is limited, and it goes through all eight steps of the buying

Exhibit 3.2
Types of Organizational Buying Decisions

	New Task	Modified Rebuy	Straight Rebuy
Customer Needs			
Information and risk reduction	Information about causes and solutions for a new problem; reduce high risk in making a decision with limited knowledge.	Information and solutions to increase efficiency and/or reduce costs.	Needs are generally satisfied.
Nature of Buying Process			
Number of people involved in process	Many	Few	One
Time to make a decision	Months or years	Month	Day
Key steps in the buying process (Exhibit 3.1)	1, 2, 3, 8	3, 4, 5, 6, 8	5, 6, 7, 8
Key decision makers	Executives and engineers	Production and purchasing managers	Purchasing agent
Selling Strategy			
For in-supplier	Monitor changes in customer needs; respond quickly when problems and new needs arise; provide technical information.	Act immediately when problems arise with customers; make sure all of customer's needs are satisfied.	Reinforce relationship.
For out-supplier	Suggest new approach for solving problems; provide technical advice.	Respond more quickly than present supplier when problem arises; encourage customer to consider an alternative; present information about how new alternative will increase efficiency.	Convince customer of potential benefits from reexamining choice of supplier; secure recognition and approval as an alternative supplier.

process. In these situations customers face considerable risk. Thus they typically seek information from salespeople and welcome their knowledge. One study found organizational buyers rate salespeople as a more important information source than the Internet, particularly when the success of the purchase is likely to be difficult to achieve and to evaluate.[12]

From the salesperson's perspective, the initial buying process steps are critical in new-task situations. During these steps the alert salesperson can help the customer define the characteristics of the needed product and develop the purchase specifications. By working with the customer in these initial steps, the salesperson can take advantage of creeping commitment and gain a significant advantage over the competition. The final step, postpurchase evaluation, is also vital. Buyers making a new purchase decision are especially interested in evaluating results and will use this information in making similar purchase decisions in the future.

STRAIGHT REBUYS

In a **straight rebuy** situation, the customer buys the same product from the same source it used when the need arose previously. Because customers have purchased the product or service a number of times, they have considerable knowledge about their requirements and the potential vendors. MRO supplies and services and reorders of OEM components often are straight rebuy situations.

Typically a straight rebuy is triggered by an internal event, such as a low inventory level. Because needs are easily recognized, specifications have been developed, and potential suppliers have been identified, the latter steps of the buying process assume greater importance.

Some straight rebuys are computerized. For example, many hospitals use an automatic reorder system developed by Baxter, a manufacturer and distributor of medical supplies. When the inventory control system recognizes that levels of supplies such as tape, surgical sponges, or IV kits have dropped to prespecified levels, a purchase order is automatically generated and transmitted electronically to the nearest Baxter distribution center.

When a company is satisfied and has developed a long-term supplier relationship, it continues to order from the same company it has used in the past. Salespeople at in-companies want to maintain the strong relationship; they do not want the customer to consider new suppliers. Thus these salespeople must make sure that orders are delivered on time and that the products continue to get favorable evaluations.

Salespeople trying to break into a straight rebuy situation—those representing an out-supplier—face a tough sales problem. Often they need to persuade a customer to change suppliers, even though the present supplier is performing satisfactorily. In such situations the salesperson hopes the present supplier will make a significant mistake, causing the customer to reevaluate suppliers. To break into a straight rebuy situation, salespeople need to provide compelling information to motivate the customer to treat the purchase as a modified rebuy.

MODIFIED REBUYS

In a **modified rebuy** situation, the customer has purchased the product or a similar product in the past but is interested in obtaining new information. This situation typically occurs when the in-supplier performs unsatisfactorily, a new product becomes available, or the buying needs change. In such situations sales representatives of the in-suppliers need to convince customers to maintain the relationship and continue their present buying pattern. In-suppliers with strong customer relationships are the first to find out when requirements change. In this case customers give the supplier's salespeople information to help them respond to the new requirements.

Salespeople with out-suppliers want customers to reevaluate the situation and to actively consider switching vendors. The successful sales rep from an out-supplier will need to influence all the people taking part in the buying decision.

WHO MAKES THE BUYING DECISION?

As we discussed previously, a number of people are involved in new-task and modified rebuy decisions. This group of people is called the **buying center,** an informal, cross-department group of people involved in a purchase decision. People in the customer's organization become involved in a buying center because they have formal responsibilities for purchasing or they are important sources of information. In some cases the buying center includes experts who are not full-time employees. For example, consultants usually specify the air conditioning equipment that will be used in a factory undergoing remodeling. Thus the buying center defines the set of people who make or influence the purchase decision.[13]

Salespeople need to know the names and responsibilities of all people in the buying center for a purchase decision, and sometimes they need to make sure the right people are participating. For example, Ron Swift, vice president for Teradata, a maker of data warehousing equipment and software, was called in by the marketing director of a cell phone services provider to discuss the problem of customer churn (customers leaving for a competitor). The marketing director believed better customer information would solve the revenue loss problem, so he wanted to consider a data warehouse, a significant investment in information systems, in which to store that information. The process began without anyone from the information systems department! Fortunately, with Ron's experience, the Teradata team was able to involve the chief information officer and the right people from his area, as well as the financial people needed to understand the budgeting implications. With the correct buying team in place, the right system was designed, resulting in a churn reduction of 20 percent and additional revenues of nearly $50 million in only a few years.[14]

USERS

Users, such as the manufacturing personnel for OEM products and capital equipment, typically do not make the ultimate purchase decision. However, they often have considerable influence in the early and late steps of the buying process—need recognition, product definition, and postpurchase evaluation. Thus users are particularly important in new-task and modified rebuy situations. Salespeople often attempt to convert a straight rebuy to a modified rebuy by demonstrating superior product performance or a new benefit to users.

INITIATORS

Another role in the buying process is that of **initiator,** or the person who starts the buying process. A user can play the role of the initiator, as in, "This machine is broken; we need a new one." In fact, often it is users' dissatisfaction with a product used by the organization that initiates the purchase process.[15] In some instances, though, such as in OEM product decisions, the initiator could be an executive making a decision such as introducing a new product, which starts the buying process.

INFLUENCERS

People inside or outside the organization who directly or indirectly provide information during the buying process are **influencers.** These members of the buying

The buying center for radiology equipment includes (clockwise from lower left) the technicians operating the equipment (users), the radiologists (gatekeepers and influencers), and the hospital administrator (the decision maker).

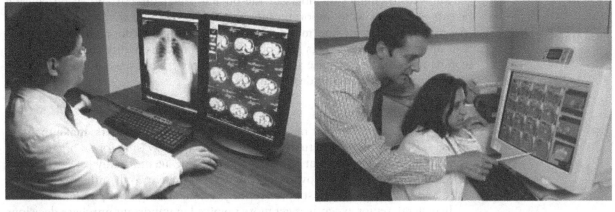

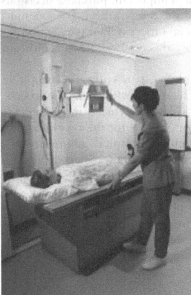

center may seek to influence issues regarding product specifications, criteria for evaluating proposals, or information about potential suppliers. For example, the marketing department can influence a purchase decision by indicating that the company's products would sell better if they included a particular supplier's components. Architects can play a critical role in the purchase of construction material by specifying suppliers, even though the ultimate purchase orders will be placed by the contractor responsible for constructing the building. Influence can be technical, such as in product specifications, but can also involve finances and how a decision is made.

Miller and Heiman, two noted sales consultants, assert that there are four types of influencers. One is the **economic influencer,** or person who is concerned about the financial aspects of the decision. Another is the user, which we will discuss later. A third is the **technical influencer,** a person who makes sure the technical requirements (including logistics, terms and conditions, quality measurements, or other specifications) are met. Miller and Heiman state that these people usually have the authority only to say no (meaning the salesperson did not meet the specifications, so the proposal is rejected), so they play a gatekeeping role (discussed more in a moment). The fourth role or type of influencer is the coach. The **coach** is someone in a buying organization who can advise and direct you, the salesperson, in maneuvering through the buying process in an effective fashion, leading to a sale. In addition, this person may advocate for you in private conversations among members of the buying center. As you can imagine, finding a coach is an important factor when decision processes are complex and involve a lot of people.[16]

GATEKEEPERS

Gatekeepers control the flow of information and may limit the alternatives considered. For example, the quality control and service departments may determine which potential suppliers are qualified sources.

Purchasing agents often play a gatekeeping role by determining which potential suppliers are to be notified about the purchase situation and are to have access to relevant information. In some companies all contacts must be made through purchasing agents. They arrange meetings with other gatekeepers, influencers, and users. Such gatekeeping activity is not a power play; rather, it ensures that purchases are consolidated under one contract, thus reducing costs and increasing quality. These single contracts are growing in popularity as a way to reduce costs globally.[17] When dealing with such companies, salespeople may not be allowed to contact members of the buying center directly. When purchasing agents restrict access to important information, salespeople are tempted to bypass the purchasing agents and make direct contact. This backdoor selling approach can upset purchasing agents so much that they may disqualify the salesperson's company from the purchase situation. In Chapter 7 we discuss ethical strategies that salespeople can use to deal with this issue.

DECIDERS

In any buying center one or more members of the group, **deciders,** make the final choice. Determining who actually makes the purchase decision for an organization is often difficult. For straight rebuys the purchasing agent usually selects the vendor and places the order. However, for new tasks many people influence the decision, and several people must approve the decision and sign the purchase order.

In general, senior executives get more involved in important purchase decisions that have a greater effect on the performance of the organization. For example, the chief executive officer (CEO) and chief financial officer (CFO) play an important role in purchasing a telephone system because this network has a significant impact on the firm's day-to-day operations.

To sell effectively to organizations, salespeople need to know the people in the buying center and their involvement at different steps of the buying process. Consider the following situation. Salespeople selling expensive intensive care monitoring equipment know that a hospital buying center for the type of equipment they sell typically consists of physicians, nurses, hospital administrators, engineers, and purchasing agents. Through experience, these salespeople also know the relative importance of the buying center members in various stages of the purchasing process (see Exhibit 3.3). With this information the intensive care equipment salespeople know to concentrate on physicians throughout the process, nurses and engineers in the middle of the process, and hospital administrators and purchasing agents at the end of the process.

SUPPLIER EVALUATION AND CHOICE

At various steps in the buying process, members of the buying center evaluate alternative methods for solving a problem (step 2), the qualifications of potential suppliers (step 4), proposals submitted by potential suppliers (step 5), and

Exhibit 3.3

Importance of Hospital Buying Center Members in the Buying Process for Intensive Care Monitoring Equipment

Step in Buying Process	Physicians	Nurses	Hospital Administrators	Purchasing Engineers	Agents
Need recognition (step 1)	High	Moderate	Low	Low	Low
Definition of product type (step 2)	High	High	Moderate	Moderate	Low
Analysis of proposal (step 5)	High	Moderate	Moderate	High	Low
Proposal evaluation and supplier selection (step 6)	High	Low	High	Low	Moderate

Exhibit 3.4
Factors Influencing
Organizational Buying
Decisions

| Organizational factors |
| Economic criteria |
| Quality criteria |
| Service criteria |

| Individual factors |
| Needs of buying center |
| members |
| Personal risks |
| Personal needs |

Buyer

the performance of products purchased (step 8). Using these evaluations, buyers select potential suppliers and eventually choose a specific vendor.

The needs of both the organization and the individuals making the decisions affect the evaluation and selection of products and suppliers (see Exhibit 3.4). Often these organizational and personal needs are classified into two categories: rational needs and emotional needs. **Rational needs** are directly related to the performance of the product. Thus the organizational needs discussed in the next section are examples of rational needs. **Emotional needs** are associated with the personal rewards and gratification of the person buying the product. Thus the personal needs of buying center members often are considered emotional needs.

ORGANIZATIONAL NEEDS AND CRITERIA

Organizations consider a number of factors when they make buying decisions, including economic factors such as price, product quality, and supplier service. In addition, organizations also consider strategic objectives, such as sustainability (choosing vendors and products that are good for the planet) and social diversity. Learn more about supplier diversity in "Building Partnerships 3.1."

Economic Criteria

The objective of businesses is to make a profit. Thus businesses are very concerned about buying products and services at the lowest cost. Organizational buyers are now taking a more sophisticated approach to evaluating the cost of equipment. Rather than simply focusing on the purchase price, they consider installation costs, the costs of needed accessories, freight charges, estimated maintenance costs, and operating costs, including forecasts of energy costs.

Life-cycle costing, also referred to as the total cost of ownership, is a method for determining the cost of equipment or supplies over their useful lives. Using this approach, salespeople can demonstrate that a product with a higher initial cost will have a lower overall cost. An example of life-cycle costing appears in Exhibit 3.5. (Approaches salespeople can use to demonstrate the value of their products to customers are discussed in more detail in Chapter 9.)

BUILDING Partnerships

3.1

DEVELOPING A DIVERSE SUPPLIER BASE

For many years, increasing supplier diversity has been an objective for businesses. According to Sherri Macko, manager of supplier diversity at American Airlines, her company believes that success comes from diversity. "The value in supplier diversity lies in the way these suppliers sometimes offer a different approach to meeting our needs and their flexibility to do whatever it takes to get the job done," she says.

Diversity in purchasing means buying from vendors owned by minorities, women, and disabled veterans. Part of the strength of diversity purchasing programs is that such vendors represent segments of the market, and as such, are able to help their customer, the buyer, understand and realize opportunities in those diverse segments. For example, Proctor & Gamble recently set a goal of spending at least 16% of its marketing budget with minority- and women-owned businesses. These marketing suppliers will bring a perspective that may be difficult for traditional vendors.

AT&T, which spends over $6 billion annually with diverse suppliers, believes that sound business benefits result from its supplier diversity program, which was recently given several awards. Margaret Rawls, executive director of AT&T, notes, "For 41 years, AT&T's

commitment to supplier diversity has been unwavering, through all economic climates, because it's built on tangible economic benefits."

Companies that seek greater diversity in their supplier base must work at it. Since most minority-, veteran-, disabled-, or women-owned businesses are small, they often need help simply finding the opportunities. That's why Delta Airlines recently launched a new Web site specifically for helping these smaller companies find opportunities to sell to Delta.

Companies like P&G, AT&T, and Delta also provide workshops to help these smaller companies operate more profitably. Such workshops deliver benefits to the bigger companies because when suppliers are more efficient, lower prices and other benefits accrue to the buyers too. As Macko says, "Overall, supplier diversity is a good business decision."

Sources: Sherri Macko, personal correspondence, used with permission; "Delta Air Lines Uses New Web site to Expand Outreach to Diverse Business Suppliers," *Airline Industry Information*, January 12, 2010; "AT&T Leads in Diversity of Businesses in Supply Chain," *RBOC Update* 21, no. 1 (January 2010), pp. 1–3; Andre McMains, "P&G Reaffirms Need for Supplier Diversity," *Adweek* 50, no. 42 (November 30, 2009), p. 6.

Quality Criteria

Many firms recognize that the quality and reliability of their products are as important to their customers as price. Firms expect their suppliers to support their efforts to provide quality products. A recent study in Japan indicates that suppliers are evaluated on both the quality of their service and the quality of their products because both impact the quality that the buyer can deliver to its customer.[18] Salespeople often need to describe how their firms will support the customer's quality objectives.

To satisfy customer quality needs, salespeople need to know what organizational buyers are looking for. For example, Lionel Dace, of Dace and Dace, was calling on an engineer who was trying to source metal containers. His company had designed a new milkshake machine, and this container was supposed to hold milk inside a milkshake machine. The engineer was beating up Dace over price, and showed him another container from a competitor at a lower price. Dace saw that it was cheaply made using a completely different process than the one he had to offer. The lower-priced version might hold up under moderate use, but Dace thought it didn't look as good as the machine the engineer and his team had designed. However, Dace had been calling on this buyer for three years and

Exhibit 3.5
Life-Cycle Costing

	Product A	Product B
Initial cost	$35,000	$30,000
Life of machine	10 years	10 years
Power consumption per year	150 MWh*	180 MWh*
Power cost at $30/MWh	$45,000	$54,000
Estimated operating and maintenance cost over 10 years	$25,000	$30,000
Life-cycle cost	$105,000	$114,000

Note: A more thorough analysis would calculate the net present value of the cash flow associated with each product's purchase and use.

*MWh = megawatt-hour

had heard nothing but price, price, price. Out of exasperation, Dace looked at the engineer and said, "Is this really what you want it to look like? Can you be proud of that?" Dace says the buyer was immediately transformed; although he had focused on low price, he really wanted something that looked as sleek as the machine he had designed. Dace got the sale, but perhaps more importantly, the nature of their relationship changed for the better.[19]

Service Criteria

Organizational buyers want more than products that are low-cost, perform reliably, and are aesthetically pleasing. They also want suppliers that will work with them to solve their problems. One primary reason firms are interested in developing long-term relationships with suppliers is so they can learn about each other's needs and capabilities and use this information to enhance their products' performance. **Value analysis** is an example of a program in which suppliers and customers work together to reduce costs and still provide the required level of performance.[20]

Representatives from the supplier and the purchasing department and technical experts from engineering, production, or quality control usually form a team to undertake the analysis. The team begins by examining the product's function. Then members brainstorm to see whether changes can be made in the design, materials, construction, or production process to reduce the product's costs but keep its performance high. Some questions addressed in this phase are the following:

- Can a part in the product be eliminated?
- If the part is not standard, can a standard (and presumably less expensive) part be used?
- Does the part have greater performance than this application needs?
- Are unnecessary machining or fine finishes specified?

Salespeople can use value analysis to get customers to consider a new product. This approach is particularly useful for the out-supplier in a straight rebuy situation. David Lenling, a sales representative for Hormel, used value analysis to sell pepperoni to a 35-unit group of pizzerias in the Cincinnati area. The owner had been using the same pepperoni and bacon topping for over 15 years and was reluctant to switch. Lenling showed how the Hormel pepperoni product cost $5 per case more but offered 1,200 more slices in a case with the same weight, which equated to an additional $12 of pepperoni or a $7 per case net savings, enough to make about 35 more pizzas per case. The owner of the chain was unaware of these differences until Lenling actually weighed his current product. Through value analysis, Lenling was able to interrupt a straight rebuy. Further, Lenling's buyer agreed that the Hormel product tasted better and was less greasy, resulting in a better-looking and tastier pizza, which might result in customers coming back more often. Because Hormel products are of high quality and sell at a premium price, Lenling and other sales representatives have to prove that the products are worth the extra money. They use value analysis to help purchasing agents determine how much it costs to use the product, rather than how much the product costs. That's why Lenling was able to win that large pizza chain's business.[21]

INDIVIDUAL NEEDS OF BUYING CENTER MEMBERS

In the preceding section we discussed criteria used to determine whether a product satisfies the needs of the organization. However, buying center members are people. Their evaluations and choices are affected by their personal needs as well as the organization's needs.

Types of Needs

Buying center members, like all people, have personal goals and aspirations. They want to get a raise, be promoted to a high-level position, have their managers recognize their accomplishments, and feel they have done something for their company or demonstrated their skills as a buyer or engineer.

Salespeople can influence members of the buying center by developing strategies to satisfy individual needs. For example, demonstrating how a new product will reduce costs and increase the purchasing agents' bonus would satisfy the purchasing agents' financial security needs. Encouraging an engineer to recommend a product employing the latest technology might satisfy the engineer's need for self-esteem and recognition by his or her engineering peers.

Risk Reduction

In many situations, members of the buying center tend to be more concerned about losing benefits they have now than about increasing their benefits. They place a lot of emphasis on avoiding risks that may result in poor decisions, decisions that can adversely affect their personal reputations and rewards as well as their organization's performance. Buyers first assess the potential for risk and then develop a risk reduction strategy.[22] To reduce risk, buying center members may collect additional information, develop a loyalty to present suppliers, or spread the risk by placing orders with several vendors.

Because they know suppliers try to promote their own products, customers tend to question information received from vendors. Customers usually view information from independent sources such as trade publications, colleagues, and outside consultants as more credible than information provided by salespeople and company advertising and sales literature. Therefore, they will search for such information to reduce risk when a purchase is important.

Advertising, the Internet, and sales literature tend to be used more in the early steps of the buying process. Word-of-mouth information from friends and colleagues is important in the proposal evaluation and supplier selection steps. Word-of-mouth information is especially important for risky decisions that will have a significant impact on the organization or the buying center member. "Sales Technology 3.1" illustrates the importance of the Internet for word-of-mouth information.

SALES Technology

WEB-ENABLED WORD OF MOUTH

Facebook, Google Buzz, Twitter. Only a few years ago, none of these brands existed. Now they are dominant ways for people to access the Internet and each other. What does this mean for buyers?

Web reviews are one implication. When a buyer wants to evaluate a potential supplier, not only are there articles about how good (or bad) the supplier is, there are also blogs, tweets, and postings on review sites such as Epinions. Most consumers, especially those under 40, use these to find information for important purchases, and business buyers are no different. In fact, one survey finds 87 percent of business buyers turning to the Internet for information about almost every purchase.

What's interesting is that the buyers are in control of much of the content that is on the Web. Make someone mad and it shows up in a blog that reaches several thousand peers. Think a couple of thousand buyers don't matter? In a B2B market, you may have only a couple thousand buyers total.

Dell, in fact, has a staff of 45 people who monitor blogs, tweets, and other social media posts by buyers. When a complaint is registered, these staff members respond directly to the individual who complained. But they also use the information to create new services that might make Dell's offerings more attractive.

Customers also want to be able to offer input into new product development and use the Web to do so. Microsoft created an advertising campaign about Windows 7, presenting stories of individuals who claim responsibility for coming up with the ideas that became new features. Whether or not customers actually created those ideas is another story, but the campaign played to the desire customers have to offer input into new product development. IdeaStorm is a Web site that Dell operates specifically to allow users to post new product or feature ideas (see www.ideastorm.com). These ideas are then sorted by Dell personnel, and the better ones are sent to engineers to make their way into products.

Buyers use the Web as an information source. But they also use it as a place to register their complaints, voice their wants and desires, and talk to each other about which vendors are the best to do business with. Smart companies dynamically participate with these Web-active buyers.

Sources: "Brands Using Twitter," *Revolution*, December 2009, p. 17; Richard Bush, "The Changing Face of B2B," *Marketing*, January 14, 2009, p. 5; David Gelles, "The New Corporate Firefighters," *Financial Times*, January 22, 2009, p. 12.

Another way to reduce uncertainty and risk is to display **vendor loyalty** to suppliers—that is, to continue buying from suppliers that proved satisfactory in the past. Converting buying decisions into straight rebuys makes the decisions routine, minimizing the chances of a poor decision. One name for this is **lost for good;** for all the out-suppliers, this account can be considered lost for good because the in-supplier has cemented this relationship for a long time. Organizations tend to develop vendor loyalty for unimportant purchase decisions, though they will often look to vendors who have proved trustworthy when beginning to search in a risky situation. In these situations the potential benefits from new suppliers do not compensate for the costs of evaluating these suppliers.

The consequences of choosing a poor supplier can be reduced by using more than one vendor. Rather than placing all orders for an OEM component with one supplier, for example, a firm might elect to purchase 75 percent of its needs from one supplier and 25 percent from another. Thus if a problem occurs with one supplier, another will be available to fill the firm's needs. If the product is proprietary—available from only one supplier—the buyer might insist that the supplier develop a second source for the component. Such a strategy is called **always a share,** which means the buyer will always allocate only a share to each vendor.

These risk reduction approaches present a major problem for salespeople working for out-suppliers. To break this loyalty barrier, these salespeople need to develop trusting relationships with customers. They can build trust by offering performance guarantees or consistently meeting personal commitments. Another approach is to encourage buyers to place a small trial order so the salesperson's company can demonstrate the product's capabilities. On the other hand, the salesperson for the in-supplier wants to discourage buyers from considering new sources, even on a trial basis.

PROFESSIONAL PURCHASING'S GROWING IMPORTANCE

The purchasing profession is undergoing dramatic changes. Companies have recognized the impact that effective purchasing can make on the bottom line. For example, if a company can save $5,000 on a purchase, $5,000 is added to net income. If sales go up $5,000, of which most is additional costs, only $500 may be added to net income. Most large firms have elevated their directors of purchasing to the level of senior vice president to reflect the increasing importance of this function. As Russ Boyd, senior procurement specialist for Perot Systems, notes, "More CEOs are bringing purchasing (departments) to the table, asking where can you help us." Phil Krotz, of Rockwell Collins, agrees, meeting regularly with his company's CEO to help create initiatives that generate significant financial returns to the company.[23] Combine recognition of the power of purchasing with technology, and you can see why trends in professional purchasing are changing the business environment. The overall strategy is called supply chain management.

SUPPLY CHAIN MANAGEMENT

Supply chain management (SCM) began as a set of programs undertaken to increase the efficiency of the distribution channel that moves products from the producer's facilities to the end user. More recently, however, supply chain management has become more than just logistics; it is now a strategy of managing inventory while containing costs. Supply chain management includes logistics systems such as just-in-time inventory control, as well as supplier evaluation processes such as supplier relationship management systems.

The **just-in-time (JIT) inventory control** system is an example of a logistics supply chain management system used by a producer to minimize its inventory by having frequent deliveries, sometimes daily, just in time for assembly into the final product. In theory each product delivered by a supplier must conform to the manufacturer's specifications every time. It must be delivered when needed, not earlier or later, and it must arrive in the exact quantity needed, not more or less. The ultimate goal is to eventually eliminate all inventory except products in production and transit.

To develop the close coordination needed for JIT systems, manufacturers tend to rely on one supplier. The selection criterion is not the lowest cost, but the ability of the supplier to be flexible. As these relationships develop, employees of the supplier have offices at the customer's site and participate in value analysis meetings with the supplier. The salesperson becomes a facilitator, coordinator, and even marriage counselor in developing a selling team that works effectively with the customer's buying center. Resellers are also interested in managing their inventories more efficiently. Retailers and distributors work closely with their suppliers to minimize inventory investments and still satisfy the needs of customers. These JIT inventory systems are referred to as **quick-response** or **efficient consumer response (ECR)** systems in a consumer product distribution channel.

(Partnering relationships involving these systems are discussed in more detail in Chapter 14.)

Automatic replenishment (AR) is a form of JIT where the supplier manages inventory levels for the customer. The materials are provided on consignment, meaning the buyer doesn't pay for them until they are actually used. These types of arrangements are used in industrial settings, where the product being consumed is a supply item used in a manufacturing process, as well as in retail settings. Efficient consumer response systems use automatic replenishment technology through **electronic data interchange (EDI),** or computer systems that share data across companies. Exhibit 3.6 illustrates the communications associated with placing orders and receiving products that are transmitted electronically through EDI. Recent research has indicated that adopting systems involving both EDI and quick response or JIT delivers a number of benefits to the firm, in addition to lower costs. These benefits include greater flexibility in manufacturing, improved stability of supply, and other operating benefits. Though EDI has been around a long time, read Sean Gardner's perspective on implementing global EDI for Nestlé in "From the Buyer's Seat 3.1."

Material requirements planning (MRP) systems are an important element in JIT programs. These systems are used to forecast sales, develop a production schedule, and then order parts and raw materials with delivery dates that minimize the amount of inventory needed, thereby reducing costs. Effective JIT requires that customers inform suppliers well in advance about production schedules and needs.

SUPPLIER RELATIONSHIP MANAGEMENT

Supplier relationship management (SRM) is a strategy by which organizational buyers evaluate the relative importance of suppliers and use that information

Exhibit 3.6
EDI Transactions

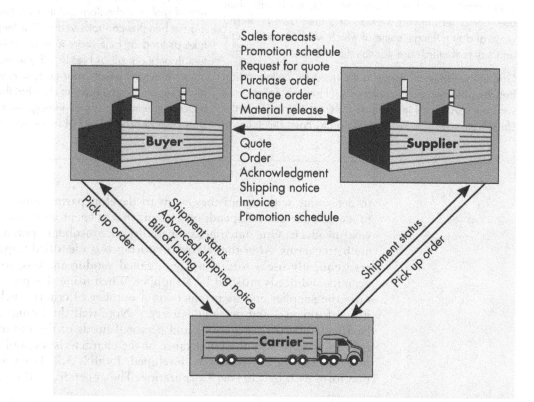

From the BUYER'S SEAT

3.1

GLOBAL EDI AT NESTLÉ

Featuring Sean Gardner, B2B Strategies

EDI, or electronic data interchange, has been around for more than three decades. Originally created to enable electronic buying, EDI was offered by vendors such as American Hospital Supply and Xerox as a way to gain competitive advantage. By offering to manage their customers' inventories automatically through EDI, including reordering supplies automatically, these companies offered EDI to their customers as a way for their customers to cut ordering costs.

Now, 30 years later, you might expect EDI to be ubiquitous. But while the basic advantages of EDI haven't changed (assured supply and lower operating costs due to automatic ordering and inventory management), global supply chain management systems have added so many layers of complexity that global EDI systems simply don't exist. At least, not yet.

Working on a global EDI system for Nestlé, Sean Gardner, Cadre Director of B2B Strategies, explains the challenges. "One size doesn't fit all. Not when you have so many markets and so many countries, each with their own computer network systems and their own preferred ways of doing things, some of which work very efficiently and some of which are not so efficient."

One tremendous challenge is the need for collaboration between Nestlé and its customers. "How we collaborate with our customers in Israel is different than it is in the United States." The EDI system has to have flexibility to

account for such collaboration across customers and across markets. "It's not just our salespeople who have to collaborate, but all of the areas of the business that drive customer service," notes Gardner.

Nor is it just collaboration with customers. "Any EDI system has to also account for collaboration up the supply chain. Our vendors, including transport, banking, and others, have to be able to collaborate with us and our customers through our EDI system."

Globalizing EDI is more than globalizing a software platform. Some markets might be paying 20 times what they would pay on a global contract made possible through global EDI, whereas some markets may only be paying 5 times. That may sound like great savings are possible for everyone; but in reality, some markets operate so efficiently that there is resistance to any new system. And existing relationships may be replaced with new suppliers or customers when a global EDI system is implemented. Not everyone wants to lose those existing relationships. "Any change that changes how people operate is not easy."

When you process millions of transactions a month, the lure of global technology solutions is tempting. But realizing the benefits can take years. Gardner estimates it may take as long as four years to fully implement an EDI system throughout all of Nestlé. "If you want to compete in an environment where your customers want to work with fewer suppliers, you have to do what they want. And that includes trimming costs all throughout the supply chain," states Gardner. Global EDI is one way to do that.

to determine with whom they want to develop partnerships. The first step is to identify the **annual spend,** or amount that is spent with each vendor and for what products. One outcome is the ability to consolidate purchases and negotiate better terms. After the relative importance is identified, organizational buyers frequently use a formal method, called **vendor analysis,** to summarize the benefits and needs satisfied by a supplier. When using this procedure, the buyer rates the supplier and its products on a number of criteria such as price, quality, performance, and on-time delivery.[24] Note that the ratings of suppliers can be affected by the perceptions and personal needs of the buyers. Then the ratings are weighted by the importance of the characteristics, and an overall score or evaluation of the vendor is developed. Exhibit 3.7 shows a vendor evaluation form used by Chrysler Corporation. The appendix to this chapter describes

Kingfisher plc, a European firm that owns and operates retail stores such as Castorama, uses supplier relationship management software from SAS Institute to track supplier performance.

the multiattribute model, which is useful in analyzing how members of the buying center evaluate and select products. The model also suggests strategies salespeople can use to influence these evaluations.

SRM software is being used by companies like Kingfisher plc, a company with some 1,400 stores across 17 countries and leading European retail brands such as Castorama and BUT. The company's Asia sourcing office in Hong Kong buys over 8,000 products from more than 150 suppliers. SRM software enables the company to identify problems, such as a delivery problem with one vendor in particular. Caterpillar, the construction and agriculture equipment manufacturer, instituted SRM software and training for all employees involved in purchasing. The training, created by Accenture, was more than just about the software; it was also about the strategy so the company could maximize its return on the software investment.[25]

SRM isn't always about improving profits. Sustainability, for example, is an important trend in purchasing and means making purchasing decisions that do not damage the environment. Bell Inc., a Sioux Falls, South Dakota, manufacturer of packaging products, worked with the U.S. Postal Service (USPS) to develop sustainable packaging products. The project required Bell to work with its suppliers, but the important element that allowed the project to flourish was the trust already built by actively managing relationships with suppliers. As Ben Graham, vice president for sales and supply chain, notes, "The project required us to work with a third-party accrediting agency that went back to our supply chain to understand the impact of the components of our packaging on the waste stream. It's a huge process, and it's not easy to go back to a supplier asking it to share its recipes. That takes confidentiality, trust, and understanding." Key for suppliers, Graham says, is to recognize the direction Bell's business is taking, the company's goals in the marketplace, and how they as suppliers fit in that strategy. "Once they understand that and see the opportunity they get very excited," he says. "Suppliers take part in our success."[26]

THE INTERNET AND BUSINESS-TO-BUSINESS SELLING

Companies like Amazon.com and eBay that sell products to consumers over the Internet are well known, but the number of business-to-business transactions over the Internet is many times greater than the number of business-to-consumer transactions.

How does the Internet affect salespeople? Most businesses view their Web sites on the Internet as a tool for supporting salespeople rather than replacing them. Buyers go to supplier Web sites to get information about product specifications and availability, place orders, and check on the status of orders. Thus salespeople will be able to spend less time on transactions and more time building relationships.

Exhibit 3.7
Sample Vendor Analysis
Form

Supplier Name: _____ Type of Product: _____

Shipping Location: _____ Annual Sales Dollars: _____

	5 Excellent	4 Good	3 Satisfactory	2 Fair	1 Poor	0 N/A
Quality (45%)						
Defect rates	—	—	—	—	—	—
Quality of sample	—	—	—	—	—	—
Conformance with quality program	—	—	—	—	—	—
Responsiveness to quality problems	—	—	—	—	—	—
Overall quality	—	—	—	—	—	—
Delivery (25%)						
Avoidance of late shipments	—	—	—	—	—	—
Ability to expand production capacity	—	—	—	—	—	—
Performance in sample delivery	—	—	—	—	—	—
Response to changes in order size	—	—	—	—	—	—
Overall delivery	—	—	—	—	—	—
Price (20%)						
Price competitiveness	—	—	—	—	—	—
Payment terms	—	—	—	—	—	—
Absorption of costs	—	—	—	—	—	—
Submission of cost savings plans	—	—	—	—	—	—
Overall price	—	—	—	—	—	—
Technology (10%)						
State-of-the-art components	—	—	—	—	—	—
Sharing research & development capability	—	—	—	—	—	—
Ability and willingness to help with design	—	—	—	—	—	—
Responsiveness to engineering problems	—	—	—	—	—	—
Overall technology	—	—	—	—	—	—

Buyer: _____ Date: _____

Comments: _____

Source: Chrysler Corporation.

In some instances, though, buyers do use the Web instead of buying through salespeople. Reverse auctions are one mechanism that buyers use on the Web. A **reverse auction** is an auction, but instead of a seller offering a product and buyers bidding, a buyer offers a contract and sellers bid. Also, instead of prices rising, they fall as sellers compete to win the sale. Reverse auctions work best when the product being purchased can be specified completely and clearly, when the purchase is large enough to attract multiple suppliers and they are competitive, and when the buying company has the infrastructure to support a reverse auction.[27] Buyers are finding that you can't just stick a product description on the Web and have a reverse auction; it takes planning, accessibility of personnel to answer sellers' questions, and other resources. When it works, though, it can save both money and time. Tata Motors, the India-based auto manufacturer and owner of the Jaguar and Land Rover brands, used reverse auctions to save over $100 million per year. Now 40 percent of Tata purchases are made through reverse auctions.[28] Heinz had a similar experience, using reverse auctions thousands of times and reducing costs by over $60 million. Heinz found that being completely open and honest with suppliers about what was needed made the auctions work more effectively, leading to greater savings and satisfaction because it gave suppliers some flexibility in what they could offer. Their experience has been supported in research showing that reverse auctions can save buyers a great deal of money when buyers know exactly what they need. [29]

Reverse auctions are just one way to use the Internet. In "Sales Technology 3.1" we discuss how buyers use the Internet and the possible effect on salespeople.

thinking it through   Review the stages in the decision-making process described earlier in the chapter. Do you go through those stages when making an important purchase? How does the Internet affect the way you buy products and services? What effect does it have on each stage of the process?

SELLING YOURSELF

When you are selling your ideas or selling yourself in a job search, recognize that there is a buying center. Although a sales manager may make the final decision on whether you are hired, chances are that you'll interview with at least four people before the job offer will come. Similarly, once you have the job and you have an idea for a new program or product, you will have to sell that idea to management. That decision will likely include someone from finance, someone from operations, and so on, creating a buying center. Each member of the center will take on different roles and may be present for only part of the decision. Each member may also have different criteria.

Further, you need to understand the process by which the decision is made. In a job search, the decision to hire someone has been made before anyone talks to you. At that point your concern is making it from the large pool of college students they've interviewed at six different campuses to the group they bring into the office, to the final selection of new employees. Similarly, management approval of your idea is likely to follow a process not unlike that of any organizational purchase. Keep in mind that your idea is competing against other ideas from other people, just as your candidacy for a sales job is compared to other college students from your school and others.

SUMMARY

Salespeople sell to many different types of customers, including consumers, business enterprises, government agencies, and institutions. This text focuses on selling to organizations rather than to consumers. Selling to organizations differs from selling to consumers because organizations are more concentrated, demand is derived, and the buying process is more complex.

The organizational buying process consists of eight steps, beginning with the recognition of a need and ending with the evaluation of the product's performance. Each step involves several decisions. As organizations progress through these steps, decisions made at previous steps affect subsequent steps, leading to a creeping commitment. Thus salespeople need to be involved in the buying process as early as possible.

The length of the buying process and the role of various participants depend on the customer's past experiences. When customers have had considerable experience in buying a product, the decision becomes routine—a straight rebuy. Few people are involved, and the process is short. However, when customers have little experience in buying a product—a new task—many people are involved, and the process can be lengthy.

The people involved in the buying process are referred to as the buying center. The buying center is composed of people who are initiators, users, influencers, gatekeepers, and deciders. Salespeople need to understand the roles buying center members play to effectively influence their decisions.

Individuals in the buying center are concerned about satisfying the economic, quality, and service needs of their organization. In addition, these people have personal needs they want to satisfy.

Organizations face an increasingly dynamic and competitive environment. Purchasing is becoming a strategic weapon with the development of supply chain management and supplier relationship management strategies.

The Internet is playing a much more important role in business-to-business transactions than it plays in the widely publicized business-to-consumer e-businesses. Business-to-business applications of the Internet are designed to support salespeople's ability to build relationships with major customers.

KEY TERMS

always a share   81
annual spend   84
automatic replenishment (AR)   83
buying center   74
capital equipment   65
coach   75
creeping commitment   71
deciders   76
derived demand   69
economic influencer   75
efficient consumer response (ECR)   82
electronic data interchange (EDI)   83
emotional needs   77
end users   65
gatekeepers   75
influencers   74
initiators   74
just-in-time (JIT) inventory control   82
life-cycle costing   77
lost for good   81
material requirements planning (MRP)   83

modified rebuy   73
MRO supplies   65
new task   72
original equipment manufacturer (OEM)   64
producers   64
profit margin   65
quick-response system   82
rational needs   77
resellers   65
reverse auction   86
services   65
straight rebuy   73
supplier relationship management (SRM)   83
supply chain management (SCM)   82
technical influencer   75
turnover   65
users   74
value analysis   79
vendor analysis   84
vendor loyalty   81

ETHICS PROBLEMS

1. You know that American Airlines and Delta Airlines both have goals for purchasing from women- and minority-owned businesses (see "Building Partnerships 3.1"). You have a product that is innovative and patented, and it will save airlines like American and Delta over 30 percent in fuel costs. But your business does not qualify as woman- or minority-owned because you are a white male, so you are thinking of bringing a partner into the business—your sister. Is this appropriate? Or would it be better to license the product to an already certified minority-owned business?

2. You are talking about this class to someone who isn't familiar with business. When you mention you are studying how people make buying decisions and that this information will help you become a better salesperson, your friend says you are just trying to learn how to manipulate people more effectively. How do you respond?

QUESTIONS AND PROBLEMS

1. In the opening profile, Jenna Weber describes the personalities of two different buyers. Are these two personalities the only two types you would expect to see? She says one is easy to get along with, yet this one didn't buy her bacon promotion. Why, in your opinion, is that? What could she have done better?

2. Michelle Obama, as First Lady, has made childhood obesity an important issue. Suppose her goals include reducing sugar content in children's cereals, making vegetables more palatable, and reducing fat in the overall diet. Identify three product categories (not including vegetables) for which derived demand would influence manufacturers and producers of consumer packaged goods (foods sold to be cooked or eaten at home). Include at least one product affected positively and one affected negatively.

3. Assume you work for a division of 3M that makes medical monitoring systems. How would the purchasing decision process differ in the following situations? Which situation is a new task? A modified rebuy? A straight rebuy? How likely is the buyer to get other people in the organization involved? Which types of people are likely to get involved in each decision? Which situation is likely to produce the slowest decision?
   a. The organization is purchasing a custom-designed machine to be used in the manufacturing of metal racks that house multiple monitoring systems.
   b. An organization reorders plastic shields that it uses in making medical monitoring equipment from a regular supplier, a supplier that it has bought from in the past.
   c. The organization is designing a new line of medical monitoring equipment and wants an improved and updated microprocessor. It is considering its past suppliers as well as some suppliers that it has not bought from before.

4. Review each purchase in question 3. What information would you need to conduct a value analysis for each? Note: You will need some different and some similar information in each situation.

5. A chain of restaurants wants to purchase a new order entry computer system tied into an accounting system that manages food inventory and automatically replenishes food items. Which criteria for evaluating supplier proposals might be used by (a) the purchasing agent, (b) the information systems department, (c) a store manager, and (d) the head of the legal department? How would this purchase differ from a purchase of the same products by a company that resells store fixtures and equipment to small restaurants?

6. Dub Oliver runs the maintenance department at the paper mill, and he buys lots of hardware to fix equipment. Right now, he orders most of it through a Web site at NCH. If you work for Home Depot, how would you try to make a sale to Oliver? Assume you have a Web site he can order through, too.

7. When is vendor loyalty important? Find at least one example in the chapter (there are several) where vendor loyalty would prove to be important, and discuss why it was important in that particular instance. What can buyers do to improve vendor loyalty? When might vendor loyalty be inefficient or wasteful?

8. Does EDI result in greater loyalty? If so, how? Reread What are the challenges in creating and implementing a global EDI system? Why might some members of a company resist the adoption of a global EDI system?

9. Mitchell's Metal Shop is considering the purchase of a new press, a machine that bends sheet metal. The cost is $10,000, which is about 25 percent of the firm's profit for the quarter. Ford Motor Company is also considering buying new presses—30 of them. Discuss how risk is different for Frank Mitchell, owner of Mitchell's Metal Shop, and Ford.

10. How are the buying criteria for an OEM the same as a reseller? Why? How are the criteria likely to be different, and why? What type of buyer is likely to have criteria that are very different? Why are these criteria so different?

CASE PROBLEMS

case 3.1

Going Out through the Backdoor

Travis Bruns is a sales representative for Crown Lift Services in Houston, Texas. In his own words, he describes an ethics issue with a buyer.

Last year I was in a real cutthroat bidding war for a $300,000-plus sales opportunity. Over the course of two months the competitive field had been narrowed down to two organizations, mine and the incumbent organization. The customer had set up a set of strict guidelines for the bidding process. One of those was that they had designated a "point of contact" (POC) that was to be the liaison through which all bids and proposals were to channel through to the VP. My organization and I had truly put our best foot forward on pricing and proposed service after the sale, and although the negotiations had been rough, we were able to sell the value of our solution, retain a fair amount of profit, and were told we had the deal: a true win–win. On the final day that the bid was open, I received a call from the point of contact asking me to lower my price. I was confused. I inquired about the previous discussions that had taken place in which we had mutually agreed that the price of our proposal was fair and good. I could hear some level of discomfort if not embarrassment in the POC's voice, so I came right out and asked him, "I get the sense that you are not comfortable with what is happening here either. What happened?"

He replied, "Well, Travis, [your competitor] called one of the other managers in the office and was able to find out the pricing in your proposal. He then went around me and called the VP directly and offered a much lower price. The VP then called me and asked me to get you to lower your price or the other company will get the business."

I was dumbfounded. I asked the customer, "If I cannot lower my price, are you telling me this deal is over for me?"

"I think so," he replied.

Source: Travis Bruns. Used with permission.

Questions

1. What would you do? Do you lower your price or walk away? Why? Write out specifically what you would say next.

2. Do buyers have to follow the same ethics principles as sellers? For example, sellers have to fully disclose all information. Do buyers? Why or why not? What ethical principle violation occurred here?

Shirley Parker, CEO of her family's pet food manufacturing company, called some of the employees together to discuss employee benefits. Mark, the human resources director, asked her to call the meeting because the company needed to hire new workers, but he was finding it difficult because there were few benefits.

"We need a health plan for our employees. The plan must have doctors who are close to where our employees work, not close to the plant," says Fred, the plant manager.

Rachael, the production supervisor, added, "I'm concerned about retirement benefits, too. This is a private company, so we can't build a pension through a stock option plan. But I'd like something for retirement."

Chuck, the CFO, said, "Yeah, but you're talking about adding costs. Where's the benefit to the company? What budget will this come out of?"

They talked some more about the situation, and Shirley closed the meeting by saying, "Look, Chuck, I'd like you to head up a committee to gather some ideas from some different companies. Mark, you should be on this committee, too. Once you guys have narrowed things down a bit, let's get together and you can show me what you found."

Questions

1. What is the likely makeup of the buying center?
2. List the roles in the buying center, based on material in the chapter. Are all of the roles filled with someone?
3. What type of purchase situation is this? What implications will that have if you are a salesperson selling employee benefit plans?

ROLE PLAY CASE

During much of the rest of the semester, you will be calling on one of three accounts. The accounts are listed here with some information. Information that you gain on each call can be used in subsequent calls as you practice the skills and apply the concepts introduced in each chapter.

Spear One: Spear One is a company that creates special marketing events for clients all across the country. For example, when a PGA golf tournament is in town, Spear One may produce a special event for a client that involves the tournament, some of the players, the client's customers, and so forth. Think party planner for a business.

McLane Properties: McLane Properties is a commercial real estate company located in a major metropolitan town. While McLane has a lot of industrial space available, its primary focus is retail development and management. It leases out about 30 percent of the city's retail space and is the largest retail property management firm in town. Clients include stores like Old Navy, Gap, Academy, Radio Shack, and others.

Dart Paper Products: Dart makes paper products like cups, plates, napkins, and other products that are sold through distributors to restaurants, caterers, and institutional cafeterias (such as at universities or prisons) or directly to government agencies. Dart is the second largest paper products maker in North America, with operations also in Europe and Asia.

Today you want to find out what you can about who is involved in the decision process. You have an appointment arranged with a sales manager, thanks to a lead from an American Marketing Association workshop where you presented a session on sales productivity and software. Start from the beginning: Introduce yourself and your company, thanking the buyer for today's meeting, and then tell the buyer you'd like to ask some questions. Ask questions about the buying process, based on what you know from this chapter. After the role play, see if you can chart the buyer's organizational structure and the buying center.

APPENDIX MULTIATTRIBUTE MODEL OF PRODUCT EVALUATION AND CHOICE

The multiattribute model is a useful approach for understanding the factors individual members of a buying center consider in evaluating products and making choices. The multiattribute model is one approach that companies can take to making purchases and is most often used in complex decisions involving several vendors.[30] Many business decisions are straight rebuys, but the original vendor selection decision may have involved a multiattribute approach. The vendor analysis form used by Chrysler (see Exhibit 3.7) illustrates the use of this model in selecting vendors. The model also provides a framework for developing sales strategies.

The multiattribute model is based on the idea that people view a product as a collection of characteristics or attributes. Buyers evaluate a product by considering how each characteristic satisfies the firm's needs and perhaps their individual needs. The following example examines a firm's decision to buy laptop computers for its sales force. The computers will be used by salespeople to track information about customers and provide call reports to sales managers. At the end of each day, salespeople will call headquarters and upload their call reports.

PERFORMANCE EVALUATION OF CHARACTERISTICS

Assume the company narrows its choice to three hypothetical brands: Apex, Bell, and Deltos. Exhibit A.1 shows information the company has collected about each brand. Note that the information goes beyond the physical characteristics of the product to include services provided by the potential suppliers.

Each buying center member, or the group as a whole in a meeting, might process this objective information and evaluate the laptop computers on each characteristic. These evaluations appear in Exhibit A.2 as ratings on a 10-point scale, with 10 being the highest rating and 1 the lowest.

How do members of the buying center use these evaluations to select a laptop computer? The final decision depends on the relationship between the performance evaluations and the company's needs. The buying center members must consider the degree to which they are willing to sacrifice poor performance on

Exhibit A.1
Information about Laptop Computers

Characteristic/Brand	Apex	Bell	Deltos
Reliability rating	Very good	Very good	Excellent
Weight (pounds)	3.0	4.5	7.5
Display size (inches)	15.0	13	10.1
Display visibility	Good	Very good	Excellent
Speed (clock rate in gigahertz)	2.4	3.0	2.4
RAM (memory in gigabytes)	2	2	4
Number of U.S. service centers	140	60	20

Exhibit A.2
Performance Evaluation
of Laptop Computers

Characteristic/Brand Rating	Apex	Bell	Deltos
Reliability	5	5	8
Weight	8	5	2
Display size	8	6	4
Display visibility	2	4	6
Speed	4	8	4
RAM	3	3	8
Service availability	7	5	3

one attribute for superior performance on another. The members of the buying center must make some trade-offs.

No single product will perform best on all characteristics. For example, Apex excels on size, weight, and availability of convenient service; Bell has superior speed; and Deltos provides the best reliability and internal memory.

IMPORTANCE WEIGHTS

In making an overall evaluation, buying center members need to consider the importance of each characteristic. These importance weights may differ from member to member. Consider two members of the buying center: the national sales manager and the director of management information systems (MIS). The national sales manager is particularly concerned about motivating his salespeople to use the laptop computers. He believes the laptops must be small and lightweight and have good screen visibility. On the other hand, the MIS director foresees using the laptop computers to transmit orders and customer inventory information to corporation headquarters. She believes expanded memory and processing speed will be critical for these future applications.

Exhibit A.3 shows the importance these two buying center members place on each characteristic using a 10-point scale, with 10 representing very important and 1 representing very unimportant. In this illustration the national sales manager and the MIS director differ in the importance they place on characteristics;

Exhibit A.3
Information Used
to Form an Overall
Evaluation

Characteristic	Importance Weights		Brand Ratings		
	Sales Manager	MIS Director	Apex	Bell	Deltos
Reliability	4	4	5	5	8
Weight	6	2	8	5	2
Display size	7	3	8	6	4
Display visibility	8	5	2	4	6
Speed	1	7	4	8	4
RAM	1	6	3	3	8
Service availability	3	3	7	5	3
Overall evaluation					
Sales manager's			168	150	141
MIS director's			137	157	163

however, both have the same evaluations of the brands' performance on the characteristics. In some cases people may differ on both importance weights and performance ratings.

OVERALL EVALUATION

A person's overall evaluation of a product can be quantified by multiplying the sum of the performance ratings by the importance weights. Thus the sales manager's overall evaluation of Apex would be as follows:

$$4 \times 5 = 20$$
$$6 \times 8 = 48$$
$$7 \times 8 = 56$$
$$1 \times 4 = 4$$
$$1 \times 3 = 3$$
$$8 \times 2 = 16$$
$$3 \times 7 = \underline{21}$$
$$168$$

Using the national sales manager's and MIS director's importance weights, the overall evaluations, or scores, for the three laptop computer brands appear at the bottom of Exhibit A.3. The scores indicate the benefit levels the brands provide as seen by these two buying center members.

VALUE OFFERED

The cost of the computers also needs to be considered in making the purchase decision. One approach for incorporating cost calculates the value—the benefits divided by the cost—for each laptop. The prices for the computers and their values are shown in Exhibit A.4. The sales manager believes Apex provides more value. He would probably buy this brand if he were the only person involved in the buying decision. On the other hand, the MIS director believes that Bell and Deltos offer the best value.

SUPPLIER SELECTION

In this situation the sales manager might be the key decision maker, and the MIS director might be a gatekeeper. Rather than using the MIS director's overall evaluation, the buying center might simply ask her to serve as a gatekeeper and

Exhibit A.4
Value Offered by Each Brand

	Overall Evaluation (Benefits Points)	Assigned Value	
		Computer Cost	Benefit/Cost
Sales manager			
Apex	167	$1,600	$0.10
Bell	152	1,800	0.08
Deltos	143	1,800	0.08
MIS director			
Apex	130	$1,600	0.08
Bell	169	1,800	0.09
Deltos	177	1,800	0.10

determine whether these computers meet her minimum acceptable performance standards on speed and memory. All three laptops pass the minimum levels she established of a 2-gigahertz clock rate and a 3-gigabyte internal memory. Thus the company would rely on the sales manager's evaluation and purchase Apex laptops for the sales force.

Even if a buying center or individual members do not go through the calculations described here, the multiattribute model is a good representation of their product evaluations and can be used to predict product choices. Purchase decisions are often made as though a formal multiattribute model were used.

thinking it through

If you were selling the Bell computer to the national sales manager and MIS director depicted in the text and in Exhibits A.3 and A.4, how would you try to get them to believe that your computer provides more value than Apex or Deltos does? What numbers would you try to change?

IMPLICATIONS FOR SALESPEOPLE

How can salespeople use the multiattribute model to influence their customers' purchase decisions? First, the model describes the information customers use in making their evaluations and purchase decisions. Thus salespeople need to know the following information to develop a sales strategy:

1. The suppliers or brands the customer is considering.
2. The product characteristics being used in the evaluation.
3. The customer's rating of each product's performance on each dimension.
4. The weights the customer attaches to each dimension.

With this knowledge salespeople can use several strategies to influence purchase decisions. First, salespeople must be sure their product is among the brands being considered. Then they can try to change the customer's perception of their product's value. Some approaches for changing perceived value are

1. Increase the performance rating for your product.
2. Decrease the rating for a competitive product.
3. Increase or decrease an importance weight.
4. Add a new dimension.
5. Decrease the price of your product.

Assume you are selling the Bell computer and you want to influence the sales manager so he believes your computer provides more value than the Apex computer. Approach 1 involves altering the sales manager's belief about your product's performance. To raise his evaluation, you would try to have the sales manager perceive your computer as small and lightweight. You might show him how easy it is to carry—how well it satisfies his need for portability. The objective of this demonstration is to increase your rating on weight from 5 to 7 and your rating on size from 6 to 8.

You should focus on these two characteristics because they are the most important to the sales manager. A small change in a performance evaluation on these characteristics will have a large impact on the overall evaluation. You would not want to spend much time influencing his performance evaluations of speed or memory because these characteristics are not important to him. Of course your objectives when selling to the MIS director would be different because she places more importance on speed and memory.

This example illustrates a key principle in selling. In general, salespeople should focus primarily on product characteristics that are important to the customer—characteristics that satisfy the customer's needs. Salespeople should not focus on the areas of superior performance (such as speed in this example) that are not important to the customer.

Approach 2 involves decreasing the performance rating of Apex. This strategy can be dangerous. Customers prefer dealing with salespeople who say good things about their products, not bad things about competitive products.

In approach 3 you try to change the sales manager's importance weights. You want to increase the importance he places on a characteristic on which your product excels, such as speed, or decrease the importance of a characteristic on which your product performs poorly, such as display visibility. For example, you might try to convince the sales manager that a fast computer will decrease the time salespeople need to spend developing and transmitting reports.

Approach 4 encourages the sales manager to consider a new characteristic, one on which your product has superior performance. For example, suppose the sales manager and MIS director have not considered the availability of software. To add a new dimension, you might demonstrate a program specially developed for sales call reports and usable only with your computer.

Approach 5 is the simplest to implement: Simply drop your price. Typically firms use this strategy as a last resort because cutting prices decreases profits.

These strategies illustrate how salespeople can adapt their selling approach to the needs of their customers. Using the multiattribute model, salespeople decide how to alter the content of their presentation—the benefits to be discussed—based on customer beliefs and needs. (Chapter 4 describes adaptive selling in more detail and illustrates it in terms of the form of the presentation—the communication style the salesperson uses.)

ADDITIONAL REFERENCES

Andersson, Svante, and Per Servais. "Combining Industrial Buyer and Seller Strategies for International Supply and Marketing Management." *European Business Review* 22 (2010), pp. 64–82.

Autry, Chad W., and Susan L. Golicic. "Evaluating Buyer–Supplier Relationship–Performance Spirals: A Longitudinal Study." *Journal of Operations Management* 28 (March 2010), pp. 87–104.

Briggs, Ellen. and Douglas Grisaffe, "Service Performance–Loyalty Intentions Link in a Business-to-Business Context: The Role of Relational Exchange Outcomes and Customer Characteristics." *Journal of Service Research* 13 (2010), pp. 37–52.

Brinkmann, Jorg. "An Analysis of Buying Center Decisions through the Salesforce." *Industrial Marketing Management* 36, no. 7 (2007), pp. 998–1012.

Glynn, Mark S., Judy Motion, and Roderick J. Brodie. "Sources of Brand Benefits in Manufacturer–Reseller B2B Relationships." *Journal of Business & Industrial Marketing* 22, no. 6 (2007), pp. 400–13.

Gonzalez-Padronn, Tracy, G. Tomas Hult, and Roger Calantone. "Exploiting Innovative Opportunities in Global Purchasing: An Assessment of Ethical Climate and Relationship Performance." *Industrial Marketing Management* 37, no. 1 (2008), pp. 69–79.

Howard, Paul, and Declan Doyle. "An Examination of Buying Centres in Irish Biotechnology Companies and Its Marketing Implications." *The Journal of Business & Industrial Marketing* 21, no. 5 (2006), pp. 266–76.

Kotabe, Masaaki, Michael J. Mol, and Janet Y. Murray. "Outsourcing, Performance, and the Role of E-Commerce: A Dynamic Perspective." *Industrial Marketing Management* 37, no. 1 (2008), pp. 37–49.

Leach, Mark. "Examining Exchange Relationships among High-Tech Firms in the Evolving Global Economy." *Journal of Business & Industrial Marketing* 24 (2009), pp. 78–94.

Lindgreen, Adam, Balazs Revesz, and Mark Glynn. "Purchasing Orientation." *Journal of Business & Industrial Marketing* 24 (2009), pp. 148–72.

Lucero, Carrete. "A Relationship Model between Key Problems of International Purchasing and the Post-Purchase Behavior of Industrial Firms." *Journal of Business & Industrial Marketing* 23 (2008), pp. 332–47.

Lynch, Joanne, and Leslie de Chernatony. "Winning Hearts and Minds: Business-to-Business Branding and the Role of the Salesperson." *Journal of Marketing Management* 23, no. 1–2 (2007), pp. 123–36.

Marshall, Roger, Peter Alan Reday, Na Woonbong , and Shashank Shekhar Agrawal. "Response Time Measurement of Group Purchasing–Decision Power Structures." *Journal of Business Research* 60, no. 7 (2007), pp. 711–24.

Moon, Mark A. , and Leff Bonney. "An Application of the Investment Model to Buyer–Seller Relationships: A Dyadic Perspective." *Journal of Marketing Theory and Practice* 15, no. 4 (2007), pp. 335–47.

Paulraj, Antony, and Injazz J. Chen. "Strategic Buyer–Supplier Relationships, Information Technology, and External Logistics Integration." *Journal of Supply Chain Management* 43, no. 2 (2007), pp. 2–14.

Paulssen, Marcel, and Matthias M. Birk. "Satisfaction and Repurchase Behavior in a Business-to-Business Setting: Investigating the Moderating Effect of Manufacturer, Company, and Demographic Characteristics." *Industrial Marketing Management* 36, no. 7 (2007), pp. 983–97.

Pels, Jaqueline, Kristian Moller, and Michael Saren. "Do We Really Understand Business Marketing?" Getting beyond the RM and BM Matrimony." *Journal of Business & Industrial Marketing* 24 (2009), pp. 322–49.

Piercy, Nigel F., and Nikala Lane. "Ethical and Moral Dilemmas Associated with Strategic Relationships between Business-to-Business Buyers and Sellers." *Journal of Business Ethics* 72, no. 1 (2007), pp. 87–99.

Ritter, Thomas. "A Framework for Analyzing Relationship Governance." *The Journal of Business & Industrial Marketing* 22, no. 3 (2007), pp. 196–209.

Roy, Subroto, and Kiva Sivakumar. "The Role of Information Technology Adoption in the Globalization of Business Buying Behavior: A Conceptual Model and Research Propositions." *Journal of Business & Industrial Marketing* 22, no. 4 (2007), pp. 220–34.

Sashi, C.M., "Buyer Behavior in Business Markets: A Review and Integrative Model," *Journal of Global Issues* 3 (Summer 2009), pp. 129–38.

Skarmeas, Dionysis, Constantine S. Katsikeas, Stavroula Pyropoulou, and Esmail Salehi-Sangari. "Market and Supplier Characteristics Driving Distributor Relationship Quality in International Marketing Channels of Industrial Products." *Industrial Marketing Management* 27, no. 1 (2008), pp. 23–29.

Svahn, Senja and Mika Westerlund. "Purchasing Strategies in Supply Relationships." *Journal of Business & Industrial Marketing* 24 (2009), pp. 173–89.

Tomas, G., M. Hult, David J. Ketchen Jr., and Brian R. Chabowski. "Leadership, the Buying Center, and Supply Chain Performance: A Study of Linked Users, Buyers, and Suppliers." *Industrial Marketing Management* 36, no. 3 (2007), pp. 393–406.

chapter **5**

ADAPTIVE SELLING FOR RELATIONSHIP BUILDING

SOME QUESTIONS ANSWERED IN THIS CHAPTER ARE

- What is adaptive selling?
- Why is it important for salespeople to practice adaptive selling?
- What kind of knowledge do salespeople need to practice adaptive selling?
- How can salespeople acquire this knowledge?
- How can salespeople adapt their sales strategies, presentations, and social styles to various situations?

PART 1

PROFILE

"When meeting with so many business owners, it is vital for me to figure out what type of social style each prospective client is."

Meggie Dominguez

PROFILE

I am Meggie Dominguez, a May 2008 graduate from Texas State University–San Marcos. I earned my BBA in management from the McCoy College of Business. I served as president of Students in Free Enterprise (SIFE) and was a Texas State representative at the National Collegiate Sales Competition, both of which were under Vicki West. Mrs. West introduced me to ADP, which is where I was hired as a district manager.

At ADP, we consider ourselves business consultants. We don't have a prescript sales pitch that is used on every call. The goal is to educate the owner on varying topics surrounding payroll to show them how a service like ADP can make them more efficient and compliant with state and federal employer laws.

Because I meet with business owners who have anywhere from 1 employee to 49 employees in every industry thinkable, the needs of the businesses are never the same. I have to customize my presentation depending on many factors. For example, a first-time restaurant owner who has 35 tipped employees will need me to explain everything we do in depth from payroll taxes and new hire reporting to FICA tip reporting. Most new business owners are not aware of all their tax liabilities and ways they can get money back from the government for having tipped employees. The owners are very appreciative that I take the time to explain all these fiduciary responsibilities and the fines they could be liable for.

On the other hand, when I meet with a longtime owner of a nonprofit company with three employees, this presentation is completely different. In this situation the owner wouldn't be interested in hearing about the "payroll 101" I was telling the new business owner. Instead he or she would want to know about payroll being directly tied to grant funding, ability to offer comprehensive benefits, and wage tracking for grant reporting. Either way, I am selling the same service but simply customizing the presentation to the buyers' needs.

When meeting with so many business owners, it is vital for me to figure out what type of social style each prospective client is. If I am meeting with someone who isn't the same style as me, I have to recognize that and change my behavior to mirror the business owner. This will set the tone for the rest of the meeting, so in order for it to be a comfortable and productive conversation, I have to be aware of what type of person I am selling to.

Being able to adapt to my prospective clients and their needs is very important! One skill that makes this easier is being knowledgeable about common concerns within certain types of businesses and confidently knowing ADP's services that will eliminate those problems. When I show the owners how seamlessly ADP can address their concerns, they trust me, which ultimately leads to them becoming a new client. With knowledge comes confidence, and confidence brings sales!

Visit our Web site at www.adp.com.

Personal selling is the most effective marketing communication medium because it allows salespeople to tailor their presentations to each customer. They use their knowledge of the customer's buying process (Chapter 3) and finely tuned communication skills (Chapter 4) to learn about their customers and select effective sales strategies. Effective salespeople adapt their selling strategies and approaches to the selling situation. This chapter examines how salespeople can communicate effectively with their customers by practicing adaptive selling.

TYPES OF PRESENTATIONS

Salespeople can choose from a number of presentation types. This text examines the three most common: (1) the standard memorized presentation, (2) the outlined presentation, and (3) the customized presentation.

STANDARD MEMORIZED PRESENTATION

The **standard memorized presentation**, also called a *canned presentation,* is a completely memorized sales talk. The salesperson presents the same selling points in the same order to all customers. Some companies insist that their inside telemarketing salespeople, for example, memorize the entire presentation and deliver it word for word. Others believe that salespeople should be free to make some minor adjustments.

The standard memorized presentation ensures that the salesperson will provide complete and accurate information about the firm's products and policies. Because it includes the best techniques and methods, the standard memorized presentation can help bring new salespeople up to speed quickly and give them confidence. However, the effectiveness of the standard memorized presentation is limited because it offers no opportunity for the salesperson to tailor the presentation to the needs of the specific customer.

OUTLINED PRESENTATION

The **outlined presentation** is a prearranged presentation that usually includes a standard introduction, standard answers to common objections raised by customers, and a standard method for getting the customer to place an order. An example of an outlined presentation appears in Exhibit 5.1.

An outlined presentation can be very effective because it is well organized. It is more informal and natural than the standard memorized presentation and provides more opportunity for the customer to participate in the sales interaction. It also permits some flexibility in the approach used to present the key points.

CUSTOMIZED PRESENTATION

The **customized presentation** is a written and/or oral presentation based on a detailed analysis of the customer's needs. This type of presentation offers an opportunity to use the communication principles discussed in Chapter 4 to discover the customer's needs and problems and propose the most effective solution for satisfying those needs.[1] The customer recognizes the sales representative as a professional who is helping solve problems, not just selling products. The customized presentation lets the salesperson demonstrate empathy. Cultivating this view is an important step in developing a partnering relationship.

Each of the presentation types just discussed involves a different level of skill, cost, and flexibility. Standard memorized presentations can be delivered at a low cost by unskilled salespeople with little training. On the other hand, the customized presentation can be costly, requiring highly skilled people to analyze the customer's needs. Salespeople have the greatest opportunity to adapt their

Exhibit 5.1
Example of an Outlined
Presentation

Scenario: A Procter & Gamble Salesperson Calling on a Grocery Store Manager	
Step in Outlined Sales Presentation	**Say Something Like This**
1. Reinforce past success.	Good morning, Mr. Babcock. I was talking with one of your stockers, and he said that our Crest end-of-aisle display was very popular with customers last weekend. He said that he had to restock it three times. Looks like you made a wise decision to go with that program.
2. Reiterate customer's needs.	I know that profits and fast turns are what you are always looking for.
3. Introduce new Sure antiperspirant campaign.	We have a new campaign coming up for our Sure line.
4. Explain ad campaign and coupon drops.	We will be running a new set of commercials on all three network news programs. . . . Also, we'll be adding an insert in the Sunday coupon section with a 35-cents-off coupon.
5. Explain case allowances.	We are going to give you a $1.20 case allowance for every case of Sure you buy today.
6. Ask for end-of-aisle display and order of cases.	I propose that you erect an end-of-aisle display on aisle 7 . . . and that you order 20 cases.
7. Thank manager for order.	Thank you, and I know the results will be just as good as they were for our Crest promotion.

presentations to customer needs when using the customized presentation and the least opportunity when using the standard memorized presentation. The next section discusses the importance of adapting sales presentations.

ADAPTIVE SELLING AND SALES SUCCESS

Salespeople practice **adaptive selling** when they react to different sales situations by changing their sales behaviors. An extreme example of nonadaptive selling is using the standard memorized presentation, in which the same presentation is used for all customers. The customized presentation illustrates adaptive selling because the presentation is tailored to the specific needs of the customer.

Adaptive selling is featured in this textbook because this approach forces the salesperson to practice the marketing concept. It emphasizes the importance of satisfying customer needs. And being adaptable increases buyer trust and commitment and results in higher sales performance. It's important for salespeople to take the initiate and be adaptive.[2] The communication principles described in Chapter 4 are required to practice adaptive selling successfully. For example, a Kohler sales representative may believe that a portable generator manufacturer is interested in buying an economical, low-horsepower gasoline motor. While presenting the benefits of a low-cost motor, the sales rep discovers, by observing nonverbal behaviors, that the customer is interested in discussing overall operating costs. At this point the rep asks some questions to find out whether the customer would pay a higher price for a more efficient motor with lower operating costs. Based on the customer's response, the rep may adopt a new sales strategy: presenting a more efficient motor and demonstrating its low operating costs. Studies show that salespeople who are able to appraise the emotions of the buyer while practicing adaptive selling have higher performance.[3]

It is sometimes hard for people to realize that the world is not made up of people just like them. Many people are much older than you, while some are younger than you. They practice different religions, enjoy different foods, and shop at stores where you would never think of shopping. They have different moral beliefs and different ideas about "the perfect product" and were raised in a totally different way. Their hopes and aspirations don't match yours. Many of them would be shocked to hear what your life's dreams and goals are.

We are not just talking about differences in people in other countries. We are talking about people who live next door to you, who are sitting next to you in your classroom. Men and women often react differently to presentations. Generation Xers are different from baby boomers, who differ from the generations before them. One salesperson reported that grocery stores that cater to migrant farmers in the San Francisco area want a different product mix (such as more demand for Hormel SPAM) than a grocery store in midtown San Francisco (more demand for upscale, specialty Hormel meat products like Cure81 ham). The sooner you realize that your world is made up of diverse people, the sooner you will realize the importance of becoming adaptive. Selecting the appropriate sales strategy for a sales situation and making adjustments during the interaction are crucial to successful selling.

Salespeople should also adapt to the customer's desire for a specific type of relationship. For example, if a customer is not interested in developing a strong, long-term relationship and is more interested in maintaining a less involved relationship, the salesperson should adapt to this desire.

Practicing adaptive selling does not mean salespeople should be dishonest about their products or their personal feelings. It does mean salespeople should alter the content and form of their sales presentation so customers will be able to absorb the information easily and find it relevant to their situation. As "Building Partnerships 5.1" illustrates, sometimes a salesperson has to adapt to a difficult situation.

thinking **it** through   Do you act and talk differently to your professor than when you talk to your friends? Why do you adapt in that way?

This salesperson has acquired extensive knowledge of the customer's systems.

The advantages and disadvantages of the three types of sales presentations illustrate the benefits and drawbacks of adaptive selling. Adaptive selling gives salespeople the opportunity to use the most effective sales presentation for each customer. However, uncovering needs, designing and delivering different presentations, and making adjustments require a high level of skill. The objective of this textbook is to help you develop the skills and knowledge required to practice adaptive selling.

KNOWLEDGE MANAGEMENT

A key ingredient in effective selling is knowledge.[4] Salespeople need to know about the products they are selling, the company they work for, and the customers they will be selling to. Knowledge enables the salesperson to build self-confidence, gain the buyer's trust, satisfy customer needs, and practice adaptive selling.[5]

BUILDING Partnerships

5.1

I'M SORRY, DOCTOR, BUT I THINK YOU'RE ABOUT TO MAKE A MISTAKE

One aspect of my selling job requires me to service what I sell, and in the case of replacement joints that means going into the operating room with the surgeon and taking the role of a technical expert when it comes to the capabilities, function, and surgical technique used with my company's hardware. This scenario occurred during a total hip replacement on an 80-year-old woman. The doctor involved was a new customer, so I had brought in a wide variety of options for him to use, as I wasn't very familiar with his preferences and I wanted to be prepared for anything.

The case was going smoothly until the surgeon was deciding which component to use in the femur. There are two different types when it comes to the method of fixation of the new joint: cemented stems and press-fit stems. The stem is inserted into the intermedullary, or IM, canal, and if it is a round stem it is secured to the bone using bone cement. If it is a press-fit stem it is squared off, and you are essentially sticking a square peg into a round hole. The press-fit stem is pounded in such a manner that the four corners dig into the surrounding bone, and that provides fixation. It also leaves some open gaps in the IM canal.

The doctor decided to use a press-fit stem but decided that the bone quality wasn't what he wanted, and he didn't feel like it was secure. He told me he wanted to cement the press-fit stem in place. I knew that this was not typically done, and my training told me that it shouldn't

be done in order to avoid having bone cement leak down into the IM canal, which could potentially cause a number of problems down the road. At the same time if it was done very carefully it could work without any issues. What should I do?

In this case I felt I had ethical obligations to the surgeon and the patient. I stepped out of the OR and called one of our engineers to ask him what his opinion was, and he told me that I should strongly recommend against it. I would have liked to call our regional manager, but when you have an open patient on the operating table, time is very limited. I returned to the OR and told the doctor that as a representative of our company I had to recommend against cementing that particular stem. I said this in the OR with several support staff around, providing witnesses to my recommendations. I also stated that he was the doctor and that the final decision obviously rested with him. I did not know how the doctor would respond.

The surgeon listened to my concerns and then decided to go ahead with his original decision, but did confirm that I had recommended against it. After the case was over we talked in the doctor's lounge, and he said that he was glad I had voiced my opinion but he felt it was the proper decision. I explained my position once again. He said he understood, and the business relationship did not suffer.

Source: Brendan Brooks, Smith & Nephew; used with permission.

PRODUCT AND COMPANY KNOWLEDGE

Salespeople need to have a lot of information about their products, services, and company. Purchasing agents rate product knowledge as one of the most important attributes of good salespeople. Effective salespeople need to know how products are made, what services are provided with the products, how the products relate to other products, and how the products can satisfy customers' needs. Salespeople also need to know about their competitors' products as well as their own because they are frequently asked to compare their products to competitors' offerings.

KNOWLEDGE ABOUT SALES SITUATIONS AND CUSTOMERS

Equally important with product and company knowledge is detailed information about the different types of sales situations and customers salespeople may encounter.[6] For example, Nextel salespeople need to be knowledgeable about networking and information technology and have overall expertise in how businesses operate in order to sell cell phone service to their unique customer types.

Successful sales managers give their salespeople diagnostic feedback.

By developing categories of customer types or types of sales situations, salespeople reduce the complexity of selling and free up their mental capacity to think more creatively.[7] The categories salespeople use can focus on the benefits the customer seeks, the person's role in the buying center, the stage in the buying process, or the type of buying situation. For example, a Colgate salesperson might divide buyers into several categories based on their decision-making style. When selling to emotional buyers, this salesperson might need to be more enthusiastic and engage in visual storytelling. When selling to rational buyers, this salesperson might want to stress the financial benefits of purchasing the new toothpaste.

HOW TO CREATE KNOWLEDGE

One source of knowledge would be top salespeople in the company you work for. Some firms will collect and share this information with you. For example, a telecommunications company conducted in-depth interviews with its top performers. Through these interviews, it learned about the types of situations these salespeople encountered and what strategies they used in each situation. The company developed role plays for each sales situation and used them when training new salespeople. Such role-playing enabled the new salespeople to experience the variety of situations they would actually encounter on the job. The strategies recommended by the top salespeople served as a starting point for the trainees to develop their own sales methods for handling these situations.

Salespeople also create knowledge by getting feedback from sales managers. This can be in the form of **performance feedback** ("Did you achieve the goals you set for this call?") or **diagnostic feedback** ("Let's talk about why you didn't achieve your goals"). Diagnostic feedback provides information about what you're doing right and wrong, instead of just whether you made a sale.

The following example illustrates diagnostic feedback:

SALESPERSON: Why do you think I didn't make the sale?

SALES MANAGER: You stressed the low maintenance cost, but he wasn't interested in maintenance cost. Did you see how he kept looking around while you were talking about how cheap it is to maintain the product?

SALESPERSON: What do you think I should do next time?

SALES MANAGER: You might try spending more time finding his hot button. Maintenance cost isn't it.

Other sources of knowledge include the Web, company sales manuals and newsletters, experts in the salesperson's firm, sales meetings, plant visits, and business and trade publications. Salespeople also collect information about competitors from customers, by visiting competitor displays at trade shows, and from viewing competitors' Web pages.

RETRIEVING KNOWLEDGE FROM THE KNOWLEDGE MANAGEMENT SYSTEM

Salespeople store much of their acquired knowledge in their memory, and as such, retrieval is merely accessing information in that memory. Many companies, like Isuzu Commercial Trucks, described in "Sales Technology 5.1," also have customer relationship management (CRM) systems to support their salespeople.[8] Salespeople use programs like NetSuite to store and retrieve critical knowledge

SALES Technology

KEEPING TRACK OF THINGS—HOW ISUZU COMMERCIAL TRUCK OF AMERICA DOES IT

In this textbook we've been providing information and end-of-chapter role plays around a product called NetSuite (see the role play case at the end of Chapter 1 for more details about NetSuite). NetSuite allows salespeople to keep track of their prospects and customers and provides a number of reports and information that help salespeople and sales managers be more effective and efficient.

Isuzu Commercial Truck of America, a manufacturer of medium- and heavy-duty trucks located in Cerritos, California, found NetSuite to be just what they needed. Their old CRM system just didn't have the power the sales reps needed and was, not surprisingly, used little by the sales force. That, combined with a downturn in industrywide sales, put pressure on Isuzu to do something. The solution? NetSuite CRM.

What about salesperson reluctance to accept the new system? Often salespeople are reluctant to adopt CRM systems because they see such a system as something that helps management but doesn't help them day-to-day. "We had some old-time people who would maintain accounts on the back of an envelope, but with NetSuite's ease of use and a little internal competition, we were able

to load hundreds of our most important customer contacts in the first month," says Todd Bloom, VP of marketing and fleet operations at Isuzu Commercial Truck of America.

Implementing NetSuite has helped Isuzu sales reps by reducing their time spent filling out reports and performing other administrative tasks. The result is more time to interact with key customers. "Our goal is to keep our field reps in front of the customers for the greatest amount of time," Bloom says. "Implementing NetSuite CRM will help us reduce the time we spend in meetings and doing paperwork and reports." And because the entry data and reports are standardized, reps can be evaluated on a more equitable plane.

NetSuite has also given both U.S. and Japanese management important information and insight into what salespeople are doing. And using such a cutting-edge tool has positioned the company well for further growth in its approximately 70 percent market share of the medium- to heavy-duty truck category.

Source: netsuite.com (including the customer success stories linked from that site at http://www.netsuite.com/portal/customers/main.shtml).

about accounts, products, and competitors. For example, salespeople for the Houston Aeros hockey franchise use NetSuite to store and access information about its customers. They use this knowledge when interacting with customers to develop sales strategies and purchase recommendations. Studies have shown that using a CRM system has a positive impact on being adaptive while selling.[9]

It is important for salespeople to be able to retrieve brochures and other business collateral from the knowledge management system. But perhaps more important is the ability to tap the knowledge of in-house experts. One writer calls this "genius management," which implies going beyond document management to the realm of tapping knowledge from genius within your firm.[10] Social computing tools are important in this regard.[11] Progressive firms are encouraging in-house experts, like engineers, product development specialists, and financial staff, to develop in-house blogs, wikis, and Web pages that are easily accessible and searchable by the sales force. Social networking sites like LinkedIn and Facebook can also be used to connect in-house experts with salespeople. Finally, firms are experimenting with tagging, which is including keywords with a person's name in company documents and on internal Web pages. The keywords indicate the areas of expertise for which that person can be contacted. The goal in all of this is to make it easier for salespeople to connect to experts in their own firms for ideas and assistance.

THE SOCIAL STYLE MATRIX: A TRAINING PROGRAM FOR BUILDING ADAPTIVE SELLING SKILLS

To be effective, salespeople need to use their knowledge about products and customers to adapt both the content of their sales presentations—the benefits they emphasize to customers and the needs they attempt to satisfy—and the style they use to communicate with customers. The **social style matrix** is a popular training program that companies use to help salespeople adapt their communication styles.

David Merrill and Roger Reid discovered patterns of communication behaviors, or social styles, that people use when interacting with one another.[12] Merrill and Reid found that people who recognize and adjust to these behavior patterns have better relationships with other people. The company Wilson Learning conducts training using these concepts.[13]

Here is a quick preview of what you will learn about the social style training program. As you know, the world is made up of diverse people. For example, some are fast decision makers, whereas others are slow to make just about any kind of decision; some like to talk, whereas others are quiet. To make it easier, this system divides all people into four different types or categories that are based on two dimensions. Your goal as a salesperson is to first identify which of the four types you are. Next you figure out which of the four types your customer is. Finally you adjust your behavior to mirror or match that of your customer. Now that you have a general idea of how the system works, let's look at it in more detail.

DIMENSIONS OF SOCIAL STYLES

This training program uses two critical dimensions to understand social behavior: assertiveness and responsiveness.

Assertiveness

The degree to which people have opinions about issues and publicly make their positions clear to others is called **assertiveness.** Simply having strong convictions does not make a person assertive; assertive people express their convictions publicly and attempt to influence others to accept these beliefs.

Assertive people speak out, make strong statements, and have a take-charge attitude. When under tension, they tend to confront the situation. Unassertive people rarely dominate a social situation, and they often keep their opinions to themselves. Exhibit 5.2 shows some verbal and nonverbal behavioral indicators of assertiveness.

Responsiveness

The second dimension, **responsiveness,** is based on how emotional people tend to get in social situations. Responsive people readily express joy, anger, and sorrow. They appear to be more concerned with others and are informal and casual in social situations. Less responsive people devote more effort toward controlling their emotions. They are described as cautious, intellectual, serious, formal, and businesslike. Exhibit 5.3 lists some indicators of responsiveness.

CATEGORIES OF SOCIAL STYLES

The two dimensions of social style, assertiveness and responsiveness, form the social style matrix shown in Exhibit 5.4. Each quadrant of the matrix defines a social style type.

Exhibit 5.2
Indicators of
Assertiveness

Less Assertive	More Assertive
"Ask" oriented	"Tell" oriented
Go-along attitude	Take-charge attitude
Cooperative	Competitive
Supportive	Directive
Risk avoider	Risk taker
Makes decisions slowly	Makes decisions quickly
Lets others take initiative	Takes initiative
Leans backward	Leans forward
Indirect eye contact	Direct eye contact
Speaks slowly, softly	Speaks quickly, intensely
Moves deliberately	Moves rapidly
Makes few statements	Makes many statements
Expresses moderate opinions	Expresses strong opinions

Exhibit 5.3
Indicators of
Responsiveness

Less Responsive	More Responsive
Controls emotions	Shows emotions
Cool, aloof	Warm, approachable
Talk oriented	People oriented
Uses facts	Uses opinions
Serious	Playful
Impersonal, businesslike	Personable, friendly
Moves stiffly	Moves freely
Seldom gestures	Gestures frequently
Formal dress	Informal dress
Disciplined about time	Undisciplined about time
Controlled facial expressions	Animated facial expressions
Monotone voice	Many vocal inflections

Drivers

Drivers are high on assertiveness and low on responsiveness. The slogan of drivers, who are task-oriented people, might be "Let's get it done now, and get it done my way." Drivers have learned to work with others only because they must do so to get the job done, not because they enjoy people. They have a great desire to get ahead in their companies and careers.

Drivers are swift, efficient decision makers. They focus on the present and appear to have little concern with the past or future. They generally base their decisions on facts, take risks, and want to look at several alternatives before making a decision. As compared to analyticals, who also like facts and data, drivers want to know how the facts affect results—the bottom line. They are not interested in simply technical information.

To influence a driver, salespeople need to use a direct, businesslike, organized presentation with quick action and follow-up. Proposals should emphasize the effects of a purchase decision on profits.

Exhibit 5.4
Social Style Matrix

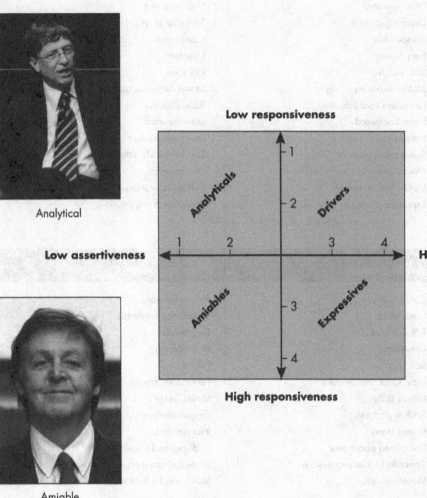

Analytical

Driver

Amiable

Expressive

Some example of social styles (Donald Trump, Barack Obama, Paul McCartney, Bill Gates). Do you agree with where they are placed? Note that all these people may switch to a different style under certain conditions.

Expressives

Expressives are high on assertiveness and high on responsiveness. Warm, approachable, intuitive, and competitive, expressives view power and politics as important factors in their quest for personal rewards and recognition. Although expressives are interested in personal relationships, their relationships are primarily with supporters and followers recruited to assist expressives in achieving their personal goals.

People with an expressive style focus on the future, directing their time and effort toward achieving their vision. They have little concern for practical details in present situations. Expressives base their decisions on their personal opinions and the opinions of others. They act quickly, take risks, but tend to be impatient and change their minds easily.

When selling to expressives, salespeople need to demonstrate how their products will help the customer achieve personal status and recognition. Expressives prefer sales presentations with product demonstrations and creative graphics, rather than factual statements and technical details. Also, testimonials from well-known firms and people appeal to expressives' need for status and recognition. Expressives respond to sales presentations that put them in the role of innovator, the first person to use a new product.

Amiables

Amiables are low on assertiveness and high on responsiveness. Close relationships and cooperation are important to amiables. They achieve their objectives by working with people, developing an atmosphere of mutual respect rather than using power and authority. Amiables tend to make decisions slowly, building a consensus among people involved in the decision. They avoid risks and change their opinions reluctantly.

Salespeople may have difficulty detecting an amiable's true feelings. Because amiables avoid conflict, they often say things to please others despite their personal opinions. Therefore, salespeople need to build personal relationships with amiables. Amiables are particularly interested in receiving guarantees about a product's performance. They do not like salespeople who agree to undertake activities and then do not follow through on commitments. Salespeople selling to amiables should stress the product's benefits in terms of its effects on the satisfaction of employees.

Analyticals

Analyticals are low on assertiveness and low on responsiveness. They like facts, principles, and logic. Suspicious of power and personal relationships, they strive to find a way to carry out a task without resorting to these influence methods.

Because they are strongly motivated to make the right decision, analyticals make decisions slowly, in a deliberate and disciplined manner. They systematically analyze the facts, using the past as an indication of future events.

Salespeople need to use solid, tangible evidence when making presentations to analyticals. Analyticals are also influenced by sales presentations that recognize their technical expertise and emphasize long-term benefits. They tend to disregard personal opinions. Both analyticals and amiables tend to develop loyalty toward suppliers. For amiables, the loyalty is based on personal relationships; analyticals' loyalty is based on their feeling that well-reasoned decisions do not need to be reexamined.

IDENTIFYING CUSTOMERS' SOCIAL STYLES

Exhibit 5.5 lists some cues for identifying the social styles of customers or prospects.[14] Salespeople can use their communication skills to observe the customer's behavior, listen to the customer, and ask questions to classify the customer. Merrill and Reid caution that identifying social style is difficult and requires close, careful observation. Salespeople should not jump to quick conclusions based on limited information. Here are some suggestions for making accurate assessments:

- Concentrate on the customer's behavior and disregard how you feel about the behavior. Don't let your feelings about the customer or thoughts about the customer's motives cloud your judgment.

- Avoid assuming that specific jobs or functions are associated with a social style ("He must be an analytical because he is an engineer").

- Test your assessments. Look for clues and information that may suggest you have incorrectly assessed a customer's social style. If you look for only confirming cues, you will filter out important information.

Exhibit 5.5
Cues for Recognizing
Social Styles

Analytical	Driver
Technical background.	Technical background.
Achievement awards on wall.	Achievement awards on wall.
Office is work oriented, showing much activity.	No posters or slogans on office walls.
Conservative dress.	Calendar prominently displayed.
Likes solitary activities (e.g., reading, individual sports).	Furniture is placed so that contact with people is across desk.
	Conservative dress.
	Likes group activities (e.g., politics, team sports).

Amiable	Expressive
Liberal arts background.	Liberal arts background.
Office has friendly, open atmosphere.	Motivational slogans on wall.
Pictures of family displayed.	Office has friendly, open atmosphere.
Personal momentos on wall.	Cluttered, unorganized desk.
Desk placed for open contact with people.	Desk placed for open contact with people.
Casual or flamboyant dress.	Casual or flamboyant dress.
Likes solitary activities (e.g., reading, individual sports).	Likes group activities (e.g., politics, team sports).

SOCIAL STYLES AND SALES PRESENTATIONS

In addition to teaching trainees how to assess social style, the Merrill and Reid program also assesses the trainees' social styles. Each person is asked to have a group of his or her customers complete a questionnaire and mail it to the director of the training program. These responses are used to determine the trainee's style. Trainees frequently are surprised by the difference between their self-perceptions and the perceptions of their customers. To get a rough idea of your own social style, you can complete the assessment in Exhibit 5.6.

Interpreting self-ratings requires great caution. Self-assessments can be misleading because we usually do not see ourselves the same way others see us. When you rate yourself, you know your own feelings, but others can observe only your behaviors. They don't know your thoughts or your intentions. We also vary our behavior from situation to situation. The indicators listed in Exhibits 5.2 and 5.3 merely show a tendency to be assertive or responsive.

Is there one best social style for a salesperson? No. None is "best" for all situations; each style has its strong points and weak points. Driver salespeople are efficient, determined, and decisive, but customers may find them pushy and dominating. Expressives have enthusiasm, dramatic flair, and creativity but can also seem opinionated, undisciplined, and unstable. Analyticals are orderly, serious, and thorough, but customers may view them as cold, calculating, and stuffy. Finally, amiables are dependable, supportive, and personable but may also be perceived as undisciplined and inflexible.

The sales training program based on the social style matrix emphasizes that effective selling involves more than communicating a product's benefits. Salespeople must also recognize the customer's needs and expectations. In the sales

Exhibit 5.6
Self-Assessment of
Social Styles

Assertiveness Ratings I perceive myself as:				Responsiveness Ratings I perceive myself as:			
Quiet . . . . Talkative				Open . . . . Closed			
1	2	3	4	4	3	2	1
Slow to decide . . . . Fast to decide				Impulsive . . . . Deliberate			
1	2	3	4	4	3	2	1
Going along . . . . Taking charge				Using opinions . . . . Using facts			
1	2	3	4	4	3	2	1
Supportive . . . . .Challenging				Informal . . . . Formal			
1	2	3	4	4	3	2	1
Compliant. . . . . Dominant				Emotional . . . . Unemotional			
1	2	3	4	4	3	2	1
Deliberate. . . . . Fast to decide				Easy to know . . . . Hard to know			
1	2	3	4	4	3	2	1
Asking questions . . . . Making statements				Warm . . . . Cool			
1	2	3	4	4	3	2	1
Cooperative . . . . .Competitive				Excitable .Calm			
1	2	3	4	4	3	2	1
Avoiding risks . . . . Taking risks				Animated . . . . Poker-faced			
1	2	3	4	4	3	2	1
Slow, studied. . . . . .Fast-paced				People-oriented . . . . Task-oriented			
1	2	3	4	4	3	2	1
Cautious. . . . . Carefree				Spontaneous. . . . . Cautious			
1	2	3	4	4	3	2	1
Indulgent. . . . . Firm				Responsive . . . . Nonresponsive			
1	2	3	4	4	3	2	1
Nonassertive. . . . . .Assertive				Humorous. . . . . Serious			
1	2	3	4	4	3	2	1
Mellow. . . . . Matter-of-fact				Impulsive . . . . Methodical			
1	2	3	4	4	3	2	1
Reserved. . . . . Outgoing				Lighthearted . . . . Intense			
1	2	3	4	4	3	2	1

Mark your answers above. Total the score for each side and divide each by 15. Then plot your scores on Exhibit 5.4 to see what social style you are. For fun, you may want to have several friends also score you.

Source: Based on work by David Merrill and Roger Reid, *Personal Styles and Effective Performance* (Radnor, PA: Chilton, 1981).

interaction, salespeople should conduct themselves in a manner consistent with customer expectations. Exhibit 5.7 indicates the expectations of customers with various social styles.

Although each customer type requires a different sales presentation, the salesperson's personal social style tends to determine the sales technique he or she typically uses. For example, drivers tend to use a driver technique with all customer types. When interacting with an amiable customer, driver salespeople will be efficient and businesslike, even though the amiable customer would prefer to deal with a more relationship-oriented and friendlier salesperson.

This sales training program emphasizes that to be effective with a variety of customer types, salespeople must adapt their selling presentations to customers'

Exhibit 5.7
Customer Expectations Based on Social Styles

Area of Expectation	Customer's Social Style			
	Driver	Expressive	Amiable	Analytical
Atmosphere in sales interview	Businesslike	Open, friendly	Open, honest	Businesslike
Salesperson's use of time	Effective, efficient	To develop relationship	Leisurely, to develop relationship	Thorough, accurate
Pace of interview	Quick	Quick	Deliberate	Deliberate
Information provided by salesperson	Salesperson's qualifications; value of products	What salesperson thinks; whom he/she knows	Evidence that salesperson is trustworthy, friendly	Evidence of salesperson's expertise in solving problem
Salesperson's actions to win customer acceptance	Documented evidence, stress results	Recognition and approval	Personal attention and interest	Evidence that salesperson has analyzed the situation
Presentation of benefits	What product can do	Who has used the product	Why product is best to solve problem	How product can solve the problem
Assistance to aid decision making	Explanation of options and probabilities	Testimonials	Guarantees and assurances	Evidence and offers of service

social styles. Versatility is the key to effective adaptive selling. "From the Buyer's Seat 5.1" gives a good illustration of a salesperson who didn't practice versatility—and the consequences of that behavior.

VERSATILITY

The effort people make to increase the productivity of a relationship by adjusting to the needs of the other party is known as **versatility**. Versatile salespeople—those able to adapt their social styles—are much more effective than salespeople who do not adjust their sales presentations. Here is a comparison of behaviors of more versatile and less versatile people:

How can a salesperson improve his or her versatility? Many companies have sales training programs, using tools like the social style matrix that help teach salespeople the differences in buyers. Role playing is also used extensively for managers to spot problems in salesperson versatility and to teach new ways to help improve it. For example, sales training might suggest that effective salespeople adjust their social styles to match their customers' styles. In role plays, salespeople with a driver orientation need to become more emotional and less assertive when selling to amiable customers. Analytical salespeople must increase

Less Versatile	More Versatile
Limited ability to adapt to others' needs	Able to adapt to others' needs
Specialist	Generalist
Well-defined interests	Broad interests
Sticks to principles	Negotiates issues
Predictable	Unpredictable
Looks at one side of an issue	Looks at many sides of an issue

From the BUYER'S SEAT

SOME SALESPEOPLE JUST DON'T ADAPT TO ME, OR TO THE SITUATION

By Tracey Brill

One thing that really irritates me is when a salesperson calls on me and doesn't adapt to the situation or to my specific needs. I could tell many stories of how this works out in practice, but perhaps one example will give you a good idea.

I was in my doorway about to leave my office to meet with a vice president. I had ended a meeting in my office about three minutes early to give myself the time to get up the three flights of stairs to her (the VP's) office in time. A salesperson, whom I had never met before, stopped me in my doorway, and I explained that I was on my way to an important meeting.

The salesperson said he understood but proceeded to take my hand and shake it and introduce himself. He continued to say that he was asked to meet with me by another coworker to introduce his services. I continued to explain that I needed to go to my meeting, but I would

take his card and call him later. He would not clear the doorway and continued to explain his services, which was "only going to take a minute." I explained that I really didn't have a minute, and I would call him later.

He continued to explain his services after I said I didn't have the time. I interrupted him and explained that he needed to allow me to leave my office. His disregard for my time and his desire "to only take a minute of my time" resulted in my being two minutes late for my meeting.

This salesperson works in a very competitive business. Many groups offer the same services, but I am usually interested in meeting with the different vendors to see if they have any unique feature we have not already evaluated. What did I do in this case? Instead of calling the rep back, I did my homework with the coworker who referred him to me. The project was bid to three vendors. But I didn't bid it to the salesperson that interrupted me in the doorway.

Source: Tracey Brill; used with permission.

their assertiveness and responsiveness when selling to expressive customers. Exhibit 5.8 shows some techniques for adjusting sales behaviors in terms of assertiveness and responsiveness.

THE ROLE OF KNOWLEDGE

The social style matrix illustrates the importance of knowledge, organized into categories, in determining selling effectiveness through adaptive selling. Sales training based on the social style matrix teaches salespeople the four customer categories or types (driver, expressive, amiable, and analytical). Salespeople learn the cues for identifying them. Salespeople also learn which adjustments they need to make in their communication styles to be effective with each customer type.

SYSTEMS FOR DEVELOPING ADAPTIVE SELLING SKILLS

The social style matrix developed by Merrill and Reid is one of several sales training methods based on customer classification schemes. Rather than using assertiveness and responsiveness, other classification schemes use dimensions like warm–hostile and dominant–submissive; dominance and sociability; relater, socializer, thinker, and director; logical (yellow), emotional (blue), conceptual (orange), and analytical (green); and skeptics, charismatics, thinkers, followers, and controllers.

Exhibit 5.8
Adjusting Social Styles

Dimension	Adjustment	
	Reduce	Increase
Assertiveness	Ask for customer's opinion.	Get to the point.
	Acknowledge merits of customer's viewpoint.	Don't be vague or ambiguous.
	Listen without interruption.	Volunteer information.
	Be more deliberate; don't rush.	Be willing to disagree.
	Let customer direct flow of conversation.	Take a stand.
		Initiate conversation.
Responsiveness	Become businesslike.	Verbalize feelings.
	Talk less.	Express enthusiasm.
	Restrain enthusiasm.	Pay personal compliments.
	Make decision based on facts.	Spend time on relationships rather than business.
	Stop and think.	Socialize; engage in small talk.
		Use nonverbal communication.

Regardless of the training system used, it is imperative that salespeople adjust to their audience. To repeat, it is also important to adjust your style when selling to diverse cultures even within your own country. For example, Hispanic salespeople may need to alter their communication style when selling to Anglo-American customers.

Expert systems have been developed to help salespeople understand their customers and develop effective sales strategies. An **expert system** is a computer program that mimics a human expert. The program contains the knowledge, rules, and decision processes employed by experts and then uses these elements to solve problems, suggest strategies, and provide advice similar to that of an expert.

Expert systems, like Insights for Sales Strategy, help salespeople understand buyers and develop effective sales strategies.

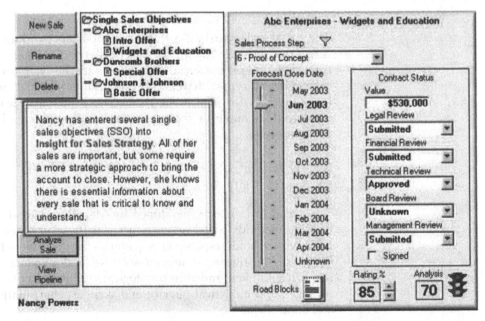

Studies show that salespeople who are willing to accept technology have higher performance.

Training methods such as the social style matrix and expert systems are simply a first step in developing knowledge for practicing adaptive selling. They emphasize the need to practice adaptive selling—to use different presentations with different customers—and stimulate salespeople to base their sales presentations on an analysis of the customer. But these methods are limited; they present only a few types of customers, and classification is based on the form of communication (the social style), not on the content of the communication (the specific features and benefits stressed in the presentation).

In addition, accurately fitting customers into the suggested categories is often difficult. Customers act differently and have different needs in different sales encounters: A buyer may be amiable in a new task buying situation and be analytical when dealing with an out-supplier's salesperson in a straight rebuy. Amiable buyers in a bad mood may act like drivers. By rigidly applying the classification rules, salespeople may actually limit their flexibility, reducing the adaptive selling behavior these training methods emphasize.

SELLING YOURSELF

Congratulations! You have an interview on campus this Thursday for an internship. You don't know a lot about the job, but you've heard other students say it's an awesome experience.

To prepare, you'll need to gain some knowledge about the internship as well as the company. You also need to learn how an interview process works and what to expect. One of the best ways to do that is to use the services of your school's outplacement office (sometimes called the career center, job center, or something like that). They are experts and have a wealth of knowledge. You want to tap that knowledge and add it to your knowledge base.

As the folks at your college's career center engage in practice interviews with you, provide constructive feedback on your résumé, or hint that perhaps your clothing or accessories might not be something you want to wear in the actual interview, accept this evaluative feedback for what it is—something to help you succeed. They're not telling you those things to hurt you or make you feel bad. The sooner you can learn not to take things personally, and accept (and even ask for) feedback on what you're doing wrong, the sooner you will start being successful. It's as simple as that. Fight feedback, and people will often stop giving it to you, making you less skilled in life.

As the meeting begins, you should start forming impressions about the social style of the interviewer. Is she an amiable or more analytical? The chapter told how you could assess this, but many of the cues you are supposed to look for won't be there because you're meeting at the school's job placement center rather than in the person's own office.

But don't give up. You can still learn a great deal from whether he wants to engage in small talk, or from whether she is taking careful written notes (or just watching you and listening to you without taking notes), or from whether he seems to have the entire interview planned out or is just adapting to your specific interview and deciding what to do next as the interview proceeds. You can also learn about her social style from how she is dressed (casually or conservatively) and from whether you are sitting across the desk from each other or next to each other. Learn from the cues that are provided and adapt your style accordingly. You'll be glad you did.

SUMMARY

Adaptive selling uses one of the unique properties of personal selling as a marketing communication tool: the ability to tailor messages to individual customers and make on-the-spot adjustments. Extensive knowledge of customer and sales situation types is a key ingredient in effective adaptive selling.

To be effective, salespeople need considerable knowledge about the products they sell, the companies for which they work, and the customers to whom they sell. Experienced salespeople organize customer knowledge into categories. Each category has cues for classifying customers or sales situations and an effective sales presentation for customers in the category.

The social style matrix, developed by Merrill and Reid, illustrates the concept of developing categorical knowledge to facilitate adaptive selling. The matrix defines four customer categories based on a customer's responsiveness and assertiveness in sales interactions. To effectively interact with a customer, a salesperson needs to identify the customer's social style and adapt a style to match. The sales training program based on the social style matrix provides cues for identifying social style as well as presentations salespeople can use to make adjustments.

The social style matrix is one example of a categorical scheme salespeople can use to improve their knowledge and adaptability. However, other schemes are used, and some have been incorporated into expert system computer programs.

KEY TERMS

adaptive selling   129
amiable   137
analytical   137
assertiveness   134
customized presentation   128
diagnostic feedback   132
driver   135
expert system   142

expressive   136
outlined presentation   128
performance feedback   132
responsiveness   134
social style matrix   134
standard memorized presentation   128
versatility   140

ETHICS PROBLEMS

1. As a salesperson, is it ethical to adjust your presentation based on social styles? Isn't that just being manipulative? Can't you just be yourself and sell?
2. You have a buyer who is a real jerk. She is in constant battles with all the salespeople who call on her, as well as with her own staff. Her business is important to you, and you don't want to lose it because you love the commissions on the sales you make. How should you adapt to her social style?[15]

QUESTIONS AND PROBLEMS

1. A salesperson stated, "I just can't stand to deal with buyers who have trouble making up their minds. I'd much rather deal with someone who shouts at me and tells me in no uncertain terms what they hate about me or my product." Based on this limited amount of information, what social style would you guess the salesperson to be? What would be your response to this salesperson?
2. In "Sales Technology 5.1" you learned how Isuzu is using NetSuite to empower its salespeople to perform more effectively and efficiently. But some salespeople, far from using the benefits of technology, were still writing

call notes on the back of envelopes. What would be your response to a salesperson who says, "I don't need all that fancy technology. My system of taking hand notes works just fine for me"?

3. A salesperson made the following comment: "I hate it when my sales manager makes calls with me. I do so much better when I'm by myself. After the call, she is always telling me what I did wrong." Based on what you learned in this chapter about knowledge systems, what would be your response to this salesperson?

4. "A good salesperson can sell any customer." Do you agree? Why or why not?

5. Would a person with an analytical social style be better at selling than a person with a driver or an expressive style? Why or why not?

6. Some people object to the social style matrix training system because they don't want to "act." Is that a valid objection? What would you say to them?

7. What social styles would you assign to the following people?
   a. Oprah Winfrey.
   b. Your favorite instructor last term.

c. The person who sits next to you in this class.
d. Your best friend.

8. The salesperson in "Building Partnerships 5.1" had to tell the surgeon that he was using a product incorrectly. Assume you are in a similar situation. You have to tell a surgeon that she is using your product incorrectly. How would you do that differently for a surgeon who is an analytical versus a driver surgeon?

9. Suppose that during a sales call, a customer says, "I'm not convinced that this new product will sell." How should you respond if this customer is a driver? An expressive?

10. Market research by a commercial cleaning company identified two types of high schools. Traditional high schools believe that teacher and staff satisfaction is based on the quality of students and that cleaning services are relatively unimportant. Private and charter high schools believe that cleaning services are important because they affect the students' and parents' perceptions of the school. What type of sales presentation would you use to sell janitorial services to each of these high school types? Which product features and benefits would you emphasize in each case?

CASE PROBLEMS

case **5.1**

Dyson Airblade

Jon TePoel is a salesperson for Dyson, Inc., in New York City, and he has been working for the company for two years. Dyson is well known for making some of the highest-quality vacuum cleaners in the world.

Recently Sir James Dyson, the owner of the company, created an air hand dryer for public restrooms, and it's one that actually works. The Dyson Airblade dries hands in only 12 seconds, uses 80 percent less energy than other air flow hand dryers, and the kills 99.9 percent of airborne bacteria with a built-in HEPA filter.

Jon is going to call on a buying team of three individuals (Marty Chuckalot, Alfred Nordstrom, and Cynthia Bergstein) for a large New York City developer. His goal is to convince them to specify Dyson Airblade hand dryers for all the public restrooms in their new construction projects. Currently the developer uses a combination of regular air dryers and paper towel dispensers.

While doing some background research, Jon has discovered a bit about his three buyers. Marty Chuckalot never arrives to a meeting without bringing his laptop, and he uses it throughout the meeting, often not seeming to pay attention to whoever is giving the presentation. Marty is quiet, never answering questions during a meeting or offering his opinions. One of his favorite phrases is, "I'm not sure if I fully understand your product. Can you tell me a bit more about it?" His personality is fairly serious, which is evident when he frequently decodes a person's message with its literal, rather than the intended, meaning. People who interact with him say they have to learn to tolerate silences and give him time to think before answering.

Alfred Nordstrom is quite a different type of buyer. Alfred seems to know everyone's first name, and everyone seems to knows him, although a few don't really like him. In conversations he often takes the lead, making his opinion well known in the group. He has been described as manipulative, but always "in a nice way." He loves to talk and can carry on a conversation about hockey for an hour if the seller will let him.

Cynthia Bergstein is the friendliest of the three buyers. She tries to make everyone feel comfortable and often softens remarks made by Alfred. She never buys from someone until she gets to know them because, as she says, "How do we know we can trust them if we don't know them well first?" She is supportive of other's decisions, even if an idea is contrary to her own point of view. She prefers to let others take the lea, and would say her strength is to be a great team player.

Questions

1. Based on the information provided in this case, identify each of the three buyers' social styles.
2. If you were Jon, what should you do to sell to this group?

case 5.2

Cedar Point Amusement Park

You have just been hired as a salesperson for Cedar Point Amusement Park in Sandusky, Ohio.

Cedar Point is the largest amusement ride park in the world. The park has 75 rides, including 17 roller coasters (3 of the top 10 steel roller coasters in the world are found in the park). There are other family attractions including a Planet Snoopy area for children, shows, and so forth.

Your job is to sell to corporate groups—either a single-day event or "good any day" passes that can be used by employees any day the park is open (employees don't have to attend the park together if they use good any day passes). Cedar Point offers many options for corporations, including the ability to cater meals for the event.

Questions

1. What kinds of knowledge do you need to do your job effectively?
2. How can you acquire that knowledge?
3. What type of system should you use to store that knowledge and retrieve it as needed?

Source: http://www.cedarpoint.com.

ROLE PLAY CASE

This role play requires some before-class preparation. Write a brief outline of how you would describe NetSuite to someone who has never seen it. Identify three features of NetSuite that you think would benefit your buyer, based on the information you've learned so far this semester. Then write down what you would want to say about each feature. You will take turns presenting your sales presentations to your buyer. After you give your presentation, determine what the other person's social style was. Identify the hints the buyer gave you.

If you have been using NetSuite role plays all along, you can use the same customer you have called on. If not, you will need to review the role play material at the end of Chapter 3. You can also review material about NetSuite in the role play case at the back of this book to understand NetSuite and what it does.

When you play the buyer, pick a social style different from your own. Interact with the seller in ways that give clues about your social style. Before the role play starts, think of at least five things you will do to hint at your new social style. Keep in mind that a social style includes both responsiveness and assertiveness, so make sure your hints combine both dimensions. After each role play, the salesperson should say what the other person's social style was and what clues were used to make that determination.

Note: For background information about these role plays, please see page 27.

To the instructor: Additional information needed to complete the role play is available in the Instructor's Manual.

ADDITIONAL REFERENCES

Amyx, Douglas, and Shahid Bhuian. "The Salesperson Service Performance Scale." *Journal of Personal Selling & Sales Management* 29, no. 4 (Fall 2009), pp. 367–76.

Aramo-Immonen, Heli, and Pasi Porkka. "Shared Knowledge in Project-Based Companies' Value Chain." *International Journal of Knowledge Management Studies* 6 (October 2009), p. 364.

Badrinarayanan, Vishag, and Sreedhar Madhavaram. "Workplace Spirituality and the Selling Organization: A Conceptual Framework and Research Propositions." *Journal of Personal Selling & Sales Management* 28, no. 4 (Fall 2008), pp. 421–34.

Barnes, Bradley R., Pete Naude, and Paul Michell. "Perceptual Gaps and Similarities in Buyer–Seller Dyadic Relationships." *Industrial Marketing Management* 36, no. 5 (July 2007), pp. 662–75.

Chakrabarty, Subhra, Gene Brown, and Robert E. Widing. "Closed Influence Tactics: Do Smugglers Win in the Long Run?" *Journal of Personal Selling and Sales Management* 30, no. 1 (Winter 2010), pp. 23–32.

Dickson, Peter R., Walfried M. Lassar, Gary Hunter, and Samit Chakravorti. "The Pursuit of Excellence in Process Thinking and Customer Relationship Management." *Journal of Personal Selling & Sales Management* 29, no. 2 (Spring 2009), pp. 111–24.

Dietvorst, Roeland C., et al. "A Sales Force-Specific Theory-of-Mind Scale: Tests of Its Validity by Classical Methods and Functional Magnetic Resonance Imaging." *Journal of Marketing Research* 46, no. 5 (2009), pp. 653–68.

Erickson, G. Scott, and Helen N. Rothberg. "Intellectual Capital in Business-to-Business Markets." *Industrial Marketing Management* 38, no. 2 (February 2009), pp. 159–65.

Goldsmith, Marshall, and Louis Carter. *Best Practices in Talent Management.* Pfeiffer, 2009.

Guenzi, Paolo, Laurent Georges, and Catherine Pardo. "The Impact of Strategic Account Managers' Behaviors on Relational Outcomes: An Empirical Study." *Industrial Marketing Management* 38, no. 3 (April 2009), pp. 300–11.

Hunter, Gary K., and William D. Perreault. "Making Sales Technology Effective." *Journal of Marketing* 71, no. 1 (January 2007), pp. 16–34.

Lamont, J. "Past and Future: Closing the Knowledge Loop." *KM World* 19, no. 1 (January 2010), pp. 8–19.

Liao S, Wu C. "System Perspective of Knowledge Management, Organizational Learning, and Organizational Innovation." *Expert Systems with Applications* 37, no. 2 (March 2010), pp.1096–1103.

Lohtia, Ritu, Daniel C. Bello, and Constance Elise Porter. "Building Trust in US–Japanese Business Relationships: Mediating Role of Cultural Sensitivity." *Industrial Marketing Management* 38, no. 3 (April 2009), pp. 239–52.

Powers, Thomas L., and William R. Reagan. "Factors Influencing Successful Buyer–Seller Relationships." *Journal of Business Research* 60, no. 12 (December 2007), pp. 1234–42.

Stanko, Michael A., Joseph M. Bonner, and Roger J. Calantone. "Building Commitment in Buyer–Seller Relationships: A Tie Strength Perspective." *Industrial Marketing Management* 36, no. 8 (November 2007), pp. 1094–103.

Stein, Dave. "Why Sales Process Gets the Shaft." *Sales & Marketing Management,* September/October 2008, pp. 22–24.

Van Hulse, J., and T. Khoshgoftaar. "Knowledge Discovery from Imbalanced and Noisy Data." *Data & Knowledge Engineering* 68, no. 12 (December 2009), pp.1513–42.

Wachner, Trent, Christopher R. Plouffe, and Yany Grégoire. "SOCO's Impact on Individual Sales Performance: The Integration of Selling Skills as a Missing Link." *Industrial Marketing Management* 38, no. 1 (January 2009), pp. 32–44.

Weitzel, Sloan R. *Feedback That Works: How to Build and Deliver Your Message.* Jossey-Bass, 2007.

The Partnership Process

2

PART

chapter

8

MAKING THE SALES CALL

SOME QUESTIONS ANSWERED IN THIS CHAPTER ARE

- How should the salesperson make the initial approach to make a good impression and gain the prospect's attention?

- How can the salesperson develop rapport and increase source credibility?

- Why is discovering the prospect's needs important, and how can a salesperson get this information?

- How can the salesperson most effectively relate the product or service features to the prospect's needs?

- Why is it important for the salesperson to make adjustments during the call?

- How does the salesperson recognize that adjustments are needed?

- How can a salesperson effectively sell to groups?

PROFILE

PROFILE My name is Jennifer VanWinkle, and I graduated from the College of St. Catherine in 2007 with a degree in medical sales. While in school, I took the Fundamentals of Selling class with Dr. Greg DiNovis and obtained an internship with Ecolab, a global cleaning and sanitation company headquartered in St. Paul, Minnesota. I later accepted a full-time position with the company as a territory sales manager. Today my job takes me to restaurants, hotels, and health care facilities, where I help customers select and use products to obtain exceptional cleaning and sanitizing results.

Good communication is an extremely important aspect of the sales call process. It all starts with the initial approach. Before I contact a customer for the first time, I like to know as much as possible about his or her operation. Think of it as a job interview. You can really gain your prospect's attention and trust and build rapport quickly if you prove you've taken the time to learn about the business before your first sales call.

During your first meeting, I believe that it's important to make a good first impression. Be on time, smile, greet them by name, and be confident. This is a great opportunity to build rapport and get your main sales goals across without being pushy. A good way to build rapport is to try and relate to your customer. Look around his or her office; see if there is anything you can use to strike up a friendly conversation. Each customer will be different. You must adapt to them. Never expect them to adapt to you.

Use this first meeting to get some key information from your prospect. Find out about his or her wants, needs, and expectations. Ask a lot of questions and listen intently. For example, it's very important for me to know what my customer is looking for before I begin presenting potential product solutions. Ecolab has hundreds of solutions to choose from, and I want to make sure I give my customer exactly what he or she is looking for to solve the cleaning issue.

One way to know precisely what a customer needs is to ask open-ended questions. The more he or she talks, the more you will learn about the situation. As you will learn in this chapter, the SPIN method of questioning can be very helpful in identifying your prospect's needs. I use the SPIN method in my position at Ecolab, and it has helped me immensely. SPIN questions help differentiate the products and service I sell from Ecolab's competitors, and it's a method that my company has helped perfect within our sales teams.

One final note about the initial sales call. Make sure you are prepared for objections from your prospect and are able to quickly adjust during your presentation. In my business, I've found that there are several standard objections that customers often give. After learning the business and meeting with several customers, it has become much easier for me to prepare for those objections and respond appropriately.

Your first few sales calls might be tough, but eventually you will become a pro at responding to objections and you will know what to expect in most situations. Objections may not always be verbal, so remember to read the prospect's non-verbal reactions and adjust when necessary. If you notice something starting to go wrong, you need to change your approach so that you can ensure a close to your sale, or at least obtain another follow-up appointment.

For more information about Ecolab, visit our Web site at www.ecolab.com.

Exhibit 8.1
Essential Elements of the Sales Call

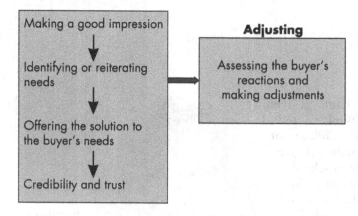

At this point in the sales process, we assume that an appointment has been made, sufficient information about the prospect and his or her organization has been gathered, and the salesperson has developed strong objectives for the call. In this chapter we discuss how to make the actual sales call. The content of a sales call depends on the specific situation the salesperson encounters as well as the extent of the relationship the salesperson has already established with the other party.[1] Exhibit 8.1 provides an organizing framework for our discussion. We start by considering how to make a good impression and begin to develop a long-term relationship. We then examine the initial needs assessment phase of a relationship and how to relate solutions to those needs. Finally, we discuss the relationship between adaptability and successful sales calls.

There are, of course, many conceptualizations of the selling process. For example, one trainer finds value in describing the selling process as the *Four A's* (*a*cknowledge, *a*cquire, *a*dvise, and *a*ssure).[2] First the seller acknowledges the buyer by greeting/welcoming/honoring and building trust. Next the seller acquires information via needs analysis and a summary of that analysis outlining the agreement between buyer and seller about the current situation and the desired solution. Advising comes next, during which the seller narrows the possible choices to specific options, sells benefits of those options (not just features), watches for buying signals, and asks for the order. Finally, the seller assures the buyer after the sale by enhancing satisfaction with the buying decision and giving proper follow-up and referrals.

MAKING A GOOD IMPRESSION

When salespeople arrive late, make a poor entrance, fail to gain the buyer's interest, or lack rapport-building skills, it is difficult for them to secure commitment and build partnerships.[3] This section discusses how salespeople can manage the buyer's impression of them, a process termed **impression management**. Most of the information presented here assumes that the salesperson is making a first call on a prospect. However, impression management continues throughout calls.

One of the most important ways to ensure a good first impression is to be well prepared (as we discussed in Chapter 7). Some salespeople prepare a checklist of things to take to the presentation so they won't forget anything.

WAITING FOR THE PROSPECT

Being on time for a scheduled sales call is critical to avoid giving the buyer a negative impression. With the advent of cell phones, there is practically no good reason for not calling if you're going to be a few minutes late to the appointment.

Salespeople should use waiting time effectively.

Every salesperson must expect to spend a certain portion of each working day waiting for sales interviews. Successful salespeople make the best possible use of this time by working on reports, studying new product information, checking e-mail and text messages, planning and preparing for their next calls, and obtaining additional information about the prospect. (Chapter 15 covers time management more fully.)

Some trainers suggest that salespeople not wait for any prospect, under normal circumstances, more than 15 minutes after the appointment time. Why? To demonstrate that the seller's time is also important. Exceptions are necessary, of course, depending on the importance of the customer, the reason the customer is running late, and the distance the salesperson has traveled. In all cases salespeople should keep the sales call in perspective, realizing that their time is also valuable. Chapter 15 discusses just how valuable that time really is.

When the salesperson arrives, the receptionist may merely say, "I'll tell Ms. Schimpf that you are here." After the receptionist has spoken with Ms. Schimpf, the salesperson should ask approximately how long the wait will be. If the wait will be excessive or the salesperson has another appointment, it may be advisable to explain this tactfully and to ask for another appointment. Usually the secretary either will try to get the salesperson in to see the prospect more quickly or will arrange for a later appointment.

FIRST IMPRESSIONS

In the first meeting between a salesperson and a prospect or customer, the first two or three minutes can be very important. Making a favorable first impression usually results in a prospect who is willing to listen. A negative first impression, on the other hand, sets up a barrier that may never be hurdled. Note that one advantage of an existing partnering relationship is that the salesperson has already established a bond and has built a reputation based on his or her prior actions.

Salespeople may make a poor impression without realizing it. They may know their customer's needs and their own product, but overlook seemingly insignificant things that can create negative impressions. As Chapter 5 related, how you dress can affect the message you send to the buyer. Also, studies have shown that the physical attractiveness and gender of salespeople can influence purchase intentions of buyers. And don't forget that according to generation gap experts, it is often quite difficult for a Generation X (born 1965–1978) salesperson to relate to a baby boomer (born 1946–1964) buyer, and even harder to relate to a traditionalist (born 1922–1946) buyer.

So what should a seller do to create a good first impression? You should be well groomed and enter confidently (but not arrogantly) by using erect posture, lengthy stride, and a lively pace; and among the first words out of your mouth should be something like, "Thanks for seeing me." And don't forget to smile. Watch what happens when you look at someone and smile. In 99 out of 100 times, you will receive a smile in return.

But here's a caveat to the counsel just offered: Observe the prospect's state and modify your behavior as needed. When customers are in a bad mood, the last thing they want is a happy, bouncy salesperson. In fact, in such a situation, the prospect might be inattentive or even refuse to meet with such a salesperson. Adapt, and even ask if this is not a good time to meet if you perceive that the buyer is very stressed. Also, be aware that many buyers are repulsed by a salesperson who enters the room with exaggerated and false enthusiasm that her product is for sure going to solve all of the buyer's problems. It's better to be humble than to be cocky.[4]

It is also important to remember prospects' names and how to pronounce them (www.hearnames.com provides verbal pronunciation of many hard-to-say names). There are many ways to try to remember someone's name—such as giving your full attention when you hear it and then repeating the name immediately, associating it with someone else you know with the same name, associating it with the person's most prominent feature or trait, using it during the conversation, and writing it down phonetically. Whatever you do, make sure to pronounce the prospect's name correctly.

Some experts argue that the customer's name should be used in the opening statement. Dale Carnegie, a master at developing relationships, said a person's name is "the sweetest and most important sound" to that person. Using a person's name often indicates respect and a recognition of the person's unique qualities. Others disagree with this logic, claiming that using the person's name, especially more than once in any short time, sounds phony and insincere. A compromise is to use the prospect's name in the opening and then to use it occasionally during the rest of the call.

thinking it through

You walk into a prospect's office confidently. Even though you've never met her before, you aren't nervous. You've done your homework and have strong objectives for this meeting. After you introduce yourself to the prospect and sit down, you suddenly remember that you left your laptop in your car. And in that laptop is your entire presentation! Your car is several blocks away. What should you do? What would you say to the prospect?

SELECTING A SEAT

When selecting a seat, it is a good idea to look around and start to identify the prospect's social style and status (see Chapter 5). For example, in the United States important decision makers usually have large, well-appointed, private offices. But be careful. In Kuwait a high-ranking businessperson may have a small office and lots of interruptions. Don't take that environment to mean he or she is a low-ranking employee or is not interested. Walmart buyers interview salespeople in rough conditions to help instill the idea that they want the lowest prices they can get.

Asking permission to sit down is usually unnecessary. The salesperson should read the prospect's nonverbal cues to determine the right time to be seated. And note that many calls will not involve sitting down at all, such as talking to a store manager in a grocery store aisle, conversing with a supervisor in a warehouse, or asking questions of a surgeon in a post-op ward.

GETTING THE CUSTOMER'S ATTENTION

Recall from Chapter 5 that there are several types of sales presentations, including standard memorized, outlined, and customized. In this chapter we assume that the salesperson has chosen a customized presentation.

Getting the customer's attention is not a new concept. It is also the goal of many other activities you are familiar with, such as advertising, making new friends, writing an English composition, giving a speech, or writing a letter to a friend.

Time is valuable to prospects, and prospects concentrate their attention on the first few minutes with a salesperson to determine whether they will benefit from the interaction. The prospect is making a decision: Do I want to give this salesperson 15 minutes of my time? 30 minutes of my time? None of my time? This decision is made even while the salesperson is walking in the door and selecting a seat. Some claim that salespeople have less than six minutes to establish credibility with a client. The first few words the salesperson says often set the tone of the entire sales call. The **halo effect** (how and what you do in one thing changes a person's perceptions of other things you do) seems to operate in many sales calls. If the salesperson is perceived by the prospect as effective at the beginning of the call, he will be perceived as effective during the rest of the call and vice versa. There are many ways to open a presentation. An **opening** is a method designed to get the prospect's attention and interest quickly and to make a smooth transition into the next part of the presentation (which is usually to more fully discover the prospect's needs). Because each prospect and sales situation is unique, salespeople should be adaptable and be able to use any or a combination of openings. Again, keep in mind that openings are generally less important with partnering customers whom the salesperson has already met. Exhibit 8.2 provides details about a number of possible openings. But remember, many prospects won't like what

Exhibit 8.2
Openings That Salespeople Can Use to Gain Attention

Opening Method	Example	Things to Consider
Introduction opening (simply introduce yourself).	Ms. Hallgren, thank you for seeing me today. My name is Daniel Mundt, and I'm with ServiceMaster.	Simple, but may not generate interest.
Referral opening (tell about someone who referred you to the buyer).	Mr. Schaumberg, I appreciate your seeing me today. I'm here at the suggestion of Ms. Fleming of Acumen Ornamental Iron Works. She thought you would be interested in our line of wrought iron products and railings.	Always get permission. Don't stretch the truth.
Benefit opening (start by telling some benefit of the product).	Mr. Penney, I would like to tell you about a color copier that can reduce your copying costs by 15 percent.	Gets down to business right away.
Product opening (actually demonstrate a product feature and benefit as soon as you walk up to the prospect).	[Carrying a tablet PC into an office] Ms. Hemming, you spend a lot of time on the road as an investigative lawyer. Let me show you how this little handheld item can transform your car (or any place you go) into an efficient, effective office.	Uses visual and not just verbal opening; can create excitement.
Compliment opening (start by complimenting the buyer or the buyer's firm).	I was calling on one of our customers, Jackson Street Books, last week, and the owner couldn't say enough good things about your service. It sure says a lot about your operation to have a customer just start praising you out of the blue.	Must be sincere, not just flattery. ethics
Question opening (start the conversation with a question).	Ms. Borgelt, what is your reaction to the brochure I sent you about our new telemarketing service?	Starts two-way communication.

they deem to be "canned" approaches and will react negatively. Prospects in one study rated the following openings overwhelmingly as either negative or neutral (unsolicited small talk, 95 percent; benefit claim, 89 percent; provocative question, 84 percent).[5]

DEVELOPING RAPPORT

Rapport in selling is a close, harmonious relationship founded on mutual trust.[6] You build rapport when the prospect perceives you to be like him or her in some way. Ultimately the goal of every salesperson should be to establish rapport with each customer. Often salespeople can accomplish this with some friendly conversation early in the call. Part of this process involves identifying the prospect's social style and making necessary adjustments (see Chapter 5).

The talk about current news, hobbies, mutual friends, and the like that usually breaks the ice for the actual presentation is often referred to as **small talk.** One of the top traits of successful salespeople is the ability to be sociable. Examples include the following:[7]

I understand you went to Nebraska? I graduated from there with a BBA in 2007.

Did you see the Houston Rockets game on TV last night?

I read in the paper that you won the bass fishing tournament last weekend. I bet that was pretty exciting!

So did you have trouble getting home from work last week with that snowstorm?

Your receptionist was very helpful when I set this appointment. I never would have found this building if she hadn't told me where to park.

You don't happen to remember Marla Jones, do you? She said she went to college with you and said to say hi.

Sharing letters from satisfied customers helps a salesperson establish credibility.

Customers are more receptive to salespeople with whom they can identify—that is, with whom they have something in common. Thus salespeople will be more effective with customers with whom they establish such links as mutual friends, common hobbies, or attendance at the same schools. Successful salespeople engage in small talk more effectively by first performing **office scanning:** looking around the prospect's environment for relevant topics to talk about. "Sales Technology 8.1" describes how several salespeople use social networking sites to learn about appropriate topics of conversation.

Be careful, however, when engaging in small talk because it can be to your detriment.[8] One salesperson told of a client who asked her opinion about the economic outlook. The seller said she thought it was going down. The buyer had a different opinion, and it took months to repair the relationship. It is generally best to avoid controversial topics like politics and religion. Don't talk about your personal problems in an effort to get sympathy. Don't complain about others

SALES Technology   8.1

USE SOCIAL NETWORKING INFORMATION TO HELP GET THE CUSTOMER'S ATTENTION

If those first few minutes in a meeting are as critical as everyone claims they are, how can a salesperson use them effectively to get the prospect's attention? By using information that has been gathered about the prospect. And one good way to do that is through such social networking sites as LinkedIn, Facebook, Twitter, and MySpace.

Divya Gugnani, a venture capitalist who also runs a media company in the culinary Web site called Behind the Burner, uses LinkedIn to investigate the people she will be contacting by reviewing their profiles carefully. She then uses that information to break the ice, get the prospect's attention, and find areas of common interests and goals. For her Web site business, Divya says, "This has been a great resource for recruiting new talent, including writers, videographers, graphic designers, and interns."

When Karen Jashinsky, a recent MBA graduate, wanted to start a teen-oriented personal fitness business, she used LinkedIn to find connections with people who had similar interests. Thanks to the use of information provided by LinkedIn profiles, she is now the owner of O2 MAX, a Santa Monica, California, fitness center for teens.

Dave Brookes is the sales and marketing department of Teusner Wines. Dave uses Twitter to connect with groups of people who tweet about wine. With Twitter he gathers feedback, builds trust with existing customers, and shares information. "There's no cost, which is fantastic for guys like us because our marketing budget is tiny," says Brookes. "And you can see that it's building. We're building relationships, and people enjoy what we're doing."

It should be noted that this social networking information gathering goes in both directions. Ken Nussbaum, a CPA, noticed that a potential client had a LinkedIn account, so he encouraged him to check out Ken's profile on LinkedIn. The man did so, and found that there would be a perfect fit between his needs and what Ken had to offer. When they met at Starbucks for coffee the first time, Ken reports that there were none of the usual worrying questions from the prospect about what Ken was able to do and what his qualifications were. As Ken stated, "LinkedIn makes it easy for potential clients to learn more about me, and having recommendations from numerous clients provides concrete examples of how I've been able to help others."

Sources: Brad and Debra Schepp, *How to Find a Job on LinkedIn, Facebook, Twitter, MySpace, and Other Social Networks* (McGraw-Hill, 2010), http://press.linkedin.com/CPANewClients, accessed March 6, 2010; http://blog.linkedin.com/2009/07/21/divya-gugnani-how-linkedin-helps-me-close-deals-and-market-myself-better, accessed March 6, 2010; http://business.twitter.com/twitter101/case_teusner, accessed March 12, 2010.

(boss, wife) or gossip about your competitors. Also, especially for first calls on prospects, you want to avoid using trite phrases like "How are you doing today?" because they don't sound sincere.

Of course salespeople should consider cultural and personality differences and adapt the extent of their nonbusiness conversation accordingly. For example, an AT&T rep would probably spend considerably less time in friendly conversation with a New York City office manager than with, say, a manager in a rural Texas town. Businesspeople in Africa place such high value on establishing friendships that the norm calls for a great deal of friendly conversation before getting down to business. Chinese customers want a lot of rapport building before they get down to business. Amiables and expressives tend to enjoy such conversations, whereas drivers and analyticals may be less receptive to spending much time in nonbusiness conversation. Studies show that salespeople who adapt and mirror their prospects are more successful in gaining desired results.[9] Also, there could be less need for small talk if the salesperson uses a question or product opening when getting the customer's attention.

At this point in the sales call, after gaining the prospect's attention and establishing some rapport, a salesperson will often share his or her goals or agenda for the meeting with the prospect. This step can help build further rapport and trust. For example:

> Just so you know, my goal today is simply to verify what your needs might be and then, as I promised in the phone call, to share with you the results of the lab test we conducted last fall.

WHEN THINGS GO WRONG

Making and maintaining a good impression is important. How nice it would be if the beginning of every call went as smoothly as we have described here. Actually, things do go wrong sometimes. The best line of defense when something goes wrong is to maintain the proper perspective and a sense of humor. It's not the first thing you have done wrong and won't be your last. A good example of a call going downhill fast is the following experience, related by a salesperson:

> I pulled my right hand out of the pocket and stuck it forward enthusiastically to shake. Unfortunately, a ball of lint, about the size of a pea, had stuck to the tip of my fingers and was now drifting slowly down onto the document he had been reading. We both watched it descend, as compelling as the ball on New Year's Eve. We shook hands anyway. I said, "Excuse me," and bent forward to blow the ball of lint off the document. As I did so, I put a dent in the front edge of his desk with my briefcase.[10]

The worst response by this salesperson would be to faint, scream, or totally lose control. A better response would include a sincere apology for the dent and an offer to pay for any repairs. Further, proper planning might have prevented this situation: If the salesperson had walked into the room with his hands out of his pockets, he would not have picked up the lint.

What if you say something that is truly embarrassing? According to Mark Twain, "Man is the only animal that blushes, or needs to." For example, one salesperson calling on an older buyer motioned to a picture of a very young lady on the buyer's desk. "Is that your daughter?" the seller asked, smiling. "That's my wife," the buyer replied, frowning. In another sales call, the salesperson saw a picture on the prospect's desk and said, "Oh wow! What a great picture! How'd you ever get a picture of yourself with John Madden, the football guy!" The buyer replied angrily, "That's not John Madden, that's my wife!"[11] Obviously both sellers made major blunders. The first thing you should do in such a situation is to apologize sincerely. Then change the subject or move on in your presentation. Try to relax and put the incident behind you. And learn this lesson: Think before you speak!

Of course you can get into trouble without even saying a word. As Chapter 4 indicated, you must be careful when using gestures in other cultures because they often take on different meanings.

IDENTIFYING THE PROSPECT'S NEEDS: THE POWER OF ASKING QUESTIONS

Once the salesperson has entered and captured the buyer's attention, it is time to identify the buyer's needs. To begin this process, a salesperson might use transition sentences like the following (assuming a product approach was used to gain attention):

> Well, I'm glad you find this little model interesting. And I want to tell you all about it. But first I need to ask you a few questions to make sure I understand what your specific needs are. Is that okay?

From the BUYER'S SEAT

WHAT MY TOP SALESPEOPLE ARE LIKE

By William Fowler, DuPont

I've been an industrial buyer for DuPont, in the textiles division, for over 15 years. I've seen some big changes over the last 15 years of buying. Sellers are getting more professional. There are still the "used car" salesman types, but most are professional now. I'm also seeing sellers get more product knowledge. The best ones have good technical skills.

I've also seen more use of team selling/team buying. I will meet with a seller, and my engineer with meet with their sales engineer. That system works great! Each of us can talk to someone at our level of expertise and knowledge. If you asked me who are my best salespeople and what makes them great, I'd have an earful for you. Let me tell you about a few.

Pete is one of the best salespeople who calls on me. He sells pipes, fittings, and valves. What impresses me is the way he takes the time to really find out my needs. Sometimes I'm not even sure what I need due to some highly technical issues related to our business. In those cases he will meet with my engineers and plant people to find out exactly what we need and then supply that product.

Dale's another great salesperson. Why? Because he really finds out what we need before telling me what he has to sell. For example, we needed an actuated valve that had some special features. Actuated simply means that something causes the valve to open or close. I needed a valve that would open, and stay open, if the power were to shut down. Otherwise the product would back up in the furnace, get too hot, and destroy the raw material. Dale worked with my engineering staff as well as those of us in procurement and developed an "open valve" solution to the problem. His solution required him to work not only with me and my team, but also with the engineers and product developers in his firm. The result was a win–win.

I ask myself sometimes, why aren't all the other sales reps who call on me more like Pete or Dale? I'm not sure, but I would point to several reasons. Often the salespeople seem too rushed, like they have a lot of places to be and not much time. I'm sure that's partly due to their quotas and the goals their managers are requiring them to achieve. Sometimes I think they don't do a good job for me because they don't view me or my business as important. Some just seem to want to get in and get out, and not build a relationship. But if more salespeople were like Pete or Dale, my life would sure be more happy.

Source: William Fowler, DuPont, personal correspondence; used with permission. Names changed to protect confidentiality.

If the buyer gives permission, the salesperson begins to ask questions about the buyer's needs. Don't be surprised if the buyer is reluctant to provide confidential information. There are many people out there trying to steal valuable company information. The seller has to establish credibility and trust.

Occasionally a salesperson makes the mistake of starting with product information rather than with a discussion of the prospect's needs. The experienced salesperson, however, attempts to uncover the prospect's needs and problems at the start of the relationship. In reality, discovering needs is still a part of qualifying the prospect.

Research continually demonstrates the importance of needs discovery. An analysis by Huthwaite, Inc., of more than 35,000 sales calls in 23 countries over a 12-year period revealed that the distinguishing feature of successful salespeople was their ability to discover the prospect's needs.[12] Discovering needs was more important than opening the call strategically, handling objections, or using closing techniques effectively. "From the Buyer's Seat 8.1" provides additional evidence of that fact.

Exhibit 8.3
Discovering the Root Cause of the Need

Need behind the need
Our competition is gaining on us, and we need to be more responsive than they are.

More strategic "root cause of the need" (buyer ends here)

Need behind the need
We need to improve our sales performance.

Need
We need to equip our sales force with laptop computers.

Initial need expressed (buyer starts here)

There is an underlying reason for every customer need, and the salesperson must continue probing until he or she uncovers the root problem or need. This process could be called "discovering the root cause of the need" and is graphically illustrated in Exhibit 8.3.

This salesperson is discovering the prospect's needs before describing the services he offers.

As you discover needs, keep in mind that this process can be uncomfortable for the prospect. The prospect may resent your suggesting that there could be a problem or a better way to do things. When faced with direct evidence that things could be better, the prospect may express fear (fear of losing her job if things are not corrected, or of things changing and the situation getting worse than it is now). Also, remember that the time needed to discuss needs varies greatly depending on the type of industry, the nature of the product, how well the salesperson and buyer know each other, and so forth. We will come back to this issue after we examine methods of identifying needs.

Chapter 4 covered most of the important communication principles regarding how to effectively ask questions of the prospect and be a better listener. Remember to speak naturally while asking questions. You don't want to sound like a computer asking a set of rote questions. Nor do you want to appear to be following a strict word-for-word outline that you learned in your sales training classes.

We now briefly describe two of the most widely used systems of needs identification taught to salespeople today.

ASKING OPEN AND CLOSED QUESTIONS
In the first method of needs discovery, salespeople are taught to distinguish between open and closed questions and then encouraged to utilize more open questions. Many highly respected sales training organizations, such as Wilson Learning and Achieve Global, use this type of approach. **Open questions**

require the prospect to go beyond a simple yes-or-no response. They encourage the prospect to open up and share a great deal of useful information. For example:

What kinds of problems have the new federal guidelines caused for your division?

What do you know about our firm?

When you think of a quality sound system, what comes to mind?

Closed questions require the prospect to simply answer yes or no or to offer a short, fill-in-the-blank type of response. Examples include the following questions:

Have you ever experienced computer downtime as a result of an electrical storm?

Is fast delivery important for your firm?

How many checks do you usually write a month?

What balance do you normally keep in your checking account?

In most cases salespeople need to ask both open and closed questions. Open questions help paint the broad strokes of the situation, whereas closed questions help zero in on specific problems and attitudes. Some trainers believe simple, closed questions are best at first. Prospects become accustomed to talking and start to open up. After a few closed questions, the salesperson moves to a series of open questions. At some point he or she may revert back to closed questions.

Angie Main, a radio advertising salesperson, likes to ask her prospects the following two open questions to discover their needs:

What misconceptions do people have about your business?

If you could tell people one thing about your business, what would you want to tell them?[13]

Notice how these questions focus on the needs of the prospect rather than the solution (how her radio station can meet those needs).

Exhibit 8.4 contains an illustrative dialogue of a bank selling a commercial checking account to a business. In this sales presentation the salesperson's questions follow a logical flow. Note that follow-up probes are often necessary to clarify the prospect's responses. At the conclusion of asking open and closed questions, the salesperson should have a good feel for the needs and wants of the prospect.

One final suggestion is to summarize the prospect's needs:

So let me see if I have this right. You write about 35 checks a month, you keep about a $5,000 balance, and you are looking for a checking account that pays interest on your unused balance and has overdraft protection.... Is that correct?

Summarizing helps solidify the needs in the prospect's mind and ensures that the prospect has no other hidden needs or wants.

SPIN® TECHNIQUE

The SPIN method of discovering needs was developed by Huthwaite, an international research and training organization, after analyzing thousands of actual sales calls.[14] The results indicated that successful salespeople go through a logical needs identification sequence, which Huthwaite labeled **SPIN**: situation questions,

Exhibit 8.4
Using Open and Closed
Questions to Discover
Needs

Salesperson's Probe	Prospect's Response
Have you ever done business with our bank before? [closed]	No, our firm has always used First of America Bank.
I assume, then, that your checking account is currently with First of America? [closed]	Yes.
If you could design an ideal checking account for your business, what would it look like? [open]	Well, it would pay interest on all idle money, have no service charges, and supply a good statement.
When you say "good statement" what exactly do you mean? [open]	It should come to us once a month, be easy to follow, and help us reconcile our books quickly.
Uh-huh. Anything else in an ideal checking account? [open]	No, I guess that's about it.
What things, if any, about your checking account have dissatisfied you in the past? [open]	Having to pay so much for our checks! Also, sometimes when we have a question, the bank can't answer it quickly because the computers are down. That's frustrating!
Sure! Anything else dissatisfy you? [open]	Well, I really don't like the layout of the monthly statement we get now. It doesn't list checks in order; it has them listed by the date they cleared the bank.
Normally, what balance do you have on hand in your account? What minimum balance can you maintain? [closed]	About $8,500 now. We could keep a minimum of around $5,000, I guess.
Are you earning interest in your account now? [closed]	Yes, 3 percent of the average monthly balance if we maintain at least a $5,000 balance.
What kind of service charges are you paying now? [closed] [*more questions*]	$25 per month, $.25 per check, $.10 per deposit.
Is there anything else that I need to know before I begin telling you about our account? [open]	No, I think that just about covers it all.

*p*roblem questions, *i*mplication questions, and *n*eed payoff questions. SPIN works for salespeople involved in a **major sale:** one that involves a long selling cycle, a large customer commitment, an ongoing relationship, and large risks for the prospect if a bad decision is made. Major sales can occur anywhere but often involve large or national accounts. For example, both Johnson Wax and Bridgestone have used SPIN for their major accounts but may use other techniques for smaller accounts.

SPIN actually helps the prospect identify unrecognized problem areas. Often, when a salesperson simply asks an open question such as, "What problems are you having?" the prospect replies, "None!" The prospect isn't lying; he or she may not realize that a problem exists. SPIN excels at helping prospects test their current opinions or perceptions of the situation. Also, SPIN questions may be asked over the course of several sales calls, especially for large or important buyers. An abbreviated needs identification dialogue appears in Exhibit 8.5; it demonstrates all components of SPIN for a salesperson selling desktop publishing programs.

Situation Questions

Early in the sales call, salespeople ask **situation questions,** which are general data-gathering questions about background and current facts. The goal of these

Exhibit 8.5
Using the SPIN
Technique to Sell
Desktop Publishing

Salesperson: Do you ever send work out for typesetting? [situation question]

Prospect: Yes, about once a month we have to send work out because we are swamped.

Salesperson: Is the cost of sending work out a burden? [problem question]

Prospect: Not really. It costs only about 5 percent more, and we just add that to the customer's bill.

Salesperson: Do you get fast turnaround? [problem question]

Prospect: Well, now that you mention it, at times the turnaround is kind of slow. You see, we aren't given very high priority because we aren't big customers for the printer. We use them only when we have to, you know.

Salesperson: What happens if you miss a deadline for your customer because the turnaround is slow? [implication question]

Prospect: That happened only once, but it was disastrous. John, the customer, really chewed me out, and we lost a lot of our credibility. As I say, it happened only once, and I wouldn't like it to happen again to John—or any of our customers, for that matter!

Salesperson: If I can show you a way to eliminate outside typesetting without having to increase your staff, would you be interested? [need payoff question]

Prospect: Sure. The more I think about it, the more I realize I have something of a time bomb here. Sooner or later, it's going to go off!

questions is to better understand the prospect's current situation. Because these questions are broad, successful salespeople learn to limit them; prospects quickly become bored or impatient if they hear too many of them. Inexperienced and unsuccessful salespeople tend to ask too many situation questions. In fact, many situation-type questions should be answered through precall information gathering and planning. If a salesperson asks too many situation questions, the prospect will think the salesperson is unprepared. Here are some examples of situation questions:

What's your position? How long have you been here?

How many people do you employ? Is the number growing or shrinking?

What kind of handling equipment are you using at present? How long have you had it?

Problem Questions

When salespeople ask about specific difficulties, problems, or dissatisfactions the prospect has, they are asking **problem questions.** The goal is to discover a problem. Here are some examples of problem questions:

Is your current machine difficult to repair?

Do your operators ever complain that the noise level is too high?

If a seller can't discover a problem using problem questions, then she might need to ask additional situation questions first to uncover more issues that might lead to better problem questions.

Implication Questions

Questions that logically follow one or more problem questions and are designed to help the prospect recognize the true ramifications of the problem are **implication questions.** Implication questions cannot be asked until some problem area has been identified (through problem questions). The goal of implication questions is for the prospect to see that the identified problem has some serious ramifications and implications that make the problem worthy of being resolved.

These questions attempt to motivate the prospect to search for a solution to the problem.

Implication questions relate back to some similar issues that were described in the multiattribute model in Chapter 3. In the multiattribute model, customers weigh various attributes differently in terms of importance. In the same way, some problems that are identified by problem questions have more weight (are more serious in the eyes of the buyer) than others. The goal of the salesperson is to identify problems that have high importance to the buyer.

Examples of implication questions include these:

What happens if you ship your customer a product that doesn't meet specs?

What does having to pay overtime do to your price, as compared to your competitors'?

Does the slowness of your present system create any bottlenecks in other parts of the process?

If the buyer answers these questions in a way that indicates she doesn't see serious implications of the problem identified, the seller would have to go back and ask additional implication questions, problem questions, and maybe even situation questions. The seller doesn't move ahead to need payoff questions until the prospect sees that there are serious ramifications if he does not solve the problem.

Need Payoff Questions

When salespeople ask questions about the usefulness of solving a problem, they are asking **need payoff questions**. In contrast to implication questions, which are problem-centered, need payoff questions are solution-centered:

If I can show you a way to eliminate paying overtime for your operators and therefore reduce your cost, would you be interested?

Would you like to see a reduction in the number of products that don't meet quality specifications?

Would an increase in the speed of your present system by 5 percent resolve the bottlenecks you currently experience?

If the prospect responds negatively to a need payoff question, the salesperson has not identified a problem serious enough for the prospect to take action. In that case, the salesperson should probe further by asking additional problem questions, implication questions, and then a new need payoff question.

Conclusions about SPIN

One critical advantage of SPIN is that it encourages the prospect to define the need. During the questioning phase the salesperson is focusing on problems and isn't focusing on her product. As a result, the prospect views the salesperson more as a consultant trying to help than as someone trying to push a product.

SPIN selling has been taught to thousands of salespeople. Many salespeople quickly master the technique, whereas others have more difficulty. The best advice is to practice each component and to plan implication and need payoff questions before each sales call. SPIN works well for buyers that have a real problem (like inventory piling up). It is perhaps more difficult to use when the seller is only discussing an opportunity (no real problems, but "my solution could help you make more money").

REITERATING NEEDS YOU IDENTIFIED BEFORE THE MEETING

The extent to which one has to identify needs during any call depends on the success of precall information gathering. The salesperson may fully identify the needs of the prospect before making the sales call. In that case reiterating the needs early in the sales call is advisable so that both parties agree about the problem they are trying to solve. For example:

> Mr. Reed, based on our several phone conversations, it appears that you are looking for an advertising campaign that will position your product for the rapidly growing senior citizen market, at a cost under $100,000, using humor and a well-known older personality, and delivered in less than one month. Is that an accurate summary of your needs? Has anything changed since we talked last? Is there anything else I need to know at this point?

Likewise, in multiple-call situations, going through a complete needs identification at every call is unnecessary. But it is still best to briefly reiterate the needs identified to that point:

> In my last call we pretty much agreed that your number one concern is customer satisfaction with your inventory system. Is that correct? Has anything changed since we met last time, or is there anything else I need to know?

ADDITIONAL CONSIDERATIONS

How many questions can a salesperson ask to discover needs? It depends on the situation. Generally, as the buyer's risk of making the wrong decision goes up, so does the amount of time the salesperson can spend asking the prospect questions. For example, a Boeing salesperson could address an almost unlimited number of questions to United Air Lines because the airline realizes the importance of having Boeing propose the right airplane configuration. A salesperson for Johnson Wax calling on a local grocery store, on the other hand, has little time to probe needs before discussing an upcoming promotion and requesting an end-of-aisle display. Regardless of the situation, the salesperson should carefully prepare a set of questions that maximizes the use of available time.

Occasionally the prospect will refuse to answer important questions because the information is confidential or proprietary. The salesperson can do little except emphasize the reason for asking the questions. Ultimately the prospect needs to trust the salesperson enough to divulge sensitive data. Chapters 13 and 14 discuss trust-building strategies.

At times buyers do not answer questions because they honestly don't know the answers. The salesperson should then ask whether the prospect can get the information. If the prospect cannot do so, the salesperson can often ask the buyer's permission to probe further within the prospect's firm.

On the other hand, some buyers will not only answer questions but also appear to want to talk indefinitely. In general, the advice is to let them talk, particularly in many cultures. For example, people in French-speaking countries tend to love rhetoric, the act and art of speaking; attempts to cut them off will only frustrate and anger them.

ethics

Prospects often provide sensitive and confidential information when they reveal facts about their situations and needs. Assume that a prospect at Allied reveals to you her firm's long-term strategy for taking business away from her number one competitor, Baker's. You are close friends with the buyer at Baker's, which is one of your biggest customers. Will you share the confidential information with the Baker's buyer?

DEVELOPING A STRATEGY FOR THE PRESENTATION

Based on the needs identified, the salesperson should develop a strategy for how best to meet those needs. This process includes sorting through the various options available to the seller to see what is best for this prospect. To do so, the salesperson usually must sort out the needs of the buyer and prioritize them. Decisions have to be made about the exact product or service to recommend, the optimal payment terms to present for consideration, service levels to suggest, product or service features to stress during the presentation, and so on. Chapter 7 also talks about developing a strategy.

Products have many, many features, and one product may possess a large number of features that are unique and exciting when compared to competitive offerings. Rather than overload the customer with all the great features, successful salespeople discuss only those that specifically address the needs of the prospect. For example, suppose that a Philips salesperson learns from SPIN questioning that a prospect is looking for a DVD recorder to use only to record new training materials. In this situation the Philips representative should not spend time discussing the DVD recorder's ability to easily record from VCRs. The buyer has no need for this feature. Talking about lots of features of little interest to the customer is a waste of time and is sometimes called **feature dumping**.[15]

OFFERING VALUE: THE SOLUTION TO THE BUYER'S NEEDS

In addition to discovering the buyer's needs, the salesperson often also learns about the decision-making process (who is involved and in what capacity—see Chapter 3 for details), the buyer's time frame for making a decision, and the money budgeted. The seller develops a strategy to effectively communicate a solution to those needs; then it is time to make a presentation that shows how they can be addressed. This step includes relating product or service features that are meaningful to the buyer, assessing the buyer's reaction to what is being said, resolving objections (covered in Chapter 10), and obtaining commitment (the topic of Chapter 11). As one best-selling author stated, "Ditch the canned 1-2-3, sometimes pushy, usually insensitive, and almost always repetitive sales strategies glamorized in the past. . . . We must be willing to learn, adapt, and listen to our customers."[16]

The salesperson usually begins offering the solution with a transition sentence, something like the following: "Now that I know what your needs are, I would like to talk to you about how our product can meet those needs." The seller's job is then to translate product features into benefits for solving the buyer's needs. To do this effectively, the salesperson must know the metrics of the prospect's decision; that is, on what criteria and in what way is the prospect evaluating possible solutions? This will be discussed more in Chapter 9 and in other chapters.

RELATING FEATURES TO BENEFITS

A **feature** is a quality or characteristic of the product or service. Every product has many features designed to help potential customers. A **benefit** is the way in which a specific feature will help a particular buyer and is tied directly to the buying motives of the prospect. A benefit helps the prospect more fully answer the question "What's in it for me?" Exhibit 8.6 shows a list of features and sample benefits for a product. The way in which a salesperson shows how a product addresses the buyer's specific needs is sometimes called the **customer benefit proposition**.[17] This concept will be described more fully in Chapter 9.

Exhibit 8.6
An Example of Features
and Benefits

THE HURON TRI-PANE CUSTOM PROFILE.

① Tri-pane units
The air between the panes of glass is your insulation from heat and cold, not the glass. Tri-pane windows are essential to maximizing energy savings on an ongoing basis. As well, they greatly reduce exterior noise filtration and allow for a comfortable level of humidity in your home. Remember to look for a true 1/2″ air space, for the ideal insulating value.

WHEN ONLY THE BEST WILL DO

Huron's Quality Construction Features have been developed to maximize the quality and performance benefits of our windows. Understanding what each feature does and the importance of reducing air infiltration is essential in making the best decision for your window needs.

HURON CONSTRUCTION ADVANTAGES

① Provisions for steel reinforcement
Every Huron vinyl window is made with a heavy walled extrusion that is 25% thicker than the industry standard. Structural cavities, steel reinforced (when needed), ensure that Huron windows never warp, twist, sag or bow. In fact, even with the heaviest triple glazed awning windows, Huron Windows always keep their shape and remain easy to open and will retain their beauty and high performance for many years.

② Count the cavities
More cavities (air spaces) means greater insulation value, strength and rigidity. Compare this to the competition's construction.

③ Co-extruded gasket seals
For long-term guaranteed window performance, the double gasket is extruded into the frame and welded in the corners. These gaskets are an integral part of the frame so they can't shrink away and fail. This means there is no shrinkage in the corners and never a need to caulk, for lasting energy performance. Wind and water resistant, tests conducted on our operating windows indicate they are just as airtight as a sealed picture window.

③ Glass units are set deeper in the frame
By setting the glass units deeper in the frame, air filtration is reduced dramatically. With the Super Spacer® seals set deeper within the frame towers, the insulating air spaces help reduce heat loss through the spacer bars at the edge of the glass. This is an important feature in reducing energy costs and helping eliminate condensation on the windows.

④ Built-in drain channel
Huron Windows have a special molded drain channel should moisture ever get past the co-extruded gasket seals. The moisture is quickly drained to the outside of the sealed unit, eliminating potential damage to the sealed glass unit and the walls of your home. Glass units sit on shims, so they never sit in water.

② Count the seals on the opening unit
Huron window opening units are triple sealed to ensure low air infiltration rates that exceed CSA standards for a standard, non-opening unit. Huron weather stripping is a build style-design, that is secured in an extruded cavity that provides a fail-safe compressed fit. The weather stripping is manufactured from a special synthetic compound that remains pliable, even at -40°C. Fusion welded corners means they can't shrink away and fail.

⑥ Super Spacer® Edgetech Warm Edge Technology
Edgetech manufactures the industry leading Super Spacer® line of thermal resistant, flexible tape insulating glass edge-seals, ensuring a long-lasting seal on every Huron Window.

The salesperson usually includes a word or a phrase to make a smooth transition from features to benefits:

This china is fired at 2,600°F, and what that means to you is that it will last longer. Because it is so sturdy, you will be able to hand this china down to your children as an heirloom, which was one of your biggest concerns.

Our service hotline is open 24 hours a day, which means that even your third-shift operators can call if they have any questions. That should be a real help to you because you said your third-shift supervisor was inexperienced in dealing with problems.

Some trainers suggest going beyond mentioning features and benefits. One variation, **FAB,** has salespeople discussing *features,* **advantages** (why that feature would be important to anyone), and *benefits.* For example:

This car has antilock brakes [*feature*], which help the car stop quickly [*advantage*], which provides the safety you said you were looking for [*benefit*].

In another variation, **FEBA** (*features, evidence, benefits, agreement*), salespeople mention the feature, provide evidence that the feature actually exists, explain the benefit (why that feature is important to the buyer), and then ask whether the buyer agrees with the value of the feature and benefit. For example:

> This car has the highest-quality antilock brakes on the market today [*feature*] as proved by this test by the federal government [*evidence*]. They will provide the safety you said you were looking for [*benefit*]; don't you agree [*agreement*]?

Buyers are not interested in facts about the product or the seller's company unless those facts help solve their wants or needs. The salesperson's job is to supply the facts and then point out what those features mean to the buyer in terms of benefits and value creation. Neil Rackham, noted sales training leader, emphasizes this theme:

> The world has changed and so has selling. Today, the primary sales job is to create value—to add problem solving and creativity, so that the customer buys the advice and expertise of the salesperson as much as they buy the product . . . [in a survey] product pitches were the number one complaint from customers, with comments such as "It's quicker, more convenient, and more objective to go to the Internet than to listen to a product pitch."[18]

Exhibit 8.7 illustrates how one trainer incorporates these concepts into a problem/solution model. The customer's needs are called "business model." The salesperson knows some, but not all, of the buyer's needs before the sales call, represented by the first three lines under "business model." However, by actively listening (see Chapter 4), the seller learns more needs during the presentation, represented by lines 4 and 5 under "Business model." Using all identified needs, the seller talks about the relevant features and benefits. While doing this, the salesperson offers proof of these assertions, based on the customer's social style (see Chapter 5). The salesperson also engages in activities to help the buyer realize the importance of meeting his or her needs sooner, providing reasons to buy now. The end result is increased sales and profits for the seller.

Buyers typically consider two or more competitive products when making a purchase decision. Thus salespeople need to know more than just the benefits their products provide. They need to know how the benefits of their products are superior or inferior to the benefits of competitive products. Of course, as you explain the benefits of your service, you must make sure the prospect is looking for those benefits.

Sometimes, when selling certain commodities, it is important to sell the features and benefits of the seller's firm instead of the product. For example, Ray Hanson of Fastenal sells fasteners such as bolts and nuts. He states, "In the fastener industry I have found that a generic product, such as a nut or bolt, doesn't have too many features and benefits. We talk to our potential customers about the features our company has and how these features could benefit them as our customers."[19]

Exhibit 8.7
The Problem/Solution Model

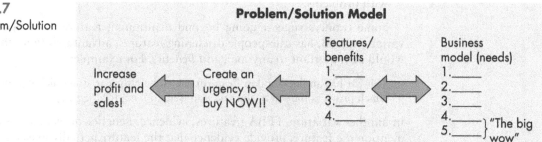

Exhibit 8.8
Features and Benefits of Yummy Earth Organic Gummy Bears, as Presented to a Grocery Store

Features	Benefits
Important to the Final Consumer	
Organic.	You want organic products, and this product is certified organic.
Only 90 calories per serving.	You can enjoy a treat without worrying about its effect on your weight.
100% of daily need for Vitamin C in every serving.	You are getting needed nutrition from a snack.
Important to the Grocery Store	
Test marketed for two years.	Because of this research, you are assured of a successful product and effective promotion; thus your risk is greatly reduced.
$500,000 will be spent for consumer advertising in the next 18 months.	Your customers will come to your store looking for the product.
40-cent coupon with front positioning in the national Sunday insert section.	Your customers will want to take advantage of the coupon and will be looking for the product in your store.

When selling to resellers, salespeople have two sets of benefits to discuss with the prospect: what the features of the product will do for the reseller and what the product features will do for the ultimate consumer of the product. Covering both sets of features and benefits is important. Exhibit 8.8 illustrates the two sets of features.

ASSESSING REACTIONS

While making a presentation, salespeople need to continually assess the reactions of their prospects. The prospect needs to agree that the benefits described would actually help his or her company. By listening to what buyers say and observing their body language (see Chapter 4 to review how to be a better listener), salespeople can determine whether prospects are interested in the product. If buyers react favorably to the presentation and seem to grasp the benefits of the proposed solution, the salesperson will have less need to make alterations or adjustments. But if a prospect does not develop enthusiasm for the product, the salesperson will need to make some changes in the presentation.

Using Nonverbal Cues

An important aspect of making adjustments is interpreting a prospect's reactions to the sales presentation. By observing the prospect's five channels of nonverbal communication, salespeople can determine how to proceed with their presentations. Chapter 4 provides more detailed information about nonverbal cues.

Nonverbal cues help salespeople know when to make adjustments. Can you interpret the cues provided by members of this buying team (the three on the right side)?

Verbal Probing

As salespeople move through a presentation, they must take the pulse of the situation. This process, often called a **trial close,** is more fully described in Chapter 11. For example, the salesperson should say something like the following:

How does this sound to you?

Can you see how these features help solve the problem you have?

Have I clearly explained our program to you?

Do you have any questions?

The use of such probing questions helps achieve several things. First, it allows the salesperson to stop talking and encourages two-way conversation. Without such probing, a salesperson can turn into a rambling talker while the buyer becomes a passive listener. Second, probing lets the salesperson see whether the buyer is listening and understanding what is being said. Third, the probe may show that the prospect is uninterested in what the salesperson is talking about. This response allows the salesperson to redirect the conversation to areas of interest to the buyer. This kind of adjustment is necessary in almost every presentation and underscores the fact that the salesperson should not simply memorize a canned presentation that unfolds in a particular sequence.

Salespeople must listen. Often we hear only what we want to hear. This behavior is called **selective perception**, and everyone is guilty of it at times. For example, read the following sentence:[20]

Finished files are the result of years of scientific study combined with the experience of years.

Now go back and quickly count the number of *f*'s in that sentence. Most non-native English speakers see all six *f*'s, whereas native English speakers see only three (they don't count the *f*'s in *of* because it is not considered an important word). The point is that once salespeople stop actively listening, they miss many things the buyer is trying to communicate.

Making Adjustments

Salespeople can alter their presentations in many ways to obtain a favorable reaction. For example, a salesperson may discover during a sales presentation that the prospect simply does not believe the seller has the appropriate product knowledge. Rather than continue with the presentation, the salesperson should redirect her or his efforts toward establishing credibility in the eyes of the prospect. Salespeople need to continually adapt to the situation at hand.

Other adjustments might require collecting additional information about the prospect, developing a new sales strategy, or altering the style of presentation. For example, a salesperson may believe a prospect is interested in buying an economical, low-cost motor. While presenting the benefits of the lowest-cost motor, the salesperson discovers the prospect is interested in the motor's operating costs. At this point the salesperson should ask some questions to find out whether the prospect would be interested in paying a higher price for a more efficient motor with lower operating costs. On the basis of the prospect's response, the salesperson can adopt a new sales strategy, one that emphasizes operating efficiency rather than the motor's initial price. In this way the sales presentation is shifted from features and benefits based on a low initial cost to features and benefits related to low operating costs.

BUILDING CREDIBILITY DURING THE CALL

To develop a close and harmonious relationship, the salesperson must be perceived as having **credibility**—that is, he or she must be believable and reliable. A salesperson can take many actions during a sales call to develop such a perception.[21]

To establish credibility early in the sales call, the salesperson should clearly delineate the time she or he thinks the call will take and then stop when the time is up. How many times has a salesperson said, "This will take only 5 minutes!" and 30 minutes later you still can't get rid of him? No doubt you would have perceived the salesperson as more credible if, after 5 minutes, he or she stated, "Well, I promised to take no more than 5 minutes, and I see our time is up. How would you like to proceed from here?" One successful salesperson likes to ask for half an hour and take only 25 minutes.[22]

Another way to establish credibility is to offer concrete evidence to back up verbal statements. If a salesperson states, "It is estimated that more than 80 percent of the households in America will own handheld Web browsers by 2015," he or she should be prepared to offer proof of this assertion—for instance, hand the prospect a letter or an article from a credible source. Ways to establish credibility are discussed in greater detail in Chapter 9.

Some trainers suggest adding a **credibility statement** early in the sales call that includes features of yourself and your company.[23] The purpose of the statement is to help the buyer realize you are capable of meeting her needs. The statement can be strengthened by proving its assertions with such items as testimonials and test results (more about these in the next chapter). Here's an example of a credibility statement:

> Hank, I don't know how much you may know about Apple Valley Savings and Loan. We were founded by a Swedish immigrant back in 1932 whose stated goal was to offer the best service in the Midwest. We've now grown into the third-largest savings bank in the upper Midwest with assets exceeding $23 billion and are the only savings bank in the Midwest earning the coveted Pinnacle Award for Excellent eight years in a row. We have over 32 branches in the five-state region. I've been with the bank for the last 14 years and have spent the last 6 years working closely with higher education institutions like yours. In terms of investments, we have focused a great deal of effort on higher education. For example, we recently provided a $2.3 million loan to West Valania State University to expand its ice hockey rink.

Of course, one way to establish credibility is to avoid making statements that do not have the ring of truth to them. For example, some suggest you should avoid using a phrase like "We're the best" or "We're number one." As one skeptical buyer noted, "Just how many number ones are there in the world, anyway?" Salespeople should also remember that, in addition to damaging credibility, truth-stretching comments can come back to haunt them in the form of legal liability (see Chapter 2 for a review of legal issues).

Many salespeople have found that the most effective way to establish credibility is to make a **balanced presentation** that shows all sides of the situation—that is, to be totally honest. Thus a salesperson might mention some things about the product that make it less than perfect or may speak positively about some exclusive feature of a competitor's product. Will this approach defeat the seller's chances of a sale? No. In fact, it may increase the chances of building long-term commitment and rapport. "Building Partnerships 8.1" provides insights about one salesperson who gives balanced presentations. Salespeople can keep customers happy and dedicated by helping them form correct, realistic expectations about a product or service.

Salespeople can build credibility by recognizing cultural differences, not only in foreign markets but also in North America. How? By demonstrating sensitivity to the needs and wants of specific subcultures and avoiding biased or racist language. See Chapter 4 for more information about cultural differences.

In selling complex products, sales representatives often must demonstrate product expertise at the beginning of the sales process—for example, by telling

BUILDING Partnerships

8.1

"I THINK YOU SHOULD USE MY COMPETITOR'S PRODUCT INSTEAD"

One aspect of my job selling replacement joints (hips, knees, and so forth) requires me to service what I sell, and in the case of replacement joints that means going into the operating room with the surgeon and taking the role of a technical expert when it comes to the capabilities, function, and surgical technique used with my company's hardware. A doctor I had worked with previously had called me to let me know that he had just seen a young man with a severe tibia fracture in the ER, and he wanted to use a set of my company's plates and screws to fix the fracture the following morning. I told him I would bring the hardware and the instruments down to the hospital that night for sterilization and that I would be there in the morning for the surgery.

Our company did not have a contract with this hospital, which means we were not allowed to keep a wide variety of equipment stocked in the hospital; rather, we were allowed to bring in only specifically requested hardware and instruments on a case-by-case basis, and then we had to remove it after the case was over. One of our competitors did have a contract, so they had basically every product they make stocked in the hospital; my company was trying to secure the same deal, which would be worth a substantial amount of money. This usually requires surgeons trying our equipment and liking the product and the service enough that they want it available at all times.

I arrived the following morning, and the surgery began on time. This type of surgery is one where the surgeon opens the area of the fracture, reduces the fracture gap, and then fixes the bone back in position with the plates and screws. Sometimes the X-rays don't provide an accurate picture of what the break will look like once the patient is open. Once this patient was opened, the fracture was somewhat more complex than the doctor had thought it would be. The doctor was examining the fracture and questioning if the plate and screw set I had brought in was going to be big enough. He said he was pretty sure he could make it work, but he wanted my opinion. I was also fairly confident that the set we had would work, but it would probably make the surgery a little more difficult. A larger plate and screw set would work with room to spare. What should I do?

In this case I recommended that the doctor use a larger set, which meant that his only option would be the competitor's set that was stocked and sterilized in the hospital. The doctor agreed that would be the safest option, so he brought in the competitor's equipment. The competitor's rep was not available because he was in another surgery, so I stayed in the OR and helped the doctor with the case and the competitor's equipment. It meant a loss of several thousand dollars by having the doctor not use our hardware; but the doctor told me afterward that he was aware of the fact that I had sacrificed a sale by recommending he use the other equipment, but that the trust I had earned with him would guarantee that he would be using more of our equipment in the future and that he would recommend to the hospital administration that our company be given a contract. This doctor has become one of our best customers.

Source: Brendan Brooks, Smith & Nephew Inc., personal correspondence; used with permission.

the customer, without bragging, about their special training or education. They can also strengthen credibility with well-conceived, insightful questions or comments.

When selling complicated technical products and services, Todd Graf notes, "You have to keep it simple. Teach as you go. Make transitions slow and smooth and always ask if they understand (half the time they don't). This is key because they may have to go back and explain some of your features to the decision maker who isn't present in this meeting."[24]

Being willing to say, "I'm sorry, I was wrong on that," or "I don't know the answer to that, but I'll get it to you," will also go a long way toward establishing credibility. A seller should never use a word if he or she doesn't know the exact definition. Some buyers may even test the salesperson. Here's an example from a real salesperson who was calling on a doctor:[25]

SALESPERSON: Because product X acts as an agonist at the kappa receptor, miosis will occur.

DOCTOR: What does *miosis* mean?

SALESPERSON: It means the stage of disease during which intensity of signs and symptoms diminishes.

DOCTOR: No! *Miosis* means contraction of the pupils.

At this point the doctor walked out of the room, and the seller thought she had lost all credibility. Actually, he had just gone out and grabbed a dictionary. The first definition was the contraction of the pupils, and the second was the seller's definition. The salesperson's definition, not the doctor's, fit the use of the term for this medication. The doctor then shook the seller's hand and thanked her for teaching him a new definition of the word. The salesperson's credibility certainly increased.

SELLING TO GROUPS

Selling to groups can be both rewarding and frustrating. On the plus side, if you make an effective presentation, every member of the prospect group becomes your ally. On the down side, groups behave like groups, with group standards and norms and issues of status and group leadership.

When selling to groups, the salesperson must gather information about the

Selling to groups requires special skills in monitoring several individuals at once, as well as being able to respond to customers with occasionally conflicting needs.

needs and concerns of each individual who will attend. Salespeople should discover (for each prospect group member) member status within the group, authority, perceptions about the urgency of the problem, receptivity to ideas, knowledge of the subject matter, attitude toward the salesperson, major areas of interest and concern, key benefits sought, likely resistance, and ways to handle this resistance. Chapter 3 discusses many things that salespeople should consider about buying centers.

It is important to develop not only objectives for the meeting but also objectives for what the seller hopes to accomplish with each prospect present at the meeting. Planning may include the development of special visual aids for specific individuals present. The seller must expect many more objections and interruptions in a group setting compared to selling to an individual.

An informal atmosphere in which group members are encouraged to speak freely and the salesperson feels free to join the group's discussion usually works best in these situations. Thus an informal location (such as a corner of a large room as opposed to a formal conference room) is preferred. Formal presentation methods, such as speeches, that separate buyers and sellers into them-versus-us sides should be avoided. If the group members decide that the meeting is over, the salesperson should not try to hold them.

Of course most things you have learned about selling to individuals apply equally to groups. You should learn the names of group members and use them when appropriate. You should listen carefully and observe all nonverbal cues. When one member of the buying team is talking, it is especially important to observe the cues being transmitted by the other members of the buying team to see whether they are, in effect, agreeing or disagreeing with the speaker.

There are several types of group selling situations. If the group meeting is actually a negotiation session, many more things must be considered. As a result, we devote an entire chapter (Chapter 12) to the topic of formal negotiations. Also, sometimes a salesperson makes a call on a prospect as part of a selling team from his firm (for example, the team might consist of his sales manager, someone from technical support, someone from customer support, and a sales executive from the firm). These situations require coordination and teamwork. Because of the importance of the various selling team scenarios, the issue of selling teams is more fully discussed in Chapter 16.

SELLING YOURSELF

It's a fact. You're going to be selling yourself while trying to get that first job right out of college. Don't forget to use everything you've read in this chapter as you do so. Otherwise you'll look and sound like the thousands of other students who merely *hope* that the company will hire them without really keying in on what the hiring company is looking for.

Always attempt to build rapport with an interviewer. Find something you have in common with her, based on information you learned from her LinkedIn profile, from your professor, or even from the staff in the career services center at your school. Someone is bound to know something about the person. Use that information to break the ice and build a sense of "liking" between the two of you. You'll be surprised how much that simple act calms you down as you realize you really do have some things in common.

Make sure you discover interviewers' needs. What exactly are they looking for in a job candidate? If you've not already discovered it, and the information is not available on their Web site, then go ahead and ask. The interviewers won't think you're weird; they'll think you are sharp. Once you find out what those needs are, sell yourself by explicitly showing how your "features" meet their needs. For example, your résumé might state the following:

> Reading with Champions Volunteer, Birchwood Elementary School: read to elementary school students two times a week to help them gain a love for books.

You're interviewing for a sales job, not a job to read books to small children. So it's your job to convert that feature into a benefit to the interviewers with something like the following:

> You said you were looking for someone with a hard work ethic and also for someone with an ability to interact with lots of different kinds of clients. Well, my volunteer work demonstrates my work ethic because I did this activity for six months, all while I was also taking 18 credits at school. I never missed a reading at that school, either! Also, the children I interacted with at that school were not like me at all. Most came from poor backgrounds and broken families. Many had never had a book read to them before. Anyway, what all of this means to you is that I am able to interact with people who are very different from me. In fact I enjoy it. I'm sure I'll be able to adapt to the many different types of customers you say you have at your firm. Did that example help you see that I am a hard worker and that I can interact with different types of people?

Finally, establish credibility by bringing your portfolio with you to the interview. The portfolio should include copies of papers you wrote, videos of presentations you gave, and any other evidence that will demonstrate that you have the skills they are looking for.

SUMMARY

Salespeople need to make every possible effort to create a good impression during a sales call. The first few minutes with the prospect are important, and care should be taken to make an effective entrance by giving a good first impression, expressing confidence while standing and shaking hands, and selecting an appropriate seat.

The salesperson can use any of several methods to gain the prospect's attention. Salespeople should adopt the opening that is most effective for the prospect's personality style. Also critical is the development of rapport with the prospect, which can often be enhanced by engaging in friendly conversation.

Before beginning any discussion of product information, the salesperson can establish the prospect's needs by using open and closed questions. The SPIN technique is very effective for discovering needs in a major sale. In subsequent calls the salesperson should reiterate the prospect's needs.

When moving into a discussion of the proposed solution or alternatives, the salesperson translates features into benefits for the buyer. The salesperson also makes any necessary adjustments in the presentation based on feedback provided by the buyer's nonverbal cues and by verbal probing.

A close, harmonious relationship will enhance the whole selling process. The salesperson can build credibility by adhering to stated appointment lengths, backing up statements with proof, offering a balanced presentation, and establishing his or her credentials.

When selling to groups, the salesperson must gather information about the needs and concerns of each individual who will attend. The seller should also uncover the ego involvement and issue involvement of each group member. It is important to develop objectives not only for the meeting but also for what the seller hopes to accomplish with each prospect present at the meeting.

Now that you know how to start the sale, discover needs, relate features to specific benefits for the buyer, and build credibility, it is time to look more closely at how to communicate your ideas more effectively. That's the topic of the next chapter.

KEY TERMS

advantages 219
balanced presentation 223
benefit 218
benefit opening 207
closed questions 213
compliment opening 207
credibility 222
credibility statement 223
customer benefit proposition 218
FAB 219
feature 218
feature dumping 218
FEBA 219
halo effect 207
implication questions 215
impression management 204

introduction opening 207
major sale 214
need payoff questions 216
office scanning 208
open questions 213
opening 207
problem questions 215
product opening 207
question opening 207
rapport 208
referral opening 207
selective perception 222
situation questions 214
small talk 208
SPIN 213
trial close 221

ETHICS PROBLEMS

1. You're an account executive for Wells Fargo Financial in Minnesota. You had an initial appointment with a customer, June, to find out what her goals were financially. The meeting went just as a typical first meeting should go, and there was a beneficial product you could create for her. However, her husband could not meet with you. After weeks of work and preparation, you have a loan that makes sense. The loan meets the goals June wanted, so you have a second appointment with her to go over exact terms . . . again without her husband. You asked when her husband could come in and sign the loan documents, and she discloses to you that her husband is not aware of the $35,000 of credit card debts the loan is going to pay off. Both the husband and wife must be present at the time of the loan. Legally you can call the husband and tell him about the loan application. What should you do?

2. You're calling on an important prospect in the paper industry, and she starts asking you how other mills are handling a specific problem. You know that this is important competitive information and that you should not provide details about a competitor. Instead you decide to give the prospect the information without specifics (like the name of the mill you're talking about). Is that OK?

Source: Erik Abrahamson, Wells Fargo Financial; used with permission.

QUESTIONS AND PROBLEMS

1. Think for a moment about trying to secure a sales job. Assume you are going to have an interview with a district manager of a consumer products firm next week for a sales position. What can you do to develop rapport and build credibility with her?

2. "I don't need to discover my prospect's needs. I sell bottled water to grocery stores and convenience stores. I know what their needs are: a high profit margin and fast turnover of products!" Comment.

3. Develop the FEBA for one of the features shown in Exhibit 8.8.

4. Assume that you are selling yard maintenance services to a homeowner. Develop a series of open and closed questions to discover the prospect's needs.

5. Assume that you represent your school's placement service. You are calling on a large business nearby that never hires graduates from your college. Generate a list of SPIN questions, making any additional assumptions necessary.

6. Prepare a list of features and benefits that could be used in a presentation to other students at your college. The objective of the presentation is to encourage them to enroll in the selling course you are taking.

7. "Sales Technology 8.1" told about the use of social networking to gain information and hence do a better job of gaining the prospect's attention. Look at the profiles of two of your friends or contacts on LinkedIn, Facebook, MySpace, or some other social networking site. Using strictly the information you find there, what are some ways you could gain that person's attention in a sales call, assuming you didn't actually know them before the call?

8. In "Building Partnerships 8.1" you read about a salesperson who told a doctor to use a competitor's product. The story has a happy ending. But what if the doctor had not become one of Brendan's best customers as a result of Brendan's actions? If Brendan knew that was going to be the outcome, should he have suggested the doctor use his product, not the competitor's product?

9. In which situations should a salesperson use a prospect's first name? When should a more formal salutation be used?

10. You're selling a new soft drink to a grocery store (choose one). Write a list of features and benefits for the grocery store, as well as a list of features and benefits for the store's customers (the shoppers who come in and buy soft drinks).

11. In "From the Buyer's Seat 8.1" you heard a buyer describe his best salespeople. The buyer said that he believes one reason more salespeople aren't great is that they are too rushed. What can a salesperson do to be less rushed and to spend the right amount of time with each customer? What can a company do to ensure that salespeople aren't too rushed?

CASE PROBLEMS

case 8.1

AirCharter (Part B)

Founded in 1985, AirCharter has provided charter flights to a wide array of customers, including business travelers worldwide. Thanks to AirCharter's online booking system, business travelers can secure reliable quotes and book both domestic and international flights. AirCharter has more than 3,000 aircraft, including jets (light, midsize, and large jets) and turboprops.

The company is known for its ability to cater to passengers' every desire, including gourmet meals, special beverages, entertainment while in the air, and other luxury accommodations. AirCharter also staffs a full-service VIP jet concierge program, similar to what major airlines offer. This service can help clients meet all their needs on the ground before and after the flight.

Felix Aleynykov is a salesperson for AirCharter. Today he will be making his first visit to Abel Espinosa, a procurement officer at the AFL-CIO. The AFL-CIO is one of the largest labor federations in the United States and has three primary executive officers: president, secretary-treasurer, and executive vice president. Both the executive officers and the executive council travel across the country a great deal in their work.

For more details about AirCharter and the AFL-CIO, see Case 7.1.

Questions

1. Develop a set of open and closed questions to fully discover Abel Espinosa's needs.
2. Develop a set of SPIN questions to discover Abel Espinosa's needs.

Sources: http://www.aircharter.net, www.aflcio.org.

case 8.2

ProPlan Software

Mark Alonzo, of ProPlan, had an important appointment with a senior buyer and her assistant at a pharmaceutical company. It had taken Mark three months to get the appointment, and he was excited about the chance to finally demonstrate his company's new system planning software. As Mark was leaving his office, his sales manager learned where Mark was going and asked to come alone. Mark had no option but to say, "Sure." However, he was worried because his manager often took control of meetings and sometimes wasn't a good listener.

When the sales team got there, the buyer, Tracey, stated that she could participate for only about 30 minutes but that her assistant, Sally, would be staying for the remainder of the time. Before Mark could begin talking, Roy, his sales manager, began taking the buyers through his sales binder that had a presentation in it. It began with the history of the company.

Tracey politely interrupted and explained that she was already familiar with ProPlan, but there were certain things that she was interested in learning about their services. Tracey asked the sales team if they could produce two items for her.

Again, before Mark could answer, Roy jumped in with, "Yes, we could, and I'm going to get there in a minute." Tracey patiently waited as he continued to take her through the company history. By now almost 10 minutes had passed.

Next Roy talked about the work that ProPlan had done for other companies. This is something that many buyers are usually interested in. However, Tracey interrupted again and said they were really looking for a vendor for a couple of specific projects, and that she wanted to see what they could do for those specific situations. Roy replied, "Hang on, Tracey. I'm almost there! I promise to get there soon."

After Roy finished showing the work ProPlan did for other companies, he began to explain the benefits of working with his company because of reputation, pricing, service, and so on. Tracey asked again about the two projects, and instead of answering her questions, Roy continued to follow his canned presentation. Tracey was becoming noticeably upset and agitated, although Sally seemed quite interested.

Questions

1. You are Mark. What will you do now?

2. How can you avoid a situation like this in future calls with your manager?

Source: Tracey Brill. Used with permission.

ROLE PLAY CASE

Today we are going to start over again, "from the top" as they say in the theater. Start from the beginning of the sales call, from when you knock on the door through the needs identification stage, ending just before your presentation. All that you have learned in previous role plays about the account continues to hold true. If you've been selling to Spear One, you'll continue to do so, but you are now meeting with a different member of the buying center. The same is true for McLane Properties and Dart Paper Products. New buyer sheets will be passed out. You can have the same person play the new role or someone else in class. (*Note:* If you have not done role plays before, you will need to review the information about the various role play customers that can be found at the end of Chapter 3.)

If your class is divided into groups of three, the person who is watching should create a check sheet. Write *S, P, I,* and *N* down the left side of the paper. As the salesperson asks a question, check whether it is a situation, problem, implication, or needs payoff question. Also note if and how he or she identified or verified the decision process. *Don't forget:* At the start of the sales call, identify the type of opening used (introduction, benefit, product, curiosity, or some other form).

Spear One: You will meet with the VP of sales and marketing. This is an appointment that was set up by the regional sales manager you called on earlier. You've never talked to this person before.

McLane Properties: Mr. McLane has asked to see you. You weren't expecting this from your earlier sales calls, but you welcome the opportunity to meet the decision maker. His secretary called and made the appointment.

Dart Paper Products: You are meeting with one of the VPs of sales. The other VP was fired, but you don't know why. The meeting was set up by the regional sales manager you called on earlier, who also told you about the firing, but she didn't know what had happened.

Note: For background information about these role plays, please see page 27.

To the instructor: Additional information needed to complete the role play is available in the Instructor's Manual.

ADDITIONAL REFERENCES

Belonax Jr., Joseph J., Stephen J. Newell, and Richard E. Plank. "The Role of Purchase Importance on Buyer Perceptions of the Trust and Expertise Components of Supplier and Salesperson Credibility in Business-to-Business Relationships." *Journal of Personal Selling & Sales Management* 27, no. 3 (Summer 2007), pp. 247–58.

Burn, Brian. *The Maverick Selling Method: Simplifying the Complex Sale.* Xlibris Corporation, 2009.

Cassell, Jeremy, and Tom Bird. *Brilliant Selling: What the Best Salespeople Know, Do, and Say.* FT Press, 2009.

Chan, Elaine, and Jaideep Sengupta. "Insincere Flattery Actually Works: A Dual Attitudes Perspective." *Journal of Marketing Research* 47, no. 1 (February 2010).

Clifford, Stephanie. "Putting the Performance in Sales Performance." *Inc.,* February 2007, pp. 87–95.

Fautsch, Leo. "Persuasion." *American Salesman* 52, no. 1 (January 2007), pp. 13–16.

Graham, John. "When the Sales Mentality Meets the Buyer Mindset." *American Salesman,* March 2007, pp. 25–30.

Griffin, Jill G., and Susan M. Broniarczyk. "The Slippery Slope: The Impact of Feature Alignability on Search and Satisfaction." *Journal of Marketing Research* 47, no. 2 (April 2010).

Johnson, Mark S., Eugene Sivadas, and Vishal Kashyap. "Response Bias in the Measurement of Salesperson Orientations: The Role of Impression Management." *Industrial Marketing Management* 38, no. 8 (November 2009), pp. 1014–24.

Keh, Hean Tat, and Yi Xie. "Corporate Reputation and Customer Behavioral Intentions: The Roles of Trust, Identification, and Commitment." *Industrial Marketing Management* 38, no. 7 (October 2009), pp. 732–42.

Laaksonen, Toni, Kalle Pajunen, and Harri I. Kulmala. "Co-evolution of Trust and Dependence in Customer–Supplier Relationships." *Industrial Marketing Management* 37, no. 8 (November 2008), pp. 910–20.

Lager, Marshall. "The Psychology of the Sale: There's a Lot Going on inside the Customer's Head, Whether You Put It There or Not. What Are Salespeople Up Against?" *CRM Magazine* 13, no. 5 (2009), pp. 34–37.

Lovas, Michael, and Pam Holloway. *Axis of Influence: How Credibility and Likeability Intersect to Drive Success.* Morgan James Publishing, 2009.

Ramani, Girish, and V. Kumar. "Interaction Orientation and Firm Performance." *Journal of Marketing* 72, no. 1 (January 2008), pp. 27–45.

Read, Nicholas A.C., and Dr. Stephen J. Bistritz. *Selling to the C-Suite: What Every Executive Wants You to Know about Successfully Selling to the Top.* McGraw-Hill, 2009.

Stoddard, James E., Stephen W. Clopton, and Ramon A. Avila. "An Analysis of the Effects of Sales Force Automation on Salesperson Perceptions of Performance." *Journal of Personal Selling & Sales Management* 27, no. 2 (Spring 2007), pp. 191–92.

Sundtoft Hald, Kim, Carlos Cordón, and Thomas E. Vollmann. "Towards an Understanding of Attraction in Buyer–Supplier Relationships." *Industrial Marketing Management* 38, no. 8 (November 2009), pp. 960–70.

Wood, John Andy, James S. Boles, and Barry J. Babin. "The Formation of Buyer's Trust of the Seller in an Initial Sales Encounter." *Journal of Marketing Theory and Practice* 16, no. 1 (Winter 2008), pp. 27–40.

The Partnership Process

PART 2

chapter 9

STRENGTHENING THE PRESENTATION

SOME QUESTIONS ANSWERED IN THIS CHAPTER ARE

- How can salespeople use verbal tools to strengthen a presentation?
- Why do salespeople need to augment their oral communication through tools such as visual aids, samples, testimonials, and demonstrations?
- What methods are available to strengthen a presentation?
- How can salespeople use visual aids and technology most effectively?
- What are the ingredients of a good demonstration?
- Is there a way to quantify the salesperson's solution to a buyer's problem?
- How can salespeople reduce presentation jitters?

PROFILE

PROFILE A few years ago I learned to fly airplanes and earned my private pilot's license. What's the most challenging is how it demands both physical and mental capabilities at the same time. You are maneuvering the airplane and abiding by countless regulations all while communicating to the air traffic controllers in an entirely different language. It is quite the experience. Once you master the proper steps you are on your way toward safe takeoffs, landings, and accident-free flying. But only when you and your flight instructor know that everything has come together is it safe for you to take to the sky and fly solo.

The same is true when it comes to selling. When I was chosen by sales instructors Nicole Howatt-Moberg and Cyndi Gundy to be part of the team representing the University of Central Florida at the National Collegiate Sales Competition, I was eager to capitalize on the opportunity and, most importantly, make UCF proud.

The sales competition was a lot like flying. Everything had to come together with precise timing and finesse in order to achieve success. We were the number one seed going into the competition and had great expectations to live up to. Our team members were each assigned research tasks to learn about NetSuite, the product we were assigned to sell in the competition. In between practice sessions and strategy meetings we dug up every feature, benefit, and statistic that we could find. We had pages and spreadsheets full of them!

As we pulled together all our tools for the competition, our coaches, Karl Sooder and Dr. Bill Callarman, and our mentors, award-winning author Jeff Lehman and founder/CEO of SalesGravy.com Jeb Blount, continually asked us to present our value proposition. They were relentless about it! We willingly played back the list of features and benefits of NetSuite. However, it was not resonating the way we all wanted it to. Then it occurred to us that reciting a list of features and benefits was not going to make for a successful value proposition. Instead it is the succinct combination of the two that creates the attention, interest, conviction, desire, and opportunity to close the prospect.

Plainly stated, having a well-crafted value proposition is the key to capitalizing on the selling opportunity. You have to be able to state your value proposition with genuine conviction. If you own the value proposition, you will do well. We practiced ours over and over. Not until everyone on our team knew it inside out were we were ready to perform successfully at the NCSC.

When preparing for a sales presentation, try putting yourself in the shoes of the buyer. When a potential client asks you, "What does your product do and how will it help my company?" can you give them a unique and well-crafted two-sentence answer that would make sense to someone who might have only briefly heard of your company? If so, does your answer also make them want to know more? The ability to deliver on both accounts is critical to a successful career in sales. That is exactly why my coaches perpetually stressed the importance of having an effective value proposition for the competition (and my sales career). An effective value proposition was part of our core strategy back at NCSC, and is also something that I actively utilize in my sales career to this day.

My coaches (who have a significant amount of practical "seat time" at high levels inside corporate America) told me that even the largest of corporations have trouble articulating their value propositions to their sales professionals and out to their customers. Yet the value proposition is an instrumental tool that, once mastered, can pay huge dividends to the sales professional. Excellent listening skills will allow you to deliver the relative features and custom-tailored benefits to the customers while keeping it easy to understand. All too often a salesperson will resort to restating feature lists and entirely miss the key benefit to the buyers. This is a sure way to confuse them and jeopardize the sale.

At NCSC I proceeded from the initial rounds all the way to the semifinals. Along with my teammate Jessica Cernell, we earned enough points to place 7th in the nation among 50+ universities. After graduating I accepted a sales position at the industry leader in document management, IKON Office Solutions. I have since put IKON's value proposition to good use. Being able to deliver a captivating value proposition has blessed me with many sales, and I wish you the same success.

Source: Andrew Eric Gaffka © 2010; used with permission.

Visit our Web page at www.ikon.com.

CHARACTERISTICS OF A STRONG PRESENTATION

Communication tools such as visual aids, samples, testimonials, demonstrations, and the use of humor are important ingredients in most sales calls. Use of such tools focuses the buyer's attention, improves the buyer's understanding, helps the buyer remember what the salesperson said, offers concrete proof of the salesperson's statements, and creates a sense of value.

KEEPS THE BUYER'S ATTENTION

How many times has your mind wandered during classroom lectures while the instructor earnestly discussed some topic? What happened? The instructor lost your attention. In contrast, your attention probably remains more focused in a class when the instructor uses visuals and humor effectively, brings in guest speakers, and finds ways to get you actively involved in the discussion.

The same is true of buyer–seller interactions. Unless you can get the buyer actively involved in the communication process and doing more than just passively hearing you talk, the buyer's attention will probably turn to other topics. "Building Partnerships 9.1" illustrates how one salesperson regained the buyer's attention in a difficult situation.

The buyer's personality can also affect his or her attention span. For example, one would expect an amiable to listen more attentively to a long presentation than, say, a driver would. Thus an effective salesperson should consider the social style of the prospect and adapt the use of communication aids accordingly (see Chapter 5 for more about personality styles).

IMPROVES THE BUYER'S UNDERSTANDING

Many buyers have difficulty forming clear images from the written or spoken word. An old Chinese proverb says, "Tell me—I'll forget. Show me—I may remember. But involve me, and I'll understand." Appeals should be made to as many of the senses (hearing, sight, touch, taste, and smell) as possible. Studies show that appealing to more than one sense with **multiple-sense appeals** increases understanding dramatically, as Exhibit 9.1 illustrates. For example, in selling Ben & Jerry's ice cream novelties to a grocery store manager, the salesperson may describe the product's merits (an appeal to the sense of hearing) or show the product and invite the merchant to taste it (appeals to sight, touch, and taste). Appeals to the grocer's fifth sense, smell, are also possible. On the other hand, salespeople who sell machinery are limited to appeals that will affect the buyers' senses of hearing, sight, and touch.

HELPS THE BUYER REMEMBER WHAT WAS SAID

On average, people immediately forget 50 percent of what they hear; after 48 hours they have forgotten 75 percent of the message. This is unfortunate

BUILDING Partnerships

I'VE GOT A BETTER IDEA

On December 5, 1933, the U.S. Congress passed a bill that would repeal the 18th Amendment and thus would end prohibition in this country. The implementation of prohibition had been linked to many negative social issues such as organized crime, bootlegging, and racketeering. Some historians have commented that the alcohol industry accepted stronger regulation of alcohol in the decades after repeal as a way to reduce the chance that Prohibition would return. Today the American beer industry is the most heavily regulated industry in the country, even more than the tobacco industry, and Minnesota is a leader when it comes to heavy regulation and high taxes. For example, here are the beer laws in Minnesota:

1. All retailers must be offered the same price at all times.
2. Beer distributors cannot pay for any cooperative advertising.
3. Beer distributors cannot give any product for free.
4. Beer distributors have a maximum of $300 per brand, per year, to promote the brand within the account (using things like neon lights and point-of-sale items), but this can't be in the form of price cuts for an individual retailer.

I was the sales representative for a beer distributor in Minnesota. My territory volume was trending down, and I was told by my manager that I needed to secure incremental activity to promote Miller Lite. My largest customer, Bill at Save-a-Lot Liquor, gave me an opportunity for an additional holiday ad in his weekly flyer. I knew this ad would yield a 200 percent lift in sales for the week and in turn would pay a nice commission to me.

To secure the ad, Bill was asking me to lower the price of my product by 50 cents per case to cover the cost of the ad. Bill also stated that if I decided not to participate, my competition had already committed to the ad. I believed that my competition had lowered the price in the past, and there had never been any repercussions from the authorities. What should I do? I had totally lost the interest of Bill, who would turn elsewhere to buy the bulk of his beer!

I had several options. I could write a personal check for the amount of the ad, but that would have repercussions down the road, and I was sure I'd be asked to do so again and again. I could try to see if Bill really did have the competitor's agreement to cut the price, but that could backfire on me and make the customer think I didn't trust his word. I could give all the other liquor stores in my territory the same 50 cent discount, but that would cut into our profit margins.

By law, entertainment is allowed in our industry as long as I go along for the entertainment also. In other words, I couldn't just give Bill two tickets for him and his wife to use without me being present also at the game. So, knowing he was a big football fan, I took Bill to a Vikings game. He appreciated the attention, and we did talk business as well. I had his attention again, and he went with my proposal. He's always been a good customer since, and I didn't break any laws. It was a win–win for everyone.

Source: Amir Permeh, Bernick's Beverages & Vending, personal correspondence; used with permission. Names of buyer changed to protect confidentiality.

because securing an order often requires multiple visits, and in many situations the prospect must relay to other people information learned in a sales call. In these circumstances it becomes more critical for the seller to help the buyer remember what was said.

Even selling situations involving one call or one decision maker will be more profitable if the buyer remembers what was said. Vividly communicated features create such a strong impression that the buyer remembers the seller's claims and is more likely to tell others about them.

Lasting impressions can be created in many ways. One salesperson swallows some industrial cleanser to show that it is nontoxic; another kicks the protective glass in the control panel of a piece of machinery to show that it is virtually

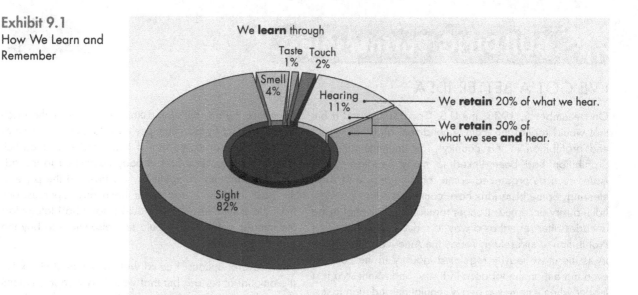

unbreakable in even the roughest conditions. Whatever the method used, the prospect is more likely to remember a sales feature if it is presented skillfully in a well-timed demonstration.

OFFERS PROOF OF THE SALESPERSON'S ASSERTIONS

Let's face it: Most people won't believe everything a salesperson tells them. Many of the communication tools we discuss in this chapter provide solid proof to back up a salesperson's claims. For example, a salesperson can easily claim that a liquid is nontoxic, but the claim is much more convincing if the salesperson drinks some of the liquid in front of the prospect.

CREATES A SENSE OF VALUE

The manner in which a product is handled suggests value. Careful handling communicates value, whereas careless handling implies that the product has little value. For example, a delicate piece of china will be perceived as more valuable if the salesperson uses appropriate props, words, and care in handling it.

HOW TO STRENGTHEN THE PRESENTATION

Salespeople should ask themselves the following questions: How can I use my imagination and creativity to make a vivid impression on my prospect or customer? How can I make my presentation a little different and a little stronger? With this frame of mind, salespeople will always try to do a better and more effective job of meeting their customers' needs. In this section we explore the many tools available to strengthen a presentation.

Before we describe the various methods, it is important to reiterate a point made in the preceding chapter. A seller should not grab a method because it sounds trendy or because it worked in a previous sales call or because it is highly entertaining. Rather, a seller should strategically select methods and media that will helpfully address the needs of the buyer. This process includes responding to the buyer's unique style (see Chapter 5 to review social styles):

- Expressives like to see strong, intense colors and lots of photos, cartoons, fancy fonts, and positive images (smiles).

- Analyticals prefer visuals that are clean and simple, a list of references, and lots of details.
- Amiables prefer visuals with people in them and a relatively slow-moving presentation.
- Drivers want crisp, professional visuals with bold lettering to highlight important points.

Strategizing also includes considering such elements as how many people will attend the presentation, which stage of the buying process they are in, what information they need, what type of situation this is (new task, modified rebuy, straight rebuy), and so on (see Chapter 3 for more buying factors to consider). In all cases, it is important to get your prospects involved and keep the focus of attention centered on them.[1]

VERBAL TOOLS

Word Pictures and Stories

The power of the spoken word can be phenomenal. To communicate effectively, the salesperson needs to remember all the hints and tools found in Chapter 4. Word pictures and stories of all types can be effective.[2] Here are some points to keep in mind when using stories:

- It is best to use stories from your own life. If you borrow one, don't act as if it is your personal story.
- Make sure you have a reason for telling the story.
- Consider using a prop, like a glove or a suitcase or something that helps tell the story and will help the prospect remember the story.
- Use the "hook" of the story to tie back directly into your presentation.
- Be accurate and vivid with the words you choose. Learn to paint a clear picture.
- Pace the story, watching your audience for cues. Use silence and pauses.
- Choose stories that fit your own style. Don't try to be someone you're not.
- Remember, stories can be short—even a few sentences.

Humor

Another way a salesperson can help keep the buyer's attention is through the use of humor. The wonderful effects of laughter will put everyone more at ease, including the salesperson. Use humorous stories from your own experience, borrowed humor, or humor adapted from another source. Here are some things to keep in mind:

- Don't oversell the joke (Here's one that'll really break you up!).
- Don't apologize before telling a joke (I wasn't ever good at telling a joke, but here goes).
- Identify any facts that are absolutely necessary for the punch line of the story to make sense (Jerry Joyner, my next-door neighbor who was always sticking his nose in other people's business,. . .).
- Use humor from your own life. Anything you got from e-mail or the Web could be circulating widely.
- Enjoy yourself by smiling and animating your voice and nonverbals.
- Practice telling the joke different ways to see which exact wording works best.
- Make sure your punch line is clear.

Beware of overdoing humor or using off-the-wall or offensive humor. Both can backfire, as one presenter found out when he used the following opening line about an overweight attendee: "Pull up two chairs and have a seat." The presenter knew right away that it was a big mistake. Always be cautious about using insider jokes, especially if you're still considered an outsider.

thinking **it** through   What humor have you seen backfire? How can you be sure the humor you are using isn't going to offend someone?

Also, understand that what is funny to one person or group may not be funny to others. For example, a foreigner from Egypt may not appreciate someone from America making fun of Egyptian culture—but someone from Egypt can tell that same joke and get plenty of laughs.

VISUAL TOOLS

A salesperson can use various visually oriented tools to strengthen a presentation. This section explores the content and use of those tools, followed by a discussion of the various media available to display the results.

Graphics and Charts

Graphics and charts help illustrate relationships and clearly communicate large amounts of information. Charts may show, for example, advertising schedules, a breakdown of typical customer profiles, details of product manufacture, profit margins at various pricing points, or the investment nature of purchasing a product.

Here are hints for developing charts and related visuals:

- Know the single point a visual should make, and then ensure that it accomplishes that point.

- Charts can easily be customized by including the name of the prospect's company in one corner or by some other form of personalization.

- Use current, accurate information.

- Don't place too much information on a visual; on text visuals, don't use more than five or six words per line or more than five lines or bullets per visual. Don't use complete sentences; the speaker should verbally provide the missing details.

- Use bullets (dots or symbols before each line) to differentiate issues and to emphasize key points.

- Don't overload the buyer with numbers. Use no more than five or six columns, and drop all unnecessary zeros.

- Clearly label each visual with a title. Label all columns and rows.

- Recognize the emotional impact of colors, and choose appropriate ones. An abundance of green connected to a humorous graph might be offensive in Islamic countries because green is a religious color. In Brazil and Mexico, purple indicates death.

- If possible, use graphics (like diagrams, pie charts, and bar charts) instead of tables. Tables are often needed if

Salespeople should use humor to get and keep the customer's attention.

actual raw numbers are important; graphics are better for displaying trends and relationships.

- Use high-quality drawings and photographs instead of clip art if possible.
- Use consistent art styles, layouts, and scales for your collection of charts and figures. Consistency makes it easier for the buyer to follow along.
- For PowerPoint slides, use 28-point type for the titles and 24-point type for the text, using Arial or Helvetica. And use transition effects and sound clips sparingly.
- Check your visuals closely for typographical errors, misspelled words, and other errors.
- Know and obey copyright laws. You can't just grab images off the Web and use them.

Models, Samples, and Gifts

Visual selling aids such as models, samples, and gifts may be a good answer to the problem of getting and keeping buyer interest. For example, Chubb Lock salespeople carry along a miniature working model of the company's electronic door locks when calling on prison security systems buyers. The model allows the salesperson to show how the various components work together to form a fail-safe security network.

Other salespeople use cross-sectional models to communicate with the buyer. For example, salespeople for Motion Industries use a cutaway model of a power transmission friction reduction product. This model helps the buyer, usually an industrial engineer, to clearly see how the product is constructed, resulting in greater confidence that the product will perform as described. Of course for some larger products the best way to display a model is to bring the customer to the selling company's manufacturing plant, as "From the Buyer's Seat 9.1" illustrates.

Depending on the service or product, samples and gifts can make excellent sales aids and help maintain the prospect's interest after the call. In a Johnson's Wax sales campaign, salespeople called on buyers of major chains to describe the promotion. Salespeople walked into each buyer's office with a solid oak briefcase containing cans of aerosol Pledge, the product to be highlighted during the promotion. During the call the sales representative demonstrated the Pledge furniture polish on the oak briefcase. At the conclusion of the visit, the rep gave the buyer not only the cans of Pledge but also the briefcase. Of course gift giving must be done with care and not violate the rules of the buyer's company.

Catalogs and Brochures

Catalogs and brochures can help salespeople communicate information to buyers effectively. The salesperson can use them during a presentation and then leave them with the buyer as a reminder of the issues covered. Brochures often summarize key points and contain answers to the usual questions buyers pose.

Firms often spend a great deal of money to develop visually attractive brochures for salespeople. Exhibit 9.2 shows an example of a brochure used by salespeople. Creatively designed brochures usually unfold in a way that enables the salesperson to create and maintain great interest while showing them.

Photos, Illustrations, Ads, and Maps

Photos are easy to prepare, are inexpensive, and permit a realistic portrayal of a product and its benefits. Photographs of people may be particularly effective. For example, leisure made possible through savings can be communicated via

From the BUYER'S SEAT

9.1

SHOW AND TELL THAT SELLS

By Regina Conner, Kinder Morgan

I'm a buyer for Kinder Morgan, one of the largest pipeline companies in the United States and Canada. I've been at this job for five years now and have learned a lot about what separates good from not-so-good salespeople.

For one thing, I'm always impressed when salespeople invite me and others in my organization to their plant or facility. This tells me they are honest by their willingness to open up their facility. Besides, we can usually tell a lot about their capabilities by visiting their facility. I'll give an example to illustrate why this is important.

We were looking at potential suppliers for modular electrical service buildings, or what are sometimes called power distribution centers. These are usually steel-framed buildings about the size of large mobile homes—just without the wheels. Anyway, they are large and expensive. One building can run about $250,000 to $300,000. We visited three suppliers that looked good on paper. And these were suppliers we had never dealt with before. If we went solely on their proposals that they submitted, any one of

them could have done the work we needed. We were purchasing 13 of these buildings.

After visiting all three suppliers, we ruled one out right away. They were basically fabricating these buildings partly in an old warehouse, and some of the work was being done outdoors in the elements. The second supplier had clear processes and nice facilities and could definitely build what we were looking for. However, they lacked the capacity we needed. They could build one building in about six weeks and only one at a time. But we needed 13 buildings in less than six months.

The third one we visited was the one we ended up actually using. They exceeded our expectations in every regard. I should note that they weren't the low-cost supplier based on the proposals submitted. I guess the point I am trying to make is that if you are truly confident in your capabilities, show us.

Source: Regina Conner, Kinder Morgan, personal correspondence; used with permission; names changed to protect confidentiality.

Exhibit 9.2
A Brochure with Great Visual Appeal

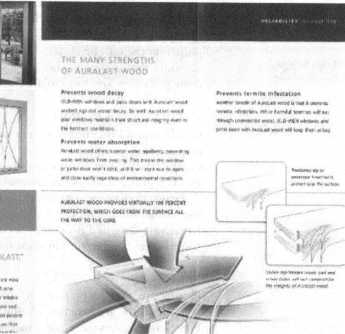

photographs of retired people at a ranch, a mountain resort, or the seashore. Illustrations drawn, painted, or prepared in other ways also help dramatize needs or benefits. Copies of recent or upcoming ads may contribute visual appeal. Detailed maps can be easily developed, for example, to show how a magazine's circulation matches the needs of potential advertisers.

Testimonials and Test Results

Testimonials are statements written by satisfied users of a product or service. For example, company representatives who sell air travel for major airlines have found case histories helpful in communicating sales points. Air Canada recounts actual experiences of business firms, showing the variety of problems that air travel can solve.

The effectiveness of a testimonial hinges on the skill with which it is used and a careful matching of satisfied user and prospect. In some situations the testimony of a rival or a competitor of the prospective buyer would end all chance of closing the sale; in other cases this type of testimony may be a strong factor in obtaining commitment. As much as possible, the person who writes the testimonial should be above reproach, well respected by his or her peers, and perhaps a center of influence (see Chapter 6). For example, when selling to certified public accountants (CPAs), a good source for a testimonial would be the president of the state's CPA association.

Before using a testimonial, the salesperson needs to check with the person who wrote it and frequently reaffirm that he or she is still a happy, satisfied customer. One salesperson for Unisys routinely handed all prospects a testimonial from a satisfied customer of a new software package. But unknown to the salesperson, the "satisfied customer" became an unsatisfied one and actually returned the software. The salesperson kept handing out the letter until one of his prospects alerted him to the situation. He will never know how many other prospects lost interest after contacting that customer.

Salespeople should not hand out a testimonial to every prospect. Such letters should be used only if they help to address the buyer's needs or concerns. Also, be aware that prospects probably discount testimonials, thinking that the seller is presenting letters only from very satisfied customers.

Salespeople can also use test results to strengthen the presentation. Tests on the product or service may have been conducted by the seller's firm or some third-party organization (such as Consumer Reports or Underwriters Laboratories). Generally, tests conducted by independent, recognized authorities have more credibility for the prospect than tests done by the seller.

Using Media to Display Visuals

Many media are available to display the types of items just mentioned. New media, and improvements to existing media, are being introduced almost every week (like 3D interactive viewing, the use of Flash for presentations, and so forth).[3] Salespeople are encouraged to choose media that are appropriate for the exact situation and not merely choose a tool because it is new or exciting. "Sales Technology 9.1" describes the use of one advanced tool that salespeople incorporate

Most salespeople have developed a **portfolio,** which is a collection of visual aids, often placed in a binder or on a computer. Salespeople do not intend to use everything in the portfolio in a single call; rather, the portfolio should contain a broad spectrum of visual aids the salesperson can find quickly should the need arise. When showing visuals in your portfolio, make sure the portfolio is turned so the buyer can see it easily. The portfolio should not be placed, like a wall,

SALES Technology

9.1

USE FLASH TO BUILD WOW INTO YOUR PRESENTATION

One of the most powerful tools for salespeople is Adobe's Flash. You're probably used Flash if you've ever watched a YouTube video on a PC. When compared to other video tools like Java, QuickTime, or Windows Media Player, the Flash player has a quick download time and can start being viewed much more quickly.

With Flash a user can also add animation and interactivity to the final product. You may have experienced this capability of Flash if someone has sent you a holiday greeting card online that changes as you click on various parts of the card.

The latest versions of Flash allow the user to create 3D object manipulation to animate objects at will. The output of Flash can be sent via the Web, on DVD, or even via iPhones. Examples of these types of files can be found on the Web (see www.adobeflash.com and http://silverlight.net).

Salespeople use Flash in many different ways. Some salespeople send a prospect Flash files before a sales meeting to generate interest and enthusiasm for an upcoming call. Flash files can also be left behind so the prospect can share information with others in the firm, especially in buying center situations. And given that Flash is interactive and interesting to use, some sales managers suggest

that pass-along use is greater than for a traditional brochure or handout.

Creating interactive Flash presentations can be costly and time-consuming. However, as technology progresses the creation costs will undoubtedly drop. Costs also have to be compared to gains. One gain is that salespeople can incorporate Flash into webinars and Web-based sales calls, reducing travel expense and time for salespeople.

One expert suggests that salespeople develop modular Flash presentations. That way, new modules can be inserted as products and market conditions change, rather than having to start over with a whole new Flash presentation. Modularity also allows a salesperson to practice adaptability during a call showing only the parts a buyer actually wants to see.

Microsoft Silverlight, HTML5, and other competitors are gaining market share, and it will be interesting to see what technological advances will be made in the coming years. To be sure, salespeople need to stay abreast of changes in technology and adopt whatever tools help buyers make better decisions.

Sources: http://silverlight.net; Izabella Iizuka, "Not Your Father's Presentation," *Sales & Marketing Management,* March/April 2008, pp. 33–35.

between you and the buyer. Remember to look at the buyer, not at your visual; maintaining eye contact is always important.

Video is another tool salespeople can use. Salespeople use video to help buyers see how quality is manufactured into a product (showing the production process at the manufacturing plant), how others use a product or service (showing a group of seniors enjoying the golf course at a retirement resort), promotional support offered with the product (showing an actual upcoming TV commercial for a product), and even testimonials from satisfied users. When using video, make sure the video is fast-paced and relatively short. Don't show more than four minutes of a video at one time.

Salespeople have adopted laptops, iPads, and other portable devices for use in sales calls. For example, Merck pharmaceutical salespeople carry laptops with a database of technical information, as well as complete copies of articles from medical journals. Progressive firms, like Aetna, are investing in **digital collateral management systems** (also called **sales asset management systems**) to archive, catalog, and retrieve digital media and text. **Collateral** is a collection of documents that are designed to generate sales, such as brochures, sales flyers and fact sheets, and short success stories. Digital collateral management systems simplify the collection and make it possible for salespeople to easily secure and adapt these selling tools for specific situations. For example, salespeople using the SAVO digital collateral management system (www.savogroup.com) can easily call up photos, videos, audio files, PowerPoint templates, Web pages, legal documents, streaming media, and just about anything else that has been digitally entered into the system.

Some salespeople use PowerPoint to give presentations. However, it is critical that salespeople not merely progress from one slide to the next. As one expert noted, "Presentations should use visuals that encourage conversation, rather than endless text that leads to the audience reading the slides."[4]

thinking it through

You turn the lights down for a PowerPoint computer slide presentation. A few minutes later, you start to panic when your eye catches an unusual jerking movement made by the buyer —she's falling asleep! What do you do now?

Computers not only offer excellent visuals and graphics but also allow the salesperson to perform what-if analyses. For example, when a grocery buyer asked a Procter & Gamble rep what would happen if a new product were sold for $2.69 instead of the $2.75 suggested retail price, the salesperson was able to easily change this number in the spreadsheet program. Instantly all charts and graphs were corrected to illustrate the new pricing point, and comparisons with the competitor's product were generated.

When using computers, be prepared. Have backup batteries, adapters, and copies of DVDs. Really get to know your hardware and software so you can recover if the system crashes. And make sure both you and your customer can comfortably view the output.

Images can also be displayed using other media. **Document cameras,** also called **visual presenters,** are capable of displaying any three-dimensional object without the use of a transparency. **Electronic whiteboards,** commonly referred

Examples of sales collateral for an industrial product.

Salespeople use electronic tools to display important information.

to as SMART boards or digital easels, are used by salespeople, especially when working with customers who prefer to brainstorm an issue or problem. These are great at encouraging a group to interact with a presentation rather than merely watching it. Hewlett-Packard executives use these to make electronic presentations to remote offices in the United States and Europe with their teleconferencing system.

PRODUCT DEMONSTRATIONS

One of the most effective methods of appealing to a buyer's senses is through product demonstrations or performance tests. Customers and prospects have a natural desire to prove a product's claims for themselves. For example, orthopedic surgeons are like carpenters for human bodies: They repair damage and build new skeletons. They don't want a salesperson merely to tell them about new products; these surgeons want to touch them, feel them, and use them to see if they are good. When selling hip replacements to such doctors, sales reps demonstrate their products right in the surgery room. Because there is a definite sterile field, sales reps have to stand outside that field and use a green laser pointer to show where the surgeon should place the appliance.

One enterprising sales representative was having trouble convincing the buyer for a national retailer that the salesperson's company could provide service at all the retailer's scattered outlets. On the next trip to the buyer, the sales representative brought along a bag of darts and a map marked with the chain's hundreds of stores and service locations. The buyer was invited to throw darts at the map and then find the nearest stores. The test pointed out that the nearest location for service was always within 50 miles. This "service demonstration" helped win the representative's company a multimillion-dollar order.

Another salesperson was selling feeding tubes to a hospital. A nurse took the salesperson to a patient's bed and stated, "Here, you do it. You said it was easier to insert. Let me see you insert it."[5]

An executive briefing center.

Some products can be sold most successfully by getting the prospect into the showroom for a hands-on product demonstration. Showrooms can be quite elaborate and effective. For example, Kohler operates a marketing showroom in Kohler, Wisconsin. Prospects (architects and designers) from across the world can view and try all of Kohler's kitchen and bath fixtures. **Executive briefing centers,** which are rooms set aside to highlight a company's products and capabilities, are the ultimate presentation room.

Here are a number of helpful hints for developing and engaging in effective demonstrations:

- Be prepared. Practice your demonstration until you become an expert. Plan for everything that could possibly go wrong.

- Secure a proper place for the demonstration, one free of distractions for both you and the buyer. If the demonstration is at the buyer's office, make sure you have everything you need (power supply, lighting, and so on). Remember, it can even be an online presentation as Chapters 7 and 8 described.

- Check the equipment again to make sure it is in good working order prior to beginning the presentation. Have necessary backup parts and supplies (like paper or bulbs).

- Get the prospect involved in a meaningful way. In a group situation, plan which group members need to participate.

- Always relate product features to the buyer's unique needs.

- Make the demonstration an integral part of the overall presentation, not a separate, unrelated activity.

- Keep the demonstration simple, concise, and clear. Long, complicated demonstrations add to the possibility that the buyer will miss the point. Limit technical jargon to technically advanced buyers who you know will understand technical terms.

- Plan what you will do during any dead time—that is, time in which the machine is processing on its own. You can use these intervals to ask the buyer questions and have the buyer ask you questions.

- Find out whether the prospect has already seen a competitor's product demonstration. If so, strategically include a demonstration of features the buyer liked about the competitor's product. Also, plan to show how your product can meet the prospect's desires and do what the competitor's product will not do.

- Find out whether any buyers present at your demonstration have used your product before. Having them assist in the demonstration may be advantageous if they view your product favorably.

- Probe during and after the demonstration. Make sure buyers understand the features and see how the product can help them. Also, probe to see whether buyers are interested in securing the product.

Remember Murphy's law: What can go wrong will go wrong! And occasionally things do go wrong during a demonstration, like when Bill Gates, CEO of Microsoft, was giving the big launch demonstration of Windows 98 and his computer froze. If a demonstration "blows up" for any reason, your best strategy usually is to appeal to fate with a humorous tone of voice: Wow, have you ever seen anything get so messed up? I should run for Congress! Don't let technical glitches embarrass or frustrate you. Life is not perfect, and sometimes things just don't work out the way you plan them. If it will help, remember that prospects also are not perfect, and sometimes they mess things up as well. Maintaining a cool and level head will probably impress the prospect with your ability to deal with a difficult situation. It may even increase your chances of a sale because you are demonstrating your ability to handle stress (something that often occurs during the after-sale servicing of an account).

HANDOUTS

Handouts are written documents provided to help buyers remember what was said. A well-prepared set of handouts can be one of the best ways to increase buyer

Getting the buyer actively involved during the call is important.

retention of information, especially over longer periods. A common practice is to make a printed copy of the presentation visuals and give that to the buyers at the conclusion of the presentation.

Others would argue that your use of handouts should be more strategically focused. Thus handouts are not a last-minute thought, but rather are a tool that needs to be carefully planned while you are preparing your presentation. For example, you could draw a line on a piece of planning paper and on the left side list the things you will do and say during the presentation, while on the right side listing the items that should go into the handout. In that way the two will work together and be complementary.

What things can go into a handout? Complex charts and diagrams can be included. Because you want to keep your presentation visuals relatively simple (see the preceding hints), your handouts can supply more complete, detailed information. You may also want to include some company reports or literature. However, to avoid making the buyer wade through a lot of nonrelevant information, include only important sections. You may even want to highlight sections of the reports. Other items to include are Web addresses with a description of each site, case studies, magazine articles, and a copy of your presentation visuals themselves (with room to take notes if you're going to give the buyer your handout during the presentation). Whatever you choose, here are some tips:

- Don't forget the goal of your meeting. That should drive all your decisions about what to include in your handouts.
- Make sure the handouts look professional. Use graphics instead of text whenever possible.
- Don't cram too much information on a page. White space is fine. Try not to fill more than two-thirds of any page with information.
- Don't drown your prospect in information. Include only helpful information in your handouts.
- Handouts are even more important for foreign buyers, especially those who are nonnative English speakers. You might even consider giving them a copy of your handouts before your meeting so they can become more comfortable and familiar with concepts and phrases. Including a glossary, with definitions, will also be appreciated by foreign buyers.

WRITTEN PROPOSALS

In some industries written proposals are an important part of the selling process. Some proposals are simple adaptations of brochures developed by a corporate marketing department. But in industries that sell customized products or require competitive bidding (as many state and local governments do), a written proposal may be necessary for the buyer to organize and compare various offerings.

The RFP Process

A document issued by a prospective buyer asking for a proposal may be called a **request for proposal (RFP)**, request for quote (RFQ), or request for bid (RFB). For brevity's sake, we will refer to all of these as RFPs.

The RFP should contain the customer's specifications for the desired product, including delivery schedules. RFPs are used when the customer has a firm idea of the product needed. From the salesperson's perspective, being a part of the specifying process makes sense. Using the needs identification process, the salesperson can help the customer identify needs and specify product characteristics.

Writing Proposals

Proposals include an **executive summary**—a one- or two-page summary that provides the total cost minus the total savings, a brief description of the problem to be solved, and a brief description of the proposed solution. The summary should satisfy the concerns of an executive who is too busy or unwilling to read the entire proposal. The executive summary also piques the interest of all readers by allowing a quick glance at the benefits of the purchase.

The proposal also includes a description of the current situation in relation to the proposed solution and a budget (which details costs). Some firms have even developed computer programs to automatically generate sales proposals in response to a set of questions the salesperson answers about a particular customer.[6] This is especially helpful because sometimes buyers use RFPs to keep their current suppliers in check. In such a case, a seller might want to minimize the amount of time spent responding to an RFP. (A familiar saying in sales is "You can't cash an RFP.")

When writing proposals, remember to use your most polished writing skills. And skip buzzwords, focusing on actual results that the prospect can gain from going with your proposal.[7]

Presenting the Proposal

Prospects use proposals in many different ways. Proposals can be used to convince the home office that the local office needs the product, or proposals may be used to compare the product and terms of sale with those of competitors. As we mentioned earlier, the intended use will influence the design of the proposal; it will also influence how the salesperson presents the proposal.

When the proposal is going to be sent to the home office, it is wise to secure the support of the local decision maker. Although that person is not the ultimate decision maker, the decision may rest on how much effort that person puts into getting the proposal accepted. Buying centers often use proposals to compare competitive offerings, and the salesperson is asked to present the proposal to the buying committee.

There are several options if you are going to give an oral presentation of your proposal. First, you can give the buyers a copy of the complete proposal before your presentation. During the meeting you would spend about 5 to 10 minutes summarizing the proposal and then ask for questions. Second, if you choose to give the written proposal to the buyers during the oral presentation, you may want to distribute the proposal a section at a time to avoid having them read ahead instead of listening to your oral presentation.

VALUE ANALYSIS: QUANTIFYING THE SOLUTION

To recap what we've described throughout this book, salespeople are selling value.[8] As mentioned in Chapter 3, one of the trends in buying is more sophisticated analyses by buyers. This section explores methods available to help the buyer conduct these types of analyses.

Quantifying a solution is more important in some situations than in others. Some products or services (like replacement parts or repairs) pose little risk for the prospect. These products are so necessary for the continuation of the prospect's business that little quantifying of the solution is usually needed. Other products pose moderate risk (such as expanding the production capacity of a plant for an existing successful product) or high risk (like programs designed to reduce costs or increase sales; these present higher risk because it is hard to calculate the exact magnitude of the potential savings or sales). For moderate-risk and high-risk situations, quantifying the solution becomes increasingly important. Finally, certain products pose super-high risk (brand-new products or services, which are riskier because no one can calculate costs or revenues with certainty). Attempts at quantifying the solution are imperative in super-high-risk situations. In summary, the higher the risk to the prospect, the more attention the salesperson should pay to quantifying the solution.

Salespeople can strengthen a presentation by showing the prospect that the cost of the proposal is offset by added value; this process is often called **quantifying the solution** or **value analysis**. Some of the most common ways to quantify a solution are value propositions, cost–benefit analysis, return on investment, payback period, net present value, and opportunity cost. For retail buyers, the seller usually must prove turnover and profit margins. The key is to offer information that will help buyers evaluate your offering based on their metrics. Thus if a buyer is evaluating proposals on the basis of ROI, that's the metric you should focus on in your presentation.

Customer Value Proposition

A **customer value proposition**, also called a *value proposition*, is the way in which your product will meet the prospect's needs and how that is different from the offerings of competitors, especially the next-best alternative.[9] The value bundle contained in a solid customer value proposition includes the features and benefits (financial and emotional) tailored to the prospect, the proof that those benefits actually exist, and the value of the seller and the seller's firm as the solutions provider. Simply having a superior product or delivering on your promises is no longer sufficient. Rather, what distinguishes you is how you make your customers feel while using your product. The experience is what bonds your customers to you.

As you write your customer value proposition, remember that what it contains is tailored to the individual prospect, so it needs to address three key issues: What is important to this specific prospect? How does our solution create value for this specific prospect? And how can we demonstrate our capability?

Here are some weak examples of customer value proposition statements, none of which tell how the prospect is really going to benefit, or how the seller can demonstrate that she is able to accomplish the goals for the account:

- It's the most technologically advanced system on the market today.
- We reduce training time more than any of our competitors.
- Our service was rated number one by an independent service lab.

Now here are examples of good customer value proposition statements, which include the elements discussed:[10]

- According to your CFO, dispatching multiple service vans to a customer site has been costing an estimated $20,000 a year in extra fuel costs. When you add that to the cost of unproductive personnel time and missed revenue, the loss is $850,000 per year. When you implement our Call Tracker system you will be able to reduce repeat customer service calls by 20 percent, resulting in a monthly savings of $250,000. This will require an investment of $2 million, which will be returned in only 8 months. We implemented a similar solution at Acme Transfer, which began achieving a monthly savings of

$500,000 within 90 days of installation. And I have personally overseen 15 such installations and will be there to ensure that all parties are fully trained in use of the new system.

- In this era of heightened airport security concerns, Advanced Engineering, a leading manufacturer of state-of-the-art explosives detective devices, offers a unique solution. The complete "Senso-37 Detection System" for major airports like yours requires a $200,000 investment, fully installed. Our superior system has been shown to save lives, lower human security guard costs, and decrease passenger processing time. My analysis reveals that Orlando International Airport will decrease its general security guard expenses at the major passenger screening area by $80,000/year for the next four years, giving you a payback in just 2.5 years, and also giving you and your passengers peace of mind that ALL passengers are being screened with state-of-the-art technology. When you install the system you also get an added advantage: my commitment and supervision, as one of the top salespeople in my company, that your system will be installed at Orlando International Airport on time and as promised, and that your security staff will be trained efficiently and effectively.

How do you create a customer value proposition?[11] Try brainstorming with your sales team and look for statements that truly tell your customers how your solution is going to solve their problems. Every time you write one down, keep asking, "So what difference does that make?" For example, if you write "saves time," ask, "So what does it matter if it saves time?" By doing so, you will eventually be able to reach the core value that your customer will achieve by adopting your product. Another helpful way to create a customer value proposition is by talking to your customers. They know what value you can bring to a prospect because they have experienced it firsthand and are usually willing to offer suggestions.

Cost–Benefit Analysis

Perhaps the simplest method of quantifying a solution is to list the costs to the buyer and the savings the buyer can expect from the investment, often called a **simple cost–benefit analysis.** For this analysis to be realistic and meaningful, information needed to calculate savings must be supplied by the buyer. Exhibit 9.3 shows how one salesperson used a chart to compare the costs and benefits of purchasing a two-way radio system.

In many situations the salesperson does a **comparative cost–benefit analysis** by comparing the present situation's costs with the value of the proposed solution or the seller's product with a competitor's product. For example, a company with a premium-priced product may justify the higher price on the basis of offsetting costs in other areas. If productivity is enhanced, the increased productivity has economic value.

Return on Investment

The **return on investment (ROI)** is simply the net profits (or savings) expected from a given investment, expressed as a percentage of the investment:

$$ROI = Net\ profits\ (or\ savings) \div Investment$$

Thus if a new product costs $4,000 but saves the firm $5,000, the ROI is 125 percent ($5,000 ÷ $4,000 = 1.25). Many firms set a minimum ROI for any new products, services, or cost-saving programs. Salespeople need to discover the firm's minimum ROI or ROI expectations and then show that the proposal's ROI

Exhibit 9.3
Cost–Benefit Analysis
for a Mobile Radio

Monthly Cost		
Monthly equipment payment (five-year lease/purchase)*		$1,555.18
Monthly service agreement		339.00
Monthly broadcast fee		+ 533.60
Total monthly cost for entire fleet		$2,427.78
Monthly Savings		
Cost savings (per truck) by eliminating backtracking, unnecessary trips (based on $.36/mile × 20 miles × 22 days/month)		$158.40
Labor cost savings (per driver) by eliminating wasted time in backtracking, etc. ($8.00/hour × 25 minutes/day × 22 days/month)		+ 73.33
Total cost savings per vehicle		231.73
Times number of vehicles		× 32
Total monthly cost savings for entire fleet		$7,415.36

	Years 1–5	**Year 6+**
Monthly savings	$7,415.36	$7,415.36
Less: monthly cost	− 2,427.78	− 872.85
Monthly benefit	4,987.58	6,542.51
Times months per year	× 12	× 12
Annual benefit	$59,850.96	$78,510.12

*Payment reflects ongoing cost of service agreement and broadcast fees.

meets or exceeds those requirements. For an ROI analysis to be accurate, it is important for the seller to collect meaningful data about costs and savings that the buyer can expect.

Payback Period

The **payback period** is the length of time it takes for the investment cash outflow to be returned in the form of cash inflows or savings. To calculate the payback period, you simply add up estimated future cash inflows and divide them into the investment cost. If expressed in years, the formula is

$$\text{Payback period} = \text{Investment} \div \text{Savings (or profits) per year}$$

Of course the payback period could be expressed in days, weeks, months, or any other period.

As an example, suppose a new machine costs $865,000 but will save the firm $120,000 per year in labor costs. The payback period is 7.2 years ($865,000 ÷ $120,000 per year = 7.2 years).

Thus, for the buyer, the payback period indicates how quickly the investment money will come back to him or her and can be a good measure of personal risk. When a buyer makes a decision, his or her neck is "on the line," so to speak, until the investment money is at least recovered. Hence it's not surprising that buyers like to see short payback periods.

For large capital outlays, the prospect usually needs to see the return on investment, payback period, and/or net present value.

We have kept the discussion simple to help you understand the concept. In reality the calculation of the payback period would take into account many other factors, such as investment tax credits and depreciation.

Net Present Value

As you may have learned in finance courses, money left idle loses value over time (a dollar today is worth more than a dollar next week) because of inflation and the firm's cost of capital. Thus firms calculate the value of future cash inflows in today's dollars (this process is called *discounting the cash flows*). One tool to assess the validity of an opportunity is to calculate the **net present value** (NPV), which is simply the net value today of future cash inflows (discounted back to their present value today at the firm's cost of capital) minus the investment. The actual method of calculating NPV is beyond the scope of this book, but many computer programs and calculators can calculate NPV quickly and easily.

$$\text{Net present value} = \text{Future cash inflows discounted into today's dollars} - \text{Investment}$$

As an example of the preceding formula, let's assume that a $50 million investment will provide annual cash inflows over the next five years of $15 million per year. The cash inflows are discounted (at the firm's cost of capital), and the result is that they are actually worth $59 million in today's dollars. The NPV is thus $9 million ($59 million − $50 million).

As with ROI and payback period, many firms set a minimum NPV. In no case should the NPV be less than $0. Again, we have kept this discussion simple to help you understand the basic concept.

Opportunity Cost

The **opportunity cost** is the return a buyer would have earned from a different use of the same investment capital. Thus a buyer could spend $100 million to buy any of the following: a new computer system, a new production machine, or a controlling interest in another firm.

Successful salespeople identify other realistic investment opportunities and then help the prospect compare the returns of the various options. These comparisons can be made by using any of the techniques we have already discussed (cost–benefit analysis, ROI, payback period, NPV). For example, a salesperson might help the buyer determine the following information about the options identified:

	NPV	Payback Period
Buying a new telecommunications system	$1.6 million	3.6 years
Upgrading the current telecommunications system	0.4 million	4.0 years

Salespeople should never forget that prospects have a multitude of ways to invest their money.

Selling Value to Resellers

When resellers purchase a product for resale, they are primarily concerned with whether their customers will buy the product and how much they will make on each sale. For example, when an Xbox salesperson meets with Walmart to sell video games, he is armed with data showing how much profit is made every time Walmart sells a game and how fast the games sell. The Walmart buyer uses this information to compare the performance of Xbox video games with objectives and with other products sold in the same category, such as Sony's PlayStation.

PROFIT MARGIN Profit margin is the net profit the reseller makes, expressed as a percentage of sales. It is calculated, and thus influenced, by many factors. For example, if Linz Jewelers bought 100 rings for $1,000 each ($100,000), spent $45,000 in expenses (for advertising, salesperson commission, store rent, and other items), and sold them all at an average price of $3,000 ($300,000 in revenue), the profit would be $155,000, with a profit margin of 52 percent ($155,000 ÷ $300,000 = .52).

INVENTORY TURNOVER Inventory turnover is typically calculated by dividing the annual sales by the average retail price of the inventory on hand. Thus it measures how fast a product sells relative to how much inventory has to be carried—how efficiently a reseller manages its inventory. The reseller would like to have in the store only the amount needed for that day's sales because inventory represents an investment. Thus large retailers such as Cub Foods receive daily delivery of some products. If the reseller is able to reduce its inventory level, it can invest this savings in stores or warehouses or in the stock market.

For example, if Linz Jewelers usually kept eight rings in stock, inventory turnover would be calculated by dividing total sales in units (100 rings) by average inventory (8 rings). Thus inventory turnover would be 100 ÷ 8, or 12.5 times. The answer represents the number of times that Linz sold the average inventory level. Another way to calculate this is to divide total sales ($300,000 in the Linz example) by the average price of inventory (8 units at $3,000, or $24,000). The answer is the same: 12.5 times.

A reseller does not necessarily want to increase inventory turnover by reducing the amount of inventory carried. Several negative consequences can result. For example, sales may fall because stockouts occur more frequently and products are not available when customers want to buy them. Expenses can increase because the reseller has to order more frequently. Finally, the cost of goods sold may increase because the reseller pays higher shipping charges and does not get as big a quantity discount.

Sellers provide resellers with information to prove that inventory turnover can be improved by buying from them. They describe their **efficient consumer response (ECR), quick response (QR), automatic replenishment (AR),** and just-in-time (JIT) inventory management systems designed to reduce the reseller's average inventory and transportation expenses but still make sure products are available when end users want them. Chapter 3 described the use of these information systems in depth.

As an example, the September 11, 2001, tragedy created an outpouring of patriotic feelings among Americans. Within 24 hours there was a shortage of American flags, and there is only one major American flag manufacturer. The company had 80,000 flags in inventory on September 11. By the close of business September 12, both Target and Walmart had completely sold out of flags—over 150,000 each. When the stores opened September 13, Walmart had 80,000 more flags, whereas Target had none. How? Walmart's QR system was updated every five minutes, whereas Target didn't update its inventory system until the stores were closed in the evening. Walmart had an order placed with expedited shipping before the stores closed and before Target knew it was out of flags! Similar situations occurred in other product categories, such as flashlights, batteries, battery-powered radios, bottled water, guns, ammunition, and other products that frightened Americans wanted. As you can see, EDI and ECR systems can give resellers significant competitive advantage.

Electronic data interchange (EDI) is a computer-to-computer transmission of data from a reseller, such as Walmart, to vendors (such as American Flag Company) and back. Resellers and vendors that have ECR or QR relationships use EDI to transmit purchase orders and shipping information.

RETURN ON SPACE A key investment that resellers make is in space—retail store space and warehouse space. A measure that retailers use to assess the return on their space investment is sales per square foot or sales per shelf foot. In a grocery store or a department store, shelf or display space is a finite asset that is used to capacity. Products therefore must be evaluated on how well they use the space allocated to them. For example, if a retailer generates $200 per square foot in sales with Tommy Hilfiger merchandise and only $150 selling Ralph Lauren merchandise, it may increase the space allocated to Tommy Hilfiger and reduce the space allocated to Ralph Lauren.

DEALING WITH THE JITTERS

Let's face it. For many people giving a presentation is a frightening experience. Even seasoned salespeople can get the jitters when the presentation is for a very important client or when the prospect has been rude in an earlier meeting. It all comes down to fear: the fear of being embarrassed or failing, the fear of exposing our lack of knowledge in some area, the fear of losing our train of thought. The reasons don't even have to be valid. If you have the jitters, you need to help resolve them.

Here are some tips from the experts on how to reduce presentation jitters:

- Know your audience well.
- Know what you're talking about. Keep up to date.
- Prepare professional, helpful visuals. These not only help your audience understand the presentation, but also can help you remember important points.
- Be yourself. Don't try to present like someone else.
- Get a good night's sleep.
- For presentations to groups, feed off the energy and enthusiasm of several friendly, happy-looking people in your audience. (Note: That's what professors often do!)
- Recognize the effect of fear on your body and reduce the accompanying stress manifestations by stretching, taking deep breaths to relax breathing, and so on.
- Visualize your audience as your friends—people who are interested and eager to hear what you have to say.
- Psych yourself up for the presentation. Think of the successes you have had in your life (previous presentations that went well or other things you have done well).
- Realize that everyone gets nervous before a presentation at times. It is natural. In fact, it can help you keep from being cocky.
- *Practice, practice, practice!* And finally, practice.

SELLING YOURSELF

You're a member of another team project for a class. Your team is going to have to give a class presentation on the findings of your research. How can the ideas found in this chapter help?

For one thing, you now realize that giving a presentation is more than merely standing up and talking. Your team is going to have to find ways to keep the attention of the other students' (who, instead of listening to your presentation, are often busy sweating about their own presentations upcoming in just a few minutes), improve their understanding of the topic, help them remember what your team said (surely this is a one of your instructor's goals!), and also offer proof that your team knows what you're talking about.

Why not come up with a powerful story to make a point? Everyone likes a story, yet so many presentations are just long, seemingly never-ending PowerPoint slides with no way for listeners to connect emotionally and deeply with the material. Stories cause people to connect with ideas. And don't be afraid to use humor, but make sure it is appropriate and that your professor isn't going to wilt or blush when you use it. People relax when they can laugh, so encourage laughter with a well-timed joke or story. You'll all be more at ease.

For any visuals, take the time to make them really stand out. Follow the guidelines shown in the chapter. For example, it's not uncommon to watch a student presentation that includes just about every transition tool in PowerPoint—rather than impress, they often make the viewer cringe in embarrassment.

Don't be afraid to use video. In fact, with new video authoring and editing tools, video can be a real asset to your presentation arsenal. But don't spend more time making the video than you did in researching the topic. Having the proper balance is always important.

Finally, think about using handouts. Sure it costs a little bit to make a few handouts for your fellow students. But do you want them to really remember what you said, or do you want them to scramble to get all the information down on paper before you click to the next slide? Especially for complicated slides or information, a handout can be a real lifesaver. You'll impress your teacher also—a goal I assume you have.

So there you go. Don't forget to review the chapter ideas about how to reduce the jitters. The last one is especially critical, so we'll reiterate it here: PRACTICE!

SUMMARY

Strengthening communication with the buyer is important. It helps focus the buyer's attention, improves the buyer's understanding, helps the buyer remember what was said, and can create a sense of value.

Many methods of strengthening communication are available. These include such items as word pictures, stories, humor, charts, models, samples, gifts, catalogs, brochures, photos, ads, maps, illustrations, testimonials, and test results. Media available include portfolios, video, computers, and visual projectors.

A backbone of many sales presentations is the product demonstration. It allows the buyer to get hands-on experience with the product, something most other communication methods do not offer. Handouts and written proposals can also strengthen presentations.

It is often important to quantify a solution so the buyer can evaluate its costs in relation to the benefits he or she can derive from the proposal. Some of the more common methods of quantifying a solution include simple cost–benefit analysis, comparative cost–benefit analysis, return on investment, payback period, net present value, and calculation of opportunity cost, turnover, and profit margins.

Salespeople should be prepared to present a clear customer value proposition that offers real value to the customer.

All communication tools require skill and practice to be used effectively. Outstanding salespeople follow a number of guidelines to improve their use of visuals, demonstrate their products more effectively, and reduce their nervousness.

KEY TERMS

ETHICS PROBLEMS

1. Men tend to respond more to jokes involving sexual innuendo than women do. Assume this statement is true for a male buyer you are going to call on next Tuesday. You learn that he loves jokes with a sexual bent. Is there any reason you should avoid using a joke with a sexual theme when calling on him?

2. Is encouraging buyers to order a large quantity so they can get a better quantity discount always a good idea? Why or why not?

QUESTIONS AND PROBLEMS

1. In "From the Buyer's Seat 9.1" you learned about a buyer's visit to several supplier production sites. Assume you were the second supplier discussed in that case (one who did not get the business). Is there any way you could have demonstrated to the buyer that you were able to make the number of units required in the time frame allotted? What tools described in this chapter would you use to strengthen your presentation of those facts? Make any assumptions necessary to answer these questions.

2. Assume you plan a demonstration to prove some of the claims you have made for a new hybrid automobile (runs off gasoline as well as electricity). How would the demonstration differ for each of these three individuals: a person who is very concerned about the environment, an economy-minded person, and a safety-minded person?

3. How could you demonstrate the following products?
   a. A textbook with a lay-flat cover (it stays open easily without having to hold it open) to a college professor.
   b. The strength of a new metal stud to an industrial construction contractor.
   c. A highly corrosion-resistant paint for bridges and overpasses to a group of civil engineers.

4. Which communication tools would you use to provide solid proof to address the following concerns expressed by prospects?

   a. I don't think that type of product would do well in a store like ours.

   b. My poorly educated workers would never be able to figure out how to use that feature.

   c. Your competitor has a much more modern, state-of-the-art plant than you do.

   d. You look too young to know what the older customers who shop in my store are looking for.

5. This chapter generally accepts the use of PowerPoint presentations as a positive, useful tool for salespeople. When should PowerPoint not be used in selling? In other words, are there any times when the use of PowerPoint could actually be detrimental to communication effectiveness? Explain.

6. Which communication tools would you use to communicate the following facts?

   a. We have been in business for over 75 years.

   b. As a salesperson, I have been certified by the state to sell this product.

   c. Even though I've been selling this product for only two months, I do possess the necessary product knowledge.

   d. I know our last product was a flop, but this product was developed with extensive test marketing.

   e. Unlike our competitors, my company has never been sued by a customer.

7. Assume that you are selling a new video security system to a manufacturing plant in your town. The system will cost $275,000. It is estimated that the new system will reduce theft and pilferage. You expect losses due to theft to drop by $19,500 each year over the next 10 years. At the manufacturing plant's cost of capital, the discounted cash inflows have a value today of $350,000. Use this information to calculate the following:

   a. Return on investment.

   b. Payback period.

   c. Net present value.

8. Are there products for which resellers wouldn't really be that concerned about turnover?

9. Are there any retail situations for which return on space is not a big deal? How about situations where return on space is extremely important?

10. In "Building Partnerships 9.1" you read how the salesperson used entertainment to help generate interest and secure business.

    a. Tell how you would have handled the described situation.

    b. What are some possible ramifications of handling the situation as the seller did?

CASE PROBLEMS

case **9.1**

BrainScope (Part A)

An estimated 1.6 million to 3.8 million sports-related traumatic brain injuries (TBIs) occur each year. Yet all too often, when a person gets hurt in sports, the team doctor asks a few questions and, assuming there are no major concerns, sends the player right back into the game. However, studies show that if a player gets another concussion before the brain has healed, there is a much greater chance of long-term brain damage.

The problem is that there isn't an MRI machine at the sidelines. But that may change if the BrainScope company has its way. It will be introducing a new product that will gauge how serious a concussion is. The tool is small enough and inexpensive enough for all teams to have one on their sidelines.

The feedback from the BrainScope is a meter that shows if brain activity is anywhere near the danger zone. The system does this by picking up brain signals and comparing them to 15,000 scans in its database. The database was created based on scans performed at New York University's Brain Research Lab.

Some doctors claim the technology isn't cutting-edge. Originally developed in the 1930s, the technology uses qEEG (quantitative electroencephalograms). However, the developers of the BrainScope claim that their new device was developed with the advice of 30 leading brain experts.

According to the company's Web site, "BrainScope's novel application of advanced mathematics and miniaturized hardware is designed to bridge the limitations of traditional EEG tools (bulky, expensive, need expert data interpretation) to provide easy-to-use, noninvasive, timely, frontline tools that can assist with an initial assessment of brain function as well as provide adjunctive assessment across the brain care path."

The BrainScope could also be used at hospitals as emergency room testing devices to see if a patient has a real problem and thus needs to have more sophisticated testing done. The company is currently focusing its efforts on military settings. For example, the U.S. Army can deploy the device in combat situations. This would be very helpful to assess soldiers who were nearby when a roadside bomb exploded.

In August 2009 BrainScope's ZOOM-100DC brain electrical activity data collection system was cleared for marketing by the U.S. Food and Drug Administration.

Questions

1. Describe how you would use the communication tools described in this chapter to sell a BrainScope ZOOM-100DC to a local football or hockey team. Make any assumptions necessary.
2. Develop a short (five-minute) slide show that you can use to introduce BrainScope's ZOOM-100DC to potential buyers at a local trade show for sports teams.

Sources: www.brainscope.com; J. Langlois, ScD, MPH, W. Rutland-Brown, MPH, M. Wald, MLS, MPH, "The Epidemiology and Impact of Traumatic Brain Injury: A Brief Overview," *Journal of Head Trauma Rehabilitation* 21, no. 5 (2006), pp. 375–78; Peter Burrows, "Don't Put Me Back In, Coach," *BusinessWeek*, February 11, 2008, p. 61.

case 9.2

Rough Customers

I was working as an outside sales rep for a restaurant supply company in southern California. This was my first job out of college. I was one of the youngest employees in the company and the only female sales rep in my region. My largest client was an upscale seafood chain. I had an arranged face-to-face presentation with the general manager and one of the owners, who flew in from the Bay Area for this meeting. I was promoting a high-end plate that was known for not chipping or cracking. Supposedly, it was the most durable plate (and one of the most expensive) on the market.

The manufacturers taught us to demonstrate the plate's durability by dropping it squarely on the base of the plate. If the weight was evenly distributed on the well of the plate, you could drop it on a tile floor and it wouldn't chip or crack. This demo was part of my standard pitch, and the owner had seen it once before. So I set up a lovely table setting of a dozen multicolored plates in an unoccupied room of the restaurant. As soon as I started to drop the first plate, the owner said, "Sit down. I know the drill." He proceeded to toss all 12 plates against the nearest wall, which was covered with leather wallpaper.

Naturally, the plates bounced off the walls and shattered on the tile floor. At first he was trying to make a point. Then he started to amuse himself. By the end, both men were laughing hysterically. The general manager said, "That was fun, what else ya got?"

Questions

1. If you were the salesperson, how would you respond in this situation?
2. What could the seller have done to prevent getting into this situation?

Source: Sarah Gottry, used with permission.

ROLE PLAY CASE

Today you will present to the same person whose needs you identified in Chapter 8. (If you have not done role plays before, you will need to review the information about the various role play customers that can be found at the end of Chapter 3. If you did not do the role play at the end of Chapter 8, choose one of the three companies to sell to.) If you sold to Spear One, you'll do so again; the same goes for McLane Properties and Dart Paper Products. Begin by summarizing the buyer's needs and gaining agreement that these are all the needs. Then make your presentation.

As a buyer, do not offer any objections today. Just listen, add your thoughts on how the product might help if asked, and agree. Ask questions if something seems vague or confusing. Further, ask for proof. For example, if the salesperson says everyone loves it, ask to see a testimonial letter or something of that sort.

When you are the odd person out and observing, look for the following:

- Did the seller tie the features to the buyer's needs? Or did the seller present features that were not needed?
- Did the seller try to gain agreement that the buyer recognized and valued the benefit?
- Did the seller use visual aids as proof sources effectively?
- Did the seller use specific language versus general or ambiguous language (for example, "It's the best")?

Note: For background information about these role plays, please see page 27.

To the instructor: Additional information needed to complete the role play is available in the Instructor's Manual.

ADDITIONAL REFERENCES

Barber, Clifford S., and Brian C. Tietje. "A Research Agenda for Value Stream Mapping the Sales Process." *Journal of Personal Selling & Sales Management* 28, no. 2 (Spring 2008), pp. 155–65.

Bradford, Kevin D., and Barton A. Weitz. "Salespersons' Management of Conflict in Buyer–Seller Relationships." *Journal of Personal Selling & Sales Management* 29, no. 1 (Winter 2008–9), pp. 25–42.

Farber, Barry. "Sales Success: Now Presenting." *Entrepreneur* 35, no. 6 (June 2007), pp. 76–77.

Jalkala, Anne, and Risto T. Salminen. "Communicating Customer References on Industrial Companies' Web Sites." *Industrial Marketing Management* 38, no. 7 (October 2009), pp. 825–37.

Matthyssens, Paul, and Koen Vandenbempt. "Moving from Basic Offerings to Value-Added Solutions: Strategies, Barriers, and Alignment." *Industrial Marketing Management* 37, no. 3 (May 2008), pp. 316–28.

McGaulley, Michael. *Sales Presentations & Demonstrations.* ChamplainHouseMedia, 2010.

Mills, Harry. *Power Points! How to Design and Deliver Presentations That Sizzle and Sell.* AMACOM/American Management Association, 2007.

Theriault, Michel. *Win More Business—Write Better Proposals.* WoodStone Press, 2010.

Williams, Robin. *The Non-Designer's Presentation Book.* Peachpit Press, 2009.

chapter 11

OBTAINING COMMITMENT

SOME QUESTIONS ANSWERED IN THIS CHAPTER ARE

- How much emphasis should be placed on closing the sale?
- Why is obtaining commitment important?
- When is the best time to obtain commitment?
- Which techniques of obtaining commitment are appropriate for developing partnerships?
- How should I prepare to be present?
- What should a salesperson do when the prospect says yes? When the prospect says no?
- What common difficulties in obtaining commitment, and how can these issues be overcome?

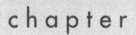

chapter **11**

OBTAINING COMMITMENT

SOME QUESTIONS ANSWERED IN THIS CHAPTER ARE

- How much emphasis should be placed on closing the sale?
- Why is obtaining commitment important?
- When is the best time to obtain commitment?
- Which methods of securing commitment are appropriate for developing partnerships?
- How should pricing be presented?
- What should a salesperson do when the prospect says yes? When the prospect says no?
- What causes difficulties in obtaining commitment, and how can these issues be overcome?

PROFILE

PROFILE All sports fans have experienced a special moment when they look around their team's stadium and see 70,000 fellow supporters passionately cheering on their team. The stadium noise is electrifying. It gives you goose bumps down your arms and raises the hair on the back of your neck. What few people begin to consider is how in the world professional sports teams are able to sell every ticket in the building to create moments like this. Welcome to the wonderful world of closing sales!

I got a taste of inside sales on the first day of my internship. After a brief training session, I was given a telephone and hundreds of people to call. My job was simple: Do whatever it took to sell as many tickets as possible. I found myself selling for boxers I'd never heard of, sports I'd never seen, and venues I'd never been to. I sold boxing, lacrosse, rugby, tennis, hockey, soccer—you name it, I tried to sell it.

After arriving in the City of Angels, my competitive, determined nature led me to strong results within a short period of time. After one month as an intern responsible for selling, hard work and lucky timing enabled me to be promoted to an account executive for the Los Angeles Kings Hockey Club. After another 13 months of more hard work and even luckier timing, I was promoted to the role of manager of ticket sales and service for the Kings.

After only 18 months of hard work, an opportunity knocked 300 miles north of Los Angeles. The five-time Super Bowl Champion San Francisco 49ers were starting a sales and service department, and I quickly jumped at the opportunity to join the National Football League. New town, new city, new sport, but the same goal in mind: Sell tickets.

Working in inside sales is very simple. Your job performance is easily quantifiable, and your peers know what kind of results you're having. Whiteboards are plastered around every office with sales representatives' names and productivity.

Everyone I interview always asks what it takes to be successful in inside sales, and the answer is quite simple: Hard work and going the extra mile. How many times have I been told "No!" and hung up on? Tens of thousands. How you respond will determine your success. Will you take the rejection personally and be fearful for the next 80 calls you need to make in a day? Make no mistake about it—burnout is extremely high in inside sales, but if you can plug away and convert the rejection into a positive learning experience for your calls and sales skills, you will be successful.

Since you'll be working with dozens of other employees in an identical position, you can make yourself stand out with hard work, organization, creativity, and humility. Be prepared to be shot down countless times, but stand back up and be ready to accomplish your goals every single time you pitch a product.

As a manager, my role as a salesperson has not diminished. Sales is a necessary tool for all employees in a sports organization, and everyone is counted on to chip in. While the athletes on the field may be the reason fans show up, the next time you see 70,000 screaming fans in your stadium, remember that it may have taken 170,000 rejections to fill the seats and ignite those goose bumps.

Visit us on the Web at www.49ers.com.

SECURING COMMITMENT TODAY

Asking for the buyer's business, often called **closing,** has always received a great deal of emphasis in sales training. Hundreds of books, DVDs, CDs, and seminar speakers have touted the importance of closing—just Google "close sales" at Amazon, and nearly 300 book titles will appear. Almost all are devoted to a method or methods that will make the decision maker say yes.

Look a little closer at those titles, however, and you'll notice that most of them are old. Some of the books may even be older than your parents! Today's sales professionals recognize that securing a sale is the reason for their existence, but getting that sale should be due to the value created, not the technique used.

Rob Keeney, training director for Frosty Acres Brands, says this about closing:

> I don't see good closers as being "pushy." Assertive, yes. Direct, yes. "Pushy" implies the customer being somehow compelled to do something they really don't want to do. By contrast, a good closer helps a customer make the decision they really want or need to make. And sooner rather than later.

Charles Cohon, president of Prime Devices and an influential speaker in the manufacturer's representation industry, says this about closing:

> Closing an order is not the end of a process, it is the beginning. Concentrate just on closing that order, and it will be the last order you get from that customer. Concentrate instead on developing a relationship with that customer that leads naturally to an order and you will earn not only that order, but also that customer's orders for many years to come.

Others also believe the traditional emphasis on getting the sale no matter what damages trust, insults the buyer's intelligence, and raises the possibility of losing commitment altogether. Customers make a buying decision, rather than the salesperson closing the sale. Buyers want to buy, not to be sold. "From the Buyer's Seat 11.1" illustrates that buyers want transparency from their salespeople and appreciate hard work that pays off with a good exchange for both sides.

Solid research provides strong evidence that questions the value of closing techniques. The research, based on more than 35,000 sales calls over 12 years, has found that in a major sale, reliance on closing techniques actually reduces the chances of making a sale.[1] Further, salespeople who were specifically trained in closing actually closed fewer sales. For very low-priced products (as in door-to-door magazine sales), however, closing techniques may increase the chances of a sale.

So why even cover closing at all? Because there are nonmanipulative and trustworthy ways to gain commitment and because obtaining commitment is critical for the success of salespeople and their firms. Without a buyer's commitment, no sale takes place. Also, buyers rarely volunteer to make a purchase even when that decision is obviously the right thing to do. This chapter covers the topic of obtaining commitment in a manner that is consistent with the theme of the book: developing and building long-term partnerships.

PART OF THE PROCESS

The process of obtaining commitment occurs throughout the natural, logical progression of any sales call. Recall from Chapter 3 that creeping commitment occurs when a customer becomes committed to a particular course of action throughout the buying process. Salespeople actually gain commitment repeatedly: when asking for an appointment, when checking to see whether the customer's entire needs have been identified, and when asking whether the prospect would like to see a

From the BUYER'S SEAT

DID I MISS THE CLOSE?

By Steve Schlesinger, Schlesinger and Associates

Just last week we had a significant purchase to make, not just because it was an expensive or large purchase but because it represented a major change in strategy. Our strategy for information technology has been to build our own. In many ways we were ahead of the market, and off-the-shelf programs did not fit our needs. But last year we needed to make some changes to one of our programs; so we thought, let's explore what's out there off-the-shelf that can be modified. We found a product that we integrated and that worked great with our proprietary software.

When it came time to do the same with our customer management software, our first thought was that it was too expensive. Two years ago we had looked at software for customer management, and it just didn't make sense. But given the success we had with the other program, we decided to take another look.

I called a friend of mine at Salesforce.com, who runs their large account business. We're about a $70 million per year company, so we don't really fit his sales team, but he was able to help us in the process. In addition to the cost, making sure their software integrated well with our custom software and work process was a big concern for us. My friend was able to help assemble a Salesforce team that could address the integration issue.

This time we learned we could accommodate what we needed. The development meeting was excellent, the integration piece was developed, and then they came back with a good cost–benefit analysis. But then the decision got tougher.

With offices across the United States and United Kingdom, we realized we needed everyone who works with clients to have access to the software. This decision increased our license from 10 users to 70 or 80. That raised the costs substantially, and suddenly that cost–benefit analysis wasn't looking so good.

I had forgotten this because I don't deal with salespeople every day. But they had a real sense of urgency to get this done.

Their year ends January 31, so they were very motivated to get the deal done. This deadline spurred more aggressive pricing and help on the integration side, and they really took care of all our needs. And on January 29 we signed the deal.

I never thought about the need to get a deal done from the salesperson's perspective. I'd thought about that when buying a car, but I hadn't really thought about it in this instance. For one thing, it wasn't a hard sell. The beauty is that they were open and honest. They were transparent—they needed to get it done and told us, and they gave me the leeway in the terms that I needed. They were very professional. Would I have gotten different or higher pricing if I had waited past their deadline? I don't know.

But I do know that it is rare to feel like you won in a negotiation. You always wonder if you could have done better. In this case, I needed these guys to win, too. I believe I got a good deal, but since this isn't a one-time purchase and I need these guys to support my integration, I want this relationship to feel good for both sides. So I was happy that we were able to close the deal in their time frame.

Source: Steve Schlesinger, Schlesinger and Associates.

demonstration or receive a proposal. Commitment, of course, is more than just securing an order. As Exhibit 11.1 illustrates, salespeople will attempt to obtain a commitment that is consistent with the objectives of the particular sales call.

Obtaining commitment is also important in moving the account through the relationship process. Once a sale is made, salespeople begin to plan for the next sale or for the next level of commitment that indicates a deepening relationship. At the same time, commitment is a two-way street. Salespeople also make commitments to buyers when the sale is made.

Exhibit 11.1
Examples of
Commitments
Salespeople May
Attempt to Obtain

Examples of Presale Commitments

- To have the prospect agree to come to the Atlanta branch office sometime during the next two weeks for a hands-on demonstration of the copier.
- To set up another appointment for one week from now, at which time the buyer will allow me to do a complete survey of her printing needs.
- To inform the doctor of the revolutionary anticlotting mechanism that has been incorporated into our new drug and have her agree to read the pamphlet I will leave.
- To have the buyer agree to pass my information along to the buying committee with his endorsement of my proposal.
- To have the prospect agree to call several references that I will provide to develop further confidence and trust in my office-cleaning business.
- To have the prospect agree on the first point (of our four-point program) and schedule another meeting in two days to discuss the second point.
- To have the prospect initiate the necessary paperwork to allow us to be considered as a future vendor.

Examples of Commitments That Consummate the Sale

- To have the prospect sign an order for 100 pairs of Levi's jeans.
- To schedule a co-op newspaper advertising program to be implemented in the next month.
- To have the prospect agree to use our brand of computer paper for a trial period of one month.
- To have the retailer agree to allow us space for an end-of-aisle display for the summer presentation of Raid insect repellent.

THE IMPORTANCE OF SECURING COMMITMENT

Overall, gaining commitment tells the salesperson what to do next and defines the status of the client. For example, gaining a needs identification appointment may mean that you have a "suspect"; at the end of that call, gaining commitment for a demonstration means you have a prospect. Gain an order and you gain a customer. Without gaining commitment, the salesperson may waste time doing the wrong things.

Salespeople need to become proficient in obtaining commitment for several other good reasons. First, if they fail to obtain commitment, it will take longer (more sales calls) to obtain a sale, if a sale occurs at all. Taking more time with one sale means fewer sales overall because you lose time for prospecting and other important activities. Second, assuming the product truly satisfies the prospect's needs, the sooner the prospect buys, the sooner she or he can realize the benefits of the product or service. Third, the company's future success depends on goodwill and earning a profit. Finally, securing commitment results in financial rewards for the salesperson; in addition, meeting needs is also intrinsically rewarding for the seller.

One thing to remember is that if you have done your job well and you have a product that the buyer truly needs, then you deserve the sale. The buyer is not doing you a favor by buying, and he or she expects you to ask for the sale if you've done your work professionally. Not only is gaining commitment important for

thinking it through

Think for a moment about a major purchase that you or a family member made, such as a new TV or a car. During the shopping process, what were some of the worst closes you experienced? What really angers you when you try to shop for major purchases? What made the difference between those experiences and the ones you found satisfying?

you and your company, it is the professional thing to do. What is not professional is a high-pressure close; typically, high-pressure closing is necessary (and inappropriate) when the salesperson has not done a good job throughout the entire process.[2]

Before we get into how to obtain commitment, some time should be spent on the importance of terms and conditions of the sale and how these influence the total cost. Sometimes terms are an important need and may be presented early in the call. But we present the credit terms here because often a buyer decides what to buy and then explores the financial terms that are available.

FINANCIAL TERMS AND CONDITIONS

Most salespeople try to hold off on presenting price until the end. Yet price is often the first question asked. The final price is really a function of the terms and conditions of the sale and depends on several factors.

Cash flow is an issue for many buyers and can stop a sale. For example, Ram Ramamurthy of RTI needed to buy a $55,000 scanner to complete a job for a customer. But the cash to buy the scanner wouldn't be available until after the customer paid for the job, which was 30 days after the job was completed and 90 days after the scanner was purchased. So Ian Wright, the salesperson selling the scanner, worked out a lease agreement that reduced Ram's cash requirements to only $5,000 up front and $1,500 per month until the job was completed. Ram then paid off the balance when his client paid him.[3]

Factors that affect price are the use of quantity and other discounts, as well as credit and shipping terms. Figuring out the final actual price can be difficult, especially in situations with many options and packages rather than standardized products. Some companies have turned to special software to manage pricing and product complexities, as discussed in "Sales Technology 11.1."

DISCOUNTS

Discounts are given for many reasons and may be based on the type of customer (such as wholesaler or retailer, senior citizen or younger adult), quantity purchased, or some other factor. The most common type of discount is the quantity discount.

Quantity discounts encourage large purchases by passing along savings resulting from reduced processing costs. Businesses offer two types of quantity discounts: (1) the single-order discount and (2) a cumulative discount. An office equipment company offering a 10 percent discount on a single order for five or more facsimile machines is an example of a single-order discount. When offering a **cumulative discount,** that same company might offer the 10 percent discount on all purchases over a one-year period, provided the customer purchases more than five fax machines. The customer may sign an agreement at the beginning of the year promising to buy five or more machines, in which case the customer will be billed for each order at the discounted price (10 percent off). If the customer fails to purchase five fax machines, a single bill will be sent at the end of the year for the amount of the discount (10 percent of the single-unit price times the number of fax machines actually purchased). Another method is to bill the customer at the full price and then rebate the discount at the end of the year, based on the actual number of fax machines purchased.

CREDIT TERMS

Most U.S. sales are made on a credit basis, with **cash discounts** allowed for early payment. These cash discounts are the last discount taken, meaning that if a

SALES Technology

11.1

NEEDED: KNOWLEDGE TO CLOSE THE DEAL

Knowledge is key to a salesperson's success. One pair of experienced sales consultants, Matt Moore and Keith De La Rue from Australia, say there is a "golden triangle" of knowledge that salespeople have to master: (1) knowledge of sales skills and processes, (2) knowledge of the customer, and (3) knowledge of the offering. Luckily for today's salesperson, there is technology to help manage each leg of the golden triangle.

For example, product configurors help salespeople manage knowledge of offerings. Anritsu, a company that makes highly technical communication devices, uses Configure One's Concept software to allow customers to configure their own products online. Salespeople can use the software, too, and the software frees salespeople to focus on selling, not on product configuration. Katherine van Diepen, Anritsu's marketing communications manager, estimates that this software saves salespeople about 45 minutes per configuration, or the equivalent of adding one sales call per day per salesperson. Increased accuracy in configuration also means more satisfied customers.

CRM systems help manage customer knowledge and knowledge of the process. Typically a CRM system will be designed around a sales process, so simply following the prompts of the system can help keep salespeople on track. But what if the situation calls for specialized

customer knowledge—say, knowledge about a particular type of customer or industry?

That's where company-based wikis come in. Just like Wikipedia, companies create Web sites where employees can post information. More sophisticated collaboration systems, like CubeTree, enable salespeople anywhere on the globe to share ideas and information. For example, the Garland Group uses it because its staff often works onsite with customers. Making the most of the company's best employees meant creating a technology solution that enabled fast and easy collaboration. That's where CubeTree comes in. Resembling a Facebook for business, the application is tailored to Garland's needs and is therefore a much more powerful tool.

Knowledge management solutions help salespeople make the most of the knowledge that is available in their organizations without having to learn it all. That's how these technology solutions help close the deal.

Sources: Matt Moore and Keith De La Rue, "Closing the Deal with the Help of Knowledge," *Knowledge Management Review* 11, no. 3 (July/August 2008), pp. 14–19; "Anritsu Case Study," http://www.configureone.com/pdf/ConfigureOnecasestudy-Anritsu.pdf, accessed March 3, 2010; "Enabling the Garland Group's Geographically Distributed Teams to Stay Continuously Connected," case study, http://www.cubetree.com/garland_group_cubetree_case_study.pdf, accessed March 3, 2010.

quantity discount is also offered, the cash discount is calculated after the quantity discount is taken off. A common discount is 2/10, n/30, which means that the buyer can deduct 2 percent from the bill if it is paid within 10 days from the date of invoice. Otherwise the full amount must be paid in 30 days. Another common discount is 2/10, EOM, which means that the 10-day period begins at the end of the month. For example, if the customer receives $1,000 worth of supplies on February 15 with terms of 2/10, EOM and pays the bill on March 5, the customer would pay $980 (that is, $1,000 at 2% = $20 discount for paying cash; $1,000 − $20 = $980). But if the customer pays on March 11, the bill would be the full $1,000.

Credit terms can be very important in capital equipment sales. Capital purchases have long lives and cost more than a buyer can afford to pay all at once. For example, the HVAC (heating, ventilation, and air conditioning) industry relies heavily on financing to sell heating and cooling systems. Johnson Controls offered a six months with no interest plan, called "same as cash." "Most consumers need some type of bridge financing to handle an unplanned $8,000 HVAC expense. That is why we feel we've seen so much business in the same-as-cash programs."[4] Easy credit terms can help salespeople close sales, but sales aren't complete until the buyer takes delivery. One home builder noticed that buyers were willing to put contracts on houses that hadn't been built yet in order to fix their credit during the nine months it took to complete the homes. So many "buyers" were unable to actually get credit and canceled sales that he quit taking orders on prebuilt homes.[5]

SHIPPING COSTS

The terms and conditions of sale include shipping costs. Recall from Chapter 2 that the term *free on board (FOB)* is used to determine the point at which the buyer assumes responsibility for both the goods and the costs of shipping them. Thus FOB destination means the buyer will take responsibility for the goods once they reach the buyer's location, and the seller will pay the freight.

Suppose Hormel quotes an FOB origin price. It will load the truck at its Chicago plant, but the buyer will pay for shipping. If Hormel sold a truckload of pepperoni to Pizza Hut under terms of FOB destination, Hormel would pay for shipping and would have the pepperoni delivered to Pizza Hut's warehouse, where warehouse personnel would unload the truck.

Another form of FOB is *FOB installed,* meaning that title and responsibility do not transfer until the equipment is installed and operating properly. In some instances FOB installed can also mean that operator training must be provided before title transfers. These are important terms because there are significant costs associated with the technical installation and operator training for many pieces of sophisticated equipment. Buyers want to know the total price and what it includes.

If Hormel quotes a price for pepperoni that's FOB origin, then Pizza Hut pays for shipping. If the price is FOB destination, then Hormel pays for shipping.

The terms and conditions of a sale, including but not limited to price, can often play as important a role as the product itself in determining what is purchased. Creative salespeople understand the terms and conditions they have to work with so they can meet the needs of their buyers while also meeting the profit objectives of their own companies.

PRESENTING PRICE

Price is often discussed at the end of the presentation simply because the salesperson may not know what that price will be until the final solution is agreed on. Because price is so important to the buyer, it is worth considering how price should be presented.

Most firms set prices after careful study of competitors' offerings, the value delivered by the product or service, and the cost of providing the product or service. For these reasons the price should represent a reasonable and fair picture of the product's or service's value. Therefore, never apologize for a price or present the price apologetically; rather, present it with confidence.

Bruce Culbert, now chief service officer with the Pedowitz Group, says that salespeople sometimes negotiate against themselves. When he was at IBM,

I had an account manager who was under pressure to make quota for the quarter. In presenting a proposal to a prospective customer, the salesperson did as was agreed and sent the proposal via e-mail a full two weeks prior to quarter end because the client said they would be able to make a decision by the end of the month. If this deal closed, the salesperson would hit quota. Several days went by, and there was no response from the prospect. A follow-up e-mail and phone went unanswered. In a panic the salesperson began to submit revised proposals each time, lowering the price in an attempt to get the prospect to respond positively. A week went by with no response. During the week two revised proposals had been submitted, each time lowering the price almost 10 percent. On the Tuesday before the quarter closed the client responded favorably to the original proposal with their apologies that they had not responded sooner but they were on vacation the past week and were just now catching up on e-mail. Needless to say the salesperson was ecstatic to learn of the good fortune just prior to quarter close. About 10 minutes later the salesperson received an additional e-mail from the client informing them to ignore the previous note and that they would like to accept proposal revision 2, which was almost 20 percent less than the original proposal.[6]

As Bruce says, here is a salesperson who panicked and lost the company 20 percent.

In addition to presenting the price with confidence, remember that price is not the focus of your presentation. The real issue is satisfying the needs of the buyer, of which budget is only one. True, a budget limitation can halt progress toward a sale. The real issue, though, is the total cost of ownership, which means the buyer should also factor in the value of the benefits delivered.

WHEN TO ATTEMPT TO OBTAIN COMMITMENT

Novice salespeople frequently ask themselves these questions: Is there a right time to obtain commitment? How will customers let me know they are ready to buy? Should I make more than one attempt? What should I do if my first attempt fails?

The right time to attempt to gain commitment is when the buyer appears ready, as evidenced by buying signals. Some salespeople say that one psychological moment in each sales presentation affords the best opportunity to obtain commitment, and if this opportunity is bypassed, securing commitment will be difficult or impossible. This belief is not true, however. Seldom does one psychological moment govern the complete success or failure of a sales presentation.

Most buyers will commit themselves only when they clearly understand the benefits and costs of such a decision. At times this point occurs early in the call. A commitment to purchase a large system, however, usually will not occur until a complete presentation and several calls have been made and all questions have been answered.

Buying signals, or indications that the buyer is ready to buy, can be evidenced both in the buyer's comments and nonverbally. Buying signals are also called **closing cues.** "Building Partnerships 11.1" presents several salespeople's experience in recognizing buying signals.

BUYER COMMENTS

A customer's comments often are the best indication that he or she is considering commitment. A prospect will seldom say, "All right, I'm ready to endorse this product to our buying committee." Questions about the product or terms of sale and comments in the form of requirements or benefit statements signal readiness to buy, as do responses to trial closes.

Buyer Questions

Here are some examples of questions that signal readiness to buy:

If I agree to go with this cooperative advertising program, do you have any ads already developed that I could use?

BUILDING Partnerships

WAIT! I'M NOT DONE YET!

Alex Homer, now with Tom James, a custom clothier, sold life insurance while he was in college. As he tells the story, "One day, I met with a prospect to discuss his life insurance. I was fairly new to the business and had just finished training. I was excited with the cache of product knowledge I had accumulated, and I wanted every person I sat down with to know it all. I would explain everything in thorough detail, and most often, it would prove favorable to a potential sale. On this particular appointment, it was very clear that the prospect was considering doing business with me, and rather than ask him to do business, I kept discussing certain features about the policy. The more details I gave him, the more complex his decision-making process became, and I received the ill-fated 'I'll think it over and call you back'."

Alex had talked himself out of the sale by talking through the buyer's closing cues. Despite having a prospect who kept indicating he was ready to buy, Alex kept right on talking.

David Appel, another insurance salesperson, experienced just the opposite situation. Instead of talking his way out of a sale over a two-year period, he couldn't seem to get the buyer to make a decision—any decision. Finally he sent a letter that said, "Dear Bill and Sue, after being in the insurance business for 16 years, I don't know what you want the ending to be—to have life insurance or to not have life insurance. Please give me a call Tuesday so we can get this thing squared away, one way or the other. And if I don't hear from you, I'll call you." David got the call and the sale. He's since used that approach with other procrastinating prospects, and it always works—but for David, what that means is that he gets a decision. Sometimes the decision is "no," but then he can move on.

Sources: Alex Homer, personal correspondence, used with permission; Julie Britt, "Dealing with Procrastinators," *Advisor Today* (December 2008), p. 60.

Do you have any facilities for training our employees in the use of the product?

How soon would you be able to deliver the equipment?

Not all questions signal a readiness to buy. But if the question concerns implementing the purchase and points toward when, not if, the purchase is implemented, the prospect may be getting ready to buy.

Requirements

Requirements are conditions that have to be satisfied before a purchase can take place. For example:

We need a cash discount for a supply order like this.

We need to get this in weekly shipments.

Requirements that are stated near the end of the presentation are need statements that reflect a readiness to buy when they relate to how the purchase will be consummated. As the examples illustrate, requirements relating to financial terms or shipping indicate that the decision to buy the product has been made and now it is time to work out the details.

Benefit Statements

Sometimes prospects offer their own benefit statements, such as these:

Oh, I like the way this equipment is serviced—it will make it much easier on my staff.

Good, that color will match our office decor.

Such positive statements reflect strong feelings in support of the purchase—a sign that the buyer is ready.

Responses to Trial Closes

Salespeople can solicit such comments by continually taking the pulse of the situation with **trial closes,** which are questions regarding the prospect's readiness to buy (first discussed in Chapter 8). Throughout the presentation, the salesperson should be asking questions:

How does this sound to you so far?

Is there anything else you would like to know at this point?

How does this compare with what you have seen of competing products?

Such questions are an important element of any sales process because trial closes serve several purposes, including identifying the customer's proximity to making the decision, gaining agreement on minor points, and creating a true dialogue in which the ultimate close is a natural conclusion. Note that these are more general questions than simply gaining agreement on benefits (discussed in Chapter 8), say as part of a FEBA.

When a seller asks a trial close question, the buyer responds, thus creating a dialogue. Issues can be raised as objections or questions by the buyer, which tell the seller what to cover. Then because the salesperson has been asking closing questions all along, the final close is just a natural part of the ongoing dialogue, as it should be.

NONVERBAL CUES

As in every phase of the presentation, nonverbal cues serve as important indicators of the customer's state of mind, as discussed in Chapter 4. While attempting to gain commitment, the salesperson should use the buyer's nonverbal signals to better identify areas of concern and see whether the buyer is ready to commit. Facial expressions most often indicate how ready the buyer is to make a commitment. Positive signals include eyes that are open and relaxed, face and mouth not covered with hands, a natural smile, and a relaxed forehead. The reverses of these signals indicate that the buyer is not yet ready to commit to the proposal.

Customers' actions also often indicate readiness to buy or make a commitment. For example, the prospective buyer of a fax machine may get a document and operate the machine or place the machine on the table where it will be used. The industrial buyer may refer to a catalog to compare specifications with competing products. A doctor, when told of a new drug, may pick up the pamphlet and begin carefully reading the indications and contraindications. A retailer considering whether to allow an end-of-aisle display may move to the end of an aisle and scan the layout. Any such actions may be signals for obtaining commitment; they should be viewed in the context of all available verbal and nonverbal cues.

HOW TO SUCCESSFULLY OBTAIN COMMITMENT

To obtain commitment in a nonmanipulative manner, salespeople need to follow several principles, including maintaining a positive attitude, letting the customer set the pace, being assertive instead of aggressive, and selling the right product in the right amounts.

Do the two buyers on the right look like they are ready to commit to a purchase?

MAINTAIN A POSITIVE ATTITUDE

Confidence is contagious. Customers like to deal with salespeople who have confidence in themselves, their products, and their companies. On the other hand, unnecessary fear can be a self-fulfilling prophecy. The student who fears essay exams usually does poorly; golfers who believe they will miss short putts usually do. So it is with salespeople: If they fear customers will not accept their proposals, the chances are good they will be right.

One manager related the example of a salesperson selling laundry detergent who unsuccessfully tried to convince a large discount chain to adopt a new liquid version of the product. When the rep's sales manager stopped by the account later in the week to follow up on a recent stockout problem, the buyer related his reasons for refusing the Liquid Tide: "Listen, I know you guys are sharp. You probably wouldn't come out with a new product unless you had tons of data to back up your decision. But honestly, the sales rep who calls on me is always so uptight and apprehensive that I was afraid to adopt the new product! Don't you guys teach them about having confidence?"

LET THE CUSTOMER SET THE PACE

Attempts to gain commitment must be geared to fit the varying reactions, needs, and personalities of each buyer. Thus the sales representative needs to practice adaptive selling. (See Chapter 5 for a complete discussion of adaptive selling.)

Some buyers who react slowly may need plenty of time to assimilate the material presented. They may ask the same question several times or show they do not understand the importance of certain product features. In these circumstances the salesperson must deliver the presentation more slowly and may have to repeat certain parts. Trying to rush buyers is unwise when they show they are not yet ready to commit.

As we discussed earlier in the book, buyers' decision-making styles vary greatly. Japanese and Chinese buyers tend to move more slowly and cautiously when evaluating a proposition. In contrast, buyers working for *Fortune* 500 firms located in the largest U.S. cities often tend to move much more quickly. The successful salesperson recognizes such potential differences and acts accordingly.

BE ASSERTIVE, NOT AGGRESSIVE

Marvin Jolson has identified three types of salespeople: aggressive, submissive, and assertive.[7] Exhibit 11.2 summarizes the differences among assertive, aggressive, and submissive salespeople's handling of the sales interview. **Aggressive** salespeople control the sales interaction but often fail to gain commitment because they prejudge the customer's needs and fail to probe for information. Too busy talking to do much listening, they tend to push the buyer too soon, too often, and too vigorously. They might say, "I can't understand why you are hesitant," but they do not probe for reasons for the hesitancy.

Submissive salespeople often excel as socializers. With customers they spend a lot of time talking about families, restaurants, and movies. They establish rapport quite effectively. They accept the customers' statements of needs and problems but do not probe to uncover any latent needs or opportunities. Submissive salespeople rarely try to obtain commitment, perhaps because they may fear rejection too much.

Assertive salespeople, the third type, are self-confident and positive. They maintain the proper perspective by being responsive to customer needs. Rather than aggressively creating new "needs" in customers through persuasion, they look for buyers who truly need their products and then use questions to acquire information. Their presentations emphasize an exchange of information rather than a one-way presentation.

Exhibit 11.2
How Aggressive, Submissive, and Assertive Salespeople Handle Sales Activities

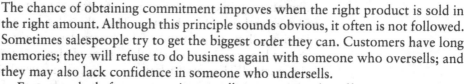

| | Selling Style | | |
Selling Activity	Aggressive	Submissive	Assertive
Defining customer needs	Believe they are the best judge of customer's needs.	Accept customer's definition of needs.	Probe for need-related information that customer may not have volunteered.
Controlling the presentation	Minimize participation by customer.	Permit customer to control presentation.	Encourage two-way communication and customer participation.
Closing the sale	Overwhelm customer; respond to objections without understanding.	Assume customers will buy when ready.	Respond to objections, leading to somewhat automatic close.

SELL THE RIGHT ITEM IN THE RIGHT AMOUNTS

The chance of obtaining commitment improves when the right product is sold in the right amount. Although this principle sounds obvious, it often is not followed. Sometimes salespeople try to get the biggest order they can. Customers have long memories; they will refuse to do business again with someone who oversells; and they may also lack confidence in someone who undersells.

For example, before attempting to sell two copiers, the office equipment sales representative must be sure that these two copiers, instead of only one copier or perhaps three, best fit the needs of the buyer's office. The chemical company sales representative selling to an industrial firm must know that one tank car of a chemical is more likely to fit the firm's needs than ten 55-gallon drums. The Johnson Wax sales rep who utilizes the firm's Sell to Potential program knows the importance of selling not too few units (the store will run out of stock during the promotion) and not too many units (the store will be stuck with excess inventory after the promotion). The chances to obtain commitment diminish rapidly when the salesperson tries to sell too many or too few units or the wrong grade or style of product.

Also, salespeople should not rely solely on trial orders. A **trial order** is a small order placed by a buyer to see if the product will work, and should not be confused with a trial close. A trial order is no commitment, and all too often a buyer will agree to a trial just to get rid of the salesperson. Further, if any learning curve is necessary, a customer who agrees to a trial might be unwilling to invest the time necessary to fully learn the product and will not fully realize the benefits. The product will be rejected often because customers don't have time to give fair trials. Trial orders can work well when the product is easy to implement (such as selling a new product to a retailer for resale) or when the benefits can be realized only by seeing the product in use.

EFFECTIVE METHODS

"If closing is seen by so many sales experts as manipulative and insulting, are effective methods those that are manipulative but not insulting?" asked one of our students. It is a fair question, and the answer has two elements. First, the salesperson's purpose is to sell the right product in the right amounts. If the prospect does not need what is being sold, the salesperson should walk to the next door and start again. Thus there should never be a need for manipulation (review Chapter 2 for a discussion of manipulation). Second, in addition to selling only what the customer needs, the salesperson should also sell in a fashion consistent with the way the buyer prefers to buy. Therefore, the salesperson should gain commitment in a manner that will help the buyer make the choice, consistent with the principle of persuasion. We use the word *choice* here to mean that the buyer can say no. Salespeople do try to persuade buyers, but with persuasion, the choice remains with the buyer. Manipulative techniques are designed to reduce or eliminate choice; partnering methods are not.

Studying successful methods and techniques enables salespeople to help prospects buy a product or service they want or need. Buyers sometimes have a need or a want but still hesitate to buy the product or service that will satisfy it. For example, an industrial buyer for a candy manufacturer refused to commit to a change in sweeteners, even though she needed better raw material. Why? Because the sweetener rep had met with her on four separate occasions, and the buyer had difficulty remembering all that was said and agreed on. (Apparently this salesperson was not using a software program like NetSuite very effectively.) Had the salesperson used the appropriate method (the benefit summary method, discussed later in this section), commitment might have been obtained. This section describes several of the most important methods for gaining commitment.

DIRECT REQUEST

The most straightforward, effective method of obtaining commitment is simply to ask for it, called the **direct request method.** However, salespeople need to be wary of appearing overly aggressive when using this direct request method. Decisive customers, such as drivers, appreciate getting down to business and not wasting time. Here are some examples:

Can I put you down for 100 pairs of model 63?

Can we meet with your engineer next Thursday to discuss this further?

Will you come to the home office for a hands-on demonstration?

Can you call the meeting next week?

BENEFIT SUMMARY

Early in the interview salespeople discover or reiterate the needs and problems of the prospect. Then, throughout the presentation, they show how their product can meet those needs. They do this by turning product or service features into benefits specifically for that buyer. As they present each benefit, they ask if that benefit meets the need. When using this approach, called the **benefit summary method,** the salesperson simply reminds the prospect of the agreed-on benefits of the proposal. This nonmanipulative method helps the buyer synthesize points covered in the presentation to make a wise decision. For example, a salesperson attempting to obtain a buyer's commitment to recommend a proposal to a buying committee might say this:

You stated early in my visit that you were looking for a product of the highest quality, a vendor that could provide quick delivery, and adequate engineering support. As I've mentioned, our fasteners have been rated by an independent laboratory as providing 20 percent higher tensile strength than the closest competitor, resulting in a life expectancy of more than four years. We also discussed the fact that my company can deliver fasteners to your location within 3 hours of your request and that this promise holds true 24 hours a day. Finally, I discussed the fact that we have four engineers on staff whose sole responsibility is to provide support and develop specifications for new fasteners for existing customers. Would you be willing to give the information we discussed to the buying committee along with your endorsement of the proposal?

One advantage of the benefit summary method over the direct request method is that the seller can help the buyer remember all the points discussed in the presentation. The summary becomes particularly important in long presentations and in selling situations involving several meetings prior to obtaining commitment. The salesperson cannot assume that the buyer will remember all the major points discussed in the presentation.

BALANCE SHEET METHOD

Sometimes referred to as the *Ben Franklin method* because Franklin described using it to make decisions, the **balance sheet method** aids prospects who cannot make a decision, even though no reason for their behavior is apparent. Such a prospect may be asked to join the salesperson in listing the pros and cons of buying now or buying later, of buying the salesperson's product or that of a competitor, or of buying the product or not buying it at all.

However, like many nonmanipulative sales techniques, this method can insult a buyer's intelligence if used inappropriately. The salesperson may start to obtain commitment with the following type of statement:

> You know, Mr. Thacker, Ben Franklin was like you, always determined to reach the right decisions and avoid the wrong ones. I suppose that's how you feel. Well, he suggested taking a piece of paper and writing all the reasons for deciding yes in one column and then listing the reasons for deciding no in a second column. He said that when you make this kind of graphic comparison, the correct decision becomes much more apparent.

That close may seem manipulative; it certainly sounds silly. A more effective start may be to simply draw a T on a plain piece of paper, place captions on each side of the crossbar, and leave space below for the insertion of specific benefits or sales points. Then ask the buyer to list pros and cons of making the purchase. For example, assume the product is National Adhesives' hot-melt adhesive used to attach paper labels to plastic lime-flavored Coke bottles. Coca-Cola is currently using a liquid adhesive made by Ajax Corporation. The top of the T might look like this:

The Ben Franklin close is a method of decision making attributed to Franklin. As a closing method, it can seem trite or cheesy.

Benefits of Adopting the National Adhesives Hot-Melt Method	Benefits of Staying with the Ajax Liquid Adhesives

The salesperson may say something like, "Making a decision like this is difficult. Let's see how many reasons we can think of for your going with the National Adhesives system." The salesperson would write the benefits (not features) in which the customer has shown interest on the left side of the T. Next the salesperson would ask the customer to list reasons to stay with the Ajax adhesive on the right side. When completed, the T lists should accurately reflect all the pros and cons of each possible decision. At that point the buyer is asked, "Which method do you think is the wisest?"

When used properly, the balance sheet method can help hesitant buyers express their feelings about the decision in a manner similar to the multiattribute matrix (see the appendix of Chapter 3), which gives the salesperson an opportunity to deal with those feelings. It is especially appropriate for a buyer who is an analytical, but would make less sense for an expressive. However, the balance sheet approach takes time and may appear "salesy," particularly if relatively unimportant benefits are considered to be equal to more important reasons not to buy. Also, the list of benefits of the product being sold will not always outnumber the list on the other side of the T.

PROBING METHOD

In the **probing method** sales representatives initially attempt to obtain commitment by another method, perhaps simply asking for it (the direct request method). If unsuccessful, the salesperson uses a series of probing questions designed to discover the reason for the hesitation. Once any reason becomes apparent, the salesperson asks a what-if question. (What if I could successfully resolve this concern? Would you be willing to commit?) An illustrative dialogue follows:

SALESPERSON: Could we make an appointment for next week, at which time I would come in and do a complete survey of your needs? It shouldn't take more than three hours.

PROSPECT: No, I don't think I am quite ready to take that step yet.

SALESPERSON: There must be some reason why you are hesitating to go ahead now. Do you mind if I ask what it is?

PROSPECT: I'm just not convinced that your firm is large enough to handle a customer of our size.

SALESPERSON: In addition to that, is there any other reason why you would not be willing to go ahead?

PROSPECT: No.

SALESPERSON: If I can resolve the issue of our size, then you would allow me to conduct a survey?

PROSPECT: Well, I wouldn't exactly say that.

SALESPERSON: Then there must be some other reason. May I ask what it is?

PROSPECT: Well, a friend of mine who uses your services told me that often your billing department sends him invoices for material he didn't want and didn't receive.

SALESPERSON: In addition to that, is there any other reason for not going ahead now?

PROSPECT: No, those are my two concerns.

SALESPERSON: If I could resolve those issues right now, would you be willing to set up an appointment for a survey?

PROSPECT: Sure.

This dialogue illustrates the importance of probing in obtaining commitment. The method attempts to bring to the table all issues of concern to the prospect. The salesperson does not claim to be able to resolve the issues but simply attempts to find out what the issues are. When probing has identified all the issues, the salesperson should attempt to resolve them as soon as possible. After successfully dealing with the concerns of the buyer, the salesperson should then ask for a commitment.

There are many modifications of the probing method. Another way to achieve the same results is the following:

SALESPERSON: Are you willing to buy this product today?

PROSPECT: No, I don't think so.

> SALESPERSON: I really would like to get a better feel of where you are. On a scale of 1 to 10, with 1 being absolutely no purchase and 10 being purchase, where would you say you are?
>
> PROSPECT: I would say I'm about a 6.
>
> SALESPERSON: If you don't mind my asking, what would it take to move you from a 6 to a 10?

Also, it is important to always keep cultural differences in mind. For example, if a Japanese businesswoman wants to tell an American salesperson that she is not interested, she might state, "Your proposal would be very difficult," just to be polite. If the seller attempts to use the probing method, the Japanese businesswoman may consider the seller to be pushy or a poor listener. In the same way, an Arab businessperson will never say no directly, a custom that helps both sides avoid losing face.[8]

ALTERNATIVE CHOICE

In many situations a salesperson may have multiple options to present to a buyer. For example, Teo Schaars sells diamonds directly from cutters in the Netherlands to consumers in the United States. When he started in sales, he would display several dozen diamonds on a purple damask–covered table. Sales were few until his father, a Dutch diamond broker, suggested that he limit his customers' choices; there were simply too many diamonds to choose from, overwhelming the buyer. Schaars found his father's comments to be wise advice. Now Schaars spends more time probing about budget and desires and then shows only two diamonds at a time, explaining the key characteristics of each. Then he allows the customer to express a preference. Schaars may have to show half a dozen or more diamonds before a customer makes the final decision, but he rarely shows more than two at a time (www.anschardiamonds.com).

OTHER METHODS

Literally hundreds of techniques and methods to obtain commitment have been tried. Exhibit 11.3 lists a number of traditional methods. Most of them, however, tend to be ineffective with sophisticated customers; nevertheless, many can be used in a nonmanipulative manner if appropriate. For example, the minor-point close can be appropriate if there really is a need to make a choice between two options; the factor that makes the method manipulative is the assumption that the minor choice is the equivalent to making the sale.

No method of obtaining commitment will work if the buyer does not trust the salesperson, the company, and the product. Gaining commitment should not require the use of tricky techniques or methods to force buyers to do something they do not want to do or to manipulate them to buy something they do not need.

IF COMMITMENT IS OBTAINED

The salesperson's job is not over when commitment is obtained. In fact, in many ways the job is just beginning. This section describes the salesperson's responsibilities that accrue after the buyer says yes.

NO SURPRISES

Customers do not like surprises, so now is the time to go over any important information they will need to fully enjoy the benefits of the product or service. For example, if you are selling life insurance and a physical is required, give the customer as much detail as possible to prepare him or her for that experience.

Exhibit 11.3
Some Traditional Closing Methods

Method	How It Works	Remark
Minor-point close	The seller assumes it is easier to get the prospect to decide on a very trivial point than on the whole proposition: What color do you like, blue or red?	This method can upset a prospect who feels he or she is being manipulated or tricked into making a commitment. Even unsophisticated buyers easily spot this technique.
Continuous *yes* close	Throughout the presentation, the seller constantly asks questions for which the prospect most logically would answer yes. By the end of the discussion, the buyer is so accustomed to saying yes that when the order is requested, the natural response is yes.	This method is based on self-perception theory. As the presentation progresses, the buyer begins to perceive himself or herself as being agreeable. At the close, the buyer wants to maintain this self-image and almost unthinkingly says yes. Use of this method can destroy long-term relationships if the buyer later feels manipulated.
Assumptive close	The seller, without asking for the order, simply begins to write it up. A variation is to fill out the order form as the prospect answers questions.	This method does not even give the buyer the courtesy of agreeing. It can be perceived as being very pushy and manipulative.
Standing-room-only close	The seller attempts to obtain commitment by describing the negative consequences of waiting. For example, the seller may state, "If you can't decide now, I'll have to offer it to another customer."	This method can be effective if the statement is true. However, if the prospect really does need to act quickly, this deadline should probably be discussed earlier in the presentation to reduce possible mistrust and the feeling of being pushed.
Benefit-in-reserve close	First the seller attempts to obtain commitment by another method. If unsuccessful, the seller says, "Oh, if you order today I can offer you an additional 5 percent for your trade-in."	This method can backfire easily. The buyer tends to think, "If I had agreed to your first attempt to obtain commitment, I would not have learned about this new enticement. If I wait longer, how much better will your offer be?" The buyer may then seek additional concessions in every future sale attempt.
Emotional close	The seller appeals to the buyer's emotions to close the sale. For example, the seller may say, "This really is a good deal. To be honest with you, I desperately need to secure an order today. As you know, I work on a straight commission basis. My wife is going to have surgery next week, and our insurance just won't cover. . ."	Many obvious problems arise with this method. It is an attempt to move away from focusing entirely on the buyer's personal needs. It does not develop trust or respect. Do not use this close!

Or if a company is going to lease a piece of heavy equipment, let the customer know that delivery will occur after a credit check and how long that credit check will take. John Branton, president of Safe Harbor Financial, requires his salespeople to make sure the client understands how the product works and, if any negative consequences can occur, make sure the client is prepared for it. No customer wants to be surprised with a tax bill later, for example, even if the purchase was still the best choice available.[9]

CONFIRM THE CUSTOMER'S CHOICE

Customers like to believe they have chosen intelligently when they make a decision. After important decisions, they may feel a little insecure about whether the sacrifice is worth it. Such feelings are called **buyer's remorse** or **postpurchase dissonance.** Successful salespeople reassure customers that their choice was the right one. For example:

> I know you will enjoy using your new office machines. You can plan on many months of trouble-free service. I'll call on you in about two weeks to make sure everything is operating smoothly. Be sure to call me if you need any help before then.

Or

Congratulations, Mr. Jacobs. You are going to be glad you decided to use our service. There is no finer service available. Now let's make certain you get off to the right start. Your first bulletin will arrive on Tuesday, March 2.

Or

You've made an excellent choice. Other stores won't have a product like this for at least 30 days.

GET THE SIGNATURE

The buyer's signature often formalizes a commitment. Signing the order is a natural part of a well-planned procedure. The order blank should be accessible, and the signing should be treated as a routine matter. Ordinarily the customer has decided to buy before being asked to sign the order. In other words, the signature on the order blank merely confirms that an agreement has already been reached. The decision to buy or not to buy should not focus on a signature.

The salesperson needs to remember several important points: (1) Make the actual signing an easy, routine procedure; (2) fill out the order blank accurately and promptly; and (3) be careful not to exhibit any excess eagerness or excitement when the prospect is about to sign.

SHOW APPRECIATION

All buyers like to think that their business is appreciated even if they purchase only small quantities. Customers like to do business with salespeople who show that they want the business.

Salespeople may show appreciation by writing the purchaser a letter. This practice especially develops goodwill after large purchases and with new customers. In some situations a small gift, such as a pen with the selling company's name on it, may also be an effective thank-you. Salespeople should always thank the purchaser personally; the thanks should be genuine but not effusive.

Is an e-mail message adequate? Eleanor Brownell doesn't think so. She says, "It (a handwritten note) makes you memorable."[10]

CULTIVATE FOR FUTURE CALLS

In most fields of selling, obtaining commitment is not the end of a business transaction; rather, it is only one part of a mutually profitable business relationship. Obtaining commitment is successful only if it results in goodwill and future commitment. Keep in mind that research shows that it is how the salesperson treats the customer that is the biggest determinant of future sales. How the customer gets treated determines loyalty, which then influences repurchase.[11]

Customers like to do business with salespeople who do not lose interest immediately after securing commitment. What a salesperson does after achieving commitment is called **follow-up.** As Jeffrey Bailey, sales director for Oracle, recognizes, "Making the sale is only the beginning." After making the sale, the salesperson must follow up to make sure the product is delivered when promised, set up appropriately, and so forth. We talk more about follow-up in later chapters. The point here is that the sale does not end with the customer's signature on the order form. Research shows that the quality of follow-up service is an important contributing factor in perceptions of salesperson quality and long-term relationships.[12]

REVIEW THE ACTIONS TO BE TAKEN

An important step, particularly when commitment is next in the buying process, is to review what each party has agreed to do. In the case of a multiple-visit sales cycle, the salesperson must review not only what the client will do but also what the salesperson will do to prepare for the next meeting. To be welcomed on repeat calls, salespeople must be considerate of all the parties involved in buying or using the product. They must pronounce and spell all names correctly, explain and review the terms of the purchase so no misunderstandings will occur, and be sociable and cordial to subordinates as well as those in key positions. In addition, the buyer or user must get the service promised. The importance of this point cannot be overemphasized. Chapter 13 provides detailed information about how to service the account and build a partnership.

IF COMMITMENT IS NOT OBTAINED

Naturally the salesperson does not always obtain the desired commitment. The salesperson should never take this situation personally (which is easier said than done). Doing everything right does not guarantee a sale. Situations change, and customers who may have really needed the product when everything started may find that other priorities make a purchase impossible.

Many times, when a buyer says no, the seller is wise to treat it as "No, not now" rather than "No, never." One salesperson for Factiva, a company that provides research services to businesses, was told no by a prospect. In talking to a gatekeeper, though, he learned of another decision maker in another area of the company who had an interest. That other decision maker bought, and the account is now one of Factiva's largest.[13]

No can mean no forever, though, if the rep isn't listening and isn't sensitive to the buyer's needs. Recall Alex Homer's story at the start of this chapter and how he talked himself out of a sale by providing more information than the buyer wanted. Similarly, Fred Brown, an attorney, had a salesperson who had a service he wanted but didn't have the budget. "When I told her that I couldn't do it now, she kept pushing, and I finally told her to leave. A few months later, when I had the money, I went to someone else because she couldn't listen."[14]

thinking **it** through   Many students report that asking for the order is the hardest part of selling. Why is it difficult? Does the customer need you to ask for the sale? Have you ever needed a salesperson to ask you to buy? Why or why not?

This section describes some of the common reasons for failing to obtain commitment and offers practical suggestions for salespeople who encounter rejection.

SOME REASONS FOR LOST OPPORTUNITIES

Wrong Attitudes

As discussed earlier in the chapter, salespeople need to have a positive attitude. A fear that obtaining commitment will be difficult may be impossible to hide. Inexperienced salespeople naturally will be concerned about their ability to obtain commitment; most of us have an innate fear of asking someone else to do anything. Some salespeople even fail to ask for the sale because if they never ask, they will never hear no. As a result, they always have more prospects but fewer customers than everyone else. But all salespeople know they need to focus on obtaining commitment to keep their jobs.

Some salespeople display unwarranted excitement when they see that prospects are ready to commit. Research suggests that nonverbals are very important cues and can signal trustworthiness or a lack thereof to buyers. A salesperson who appears excited or overly eager may display nonverbal cues that suggest dishonesty or a lack of empathy.[15] At this point wary buyers may change their minds and refuse to commit.

One of the main reasons for salespeople's improper attitudes toward obtaining commitment is the historical importance placed on closing the sale. Closing has often been viewed as a win–lose situation (if I get the order, I win; if I don't get the order, I lose). Until salespeople see obtaining commitment as a positive occurrence for the buyer, these attitudes will persist.

Poor Presentation

Prospects or customers who do not understand the presentation or see the benefits of the purchase cannot be expected to buy. The salesperson must use trial closes (see Chapter 8) and continually take the pulse of the interview.

A poor presentation can also be caused by haste. The salesperson who tries to deliver a 60-minute presentation in 20 minutes may skim over or omit important sales points. Forgoing the presentation may be better than delivering it hastily. Further, a sales presentation given at the wrong time or under unfavorable conditions is likely to be ineffective.

Another reason for not obtaining commitment is lack of product knowledge. In fact, lack of product knowledge is often cited as an important barrier to obtaining commitment.[16] If the salesperson does not know what the product does, you can be certain the buyer will not be able to figure it out either.

Poor Habits and Skills

Obtaining commitment requires proper habits and some measure of skill. The habit of talking too much rather than listening often causes otherwise good presentations to fail (recall Alex's story). Knowing when to quit talking is just as important as knowing what to say. Some salespeople become so fascinated by the sound of their own voices that they talk themselves out of sales they have already made. A presentation that turns into a monologue is not likely to retain the buyer's interest.

DISCOVERING THE CAUSE

The real reasons for not obtaining commitment must be uncovered. Only then can salespeople proceed intelligently to eliminate the barriers. Some firms have developed sophisticated systems to follow up on lost sales. Sales software, such as NetSuite or salesforce.com, can also identify points in the selling process where a salesperson may be having difficulty. If the sales cycle involves a demonstration, for example, and the salesperson turns fewer leads into demonstrations, the fault may lie in the needs identification skills of that salesperson.

Dave Alexander, account executive for Accenture, says his company does a postsale analysis whether it wins or loses the sale. This discipline causes the sales team to focus on the factors that really lead to success. Dave Stein, author of *How Winners Sell*, says that all too often salespeople will lay the blame for failure on price or the product but will take personal credit for any successes.[17] Both Stein and Alexander agree, however, that an effective win/loss system forces the salesperson to examine the real causes and, if the sale was not won, consider personal strategies for improvement.

SUGGESTIONS FOR DEALING WITH REJECTION

Maintain the Proper Perspective

Probably the inexperienced salesperson's most important lesson is that when a buyer says no, the sales process has not necessarily ended. A no may mean "Not now," "I need more information," "Don't hurry me," or "I don't understand." An answer of no should be a challenge to seek the reason behind the buyer's negative response.

In many fields of selling, most prospects do not buy. The ratio of orders achieved to sales presentations may be 1 to 3, 1 to 5, 1 to 10, or even 1 to 20. Salespeople may tend to eliminate nonbuyers from the prospect list after one unsuccessful call. This practice may be sound in some cases; however, many sales result on the second, third, fourth, or fifth call. Dean Yeck, sales manager with Qwest, says one sale took 15 sales calls.[18] When an earlier visit has not resulted in commitment, careful preparation for succeeding calls becomes more crucial.

Another perspective is that when a buyer says no it is because the buyer is not yet fully informed; otherwise the buyer would have said yes. Consequently, if the buyer has given the salesperson the opportunity to make a presentation, the buyer recognizes that a need exists or is going to exist. What has not happened yet is that match between the offering and the need. At the same time, however, no does not mean "Sell me again right now." It may mean "Sell me again later." Illiki Rai, publisher of *Rising Women* magazine, agrees, noting that when she sells her magazine to prospective advertisers, rejection is often temporary and can lead to referrals as well as future sales opportunities.[19]

The salesperson should have a clear objective for each sales call. When commitment cannot be obtained to meet that objective, the salesperson will often attempt to obtain commitment for a reduced request (a secondary or minimum objective). For example, the salesperson may attempt to gain a trial order instead of an actual order, although, as we discussed earlier, this opportunity should be offered as a last resort.

Some companies use promotional products, such as pens with the company's name and phone number on them, as something to leave behind and remind the customer of the salesperson's company.

Recommend Other Sources

A sales representative who uses the consultative selling philosophy (as described in Chapter 5) may recommend a competitor's product to solve the prospect's needs. When recommending other sources, the sales rep should explain why his or her product does not meet the prospect's needs and then provide the name of the competitive product. The goodwill generated by such a gesture should lead to future opportunities when the timing and needs are right.

After recommending other sources, the salesperson usually should ask the prospect for names of people who might be able to buy the seller's product. Also, the salesperson should emphasize the desire to maintain contact with the prospect in the event the seller's firm develops a competitive offering.

Good Manners Are Important

If obtaining commitment fails for any reason, the salesperson should react good-naturedly. Salespeople have to learn to accept no if they expect to call on prospects again. Even if salespeople do not obtain commitment, they should thank prospects for their time. Arguing or showing disappointment gains nothing. The salesperson may plan to keep in contact with these prospects through an occasional phone call, a follow-up letter, or product literature mailings. One salesperson likes to make the following statement at the conclusion of any meeting that does not result in commitment: "I'll never annoy you, but if you don't mind, I'm going to keep in touch."

Many salespeople consider leaving something behind that will let the prospect contact the salesperson in the future. Some firms use promotional products, such as a pen with the company's name and phone number, as a gift after each call to remind the prospect of the salesperson's company. Others may simply use brochures and business cards.

BRINGING THE INTERVIEW TO A CLOSE

Few buyers are interested in a prolonged visit after they commit. Obviously the departure cannot be abrupt; the salesperson should complete the interview smoothly. But goodwill is never built by wasting the buyer's time after the business is concluded.

Remember that most sales take several calls to complete. If an order wasn't signed (and often getting an order isn't even the objective of the call; see Chapter 7) and the prospect wishes to continue considering the proposal, the salesperson should leave with a clear action plan for all parties. An example of the kind of dialogue the salesperson might pursue follows:

SALESPERSON: When will you have had a chance to look over this proposal?

BUYER: By the end of next week, probably.

SALESPERSON: Great, I'll call on you in about 10 days, OK?

BUYER: Sure, set up something with my secretary.

SALESPERSON: Is there anything else I need to do for you before that next meeting?

The salesperson should always make sure the next step is clear for both parties. Therefore, review what you will do next, what the customer will do next, and when you will meet again.

Follow up promptly with a thank-you and reminder note after the sales call. If you are following up after a sales call in which you gained commitment for the next sales call, an e-mail message is not only sufficient but the best idea. Emily Tanner, of e-Rewards in Dallas, follows up after each sales call with an e-mail message laying out what each person promised to do, including the buyer. If she was told no, the follow-up e-mail message is a simple thank-you with a request to be considered again if the opportunity arises. But if she gets the sale, she sends FairyTale brownies (www.brownies.com) to the buyer's office, along with a personal thank-you.

Similarly, Shirley Hunter, an account executive with Teradata, will also follow up a sale with a handwritten thank-you note. She may also personally present a thank-you gift (her product costs half a million dollars, so a sale is worth celebrating). Her choice of a gift, though, will reflect the situation—a box of Lifesavers for the executive who got behind the purchase, a box of crayons for an architect, or something equally creative.

SELLING YOURSELF

When Carter Simon felt his fraternity needed a stronger recruiting program to attract new members, he had to gain the support of the senior leadership of the chapter. In addition, he had to convince the older members to take on a more active role with the recruiting process. "Getting someone to say they will do something is a lot easier than actually getting them to do it," says Simon.

Laura Carros, marketing manager for JCPenney, had a similar need when she wanted to create a new approach to marketing Penney's own branded products. Her first task was to convince her boss that this new approach was worthwhile. But getting his commitment was insufficient. For the new approach to really work, it would require participation from a broad array of Penney marketing and merchandising professionals—people who would have to volunteer their time and effort to the approach. To secure that participation, she had to get them to buy into her new approach. "It was really a long process. In some instances, I would visit with them personally and we would work out a strategy together. In others, we would hold meetings and I'd have to sell an entire department." The results, though, were worth it. Penney used the new approach to completely rebrand its women's lingerie line. The new product line, Ambrielle, and Carros's new approach became the models for other new product lines and new product launches.[20]

When selling internally, gaining real commitment can mean the difference between a program's success or failure. Just because the choice seems obvious to you—"It's the best decision for our customer and our company!"—doesn't mean that others in the company see it the same way. Nor can someone always order an employee to do something and expect the task to be done well. Commitment skills when selling yourself are critical to a successful career.

As with external customers, though, understanding and selling to others' needs has to come first. If you are interested only in your own needs, no closing skills will carry you.

What's also important to remember is that when selling internally, you have to live with the consequences of the selling process much more intimately than when selling to a customer. Using pushy or cheesy techniques contributes to a reputation that makes future decisions or actions more difficult to secure.

Earlier we noted Shirley Hunter's perspective on thanking a customer for a sale. She also believes, though, that internal celebrations are necessary to say thank you to those who contributed either to a sale or to a successful customer implementation. Cultivating for future calls or decisions is also important. You may not win on this decision, but there will be other opportunities to use your closing skills when selling yourself.

SUMMARY

Commitment cannot be obtained by some magical or miraculous technique if the salesperson has failed to prepare the prospect to make this decision throughout the presentation. Salespeople should always attempt to gain commitment in a way that is consistent with the objectives of the meeting. Obtaining commitment begins with the salesperson's contact with the prospect. It can succeed only when all facets of the selling process fall into their proper place. All sellers need to keep in mind this old saying: "People don't buy products or services; they buy solutions to their problems!"

The process of obtaining commitment is the logical progression of any sales call. Commitment is important for the customer, the seller's firm, and the seller. Commitment should result in a win–win situation for all parties concerned.

Pricing is an important element of any sale and is usually presented at the time of closing. Quantity discounts, payment terms, and shipping terms can affect the final price charged to the buyer as well as influence the decision.

There is no one "right" time to obtain commitment. Salespeople should watch their prospects closely and recognize when to obtain commitment. Successful salespeople carefully monitor customer comments, their buyers' nonverbal cues and actions, and their responses to probes. Comments can be in the form of questions, requirements, benefits, and responses to trial closes.

To successfully obtain commitment, the salesperson needs to maintain a positive attitude, allow the customer to set the pace, be assertive rather than aggressive, and sell the right item in the right amounts. Engaging in these practices will result in a strong long-term relationship between buyer and seller.

No one method of obtaining commitment works best for all buyers. The direct request method is the simplest to use; however, the prospect often needs help in evaluating the proposal. In those instances other methods may be more appropriate, such as the alternative choice, the benefit summary, the balance sheet method, or the probing method. No method of obtaining commitment will work if a buyer does not trust the salesperson.

If commitment is obtained, the salesperson should immediately assure the buyer that the choice was judicious. The salesperson should show genuine appreciation as well as cultivate the relationship for future calls.

If commitment is not obtained, the salesperson should analyze the reasons. Difficulties in obtaining commitment can be directly traced to wrong attitudes, a poor presentation, and/or poor habits and skills. Even if no commitment is obtained, the salesperson should thank the prospect for his or her time.

KEY TERMS

aggressive   301
assertive   301
balance sheet method   304
benefit summary method   303
buyer's remorse   307
buying signals   298
cash discount   295
closing   292
closing cues   298

cumulative discount   295
direct request method   303
follow-up   308
postpurchase dissonance   307
probing method   305
requirements   299
submissive   301
trial close   300
trial order   302

ETHICS PROBLEMS

1. One buyer stated, "All closing methods are devious and self-serving! How can a salesperson use a technique but still keep my needs totally in mind?" Comment. Integrate into your discussion the concepts of persuasion versus manipulation.

2. Reread David Appel's letter in "Building Partnerships 3.1." Do you have any ethical concerns about the letter? Do buyers have an ethical obligation to respond—to make a decision in a timely fashion one way or the other? Why or why not?

QUESTIONS AND PROBLEMS

1. Review the closing methods in Exhibit 11.3, and write a nonmanipulative and a manipulative version of each. What is the difference?

2. "The ABCs of closing are 'Always be closing.'" Another version is "Close early—close often." What is your reaction to these time-honored statements?

3. Harold Bumpurs, a professional purchasing agent, says he has never noticed any tricky closes. His perception is due not to the smooth closing skills of the salespeople who call on him but to the total skill sets they have developed. Prioritize a list of selling skills, from most important to least. How much time should be spent improving commitment-gaining skills as opposed to developing other skills? Why?

4. Reread "Building Partnerships 3.1." Suppose the prospect Alex Homer describes in the opening paragraph said, "What you say sounds interesting, but I want some time to think it over." You answer, "Well, OK. Would next Tuesday be a good day for me to come back?" How can you improve on your answer?

5. One sales manager who worked for a refrigeration equipment company taught his salespeople the following close: Ask questions that allow you to fill out the contract. Assume the sale is made and hand the contract to the buyer, along with a pen. If the buyer doesn't immediately take the pen, drop it and make the buyer pick it up. Once the buyer has the pen in hand, he or she is more likely to use it to sign the contract, so just wait silently until the buyer does.
   a. Would you label this seller as assertive or aggressive?
   b. Is this a trick (manipulative) or merely dramatization (persuasive)?
   c. How would you respond to this behavior if you were the buyer?

6. You've identified a process by which your company could recycle packaging material, saving the company about 10 percent of the packaging costs. But when you talk this over with the person in charge of shipping, he says,

"You're just a sales rep! Go sell something and let me do my job!" What do you think is driving his reaction? How would you respond? What would you do next?

7. What makes a Mercedes-Benz worth more than a Volkswagen? How would you convince someone that it is worth more if she or he knew nothing about the various brands of cars? How would the buyer's lack of knowledge influence how you try to gain commitment?

8. Read Todd Pollock's comments at the start of the chapter. How can you handle that much rejection? What is it that people are rejecting? What difference does your answer to that question make?

9. What would you say to a friend to gain his or her commitment to go on a spring break trip? Describe exactly what you would say to your friend using each of the following methods (make any assumptions necessary):
   a. Alternative choice.
   b. Direct request.
   c. Benefit summary.
   d. Balance sheet.
   e. Probing.

10. A customer is willing to order 100 cases listed at $20 per case to get a 15 percent quantity discount. Terms are 2/10, n/30. The customer pays five days after receiving the invoice. How much did the customer pay?

CASE PROBLEMS

case 11.1

AB Reddy

AB Reddy manufactures handheld scanning devices that are used in inventory management. Used in any environment where tracking inventory is important, these devices scan the UPC bar code and are used to track movement of products within a warehouse or business. Ginger Conlon is calling on Paul Greenberg, senior purchasing director for Advent Systems. Paul has global responsibility for purchasing standardization, and developing a common inventory management system across all of Advent's 32 locations in 12 countries is a task he has to complete this year. Ginger's primary call objective is to have Paul agree to set up an appointment in the next several weeks for Ginger to present to the supply chain committee that will review proposals and narrow the choices down to three systems.

GINGER: Our scanning systems can support the digital standards of both the United States and Europe, which means that, with some engineering changes in your computer network, your locations can use the same scanners.

PAUL: Ginger, I've really been thinking that the scanners built by Nortel are industry standard. What has Reddy done differently with these scanners?

GINGER: Quality is something we take very seriously at Reddy, but having the best-built old product isn't enough, is it? So we've also built probably the finest engineering staff over the past five years that you'll find anywhere. The result is a product line that was just awarded the Sultan's Engineering Award for Innovation in Egypt last month.

PAUL: That's impressive, and you're right. A well-built product using yesterday's technology is of no benefit to us. But how important is bicontinental use at the scanning level? Can't we just scan and convert the data into a common format later?

GINGER: Yes, you can, but that's really inconsistent with the overall strategy of minimizing the number of vendors and having global suppliers. Plus, you may have seen a report issued by DataMark that indicates some users have had data problems that have been difficult to identify until something goes horribly wrong.

PAUL: I've seen that report from DataMark, as well as an article in the last issue of *Supply Chain Management*. But we've had no plans for such scanners.

GINGER: Why is that?

PAUL: We don't know that it is necessary—we don't think we've got that many locations where scanning is a necessity.

GINGER: What would be considered a significant percentage—of your total sites, I mean?

PAUL: I would guess 50 percent would be acceptable. What are others experiencing?

GINGER: We've got several, maybe four, that have standardized with us globally, and another group of about two dozen that use us in the United States or North America. How does that sound?

PAUL: Intriguing, though we're not the same as others.

GINGER: I know. That's why I'd like to set up a meeting with your supply chain team in the near future. But we'll probably also need someone there from logistics, right?

PAUL: Yes, I suppose we would.

GINGER: Will I have your endorsement at the meeting?

PAUL: We'll have to wait and see. I'll need some documentation on the figures you've given me, and I'd like that before we set up the meeting.

Questions

1. What form of closing did Ginger use to gain Paul's commitment to the idea? Was that appropriate? Why or why not?

2. List how you would attempt to obtain commitment using three other methods of your choice. Write out exactly what you would say for each method (and be sure to identify the method).

3. Although you have been shown only a portion of the conversation, evaluate Ginger's performance in terms of the following:

   a. Selling benefits, not features.
   b. Using trial closes.
   c. Using communication aids to strengthen the presentation.
   d. Responding to objections.
   e. Attempting to gain commitment at the proper time.

case **11.2**

Blue Onion

Blue Onion is a systems integrator, meaning that it helps companies integrate new software into the old systems and the customer's processes. So when a customer buys SAP software, for example, Blue Onion customizes the software to fit the customer's work processes and to work with the customer's old software.

Sean Thornton just joined the company as an account executive. After five years of systems analysis and sales support for Oracle, a major software provider, he wanted to earn a salesperson's living, so he made the switch. As part of his training he spent some time working with several experienced salespeople. One such salesperson was Mary Kate Danaher.

She filled him in on the client they were about to see as they entered a large office building. "They are buying a system called BOSS," she said. "This is going to be a massive change for them, and it looks like they'll implement in three phases over a two-year period."

"In other words, a big sale for us, right?" replied Sean.

"Yup. And I'm not going to let them get away. They are considering doing the integration on their own, using temporary employees, and that never works well. So I've already filled out a contract and today, when we meet with the CEO, we'll get it signed." The determination in her voice matched the purpose in her step as she strode to the bank of elevators in the center of the lobby.

Once in the CEO's office, sitting around a small conference table with the head of MIS and the CFO, Mary Kate reviewed the key points of the agreement, saying, "Shirley, you know that this is a critical implementation and you can't afford any mistakes. That's why you should rely on Blue Onion," and handed the contract to the CEO.

The head of MIS squirmed uncomfortably. Shirley looked at him, and he said, "Shirley, I really think we can do this ourselves and save a lot of money."

"With all due respect, Jack, my experience would say that you can't. Temporaries just don't care as much as your own people do, nor as much as our people do," said Mary Kate, with conviction.

Silence draped over the table. Sean could hear an antique clock ticking away on the shelf behind Shirley's desk. After what seemed like an hour but was probably only a few seconds, Shirley looked at the CFO, who nodded almost imperceptibly. She took out her pen, signed the contract, and handed it back to Mary Kate.

"Thank you, Shirley. I will personally see this project through to completion, on time and on budget, and at the end, you'll get all you hoped for and more," said Mary Kate.

The MIS director stood, looking at the CEO and then the CFO, then back to the CEO. Then he stuck out his hand, saying, "Congratulations, Mary Kate and good luck." Then he turned, and left the room.

An awkward pause was broken first by Mary Kate. "Shirley, I will set up a meeting with our engineering manager and Jack for next week so that we can lay out the plan for integration. I'm sure that Jack will enjoy meeting her." Small talk ensued, and within five minutes, Mary Kate and Sean were back in the lobby.

"Well, rookie, we got it!" exclaimed Mary Kate. They exchanged high fives and headed to the parking lot.

Questions

1. Assess Mary Kate's style. Is her style something Sean should emulate?
2. Blue Onion's implementation team will need to work very closely with Jack and his people, and it doesn't appear that Jack wants to be helpful. What could Mary Kate have done to avoid this situation? Assume this meeting was called by Shirley. How could Mary Kate have handled it differently?

ROLE PLAY CASE

Once again you will give your presentation to the same buyer (Spear One, McLane Properties, Dart Paper Products) that you did after Chapters 9 and 10 (if you did not do role plays after those chapters, review that material now). This time you will complete your presentation, first summarizing the needs and going all the way to asking for the sale. You will have an opportunity to work on presentation, objection handling, and closing skills.

If two people are involved in the sale (a seller and a buyer) while a third observes, the observer should do the following:

1. Identify any objection-handling methods used.
2. Determine whether the seller is focused on benefits or only features.
3. Note when trial closes are used.
4. Identify the closing method used.

The professor will pass out new buyer sheets.

ADDITIONAL REFERENCES

Aggarwal, Praveen, Stephen B. Castleberry, Rick Ridnour, and C. David Shepherd. "Salesperson Empathy and Listening: Impact on Relationship Outcomes." *Journal of Marketing Theory and Practice* 13 (2005), pp. 16–31.

Agnihotri Raj, Adam Rapp, and Kevin Trainor. "Understanding the Role of Information Communication in the Buyer–Seller Exchange Process: Antecedents and Outcomes." *The Journal of Business & Industrial Marketing* 24, no. 7 (2009), pp. 474–89.

Bradford, Kevin D., J. Michael Crant, and Joan M. Phillips. "How Suppliers Affect Trust with Their Customers: The Role of Salesperson Job Satisfaction and Perceived Customer Importance." *Journal of Marketing Theory & Practice* 17, no. 4 (Fall 2009), pp. 383–94.

Fu, Frank, Willy Bolander, and Eli Jones. "Managing the Drivers of Organizational Commitment and Salesperson Effort: An Application of Meyer and Allen's Three-Component Model." *Journal of Marketing Theory and Practice* 17, no. 4 (Fall 2009), pp. 335–50.

Gough, Orla, and Mohamed Nurullah. "Understanding What Drives the Purchase Decision in Pension and Investment Products." *Journal of Financial Services Marketing* 14, no. 2 (September 2009), pp. 152–72.

Luo, Xueming, and Naveen Donthu. "The Role of Cyber-Intermediaries: A Framework Based on Transaction Cost Analysis, Agency, Relationship Marketing, and Social Exchange Theories." *The Journal of Business & Industrial Marketing* 22, no. 7 (2007), pp. 452–64.

Rutherford, Brian N., James S. Boles, Hiram C. Barksdale Jr., and Julie T. Johnson. "Buyer's Relational Desire and Number of Suppliers Used: The Relationship between Perceived Commitment and Continuance." *Journal of Marketing Theory and Practice* 16, no. 3 (Summer 2008), pp. 247–57.

Turner, Roger, Christophe Lasserre, and Pascal Beauchet. "Marketing Metrics: Innovation in Field Force Bonuses: Enhancing Motivation through a Structured Process-Based Approach." *Journal of Medical Marketing* 7, no. 2 (2007), pp. 126–35.

Weber, John A. "Business Ethics Training: Insights from Learning Theory." *Journal of Business Ethics* 70, no. 1 (2007), pp. 61–85.

Zallocco, Ronald, Ellen Bolman Pullins, and Michael L. Mallin. "A Reexamination of B2B Sales Performance." *The Journal of Business & Industrial Marketing* 24, no. 8 (2009), pp. 598–614.

chapter **15**

MANAGING YOUR TIME AND TERRITORY

The Salesperson as Manager

PART 3

SOME QUESTIONS ANSWERED IN THIS CHAPTER ARE

- Why is time so valuable for salespeople?
- What can you do to "create" more selling time?
- What should you consider when devising a territory strategy?
- How does territory strategy relate to account strategy and building partnerships?
- How should you analyze your daily activities and sales calls?
- How can you evaluate your own performance so you can improve?

PROFILE

PROFILE

Just five short weeks after graduating from Elon University in May 2008, I began my own personal sales journey. ConvaTec, a market leader in medical devices, was brave enough to appoint me into its Sales Select Program. This program has been the most invaluable experience in my short career and has opened many doors that would typically be considered unreachable for a person of my tenure and level of experience in the medical device industry.

Headquartered just 10 miles away from my childhood hometown, ConvaTec was part of Bristol-Myers Squibb Co. when I began. The Sales Select Program is a highly competitive "fast track" into the world of medical sales with six months of exclusive product/clinical training in all of our core business units, the opportunity to work with both global and U.S. marketing on brand management projects, and most importantly, the development of priceless relationships acquired both in-house and in the field. By the commencement of the program, numerous changes were occurring within the company and within me. ConvaTec divested from Bristol-Myers Squibb Co. and became a stand-alone company composed of three business units while I was fired up, hungry to get into the field, to start banging down doors and making sales. I was creating and making hour-long sales presentations about ConvaTec's products and services meant for an audience of chief surgeons, residents, and executive suite financial decision makers, interviewing for positions in the sales force, and learning the most complex nature of sales in the acute hospital setting: pricing and contracting.

I accepted the territory manager position in the Boston area for our Wound Therapeutics Division, calling on hospitals and outpatient clinics in southeastern Massachusetts. Because I was completely unfamiliar with the area, initially creating my business plan and zoning my key accounts were beyond a challenge. I found it helpful to use a combination of resources in order to make my "strategic plan" in my first territory: sales tracking numbers from the previous year, gathering information from territory managers in the other business units that share a few of the same call points within the facilities, working closely with my manager, and the most helpful contributor—asking the right questions of my customers.

Every account is different in any area of sales; but within clinical settings, not only are the policies on vendor access within each individual hospital dissimilar, but so are the most important things to the salesperson—the decision-making processes. Questions like "How are you involved in the decision-making process?" or "What is the procedure here for evaluating new product technologies?" are absolutely imperative when trying to figure out how to, where to, and with whom to spend the most of your time in each account. At times it is relatively easy to hit a roadblock when you are spending time with customers who believe that their opinions are key in the decision-making process, but over time you may come to realize that their involvement is minimal or even nonexistent. Approaching each account from multiple angles is something I try to practice. I develop relationships within several settings in the hospital: the nursing staff, critical care, hospitalists, surgeons, wound care, purchasing, storeroom, central supply, and so on in order to make sure I don't pigeonhole myself into a specific area of the account and potentially hit a dead end that I would not be able to recover from. The worst thing that happens is that I realize this person is not going to be able to make a decision, but he or she may be able to lead me to the person who does; and having his or her support will only help me in the future.

Selling in the medical device industry can be a complicated, long process. Close, trusting relationships with my customers are crucial. Not only do I create solutions to save them time and increase positive patient outcomes in their practice, but I am in charge of coordinating the education for these solutions to their entire staff. Allocating resources and acquiring the proper tools to service my customers can take up a lot of time, and subsequently this is time I cannot recreate to call on my other customers. This is one of the many reasons why time management and analyzing how you spend your time are vital. In order to prioritize your efforts and measure your performance, it is important to track and constantly alter your weekly, monthly, and quarterly goals. At ConvaTec we have a tool to assist in tracking and update this information for each call. At the end of each week you can see where you spent your time, whom you spoke with, what you intended to accomplish in the meeting, and then what actually happened. By working hard all week to hit this goal and to set up the next week, it feels like an accomplishment to sit down on Friday and enter the outcome of each presentation to see where you stand. If there is a week where you spent a large amount of your time taking care of matters that did not move the sales process forward, which happens from time to time, it is almost refreshing to start the new week off with a clean slate.

In my Boston territory, I had nearly 40 accounts, which subsequently produced a large amount of windshield time driving from hospital to hospital. By using that time to catch up on voice mail, check in with my manager, make sure my distributors are able to fill orders, and prepare for the rest of my weekly presentations, I reduced stress and workload for when I would get home that evening. Not only is managing your sales time important, but managing your work–life balance let you successfully coexist with your career rather than let it define you.

With countless competitors in the market that know your products almost as well as you do, barriers of access to key decision makers due to hospital vendor policies, and around-the-clock needs of customers caring for patients, the thing that sets ConvaTec ahead of the competition are not only our evidence-based products and solutions for clinicians and physicians, but also our clinical and educational support team teeming with renowned and respected consultants who are geared to help our customers achieve their goals.

In January ConvaTec relocated me from Boston to New York to be a territory manager for its new Critical Care Division. My role, territory, and account sizes are extremely different, but I am finding that the same lessons I learned in my first territory apply to a larger scale: Have a business plan, use it as an ever-evolving and changing blueprint, and manage your time effective and efficiently. In sales, each move you make must be deliberate, as it is for your competitor. I always assume if I am not in an account that my competition is; that's what makes me jump out of bed in the morning.

**Visit our Web site at
www.convatec.com.**

THE VALUE OF TIME

The old axiom "Time is money" certainly applies to selling. If you work 8 hours a day for 240 days of a year, you will work 1,920 hours that year. If you earn $50,000, each of those hours will be worth $26.05. An hour of time would be worth $31.25 if your earnings climb to $60,000. Looking at your time another way, you would have to sell $260 worth of product per hour to earn $50,000 if you earned a 10 percent commission!

The typical salesperson spends only 920 hours a year in front of customers. The other 1,000 hours are spent waiting, traveling, doing paperwork, or attending sales meetings. Thus, as a typical salesperson, you really have to be twice as good, selling $520 worth of products every hour to earn that $50,000 commission.

The lesson from this analysis is clear: Salespeople must make every hour count to be successful. Time is a resource that cannot be replaced if wasted. But time is just one resource, albeit a critical resource, at the salesperson's disposal.

Managing time and territory is often a question of how to allocate resources. Allocating resources such as time is a difficult management process, but when done well, it often spells the difference between stellar and average performance. Many times it is difficult to know what is really important and what only seems

Salespeople have to carefully allocate resources such as time. Although every job will occasionally require burning the midnight oil, carefully planning one's time can make for a more balanced and enjoyable life.

important. In this chapter we discuss how to manage your time. Building on what you have learned about the many activities of salespeople, we also provide strategies for allocating resources among accounts—that is, managing your territory.

THE SELF-MANAGEMENT PROCESS

The self-management process in selling has four stages. The first stage is setting goals, or determining what is to be accomplished. The second stage is allocating resources and determining strategies to meet those goals. In the third stage the salesperson implements the time management strategies by making sales calls, sending e-mail or direct mail pieces, or executing whatever action the strategy calls for. In the fourth and final stage, the salesperson evaluates performance to determine whether the goals will be reached and the strategies are effective or whether the goals cannot be reached and the strategies must change. This process is illustrated in Exhibit 15.1 and will serve as an outline for this chapter.

SETTING GOALS

THE NEED FOR GOALS

The first step in managing any worthwhile endeavor is to consider what makes it worthwhile and what you want to accomplish. Salespeople need to examine their careers in the same way. Career goals and objectives should reflect personal ambitions and desires so the individual can create the desired lifestyle, as illustrated in Exhibit 15.2. When career goals reflect personal ambitions, the salesperson is more committed to achieving those goals.

Exhibit 15.1
The Self-Management Process

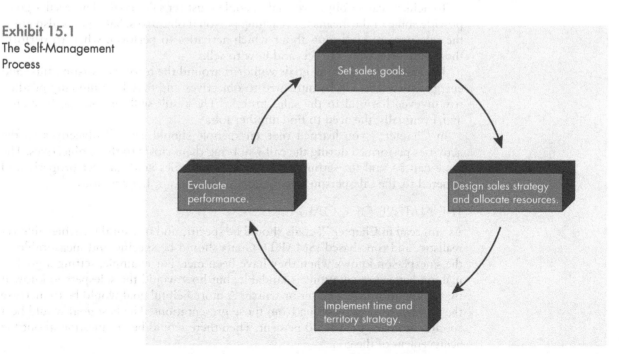

Exhibit 15.2

The Relationship of Goals
Career goals are devised from lifestyle objectives. Sales goals should reflect career goals. Although activities lead to sales, performance goals are usually set first. Then, using conversion goals, activity goals are set.

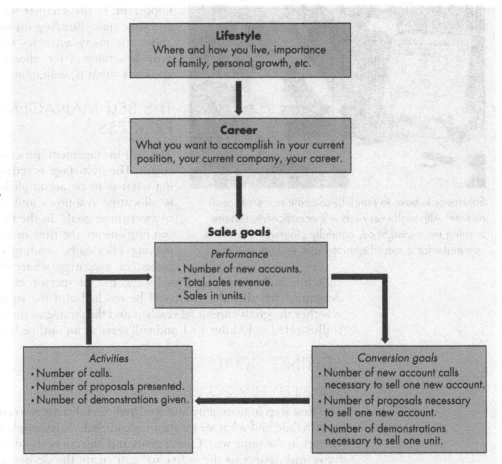

Lifestyle
Where and how you live, importance of family, personal growth, etc.

Career
What you want to accomplish in your current position, your current company, your career.

Sales goals

Performance
• Number of new accounts.
• Total sales revenue.
• Sales in units.

Activities
• Number of calls.
• Number of proposals presented.
• Number of demonstrations given.

Conversion goals
• Number of new account calls necessary to sell one new account.
• Number of proposals necessary to sell one new account.
• Number of demonstrations necessary to sell one unit.

To achieve career objectives, salespeople must set sales goals. These sales goals provide some of the means for reaching personal objectives. Sales goals also guide the salesperson's decisions about which activities to perform, when to perform those activities, whom to see, and how to sell.

The salesperson lacking goals will drift around the territory, wasting time and energy. Sales calls will be unrelated to objectives and may be minimally productive or even harmful to the sales process. The result will be poor performance and, eventually, the need to find another job.

In Chapter 7 you learned that salespeople should set call objectives so the activities performed during the call will bring them closer to those objectives. The same can be said for setting sales goals: When sales goals are set properly and adhered to, the salesperson has a guide to direct his or her activities.

THE NATURE OF GOALS

As you read in Chapter 7, goals should be specific and measurable, achievable yet realistic, and time-based (SMART). Goals should be specific and measurable so the salesperson knows when they have been met. For example, setting a goal of making better presentations is laudable, but how would the salesperson know if the presentations were better or worse? A more helpful goal would be to increase the number of sales resulting from those presentations. The best goal would be a specific increase, such as 10 percent. Then there would be no question about the achievement of the goal.

Some salespeople keep a reminder, like a photo of a new house, of their personal goals in front of them to help motivate themselves.

Goals should also be reachable yet challenging. One purpose of setting personal goals is to motivate oneself. If goals are reached too easily, little has been accomplished. Challenging goals, then, are more motivating. But if the goals are too challenging, or if they are unreachable, the salesperson may give up.

Goals should be time-based; that is, goals should have deadlines. Putting a deadline on a goal provides more guidance for the salesperson and creates a sense of urgency that can be motivating. Without a deadline, the goal is not specific enough, and the salesperson may be able to drag on forever, never reaching the goal but thinking progress is being made. Imagine the motivational difference between setting a goal of a 10 percent increase in sales with no deadline and setting a goal of a 10 percent increase for the next month. The first instance lacks a sense of urgency, of needing to work toward that goal now. Without a deadline, the goal has little motivational value.

One problem some people have is periodically creating goals and then forgetting them. Goals should be written down and then posted. For example, each month Will Pinkham has a goal for selling five new accounts (Will sells office equipment for Ikon Office Solutions). At the start of each month, he puts a new list on the wall over his desk, and as he sells each new account, he adds it to the list starting at the bottom. He starts the list at the bottom to remind him that his goal is to sell five, so when he sells one, his goal becomes four, and so forth. Probably not all goals should be posted in highly public areas, but the idea is to keep the goal in front of you so it continues to direct your activities.

thinking it through

What types of goals have you set for yourself in your college career? For specific classes? How would these goals meet the criteria of specific and measurable, reachable yet challenging, and time-based? How do you keep these goals in front of you? What would you do differently now?

TYPES OF SALES GOALS

Salespeople need to set three types of sales goals: performance, activity, and conversions (refer back to Exhibit 15.2). Although many salespeople focus only on how many sales they get, setting all three types of goals is necessary to achieve the highest possible success.

Performance Goals

Goals relating to outcomes are **performance goals.** In sales, outcomes such as the size of a commission or bonus check, the amount of sales revenue generated or number of sales generated, and the number of prospects identified are common performance goals. For example, the salesperson in Exhibit 15.3 set a performance goal of $6,000 in commissions and another performance goal of eight sales. Revenue quotas are an example of goals set by the company, but each salesperson should also consider setting personally relevant goals. For example, you may want to set higher goals so you can achieve higher earnings. People are more committed to achieving goals they set themselves; that commitment makes

Exhibit 15.3
Goal Calculations

Monthly earnings goal (performance goal):	$6,000
Commission per sale:	$750
$6,000 earnings ÷ $750 per sale = 8 sales	
Monthly sales goal (performance goal):	8
Closings goal (conversion goal):	10%
8 sales × 10 prospects per sale = 80 prospects	
Monthly prospects goal (performance goal):	80
Prospects per calls goal (conversion goal):	1 in 3
80 prospects × 3 calls per prospect = 240 calls	
Monthly sales calls goal (activity goal):	240
240 calls × 20 working days per month = 12 calls	
Daily sales calls goal (activity goal):	12

achieving them more likely. Performance goals should be set first because attaining certain performance levels is of primary importance to both the organization and the salesperson.

Personal development goals, such as improving presentation skills, are important to long-term professional growth and are a form of performance goals. Every person, whether in sales or other fields, should have some personal development goals. Reaching those goals will not only improve overall job performance but also increase personal satisfaction. Like all performance goals, however, these goals should meet the criteria of being specific, challenging, and time-based. Further, it helps to make these goals measurable. For example, if you set improving presentation skills as a performance goal, some outcome such as increased sales or fewer objections should occur that you can measure to determine if your skills are truly improving.

Activity Goals

Salespeople also set activity goals. **Activity goals** are behavioral objectives: the number of calls made in a day, the number of demonstrations performed, and so on. Activity goals reflect how hard the salesperson wants to work. The company may set some activity goals for salespeople, such as a quota of sales calls to be made each week. Exhibit 15.3 lists two activity goals: 240 sales calls per month and 12 calls per day.

All activity goals are intermediate goals; that is, achieving them should ultimately translate into achievement of performance goals. As Teradata discovered by auditing sales performance, activity goals such as a specific number of telephone calls per day are needed for the salespeople to achieve the overall performance goals.[1] Activity goals help salespeople decide what to do each day, but those goals must ultimately be related to making sales.

However, activity goals and performance goals are not enough. For example, a salesperson may have goals of achieving 10 sales and making 150 calls in one month. The salesperson may get 10 sales but make 220 calls. That salesperson had to work much harder than someone who managed to get 10 sales in only 150 calls. What caused the difference? Answer that question and you, too, can work smarter rather than harder; but the answer presupposes that you first measured conversions and then set goals based on what should be achieved.

Conversion Goals

Conversion goals are measures of a salesperson's efficiency. Conversion goals reflect how efficiently the salesperson would like to work, or work smarter. Unlike performance goals, conversion goals express relative accomplishments, such as the number of sales relative to the number of calls made or the number of customers divided by the number of prospects. The higher the ratio, the more efficient the salesperson. Exhibit 15.3 lists two conversion goals: closing 10 percent of all prospects and finding one prospect for every three calls. In the preceding example, a rep earning 10 sales while making 150 calls could close 4 or 5 more sales by making 220 calls because that rep gains a sale every 15 calls.

Conversion goals are important because they reflect how efficiently the salesperson uses resources, such as time, to accomplish performance goals. For example, Freeman Exhibit Company builds custom trade show exhibits. Customers often ask for booth designs (called speculative designs) before making the purchase to evaluate the offerings of various competitors. Creating a custom booth design is a lot of work for a designer, and the cost can be high, but it does not guarantee a sale. If a salesperson has a low conversion rate for speculative designs, overall profits will be lower because the cost for the unsold designs must still be covered. If the rep can increase the conversion rate, the overall costs for unsold designs will be lower, hence increasing profits.

Working harder would show up as an increase in activity; working smarter should be reflected in conversion goals. For example, a salesperson may be performing at a conversion rate of 10 percent. Reaching a conversion goal of 12 percent (closing 1 out of 8 instead of 1 out of 10) would reflect some improvement in the way the salesperson operates—some method of working smarter.

Measuring conversions tells salespeople which activities work best. For example, suppose a salesperson has two sales strategies. If A generates 10 sales and B generates 8 sales, the salesperson may think A is the better strategy. But if A requires 30 sales calls and B only 20, the salesperson would be better off using strategy B. Thirty sales calls would have generated 12 sales with strategy B.

Comparing your performance with the best in your organization is a form of **benchmarking.**[2] Benchmarking can help you see where you are falling short. For example, if your conversion ratio of leads to appointments (the number of leads needed to get one appointment) is the same as that of the top seller but you are closing only half of your spec designs and that person is closing 80 percent, you know you are losing sales at the spec design stage. You can then examine what that person does to achieve the higher conversion ratio.

SETTING SALES GOALS

Performance and conversion goals are the basis for activity goals. Suppose a sale is worth $500 in commission. A person who wants to earn $4,000 per month (a performance goal) needs to make eight sales each month. If the salesperson sees closing 1 out of 10 prospects as a realistic conversion goal, a second performance goal results: The rep must identify 80 prospects to yield eight closings. If the rep can identify one prospect for every three sales calls (another conversion goal), 240 sales calls (an activity goal) must be made. Assuming 20 working days in a month, the rep must make 12 sales calls each day (another activity goal). Thus activity goals need to be the last type of goals set because they will be determined by the desired level of performance at a certain rate of conversion.

Even though the conversion analysis results in a goal of 12 calls each day, that conversion rate is affected by the strategy the salesperson employs. A better strategy results in a higher conversion rate and better allocation of time, one of many important resources that must be allocated properly to achieve sales goals. We discuss how to allocate resources in the next section.

ALLOCATING RESOURCES

The second stage of the time and territory management process is to develop a strategy that allocates resources properly. These resources are allocated to different sales strategies used with different types of accounts with the purpose of achieving sales goals in the most effective and efficient manner possible.

RESOURCES TO BE ALLOCATED

Salespeople manage many resources. Some of these are physical resources, such as free samples, demonstration products, trial products, brochures, direct mail budgets, and other marketing resources. Each of these physical resources represents a cost to the company, but to the salesperson they are investments. Salespeople consider physical resources as investments because resources must be managed wisely to generate the best possible return. Whereas financial investments may return dividends or price increases, the salesperson's investments should yield sales.

A key resource that salespeople manage is time. Time is limited, and not all of a salesperson's work time can be spent making sales calls. Some time must be spent attending meetings, learning new products, preparing reports for management, traveling to sales calls, and handling other nonselling duties; in fact, nonselling activities can take up to 70 percent of a salesperson's time. Thus being able to manage time wisely is important. As we discuss in the next chapter, salespeople also coordinate many of the company's other departments to serve customers well. Salespeople must learn how to allocate these resources in ways that generate the greatest level of sales.

WHERE TO ALLOCATE RESOURCES

For salespeople the allocation of resources is often a question of finding the customers or companies that are most likely to buy and then allocating selling resources to maximize the opportunities they offer. As you may have learned in your principles of marketing course, some market segments are more profitable than others. And just as the company's marketing executive tries to determine which segments are most profitable so that marketing plans can be directed toward those segments, salespeople examine their markets to allocate their selling resources.

Maximizing the opportunity means finding profitable ways to satisfy the greatest number of customers, but not necessarily everybody.[3] One study of services customers found that only 44 percent were profitable; the rest cost the company money.[4] In the following section we discuss how to analyze the market to identify potential customers that are most likely to buy so resources will be allocated properly.

ACCOUNT CLASSIFICATION AND RESOURCE ALLOCATION

Not all customers have the same buying potential, just as not all sales activities produce the same results. The salesperson has to concentrate on the most profitable customers and minimize effort spent with customers that offer little opportunity for profitable sales. The proportion of unprofitable accounts is usually greater than one would think. As a rule, 80 percent of the sales in a territory come from only 20 percent of the customers. Therefore, salespeople should classify customers on the basis of their sales potential to avoid spending too much time and other resources with low-potential accounts, thus helping to achieve sales goals.

Customer management is not just a time management issue. Managing customers includes allocating all the resources at the salesperson's disposal in the most productive manner. Time may be the most important of these resources, but salespeople also manage sample and demonstration inventories, entertainment and travel budgets, printed materials, and other resources.

ABC Analysis

The simplest classification scheme, called **ABC analysis,** ranks accounts by sales potential. The idea is that the accounts with the greatest sales potential deserve the most attention. Using the 80/20 rule, the salesperson identifies the 20 percent of accounts that (could) buy the most and calls those A accounts. The other

80 percent are B accounts, and noncustomers (or accounts with low potential for sales) are C accounts. Eli Lilly (a pharmaceuticals company) classifies physicians and SC Johnson Wax classifies retail stores this way. One use is planning sales calls; so for example, A accounts could be seen every two weeks, B accounts every six weeks, and C accounts only if there is nothing else to do. An example of an account analysis appears in Exhibit 15.4. As you can see, Sam Thompson has used estimated potential to classify accounts so he can allocate sales calls to accounts with the greatest potential.

ABC classification schemes work well only in industries that require regular contact with the same accounts, such as consumer packaged goods and pharmaceuticals. Some industries (plant equipment, medical equipment, and other capital products) may require numerous sales calls until the product is sold. After that sale, another sale may be unlikely for several years, and the number of sales calls may diminish. Then the A, B, and C classification may not be helpful.

Salespeople in some industries find grid and customer relationship analysis methods more useful than ABC analysis. They have learned that simply allocating sales activities on the basis of sales potential may lead to inefficiencies. For example, to maximize great potential, satisfied customers may need fewer calls than accounts of equal potential that are loyal to a competitor.

Exhibit 15.4
Account Classification

Salesperson: Sam Thompson   A. Analysis of Call Pattern: 2011

Customer Type	Number of Customers Contacted	Number of Calls	Average Calls per Customer	Sales Volume	Average Sales per Call
A	15	121	8.1	$212,515	$1,756
B	21	154	7.3	115,451	756
C	32	226	7.0	78,010	345
D	59	320	5.4	53,882	168
Total	127	821		$460,859	561

B. Annual Territory Sales Plan (dollars in thousands)

Account	Actual Sales			2012 Estimated Potential Sales	Forecast	Number of Calls Allocated	Classification
	2009	2010	2011				
Allied Foods	$100	$110	$150	$250	$150	48	A
Pic N-Save	75	75	90	300	115	48	A
Wright Grocers	40	50	60	175	90	24	B
H.E.B.	20	30	30	150	30	24	B
Piggly Wiggly	10	10	25	100	55	18	C
Sal's Superstore	0	0	30	100	80	18	C
Buy-Rite	0	0	0	80	75	18	C
Tom Thumb	0	10	20	75	70	18	C
Apple Tree	0	5	12	60	60	12	D
Buy Lo	0	0	10	60	50	12	D
Whyte's Family Foods	10	8	9	50	40	12	D

Although Dr. Liu's practice may appear smaller than that of the clinic on the right, the astute salesperson would determine each business's sales potential before classifying either as an A, B, or C account.

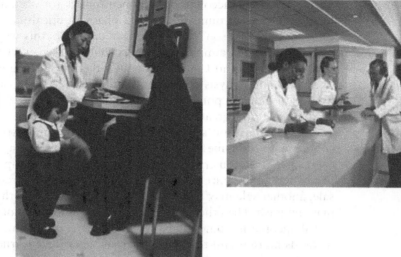

Grid Analysis

The **sales call allocation grid** classifies accounts on the basis of the company's competitive position with an account, along with the account's sales potential. As with ABC analysis, the purpose of classifying accounts through grid analysis is to determine which accounts should receive more resources. By this method, each account in a salesperson's territory falls into one of the four segments shown in Exhibit 15.5. The classification is determined by the salesperson's evaluation of the account on the following two dimensions.

First, the **account opportunity** dimension indicates how much the customer needs the product and whether the customer is able to buy the product. Some factors the salesperson can consider when determining account opportunity are the account's sales potential, growth rate, and financial condition. This rating is similar to the ABC analysis and is a measure of total sales potential. Again, the idea is that accounts with the greatest opportunity deserve the greatest resources.

Second, the **strength of position** dimension indicates how strong the salesperson and company are in selling the account. Some factors that determine strength of position are the present share of the account's purchases of the product, the attitude of the account toward the company and the salesperson, and the relationship between the salesperson and the key decision makers in the account. The strength of position helps the salesperson understand what level of sales is likely in the account. The account opportunity may be tremendous—say, $1 million. But if the account has always purchased another brand, the salesperson's strength of position is weak, and his or her real potential is something much less than $1 million.

Global accounts represent a difficult challenge in terms of determining potential and position. Position may be strong in one location and weak in another; potential may also vary. Marvin Wagner, an engineer with John Deere, has been working with Deere engineers and suppliers to Deere to standardize products globally. He's had to help suppliers negotiate buying centers involving engineers in as many as four different countries, all with different expectations and preferences for different vendors. What may be preferred by engineers at the Arc-les-Gray plant in France may not even be considered by engineers in Ottumwa, Iowa.

Exhibit 15.5
Sales Call Allocation
Grid

		Strength of Position	
		Strong	**Weak**

Account Opportunity — High		**Segment 1**
		
		Attractiveness:
		  Accounts are very attractive because they offer high opportunity, and the sales organization has a strong position.
		
		Sales call strategy:
		  Accounts should receive a high level of sales calls because they are the sales organization's most attractive accounts.
			Segment 2
			
			Attractiveness:
			  Accounts are potentially attractive because they offer high opportunity, but the sales organization currently has a weak position with accounts.
			
			Sales call strategy:
			  Accounts should receive a high level of sales calls to strengthen the sales organization's position.

Account Opportunity — Low		**Segment 3**
		
		Attractiveness:
		  Accounts are somewhat attractive because the sales organization has a strong position, but future opportunity is limited.
		
		Sales call strategy:
		  Accounts should receive a moderate level of sales calls to maintain the current strength of the sales organization's position.
			Segment 4
			
			Attractiveness:
			  Accounts are very unattractive because they offer low opportunity, and the sales organization has a weak position.
			
			Sales call strategy:
			  Accounts should receive a minimal level of sales calls, and efforts should be made to selectively eliminate or replace personal sales calls with telephone sales calls, direct mail, etc.

Source: Raymond W. LaForge, Clifford E. Young, and B. Curtis Hamm, "Increasing Sales Productivity through Improved Sales Call Allocation Strategies," *Journal of Personal Selling and Sales Management*, November 1983, pp. 53–59.

The appropriate sales call strategy depends on the grid segment into which the account falls. Accounts with high potential and a strong position are very attractive because the salesperson should be able to sell large amounts relatively easily. Thus these attractive accounts should receive the highest level of sales calls. For example, if you have an account that likes your product and has established a budget for it, and you know that the customer needs 300 units per year, you may consider that customer to be a segment 1 account (assuming 300 units is a high number) and plan to allocate more calls to that account. But if a competitor has a three-year contract with the account, you might be better off spending less time there. The account may buy 3,000 units per year, but you have little chance of getting any of that business. By classifying the account as a segment 2, you would recognize that the most appropriate strategy is to strengthen your position in the account. The sales call allocation grid, then, aids salespeople in determining where, by account, to spend time in order to meet sales goals.

THE GRID AND CURRENT CUSTOMERS The sales call allocation grid is a great tool for analyzing current customers. Recall the value of a customer that was discussed in Chapter 13; many businesses experience little or no profit in the first year of a customer's life. But over time profit grows if the salesperson can increase sales in the account, find ways to reduce the cost to serve the account (for example, shipping more can lower shipping costs), and so on.

From the BUYER'S SEAT

THE VALUE OF JUST SHOWING UP

John Ragsdale is vice president of the Service and Support Professionals Association, and he helps companies make technology purchases. In this position, he has the rare opportunity to observe what happens in buying decisions from both sides.

I don't think developers and marketers at high-tech companies have any idea how many deals they are losing based on the personality of the sales rep. What is really shocking is how many times the obvious "best fit" vendor is dismissed from the deal because

- The sales rep was arrogant (I've heard this a dozen times about one vendor in particular).
- The sales rep was late to multiple meetings and conference calls, and the company felt the vendor didn't want the business.
- The sales rep didn't know bubkes (sic) about the product functionality and tried to BS his or her way through.

These reasons are simply inexcusable. Reagan Ramsower, chief technology officer for Baylor University, recalls a similar frustration in dealing with a company that sells sales force automation. "We arranged a meeting to look at their software to manage our fund-raising officers. The rep called 15 minutes after the scheduled start time of the meeting to say that it was raining and he couldn't come." Raining? Really? Does that mean his customers can get service only on sunny days?

Helene Kennedy purchased a $30,000 annuity from an insurance salesperson. Gave him the check and everything, then didn't hear from him for nearly 30 days. "I found out he hadn't completed all of the paperwork when I called the company." After another week of delays, she rescinded the sale and got her money back. "I asked the company how much commission he would get, and it was over $1,000. I guess he didn't need the money badly enough to complete the job."

Ragsdale says he's actually called some of the vendors to get their side, but all he gets are excuses. He suggests that someone outside of sales conduct a win/loss review so companies have more accurate information about problems stemming from lack of salesperson effort and other problems.

Rob Keeney, director of training for the food distributor Frosty Acres Brands, wonders if sales managers are just getting lazy. "Too many are going to phone call reviews with their salespeople instead of riding with them in the field and coaching them based on actual observation." Ragsdale asks the same question, but the root of the question is simply based on laziness that starts with the sales manager and flows to the rep.

Woody Allen says, "80 percent of success is just showing up." If that's the case, then opportunities abound in sales simply by just working a full workweek.

Sources: Ragsdale quotes are from Marshall Lager, "The Psychology of the Sale," *Customer Relationship Management* 13, no. 5 (May 2009), pp. 34–37; all other quotes are from personal interviews.

In a landmark study of the paper and plastics industry, the key to a company's profit was found to be customer share, not market share. **Customer share,** also called **account share,** is the average percentage of business received from a company's accounts in a particular category. A similar term is **share of wallet,** which is the same thing but usually for an individual consumer. Over 15 years ago, an analysis of companies in that industry indicated that even if a company was the dominant supplier to a group of buyers, another company could be more profitable if it served fewer customers but had all their business.[5] Since that study, numerous studies have found similar insights. As a result, many companies are looking for how to increase account share, rather than the number of accounts.[6]

SALES Technology

LEAD SCORING AND PREDICTIVE MODELING IN SALES

For finding opportunities for new sales, there are two broad types of sales situations. The first is a finite and known customer universe. For example, if you sell to hospitals, there is a known and finite list of hospitals in the world. New hospitals don't suddenly spring up; salespeople don't drive around hoping to spot a new hospital. The other situation, though, is a customer universe that is broad, not known, and seemingly limitless. But no matter the situation, salespeople are limited in their time and have to make good decisions about how to use that time, including choosing accounts to call.

IBM's Software Group has the first situation. Although it sells to all types of companies, and companies can come and go, the universe of companies it would sell to is small enough to be finite and known. The group developed a set of analytical models designed to predict revenue based on current customers' purchase history. Factors such as market segment, economic leading indicators, and other variables were added to models to increase predictive accuracy. The models were then applied to existing customers and noncustomers, predicting future sales. The models predict future sales for each account individually. The accounts are ranked, and salespeople can focus on accounts with the greatest probability of sales. The process has been extended to serve over 13,000 IBM salespeople.

Profiles International falls into the second group. It sells hiring services, such as testing, to companies of any size all over the world. This potential customer universe is too large and too rapidly changing to be known. As a result, Profiles engages in marketing designed to create some initial interest on the part of a human resources or other hiring manager working for potential customers. If the person responds, say to an e-mail message or a direct mail piece, by visiting the Web site, Eloqua software tracks the person's behavior on the Web site. Eloqua recognizes the visitor if he or she clicked through an e-mail message or logs into the site, and Eloqua has predictive models built in to consider that person's behavior. Eloqua calls the buyer's online activity "digital body language." If the digital body language appears to show enough interest, based on the predictive model, the person is designated as a lead. In addition, based on that digital body language, the model can determine exactly what the prospect is interested in. A salesperson is then given a lead that not only says who the buyer is and how to contact the buyer, but also what the buyer is interested in. This system enabled Profiles to grow by over 20 percent in 2009—a year when most companies were experiencing falling sales.

Sources: Dario Parolo, interview February 4, 2010; Rick Lawrence, Claudia Perlich; Saharon Rosset, and Ildar Khabibrakhmanov, "Operations Research Improves Sales Force Productivity at IBM," *Interfaces* 40, no. 1 (2010), pp. 33–53.

INVESTING IN ACCOUNTS

Planning based on customer analysis should result in more effective use of the opportunities presented by accounts. This improvement relates to better use of time, which is allocated to the appropriate accounts. But developing good strategies entails more than developing good time use plans; strategies require the use of other resources as well.

Salespeople invest time, free samples or trials, customer training, displays, and other resources in their customers. As you can see in "Sales Technology 15.1," companies such as IBM use predictive modeling to determine which accounts are likely to be more productive. This knowledge helps salespeople determine where to invest resources—time, samples, displays, and so forth. Sales costs, or costs associated with the use of such resources, are not always costs in the traditional sense, but rather are investments in the asset called customers. This asset generates nearly all of a firm's revenue. Viewed from this perspective, formulating a strategy to allocate resources to maintaining or developing customers becomes vitally important.

Salespeople must determine not only which customers require sales effort, but also what activities should occur. CRM software can assist through **pipeline analysis**: a process for identifying and managing sales opportunities, also known as *opportunity management*. Recall that in Chapter 6 we discussed how accounts can move through stages from lead to prospect to customer. NetSuite, for example, can complete a pipeline analysis, telling the salesperson how well she is moving accounts from one stage to the next. In addition to being useful in determining conversion ratios and ensuring that a salesperson is creating enough opportunities to reach sales goals, pipeline analysis requires identifying which stage an account is in. Recognizing the account's stage in the pipeline is useful to determine what steps are appropriate. You don't want to try to do a spec design with a prospect for whom you haven't finished identifying needs, for example.

IMPLEMENTING THE TIME MANAGEMENT STRATEGY

Time is a limited resource. Once spent, it cannot be regained. How salespeople choose to use their time often means the difference between superstar success and average performance. Susan Flaviano, a sales manager for Lonseal, offers the following tips for managing your time as a salesperson; keep these in mind as you read through this section:

- Start early. Get a jump start to the day before anyone else. Then you control the day without the day controlling you.

- Manage responsiveness. Although responsiveness is key to being successful, you cannot let customer calls, e-mail messages, and voice mail consume your day. We now have the ability to respond immediately, but it is important to choose specific times during the day to reply to correspondence.

- Schedule in advance. I set most of my appointments one week in advance, which helps me stay on target. Usually, if there is not a set commitment, it is easy to justify staying in the office to get caught up on paperwork.

- Use downtime wisely. If you have a canceled appointment or extra time over lunch, or you arrive to an appointment early, use this time to plan or follow up. With our laptops and sophisticated project tracking tools, you can use this time anywhere and reduce the amount of time spent in your office or at home on Saturday catching up on paperwork![7]

Remember that your time is worth $30 to $40 an hour, but only if you use it to sell. Use it to hone a golf game or spruce up the yard, and opportunities to sell disappear. Although no manager really knows how a salesperson uses time, when the results are posted, accurate conclusions can be drawn.

thinking **it** through   How do you plan your time now? Do you use a computer to help you manage your time? How much of your time is planned by others, and how much of it are you free to allocate? What do you do to make sure you use your time wisely?

DAILY ACTIVITY PLANNING

To be effective time planners, salespeople must have a good understanding of their own work habits. For example, some people tend to procrastinate in getting the day started, whereas others may want to knock off early. If you are a late riser, you may want to schedule early appointments to force yourself to get started.

On the other hand, if your problem is heading for home too early, schedule late appointments so you work a full day.

Many salespeople have the opposite problem—they never seem to stop working. One study found that 81 percent of salespeople felt like they had to be available to their customers 24/7.[8] The BlackBerry, iPhone, and other similar products make the Internet and phone ubiquitous, but that is no excuse for failing to plan adequately. Susan Flaviano, now a sales manager for Lonseal, believed quantity of calls was the most important thing. But after a while, she realized she had no personal life and, more importantly, no more success than anyone else. She backed off the quantity of calls and began to spend more time planning her activities; the result was an increase in both sales and personal time.[9]

GUIDELINES

Salespeople need to include time for prospecting and customer care in their daily activities. Some minimize the time for such activities because they think sales do not occur on such calls, but prospects and happy customers feed future sales. Ikon, an office equipment dealer, requires salespeople to handle customer care calls before 9 a.m. and after 4 p.m. and to schedule prospecting activities between 10 a.m. and noon and between 2 p.m. and 3 p.m. Scheduled appointments are worked in when customers require them. The company bases these guidelines on its experience with buyers and when they are available.

Such planning guides are designed to maximize **prime selling time**—the time of day at which a salesperson is most likely to see a buyer. One salesperson, Lee Brubaker with Sandler Systems, calls this "pay time."[10] Prime selling time depends on the buyer's industry. For example, a good time to call on bankers is late afternoon, after the bank has closed to customers. However, late afternoon is a bad time to call on physicians, who are then making rounds at the hospital or trying to catch up on a full day's schedule of patients. Prime selling time should be devoted to sales calls, with the rest of the day used for nonselling activities such as servicing accounts, doing paperwork, or getting information from the home office.

Prime selling time varies from country to country. In the United States prime selling time is usually 9 a.m. to 4 p.m. with the noon hour off for lunch. In Mexico lunch starts and ends later, generally from 12:30 to 2:00 p.m.; offices may not close until 7 p.m. or later. In Great Britain prime selling time starts later; a British Telecom rep may not begin making calls until 10 a.m.

PLANNING PROCESS

A process exists to help you plan your daily activities, with or without the aid of planning guides. This process can even help you now, as a student, take more control of your time and use it effectively.

As Exhibit 15.6 shows, you begin by making a to-do list. Then you determine the priority of each activity on your list. Many executives rank activities as A, B, or C, with A activities requiring immediate action, B activities being of secondary importance, and C activities being done only if time allows. You can correlate these A, B, and C activities with the A, B, and C accounts discussed earlier, as well as activities such as paperwork and training. Prioritizing activities helps you choose which activities to perform first.

Note the difference between activities that seem urgent and activities that truly are important. For example, when the phone rings, most people stop whatever they are doing to answer it. The ringing phone seems urgent. Activities such as requests from managers or even customers may have that same sense of urgency; the desire to drop everything else to handle the request is called the "tyranny of the urgent." And the "urgent" can get overwhelming: The average businessperson

Exhibit 15.6
Activities Planning
Process

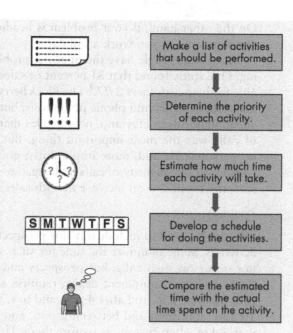

Make a list of activities
that should be performed.

↓

Determine the priority
of each activity.

↓

Estimate how much time
each activity will take.

↓

Develop a schedule
for doing the activities.

↓

Compare the estimated
time with the actual
time spent on the activity.

receives 274 personal e-mail messages and 304 business e-mail messages weekly, and according to another study, that number will grow as marketers increase their use of e-mail marketing.[11] Of course these statistics do not include telephone requests from customers. Yet, like most phone calls, even requests from customers may be less important than other tasks. Successful businesspeople learn to recognize what is truly urgent and prioritize those activities first.

The next step in the planning process is to estimate the time required for each activity. In sales, as we mentioned earlier, time must be set aside for customer care and prospecting. The amount of time depends on the activity goals set earlier and on how long each call should take. However, salespeople often have unique activities, such as special sales calls, demonstrations, customer training, and sales meetings, to plan for as well. Time must also be set aside for planning and paperwork.

The next step, developing an effective schedule, requires estimating the amount of time such activities will require. As follow-up, be sure to compare how long an activity actually took with how long you thought it would take. Comparing actual time to planned time with the aid of planning devices such as a DayRunner or DayTimer (paper-based calendars and planners) or computer software like NetSuite can help you plan more accurately in the future.

Using the Computer for Planning

Many of the same customer management programs that salespeople use to identify and analyze accounts incorporate time-planning elements. This software can generate to-do lists and calendars through a tickler file or by listing certain customer types. A **tickler file** is a file or calendar that salespeople use to remember when to call specific accounts. For example, if customer A says to call back in 90 days, the computer will remind ("tickle") the salesperson in 90 days to call that customer. Or if the company just introduced a product that can knock out competitor B, the computer can generate a list of prospects with products from competitor B; the salesperson then has a list of prospects for the new product.

Need for Flexibility

Although working out a daily plan is important, occasions will arise when the plan should be laid aside. You cannot accurately judge the time needed for each sales call, and hastily concluding a sales presentation just to stick to a schedule would be foolish. If more time at one account will mean better sales results, the schedule should be revised.

To plan for the unexpected, your first visit of the day should be to a prime prospect (in the terms discussed earlier, this would be an A account or activity); then the next best potential customer should be visited (provided the travel time is reasonable); and so forth. If an emergency causes a change of plans, at least the calls most likely to result in sales will have been made.

MAKING MORE CALLS

Making daily plans and developing efficient routes are important steps toward better time use. But suppose you could make just one more call per day. Using our analysis from the beginning of this chapter and Exhibit 15.3, this change would mean 240 more calls per year, which is like adding one month to the year!

Some salespeople develop an "out Tuesday, back Friday" complex. They can offer many reasons why they need to be back in the office or at home on Monday and Friday afternoons. Such a behavior pattern means the salesperson makes 20 to 30 percent fewer calls than a salesperson who works a full week. John Plott, with DG Vault, got one large sale by working the full week. He was making cold calls on a Friday afternoon, trying to set up appointments for the following week, when he reached an attorney whose current vendor was unable to meet a deadline. The attorney said if he could get the software set up that afternoon, he could have the business. The result was a $30,000 account and $4,500 in commission.[12]

To get the most out of a territory, the sales representative must make full use of all available days. For example, the days before or after holidays are often seen as bad selling days. Hence, while the competition takes those extra days off, the salesperson can be working and making sales calls he or she would otherwise miss. The same reasoning applies to bad weather: Bad weather reduces competition and makes things easier for the salesperson who doesn't find excuses to take it easy. On the other hand, good weather can tempt the salesperson to the golf course, doing yard work, or otherwise avoiding the job. No matter the weather, the professional salesperson continues to work.

Salespeople who make calls in bad weather often find that their competition has taken the day off, leaving the field wide open for those who want to succeed.

Salespeople can use certain techniques to increase the time they spend in front of customers selling instead of traveling. We mentioned Susan Flaviano's (Lonseal sales manager) challenges in managing her time earlier. One of her solutions, in addition to planning her time more effectively, was to use GPS routing software to help her plan her travel time more efficiently. Using routing techniques means she spends less time in the car and more time in front of customers.[13]

Routing

Routing is a method of planning sales calls in a specific order to minimize travel time. Two types of sales call patterns, routine and variable, can be more efficient with effective routing. Using **routine call patterns,** a salesperson sees the same customers regularly. For example, Eli Lilly pharmaceutical salespeople's call plans enable them to see all important doctors in their territory at least once every six weeks. Some doctors (those who see large numbers of certain types of patients) are visited every two weeks. The salesperson repeats the pattern every six weeks, ensuring the proper call level.

Variable call patterns occur when the salesperson must call on accounts in an irregular order. In this situation the salesperson would not routinely call on each account within a specified period. Routing techniques are useful, but the salesperson may not repeat the call plan on a cyclical basis.

The four types of routing plans, **circular routing, leapfrog routing, straight-line routing,** and **cloverleaf routing,** are illustrated in Exhibit 15.7. If an Eli Lilly salesperson used the cloverleaf method (with six leaves instead of four) for a routine call pattern, every sixth Tuesday would find that salesperson in the same spot. But

Exhibit 15.7
Types of Routing Plans

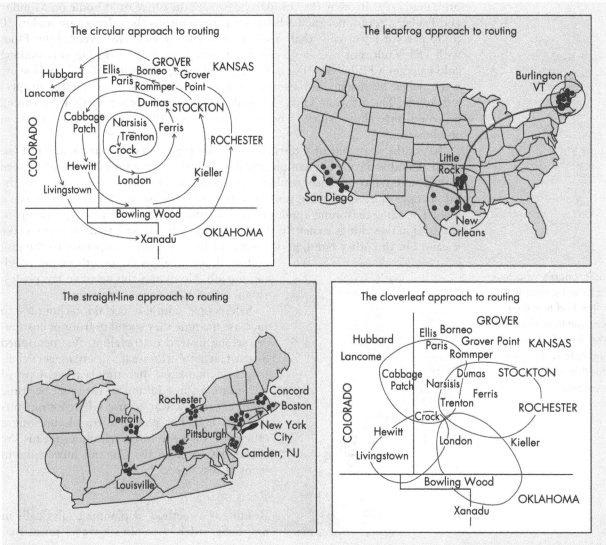

Exhibit 15.8
Zoning a Sales Territory
A salesperson may work in zone 1 on Monday, zone 2 on Tuesday, and so forth.

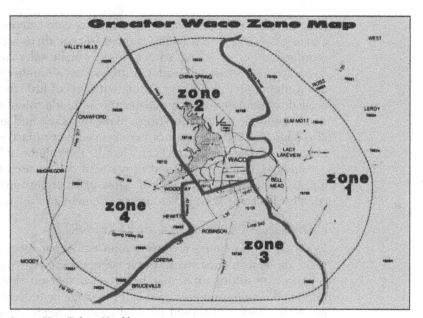

Source: *Waco Tribune Herald.*

a salesperson with variable call patterns could use the cloverleaf method to plan sales calls for an upcoming week and then use the straight-line method the next week. The pattern would vary depending on the demands of the customers and the salesperson's ability to schedule calls at convenient times.

Zoning

Zoning means dividing the territory into zones, based on ease of travel and concentration of customers, to minimize travel time. First the salesperson locates concentrations of accounts on a map. For example, an office supply salesperson may find that many accounts are located downtown, with other concentrations around the airport, in an industrial park, and in a part of town where two highways cross near a rail line. Each area is the center of a zone. The salesperson then plans to spend a day, for example, in each zone. In a territory zoned like the one in Exhibit 15.8, the salesperson might spend Monday in zone 1, Tuesday in zone 2, and so forth.

Zoning works best for compact territories or for situations in which salespeople do not call regularly on the same accounts. (In a large territory, such as the entire Midwest, a salesperson is more likely to use leapfrog routes, but the principle is similar.) Calling on customers that are in a relatively small area minimizes travel time between calls.

Salespeople can also combine zoning with routing, using a circular approach within a zone, for example. When zones are designed properly, travel time between accounts should be minimal.

Using E-Mail and Telephone

Customer contacts should not always be in-person sales calls—the phone or e-mail can be effective. For example, some customer care calls can be handled by simply sending the customer an e-mail message asking whether everything is OK. The customer may appreciate the e-mail more than a personal visit because it can be read and responded to when the customer has time and doesn't interfere with other pressing responsibilities. The salesperson may be able to make more customer care calls by e-mail, increasing the number of contacts with customers.

Keep in mind, though, that not all customer care activities should be handled by e-mail or phone. Recall from Chapter 14 that there are many reasons, such as reorders and cross-selling, to continue to make sales calls in person to current customers. For example, Jenifer Rutter serves a number of nonprofit agencies as a consultant. One client kept calling with lots of little problems. "I realized I just needed to jump in the car and drive the 200-mile round trip to see them, or they would continue to have questions, make mistakes, and grow frustrated." But she also adds that because most of her clients are even farther away, "I've got to use phone and e-mail as well, or I can't handle the volume of business I need to do."[14]

Similarly, the telephone and direct mail can be used profitably for prospecting, as we discussed in Chapter 6. More calls, or customer contacts, can be made equally effectively with judicious use of e-mail and the telephone.

HANDLING PAPERWORK AND REPORTS

Every sales job requires preparing reports for management. All salespeople complain about such paperwork, but it is important. As we discuss later, paperwork can provide information that helps a salesperson determine what should be improved. The information also helps management decide what types of marketing plans work and should be used again. Therefore, every salesperson should learn to handle paperwork efficiently.

Paperwork time is less productive than time spent selling to customers, so completing it quickly is important. Salespeople can do several things to minimize the impact of paperwork on their prime selling time.

First, salespeople should think positively about paperwork. Although less productive than selling, it can increase their productivity and the productivity of the company's marketing programs by facilitating a detailed review of selling activities and marketing programs.

Second, salespeople should not let paperwork accumulate. We once knew of a salesperson who never did expense reports. He finally offered a summer intern 10 percent if she would complete his expense reports for the previous 12 months. This deal cost him $600; in addition, he was essentially lending the company $500 per month, interest free.

Routine reports should be completed daily. Nonproductive time (like time spent waiting for a customer) can be used for paperwork. Call reports and account records should be updated immediately after the calls so that important points are remembered and any follow-up actions can be planned.

Finally, salespeople should set aside a block of nonselling time for paperwork. The quickest way to do this job is to concentrate on it and avoid interruptions. Setting aside a small amount of time at the beginning or end of each day for writing thank-you and follow-up notes and completing reports saves prime selling time for selling activities while ensuring that the salesperson keeps up with paperwork.

Using the Computer to Handle Paperwork and Communications

Many companies, such as McGraw-Hill, give their salespeople laptop or notebook computers. These computers can be hooked up to the company's network to access customer information and process other paperwork automatically. Salespeople who travel can thus complete their paperwork while in a hotel, an airport waiting area, and other places. Voice recognition systems enable salespeople to do paperwork without any paper. Companies such as Giant Eagle, a grocery distributor, use such systems to enable salespeople to call orders in and handle other paperwork from their cell phones.[15]

Many companies now provide their salespeople with wireless notebook or pad computers so they can access customer information and complete paperwork in the field, sometimes even in the car.

Salespeople calling on overseas accounts can also file reports or check the status of orders, even though the home office in another time zone may be closed for the night. Computers can help international selling organizations operate smoothly by reducing communication barriers between the field and the home office. Computers and fax machines enable salespeople to communicate with colleagues and customers all around the world, despite significant time differences.

Some customer relationship management packages, like NetSuite, include territory management capabilities. These packages allow salespeople to track their performance by calculating conversion rates, commissions, expenses, and other important figures. Such technology enables salespeople to file reports quickly. Salespeople for J&K Sales Associates (Manchester, New Hampshire) input detailed call information into a simple Outlook file. The detail includes the buyer's stage in the buying cycle (J&K uses five stages, from introduction to postsale follow-up) based on the purpose of the sales call. The company has seen greater than 20 percent productivity improvement throughout the organization simply because all company members, from the purchasing department to customer billing, have the information they need at their computers.[16]

To manage your time wisely, you must exploit a scarce resource in the most effective manner possible. Your objective is to make as many quality calls as possible by reserving prime selling time for selling activities. Routing, zoning, goal setting, and other methods of planning and scheduling time will help you maximize your prime selling time.

EVALUATING PERFORMANCE

Success in sales is a result of how hard and how smart a salesperson works. Unlike many other workers, salespeople have a great deal of control over both how hard and how smart they work. Evaluating performance is the component of self-management that provides direction for how hard the salesperson should be working as well as an opportunity to determine which strategies work best. Salespeople should evaluate each sales call individually but also look at which activity leads to desired outcomes and at what rate. Let's examine each component in more detail.

POSTCALL ANALYSIS

At the end of each call, many salespeople take a moment to write down what occurred and what needs to be done, perhaps using a printed form or entering the information into a territory management program such as NetSuite. Information such as the customer's purchase volume, key people in the decision process, and current vendors is important to have, but so is personal information such as the fact that the buyer's three children play soccer. The salesperson can use that information when preparing for the next call.

Remember the plan you made for each sales call? That plan included one or more objectives. Postcall analysis should include reflecting on whether those objectives were reached. The professional salesperson not only looks for specific areas to improve but also evaluates the success of the overall sales call.

ACTIVITY ANALYSIS

When planning their time, salespeople set certain activity goals. They use these goals not only as guidelines but also to evaluate their own performance. At the end of each day, week, and month, salespeople should review their activities in relation to the goals they set. Goals are written down or entered into NetSuite when they are set—say, Sunday evening when planning the following week. Then, on Friday evening, the actual activities from each day would be tallied and totaled for the week and compared to the goals. The salesperson could then evaluate whether more calls of a certain type are needed in the following week.

Merrill Lynch, for example, recommends that new brokers make 100 telephone calls each day (calls count even if no one answers). Frank Baugh, a new broker in central Texas, made 7,544 calls in his first 92 working days, or 82 calls per day. His goal is now 120 calls per day to bring his average up to 100 in the next quarter.

PERFORMANCE ANALYSIS

Salespeople also need to evaluate performance relative to performance goals set earlier. For example, they often evaluate sales performance in terms of percentage of quota achieved. Of course a commission or a bonus check also tells the salesperson if the earnings goal was met.

An earnings goal can be an effective check for overall performance, but salespeople also need to evaluate sales by product type, as outlined in Exhibit 15.9.

Exhibit 15.9
Sales Evaluation Measures

Evaluation Measure	Calculation	How to Use It

Conversion rate
  For total performance
  By customer type
  By product type
	Number of sales
	Number of calls
		Are your strategies effective? Do you need to improve by working smarter (i.e., a better strategy to improve your hit rate)? Compare yours to your company and/or industry average.

Sales achievement	$ Actual sales $ Sales goal	Is your overall performance where you believe it should be? Are you meeting your goals? Your company's goals?
Commission	$ Actual commission $ Earnings goal	
Sales volume (in dollars)		
By customer type		Where are you most effective? Do you need help with a customer type?
By product category		Are you selling the whole line?
By market share		How are you doing relative to your competition?
By new customers		Are you building new business?
By old customers		Are you servicing your accounts properly?
Sales calls		
Prospecting calls		Are your efforts in the right place?
Account calls		
Sales presentations		
Call frequency by customer type		

BUILDING Partnerships

RELEVANCE AND THE SALES TEAM

Lydia Pearce, account executive for Teradata, believes relevance is the foundation of her success. "At a high level relevance means knowing your customer's business, aligning its business drivers to your products and services, and articulating this to each and every person from a perspective that is meaningful to him or her," says Pearce.

Teradata is the leading provider of data warehouses—special computers created specifically to store massive amounts of data and to make those data available on demand as quickly as they are entered into the system. Companies like Continental Airlines and Bank of America use Teradata systems to manage all their data.

While the average sales cycle is 18 months, the initial Teradata sale is simply the start of a long relationship. Account executives manage only one to three customers and/or prospects. The core sales team consists of an account executive who owns the account (and quota!) and drives all activities—"in this case, me," laughs Pearce. "The other two core members of the team include a solution architect and an industry consultant. Solution architects are technologists well versed in how our technology works and where it fits within various IT environments. They can articulate our value proposition and key differentiators to a variety of audiences. From business users who are concerned about query complexity to IT executives concerned about leveraging their existing infrastructure, the solution architect's expertise is leveraged throughout the sales cycle."

Industry consultants bring industry-specific experience to the team to address the particular various business challenges that can be overcome with Teradata's technology. They are often called upon to conduct business discovery and build business cases that include revenue and cost impact models and deployment roadmaps based on the customer's financial metrics and business processes,

respectively. In addition, there is the rich pool of subject domain experts that Teradata has assembled to augment the core sales team. These folks routinely share best practices with customers on a wide range of specialized subject areas including customer relationship management, finance and performance management, data mining for predictive analytics, and industry-specific logical data models.

Each new sales effort begins with an opportunity plan. Here the team plans how to create demand through careful execution of effective and highly tailored messaging to a targeted group of people high, wide, and deep. Once executed, the opportunity plan becomes the foundation from which the account executive begins to map the customer's organizational structure. As initial points of contacts are made, account executives begin building their network of intelligence that links specific people to specific business functions, business functions to business challenges, and the alignment of these functions to products and service offers. When initial points of contact give way to genuine interest, more frequent and narrowly focused meetings begin to take place. At this point Pearce, along with her team, develops a strategic plan for winning the business. The strategy encompasses what the first solution will include, the specific business challenges it will address along with a means to quantify its value, and how it will be sold. The "how" includes a time line of meetings, critical messaging, technology benchmarks, and proof of concepts and/or pilots, along with the objectives and the essential "close" for each. Strategic plans need to be continuously modified based on the outcome of each activity. Because the exact composition of the sales team changes throughout the sales process, the strategic plan also keeps everyone who will be interacting with the customer apprised of the previous and planned activities.

Source: Contributed by Lydia Pearce; used with permission.

Salespeople who sell only part of the product line may be missing opportunities for cross-selling or full-line selling, which means they have to work harder to achieve the same level of sales as the salesperson who successfully integrates cross-selling and full-line selling in the sales strategy.

PRODUCTIVITY ANALYSIS

Salespeople also need to identify which strategies work. For example, if using a certain strategy improved the ratio of appointments to cold calls made, that approach should be continued. Otherwise the salesperson should change it or go back to a previous approach. Frank Baugh, the Merrill Lynch broker, tried several approaches before settling on one that works well for him. Of course Baugh keeps good records so he knows what works and what does not.

The **conversion ratio,** or number of sales per calls, is an important measure of effectiveness. Conversion ratios should also be calculated by account type; for example, a conversion ratio for type A accounts should be determined. Other conversion ratios can also pinpoint effective strategies and areas that need improvement.

Conversion ratios can also be calculated for each step of the sales cycle. Profiles International, for example, calculates the conversion ratio of leads to prospects to determine which marketing activities generate the highest number of qualified sales leads. These leads can be tracked all the way to the close, too, telling Dario Parolo, vice president of marketing, where to invest his marketing activities.

SELLING YOURSELF

A theme for this chapter is self-analysis to improve performance. As a student, engaging in self-analysis is important so you repeat activities that are successful (lead to good grades) and avoid those that are not. Did pulling an all-nighter improve your exam performance? Or did you do better when you studied for shorter periods each day beginning a week ahead?

Similarly, if you are in an organization and examine the organization's recruiting practices, you'll find that some methods work better than others. What method of finding leads worked best—posting a flyer in the dorms or posting an e-vite on Facebook? What events attracted the largest crowds, and which events provided the best prospective members? By applying what you've learned in this chapter to organizational recruiting (or fund-raising or other activities that mimic the sales process), you'll be able to improve your organization's performance.

But what about you? Do you set goals for your academic performance each semester? Do you track your progress toward those goals and keep the goals visible as a way to motivate yourself? One sales trainer said, "I have to know myself—what makes me work, when I want to slack, and even what tricks I can pull on myself to do what I need to do to reach my goals because there is no one else who will do it for me." Although his comments were aimed at salespeople, they apply to students as well.

SUMMARY

A sales territory can be viewed as a small business. Territory salespeople have the freedom to establish programs and strategies. They manage a number of resources, including physical resources such as sample inventory, displays, demonstration equipment, and perhaps a company vehicle. More important, they manage their time, their customers, and their skills.

Managing a territory involves setting performance, activity, and conversion goals. Salespeople use these goals to allocate time to various activities and to manage customers.

To manage customers well, the salesperson must analyze their potential. Accounts can be classified using the ABC method or the sales call allocation grid. These analyses tell how much effort should be put into each account. Some organizations use CRM software to conduct these analyses on the entire customer database, which helps identify patterns within a territory. Salespeople can use these patterns to develop account sales strategies.

More calls (working harder) can be accomplished by moving nonselling activities, such as paperwork, to nonselling time. Also, selling time can be used more efficiently (working smarter). For example, routing and zoning techniques enable the salesperson to spend more prime selling time in front of customers instead of behind the steering wheel of a car.

Effective planning of the salesperson's day requires setting aside time for important activities such as prospecting and still making the appropriate number of sales appointments. Using the full workweek and employing technology such as telephones, computers, and fax machines can help the salesperson stay ahead of the competition.

Finally, salespeople must manage their skills. Managing skills involves choosing how to make sales calls and improving the way one sells. Improvement requires that salespeople first understand what they do well and what needs improvement. Evaluating their performance can provide them with that insight.

KEY TERMS

ABC analysis 412
account opportunity 414
account share 416
activity goals 410
benchmarking 411
circular routing 422
cloverleaf routing 422
conversion goals 410
conversion ratio 428
customer share 416
leapfrog routing 422
performance goals 409

pipeline analysis 418
prime selling time 419
routine call patterns 422
routing 421
sales call allocation grid 414
share of wallet 416
straight-line routing 422
strength of position 414
tickler file 420
variable call patterns 422
zoning 423

ETHICS PROBLEMS

1. A sales manager schedules all sales training and sales meetings on the weekend so salespeople lose no selling time. Is this ethical? Does your answer depend on how they get paid—straight salary, salary plus commission, or straight commission?
2. One company's culture is "flashy," meaning salespeople are expected to wear custom-tailored clothing, flaunt expensive jewelry and watches, and drive expensive cars. Assume you are about to graduate and go to work for this company. Consider this culture, and relate it to your goals—how might this culture influence your goals? Is that influence healthy? Why or why not?

QUESTIONS AND PROBLEMS

1. Look over "Building Partnerships 15.1." How does the concept of relevance apply to understanding where an account is on the sales call allocation grid?
2. Lydia Pearce, Susan Flaviano, and many other salespeople work out of their homes. Pearce and Flaviano both recognize how tempting it is to work longer and to put off paperwork until

the weekends because it is so convenient. What problems might succumbing to such temptation cause? What safeguards can they put into place?

3. Compare and contrast the special problems of self-management for a computer salesperson who works in a computer store with those of a computer salesperson who calls on customers in their offices.

4. Shakespeare wrote, "To thine own self be true." How would you apply this statement to your planning and development activities?

5. Which factors are important for classifying customers? Why? How would these factors change depending on the industry?

6. Distinguish between routing and scheduling and between routing and zoning. Explain how routing and scheduling can interact to complement the planning of an efficient day's work.

7. How might a pharmaceutical salesperson increase the number of calls made per day? A financial services representative selling pension plans to companies? A financial services representative selling retirement plans to consumers? A representative who sells golf clubs to retailers and pro shops?

8. One sales manager said, "Sales is a numbers game. To make more sales, make more sales calls." Should sales managers encourage salespeople to continually increase the number of calls made each week? Explain your answer. Reread "From the Buyer's Seat 15.1." How does this essay relate to your answer?

9. One recruiter told a class that students are used to getting feedback on how they are doing every couple of months, but salespeople do not get a "final grade" until a year has gone by. He claims that students have a hard time making that adjustment when they enter the work world. What do salespeople do to know where they stand at any given time? What do you do now that helps you know where you stand in your classes? Why is such knowledge important?

10. How would you use the sales call allocation grid to determine a prospecting plan? Be specific, and number each step of the process you would use.

11. How does predictive modeling improve salesperson performance? You may want to review "Sales Technology 15.1" as you develop your answer.

CASE PROBLEMS

case 15.1

MicroDyne

When Bill Maguire saw the headline that Micro-Automation and Dynamic Tools merged, he almost passed out. MicroDyne, the new company, would be his account, but what kind of account would it be?

Two years ago Bill landed the Dynamic Tools business after a hard-fought negotiation and sales process. First, the company had been using Bill's strongest competitor, Target Supply, for almost 10 years. Although some minor issues had arisen, overall Dynamic Tools was pretty satisfied. The director of manufacturing, Jack Reilly, really liked the Target Supply rep and fought hard against Bill. In one meeting Jack not only shouted at Bill, he told the head of purchasing that he resented Bill's company even getting a chance to bid! But in the end Bill's lower price and several customer testimonials, including one from a good friend of the CFO, won the business.

Over the two years since, Bill made a lot of progress in strengthening the relationship, except with Jack. But then, six months ago, Jack left Dynamic to take a position with Micro-Automation, also one of Bill's accounts. The first thing he did was call Bill. "Well, guess what, Bill. I'm canceling all outstanding orders with your company as of now. And that pallet of sweepers you sent yesterday? You can come get it. I switched all our business to Target."

Micro-Automation's business for Bill was much smaller than that of Dynamic, so the loss wasn't so bad. But Micro-Automation is bigger overall, and Dynamic Tool was acquired by Micro. Jack was back, as the movie promos say, "bigger and badder than ever."

Suddenly Bill's cell phone rang. The caller ID showed Micro-Dyne. Was Jack calling to cancel already?

Questions

1. Assess the new Micro-Dyne account in terms of the sales call allocation grid.
2. Assume the call is not from Jack but from the former Dynamic Tool CFO. She tells you that she is the new CFO, and they will be reviewing all vendors. You ask about Jack's responsibility and job title, and she laughs. "I know what you're thinking. But don't worry. You've done a great job for us. We just want to consolidate all purchases so we know we're getting the best deal." How should Bill respond? What should he do?

case 15.2

McGraw-Hill

Pierce Totten is a salesperson for McGraw-Hill, the company that publishes this textbook. Pierce works from Minneapolis–St. Paul; his territory includes northern Minnesota and the following accounts:

Bemidji State, Bemidji: This school has 12 faculty members in the business administration program. It offers five majors: finance, generalist, management, marketing, and small business. It is a small school with approximately 400 undergraduate business students.

Central Lakes College, Brainerd: There are 11 faculty members at the Brainerd campus of Central Lakes in the business department. The school offers eight majors: finance, management, marketing, accounting, information systems, insurance, economics, and entrepreneurship in a two-year associate program. This pre-BBA program can be combined with programs at schools such as St. Scholastica. The school has 350 students at the Brainerd campus and another 100 taking courses online.

Lake Superior College, Duluth: There are approximately 8,500 students at Lake Superior. The business department has 10 full-time faculty members and offers 19 majors in the bachelor's program. There are approximately 30 adjunct professors who teach one class each, but in almost all cases the full-time faculty decides what books to use.

University of Minnesota Duluth: There are over 9,000 students total at UMD. The school of business and economics has over 40 faculty members (full-time) in four departments, and approximately 60 percent of all undergraduates are business majors.

St. Cloud University, St. Cloud: There are five departments offering 10 majors at St. Cloud. Over 70 faculty members teach in the undergraduate program, serving approximately 3,500 students.

Source: Based on information and a scenario suggested by Dr. Jeff Totten, Southeastern Louisiana University, and a sales representative from another textbook publisher.

Questions

1. Plan an appropriate schedule for Pierce.
2. What are the three most important issues Pierce needs to consider in scheduling his time? Why are these issues so important?

Map of Pierce Totten's Territory

ROLE PLAY CASE

Six months ago, you went through your accounts and determined that how you've allocated your effort is not consistent with the potential of each account and your relative position. In one instance, National Barns, you've got a great relationship with the CIO (chief information officer or head of information technology) and have called on National Barns once or twice a month. There are, however, only 24 salespeople there, and the company isn't growing, so there isn't much opportunity. You decided that this is an account you no longer plan to visit in person but will check by phone.

Another account, Maguire Manufacturing, merited more calling. It had 34 salespeople six months ago and has 44 now. Because it continues to grow and has indicated that it may grow through acquisition of other companies, you've decided to visit it once or twice a month.

Grafton Gifts, a distributor of gifts and greeting cards, has been a tough account to understand. Its 120 salespeople who call on retailers around the country use a paper-based system to keep track of their accounts. Orders are placed on special handheld computers that are downloaded at night. The VP of sales says that's all the company needs, but the VP of marketing wants more information so a CRM marketing strategy can be used. Today you will visit the VP of marketing to determine whether you want to continue with this account.

Your professor will give you buyer sheets for your turn as a buyer.

ADDITIONAL REFERENCES

Berry, Julian. "How Should Goals for 'Contact Optimisation' Be Set, and How Should Contact Optimisation Be Managed in a Multi-Channel Inbound and Outbound Environment?" *Journal of Database Marketing & Customer Strategy Management* 16, no. 4 (2009), pp. 241–46.

Eggert, Andreas, Wolfgang Ulaga, and Sabine Hollmann. "Benchmarking the Impact of Customer Share in Key Supplier Relationships." *Journal of Business & Industrial Marketing* 24, no. 3–4 (2009), pp. 154–69.

Fleischer, Mark. "Key Account Management in the Managed Markets: Visibility and Collaboration for Greater Effectiveness." *Journal of Medical Marketing* 10, no. 1 (January 2010), pp. 53–60.

Helm, Sabrina, Ludger Rolfes, and Bernd Gunter. "Suppliers' Willingness to End Unprofitable Customer Relationships: An Exploratory Investigation in the German Mechanical Engineering Sector." *European Journal of Marketing* 40, no. 3–4 (2006), pp. 366–83.

Koller, Monika, and Thomas Salzberger. "Benchmarking in Service Marketing: A Longitudinal Analysis of the Customer." *Benchmarking* 16, no. 3 (2009), pp. 401–20.

Lambert, Douglas M. "Customer Relationship Management as a Business Process." *Journal of Business & Industrial Marketing* 25 no. 1 (2010), pp. 4–17.

Sweet, Catherine, Tim Sweet, Beth Rogers, Valerie Heritage, and Mike Turner. "Developing a Benchmark for Company-wide Sales Capability." *Industrial and Commercial Training* 39, no. 1 (2007), pp. 18–28.

Zallacco, Ronald, Ellen Bolman Pullins, and Michael L. Mallin. "A Reexamination of B2B Sales Performance." *Journal of Business & Industrial Marketing* 24, no. 8 (2009), pp. 598–611.

PART 3

The Salesperson as Manager

chapter 16

MANAGING WITHIN YOUR COMPANY

SOME QUESTIONS ANSWERED IN THIS CHAPTER ARE

- Which areas of the company work with salespeople to satisfy customer needs?
- How do salespeople coordinate the efforts of various functional areas of the company?
- How do salespeople work with sales managers and sales executives?
- How do company policies, such as compensation plans, influence salespeople?
- How do salespeople work within the company to resolve ethical issues?
- What is the organizational structure, and how does it influence salesperson activities?

PROFILE

PROFILE International logistics is a $3 trillion a year industry that is highly regulated and changing on a routine basis. Phoenix International is a privately owned freight forwarder and customs broker that supports companies involved in international trade. As a sales executive at Phoenix International my role extends beyond selling new business. On a daily basis my focus is to ensure that my client's needs and wants are met. This may seem like an easy task, but it takes a solid relationship and strong management to be successful. Each client, commodity, and country I work with is a new canvas. Through active listening, research, and building a relationship with my clients, I am able to learn their business processes, specific requirements, frustrations, and wants. This knowledge allows me to create customized solutions that improve my customers' supply chains.

Once I have earned the trust of my clients and they choose to enter a partnership with Phoenix International, it is my responsibility to act as their advocate. Before working with a new client, I ensure that all departments have an understanding of the company, the client's needs, and any specific handling instructions. I develop standard operating procedures with the operational staff to make the customer's needs transparent. I work with the credit department and account receivables to establish appropriate credit levels and payments terms. My information systems team and I work together to provide the customer real-time visibility and reporting capabilities. Internally we all know sales can bring the first shipment in the door, but it is operations that play a vital role in maintaining and growing the business. The relationship between the operational coordinator and the customer is extremely significant, but more important is that the relationship is well managed.

Specifically here is an example of how I work with the operational coordinator: Today I received a phone call from one of my clients, Jon. He was upset because his shipment was not going to arrive on the original estimated day due to a number of events. As his representative I knew how critical this deadline was for him, and I wanted to assure him that we would use all possibilities to meet his deadline. I called his coordinator at Phoenix International to discuss various scenarios we could take to overcome the obstacle. The solution was simple and didn't take much time to resolve; with teamwork we were able to meet the customer's demands and make him happy.

Had I not worked with the operations coordinator and let the customer take a late delivery, how would my reaction have affected the business relationship between the client and Phoenix International? In my industry one small mistake, even if it was made by the customer, can cost you the account. In a company that prides itself on customer service, it is important for the sales executive to act in the best interest of the client and ensure that the coordinator is doing everything possible to make the shipment happen as smoothly as possible.

Typically when a problem arises the operational staff are the first to be made aware of it, and then the customer finds out. It is critical for the person in operations to notify me of what is going on because the next phone call I receive is going to be an upset customer. International trade is a complex business arena full of pitfalls and potential problems. My job in supporting my clients is to help the clients navigate through those pitfalls. When customers call with a concern and you have a logical explanation along with a solution, you save their day.

As a sales executive I have a number of individuals I report to. My sales manager, general manager, and all the way to the CEO of the company have a vested interest in how I am performing. Our internal systems allow management to easily track my productivity through the number of client visits and scheduled appointments, as well as my gross profit.

This visibility gives them the transparency to track my progress and determine where there may be room for improvement. This tool is very useful for my superiors to manage me; it also helps me manage myself.

Managing yourself is one of the most important roles for a sales executive. In sales you don't punch a time clock and receive a "to do" list when you walk through the door. Managing your priorities is the number one task where most people fail. There are several duties that consume your day, taking away from your core responsibilities: to sell new business and retain current customers. Once you have developed the skills to manage yourself, you are on the road to success!

Finally, no matter what position you are in or what company you work for, remember that your clients, no matter how big or small, deserve to be treated with respect and dignity and to be your number one concern. In addition the people you work with deserve the same treatment because without their support and hard work the company and you will not succeed.

Visit our Web site at
http://www.phoenixintl.com.

BUILDING INTERNAL PARTNERSHIPS

To effectively coordinate the efforts of various areas of a company, a salesperson must develop partnerships with the individuals in those areas. **Internal partnerships** are partnering relationships between a salesperson and another member of the same company. These partnerships should be dedicated to satisfying customer needs.

THE IMPORTANCE OF INTERNAL PARTNERSHIPS

By definition, a sales representative represents something. Students often think the title means that the salesperson represents only a company or a product, but at times the salesperson must represent the customer to the company. For example, the salesperson may have to convince the warehouse manager to ship a customer's product next to meet a special deadline. The salesperson does not have the authority to order the manager to ship the product, but he or she must use persuasion. Or the rep may have to negotiate with production to get a product manufactured to a customer's specifications. Sometimes success in landing a sale may depend on the salesperson's ability to manage such company efforts.

This ability to work with groups inside the company can directly affect the rep's pocketbook. One of the authors, while selling for a major corporation, had an opportunity to earn a large bonus by making 30 sales. He had 31 orders, but a sale didn't count until the product was delivered. Unfortunately two orders were delivered after the deadline, and he did not get the bonus. In tracking down the slow deliveries, the hapless salesperson learned that the order entry clerk had delayed processing the orders. A little probing uncovered the reason: She was upset with the way he prepared his paperwork! Her performance was evaluated on how quickly an order was delivered, but his sloppy paperwork always slowed her down and got her into trouble. Delaying work on his orders was her way of getting his attention.

It worked! For several months after that, he enlisted her help in filling out the paperwork properly before he turned it in. After that, she never had a problem with his orders. And when necessary to meet a customer's requirements, she would prioritize his orders.

THE ROLE OF SALES

Salespeople not only sell a company, its products, and its services to customers but also sell their customers' needs to their companies. Carrying the customer's voice across the organization is one of the most important functions of the sales force. Although many companies work to increase the customer contact time for support personnel so they will understand customers, often the only person who really understands what the customer needs and why is the salesperson. The salesperson's ability to carry the voice of the customer across the organization is key to any firm.

Nucor Fastener uses its CRM system to capture the voice of the customer. Salespeople's notes, along with a deep analysis of data from other systems, helped the company identify specific customer needs that required special treatment. For example, 50 percent of all rush orders were generated by only 12 customers. The account executives for those accounts were able to identify customer requirements that led to new service offerings, greater revenue, and higher customer satisfaction.[1]

But when companies do not have a formal voice of the customer process, salespeople still have a responsibility to their customers to ensure that the company is responsive to their changing needs. In "Building Partnerships 16.1" Dave Brock describes an experience he had with a salesperson for a marketing agency who had not taken the time and effort to make sure his company was meeting customers' needs.

SELLING INTERNALLY

To service customers well, salespeople must often rely on personnel in other areas of the firm to do their respective jobs properly. But how well those other employees assist salespeople may be a function of the relationship the salesperson has already established with them. That relationship should be a partnership, just like the one the salesperson wants to establish with appropriate customers. To establish the appropriate partnership, the salesperson must invest time in understanding the customer's needs and then work to satisfy those needs.

thinking it through

Consider the impact electronic forms of communication have had on your life so far. How do such forms of communication help build internal partnerships, particularly when a salesperson is stationed far from company headquarters? How can such forms of communication hinder a salesperson's efforts to build internal partnerships?

As summarized in Exhibit 16.1, the first step of selling laterally is to recognize that it is the salesperson's responsibility to develop relationships with other departments. Rarely do other departments have an incentive to take the initiative. Salespeople who expect other workers to serve them are frustrated by the lack of support they receive. The better perspective is, How can I serve them so we can serve the customer better?

Use questioning skills such as SPIN to understand the personal and professional needs of personnel in other departments. Salespeople should have excellent communication skills but sometimes fail to use these skills when dealing with internal customers and support groups. SPIN and active listening are just as important to understanding the needs of colleagues as they are to satisfying customer needs. For example:

SALESPERSON: What do you do with these credit applications? (*Situation*)

CREDIT REP: We key the information into the computer system, and then it is processed by a credit company each night. The next morning we get a report that shows who has been approved and who hasn't. That's why it is so important to have a clean copy.

BUILDING Partnerships

16.1

SOMETIMES I'M ASHAMED TO BE A SALESPERSON

I like talking to salespeople trying to sell me something. It's always interesting to be on the customer side and to be able to look at how I am being sold to. Often I talk to really great salespeople. They are professional, they listen well, they execute their sales process well. Even though I may not buy, I'll find a way to point those people to an opportunity, or at least thank them for their professionalism. Then I get the calls like I got today.

The phone call actually started well because it was short. The salesperson was trying to sell me some marketing services. Like every company, we are interested in opportunities to extend our reach and attract interest. The sales guy told me about his company's great capability to create content, interesting designs, powerful graphics, and compelling messages. He further talked about getting that content into multiple channels in a cohesive way.

I was interested in what he had to say. I asked him to send information and some references I could talk to. We set a follow-up for next week. Within a few minutes I got the e-mail—things were going well. He was meeting my expectations, though I did set the bar pretty low.

I received a series of Word documents. I opened the first one. It was poorly written and confusing and had major formatting problems and even a few spelling errors. Hmm.

I opened the second; it was no better; same with the third. I was beginning to wonder. Here is a company that presented itself as creating compelling content, powerful messages, and high-impact materials. If its own marketing materials represented the firm so poorly, would it represent my company any better?

I was curious, so I opened the list of references. The salesperson, in the e-mail, had told me to feel free to contact any directly. The references were four pages of testimonials—but by only four people. Three pages were two testimonials from the same person. The formatting and flow were terrible. It looked like exactly what it was: a cut-and-paste job. There were people's names, but no contact information—I guess the salesperson wanted me to work for the information.

I clicked on the first link, hoping to be taken to the reference's Web site. The site I was taken to was one that declared the company's offerings a scam! It had many testimonials about how the salesperson's company took your money but either failed to deliver the service or delivered the poorest quality of service.

This was an interesting approach; never saw this one before; I thought I'd seen just about everything! I read the dismal reviews. What they said about the company's marketing programs was actually reinforced by the poor-quality marketing materials the company had developed for itself. The other reference that I could link to took me not to the reference's Web site but to a completely different company, having nothing to do with the reference. 0 for 2, so far. I decided to stop wasting my time.

I wonder if the salesperson ever looked at the materials he sent. I wonder if he ever bothered to click on the links. He clearly did not take my request for references seriously because there were no portfolio examples, the collateral he had sent was garbage, and I had no means of finding a legitimate reference.

The company was a legitimate company. I actually pulled its D&B (a financial report available from Dunn & Bradstreet). It wasn't big, but nothing stood out as saying it wasn't real. The story wasn't good when I went to the Better Business Bureau site; there were a number of complaints there.

You might ask, Why are you blaming the salesperson, the company is bad? After all, it's providing him with bad materials and poor references. Absolutely, I agree, this company is terrible! But the salesperson bears responsibility as well. He had so little pride in what he was doing that he did not bother to look at the documents and fix them. He never bothered to look at the references and where the links went. He was simply going through the motions but not paying attention to what he was doing.

Doing your homework includes knowing your own materials, proposals, and other collateral. Make sure they respond to what the customer has requested. Make sure they present the image of the company that you want to present. If they don't, take the time to fix it.

Salespeople cannot just go through the motions! True professionals take pride in what they do, execute with precision, and always present themselves and their companies professionally. I like being around professionals—they make me want to be better. Every encounter with companies and salespeople that aren't discourages me. If they are salespeople, it makes me ashamed to be called a salesperson.

Source: Dave Brock is president and CEO of Partners in EXCELLENCE, a global consulting company focused on helping its clients achieve profound improvements in the performance of their sales organizations. Used with permission.

Exhibit 16.1

Seven Principles of Selling Internally

1. Understand that it's your problem. **Accept responsibility** for gaining the support of the internal staff.

2. **Appeal to a higher objective.** For example, show how what you are asking for meets an important company objective.

3. Probe to find out and **understand the personal and professional needs** of the internal customer. Use SPIN and active listening techniques.

4. Use arguments for support that adequately **address the internal customer's needs** as well as your own. Use your presentation skills.

5. Do not spend time or energy resenting the internal customers' inability to understand or accept your sense of urgency. Rather, spend this time fruitfully by trying to figure out how you can better communicate your needs in a manner that will **increase the internal customer's sense of urgency** to the level you need.

6. **Never personalize** any issues. Don't call names, blame the person in public, or hold a grudge.

7. Be prepared to **negotiate**.

SALESPERSON: So the quality of the copy we give you is a problem? (*Problem*)

CREDIT REP: That's right.

SALESPERSON: What happens when you can't read the copy we give you? (*Implication*)

CREDIT REP: We put in incorrect information, which can result in a customer's credit application being rejected when it should have been accepted.

SALESPERSON: What happens when that happens? (*Implication*)

CREDIT REP: That's when we call you. Then we get the right information and reenter it. But we get in trouble because the approval cycle was made longer, and you know that the goal is to have a customer's order shipped in three days. We can't meet that goal if we're still working on its credit application.

SALESPERSON: So you need legible applications—and probably e-mail would be better than handwritten, right? (*Needs payoff*)

CREDIT REP: Yes, that would help a lot.

Keep in mind too that the salesperson cannot simply order a colleague to do what the salesperson wants, such as approving a customer's credit application. But if a salesperson can show that doing what he or she wants will also meet the needs of the colleague, the salesperson is more likely to receive the desired aid. Just as when selling to an external customer, persuasion requires the salesperson to meet the other person's needs as well. For example, if a salesperson can show a plant manager how an expedited order will result in a higher profit margin, thereby more than covering the plant manager's higher costs and helping that manager make production targets, both the plant manager's needs and the customer's needs will be met.

People from other departments, except for billing and customer service, do not have direct contact with the customer. Therefore, they do not feel the same sense of urgency the customer or the salesperson feels. Successful internal sellers can communicate that sense of urgency by relating to the needs of the internal customer. Just as they do with external customers, salespeople need to communicate the need to act now when they sell internally. They need to secure commitment to the desired course of action. Also, just as with external customers, the salesperson should be sure to say thank you when someone agrees to provide the support requested.

Selling to internal customers also means keeping issues professional. Personal relationships can and should be developed. But when conflicts arise, focus on the issue, not the person. Personalizing conflict makes it seem bigger and harder to resolve. For example, rather than saying, "Why won't you do this?" ask, "If you can't do this, how can we resolve the customer's concern?" This type of statement focuses the other individual on resolving the real problem rather than arguing about company policy or personal competence.

Be prepared to negotiate. Remember from Chapter 12 that negotiation is a set of techniques to resolve conflict. Conflicts between salespeople and members of the firm representing other areas will occur, and negotiation skills can be used to respond to conflicts professionally.

Salespeople must work with many elements of their organization. In fact, few jobs require the boundary-spanning coordination and management skill that the sales job needs. In the next section we examine the many areas of the company with which the salesperson works, what their needs are, and how they partner with the salesperson to deliver customer satisfaction.

COMPANY AREAS IMPORTANT TO SALESPEOPLE

The sales force interacts with many areas of the firm. Salespeople work with manufacturing, sales administration, customer service, and personnel. In some industries requiring customization of products, engineering is an important department for salespeople. Finance can get into the picture as well when that department determines which customers receive credit and what price is charged. In addition, salespeople work with members of their own department and the marketing department.

MANUFACTURING

In general, manufacturing is concerned with producing product at the lowest possible cost. Thus in most cases manufacturing wants long production runs, little customization, and low inventories. Customers, however, want their purchases shipped immediately and custom-made to their exact specifications. Salespeople may have to negotiate compromises between manufacturing and the customer. Salespeople should also develop relationships with manufacturing so they can make accurate promises and guarantees to customers.

In addition, we've already discussed the importance of the salesperson in ensuring that customers' needs are heard and products designed that fit their needs. Research shows that close, collaborative relationships between salespeople and manufacturing yield better new product designs—better in the sense of greater market acceptance and sales volume.[2] Hose Master Inc., a manufacturer of industrial hoses, actually brings salespeople and customers together with manufacturing for training on products. Frank Caprio, major market specialist for Hose Master, says these training sessions always yield new ideas for products or product enhancements that manufacturing can implement quickly.[3]

Salespeople who develop internal partnerships with people in areas such as manufacturing and service can count on their internal partners for support.

ADMINISTRATION

The functions of order entry, billing, credit, and employee compensation require each company to have an administrative department. This department processes orders and sees that the salesperson gets paid for them. Employees in this area (as discussed earlier) are often evaluated on how quickly they process orders and how quickly the company receives customer payment. Salespeople can greatly influence both processes and realize substantial personal benefit for themselves.

The credit department is an important part of administration. Understanding the needs of the credit department and assisting it in collecting payments can better position the salesperson to help customers receive credit later. A credit representative who knows that you will help collect a payment when a problem arises is more likely to grant credit to one of your customers. Some companies do not pay commission until after the customer has paid to ensure that salespeople sell to creditworthy accounts. These companies, such as Ruhrpumpen Inc. (an industrial pump manufacturer) and General Electric, believe a close working relationship between sales and credit is critical to the financial health of the company. In fact, GE has a "Walk a Mile" program where salespeople spend a day in credit, and credit personnel spend a day in the field with salespeople. This program leads to greater understanding and communication that last long after the day of walking a mile in someone's shoes.[4]

SHIPPING

The scheduling of product shipments may be part of sales administration or manufacturing, or it may stand alone. In any case salespeople need the help of the shipping department. When salespeople make special promises to expedite a delivery, they actually must depend on shipping to carry out the promise. Shipping managers focus on costs, and they often keep their costs under control by planning efficient shipping routes and moving products quickly through warehouses. Expedited or special-handling deliveries can interfere with plans for efficient shipping. Salespeople who make promises that shipping cannot or will not fulfill are left with egg on their faces. That's why Andrea Kinnard, sales representative for Konica-Minolta in Fort Worth, has been known to help load a delivery truck so a customer could get a much-needed copier.

CUSTOMER SERVICE

Salespeople also need to interact with customer service. The need for this relationship should be obvious, but many salespeople arrogantly ignore the information obtained by customer service representatives. A technician who fixes the company's products often goes into more customers' offices or plants than the salesperson does. The technician often has early warning concerning a customer's switch to a competitor, a change in customer needs, or failure of a product to satisfy. For example, if an IBM technician spies a competitor's computer in the customer's office, the technician can ask whether the unit is on trial. If a good working relationship exists between the technician and the salesperson, the technician will warn the salesperson that the account is considering a competitive product. Close relationships and support of customer or technical service representatives mean not only better customer service but faster and more direct information flow to the salesperson. This information will help the salesperson gain and keep customers.

Salespeople, in turn, can help customer service by setting reasonable expectations for product performance with customers, training customers in the proper use of the product, and handling complaints promptly. Technicians are evaluated on the number of service calls they make each day and how long the product works between service calls, among other things. Salespeople can reduce some service calls by setting the right expectations for product performance. Salespeople can also extend the amount of time between calls by training customers in the proper use of the product and in preventive maintenance. An important by-product of such actions should be higher customer satisfaction.

MARKETING

Sales is part of marketing in some firms and separate from marketing in others. Marketing and sales should be highly coordinated because their functions are closely related. Both are concerned with providing the right product to the customer in the most efficient and effective manner. Sales acts as the eyes and ears of marketing, while marketing develops the promotions and products that salespeople sell. Salespeople act as eyes and ears by informing the marketing department of competitor actions, customer trends, and other important market information. Marketing serves salespeople by using that information to create promotional programs or design new products. Marketing is also responsible for generating leads through trade show exhibiting, direct mail programs, advertising, and public relations.

Unfortunately not all marketing and sales departments just naturally get along. A study of Dutch firms found one reason to be simply that no one is responsible for interfacing between the departments.[5] Several other studies have shown that sales and marketing departments fail to communicate, don't trust each other, and even sabotage each other.[6] One study suggested that the biggest problem seems to be a lack of communication.[7] Other studies, however, suggest that the differences run deeper than communication; the differences are driven by beliefs about what should be done and by whom, the perceived value of marketing versus sales, and other basic differences.[8] Proactive salespeople won't wait for marketing managers to make the first move. Rather than complain about poor marketing programs, proactive salespeople and sales managers prefer to participate in marketing decisions and keep communication lines open. When sales and marketing work together, salespeople have better programs with which to sell.[9]

SALES

Within any sales force, there may be several types of salespeople. As you learned in earlier chapters, global account managers may work with the largest accounts while other representatives handle the rest of the customers, and the salesperson must interact with certain sales executives and sales managers. How these people work together is the subject of the next section.

PARTNERS IN THE SALES ORGANIZATION

The sales function may be organized in many different ways, but no matter how it is organized, it is rarely perfect. Usually some customer overlap exists among salespeople, meaning several salespeople have to work together to serve the needs of one account. Customer needs may require direct customer contact with the sales executive as well as the salesperson. At the same time, the salesperson must operate in an environment that is influenced by the policies and procedures created by that same sales executive and executed by the salesperson's immediate manager. In this section we examine how the activities of sales management affect salespeople.

SALES MANAGEMENT

Salespeople should understand the roles of both sales executives and field sales managers. Salespeople who are able to develop partnerships with their managers will have more resources available to perform at a higher level.

The Sales Executive

The sales executive is the manager at the top of the sales force hierarchy. This person is a policy maker, making decisions about how the sales force will accomplish corporate objectives. Sales executives play a vital role in determining the company's strategies with respect to new products, new markets, sales forecasts, prices, and competition. The executives determine the size and organization of the sales force, develop annual and long-range plans, and monitor and control sales efforts. Sales executives also strive, or should strive, to create a corporate culture that supports appropriate behaviors by their sales managers and salespeople—behaviors that are both ethical and customer-oriented.[10] Duties of the sales executive include forecasting overall sales, budgeting, setting sales quotas, and designing compensation programs.

Size and Organization of the Sales Force

The sales executive determines how many salespeople are needed to achieve the company's sales and customer satisfaction targets. In addition, the sales executive must determine what types of salespeople are needed. For example, the sales executive determines whether global account management is needed. Many other types of salespeople can be selected, which we discuss later in this chapter. For now, keep in mind that the sales executive determines the level of customer satisfaction necessary to achieve sales objectives and then designs a sales force to achieve those goals. How that sales force is put together is important because salespeople often have to work together to deliver appropriate customer service and successfully accomplish sales goals.

Forecasting

Sales executives use a number of techniques to arrive at sales forecasts. One of the most widely used techniques is **bottom-up forecasting,** or simply adding each salesperson's own forecast into a forecast for total company sales. At each level of management, the forecast would normally be adjusted based on the manager's experience and broader perspective. This technique allows the information to come from the people closest to the market: the salespeople. Also, the forecast comes from the people with the responsibility for making those sales. But salespeople tend to be optimistic and may overestimate sales, or they may underestimate future sales if they know their bonuses depend on exceeding forecasts or if they think their quotas will be raised. Wise managers should quickly realize when salespeople are underestimating forecasts, though the salespeople may be able to obtain significant earnings the first time. Such behavior, though, not only is unethical but also creates many problems for the organization.[11]

Salespeople are especially important to the forecasting process when the executive is attempting to forecast international sales. Statistics used in the United States to forecast sales are often not available in other countries or, if available, may be unreliable. Companies in Europe operate in so many different countries that the only consistent numbers available may come from the sales force. One candy company found that its salespeople provided the best forecast possible, in part because they were closest to the customer but also because each country's data were collected and compiled in different ways, making comparisons impossible.[12] But even companies in the United States are pushing forecasting to the field. Coty Fragrance, makers of such fragrance brands as Jennifer Lopez, Vera Wang, and Kenneth Cole, began requiring salespeople to develop forecasts based on the data in their CRM system. Coty's forecasting improved, leading to a significant reduction in stockouts, which also accounted for an increase in sales when the industry was hit by the recession.[13]

Expense Budgets

Managers sometimes use expense budgets to control costs. An expense budget may be expressed in dollars (for example, the salesperson may be allowed to spend up to $500) or as a percentage of sales volume (such as expenses cannot exceed 10 percent of sales). A regional manager or salesperson may be awarded a bonus for spending less than the budget allocates. However, such a bonus may encourage the salesperson to underspend, which could hurt sales performance. For example, if a salesperson refuses to give out samples, customers may not be able to visualize how a product will work; thus some may not buy. The salesperson has reduced expenses but hurt sales.

Although salespeople may have limited input into a budget, they do spend the money. Ultimately it is the salesperson's responsibility to manage the territorial budget. The salesperson not only has control over how much is spent and whether expenditures are over or under budget but also, and more important, decides where to place resources. Recall from Chapter 15 that these resources, such as samples and trial units or trips to the customers' location, are investments in future sales. If they are used unwisely, the salesperson may still meet the expense budget but fail to meet his or her sales quota.

Control and Quota Setting

The sales executive faces the challenge of setting up a balanced control system that will encourage each sales manager and salesperson to maximize his or her individual results through effective self-control. As we have pointed out throughout this text, salespeople operate somewhat independently. However, the control system management can help salespeople manage themselves more effectively.

Quotas are a useful technique for controlling the sales force. A **quota** represents a quantitative minimum level of acceptable performance for a specific period. A **sales quota** is the minimum number of sales in units, and a **revenue quota** is the minimum sales revenue necessary for acceptable performance. Often sales quotas are simple breakdowns of the company's total sales forecast. Thus the total of all sales quotas equals the sales forecast. Other types of quotas can also be used. Understanding quotas is important to the salesperson because performance relative to quota is evaluated by management.

Profit quotas or **gross margin quotas** are minimum levels of acceptable profit or gross margin performance. These quotas motivate the sales force to sell more profitable products or to sell to more profitable customers. Some companies assign points to each product based on the product's gross margin. More points are assigned to higher-margin products. The salesperson can then meet a point quota by selling either a lot of low-margin products or fewer high-margin products. For example, assume an office equipment company sells fax machines and copiers. The profit margin (not including salesperson compensation) is 30 percent on copiers but only 20 percent on fax machines. Copiers may be worth three points each, whereas faxes are worth two. If the salesperson's quota is 12 points, the quota can be reached by selling four copiers, or six faxes, or some combination of both.

One challenge sales managers face is recognizing that performance quotas can negatively influence a customer orientation as salespeople put the need to make quota ahead of their customers' needs.[14] One type of quota that can avoid this dilemma is an activity quota. **Activity quotas,** similar to the activity goals we discussed in the preceding chapter, are minimal expectations of activities for each salesperson. The company sets these quotas to control the activities of the sales force. This type of quota is important in situations where the sales cycle is long and sales are few because activities can be observed more frequently than sales. For example, for some medical equipment, the sales cycle is longer than one year, and a salesperson may sell only one or two units each quarter. Having a monthly sales target in this case would be inappropriate, but requiring a certain minimum number of calls to be made is reasonable. The assumption made by management is that if the salesperson is performing the proper activities, sales will follow with the customer's needs in mind. Activities for which quotas may be established include number of demonstrations, total customer calls, number of calls on prospects, or number of displays set up.

Compensation and Evaluation

An important task of the sales executive is to establish the company's basic compensation and evaluation system. The compensation system must satisfy the needs of both the salespeople and the company. You, as a salesperson, need an equitable, stable, understandable system that motivates you to meet your objectives. The company needs a system that encourages you to sell products at a profitable price and in the right amounts.

Salespeople want a system that bases rewards on effort and results. Compensation must also be uniform within the company and in line with what competitors' salespeople receive. If competitors' salespeople earn more, you will want to leave and work for that competitor. But your company expects the compensation system to attract and keep good salespeople and to encourage you to do specific things. The system should reward outstanding performance while achieving the proper balance between sales results and costs.

Compensation often relates to quotas. As with quotas, salespeople who perceive the system as unfair may give up or leave the firm. A stable compensation system ensures that salespeople can reap the benefits of their efforts, whereas a constantly changing system may lead them to constantly change their activities but never make any money. A system that is not understandable will be ignored.

The sales executive decides how much income will be based on salary or incentive pay. The salesperson may receive a **salary,** which is a regular payment regardless of performance, or **incentive pay,** which is tied to some level of performance. There are two types of incentives: commission and bonus. A **commission** is incentive pay for an individual sale, whereas a **bonus** is incentive pay for overall performance in one or more areas. For example, a bonus may be paid for acquiring a certain number of new customers, reaching a specified level of total sales in units, or selling a certain amount of a new product.

Sales executives can choose to pay salespeople a straight salary, a straight commission, or some combination of salary, commission, and/or bonus. Most firms opt for some combination of salary and bonus or salary and commission. Fewer than 4 percent pay only commission, and slightly fewer than 5 percent pay only salary. Exhibit 16.2 illustrates how various types of compensation plans work.

Under the **straight salary** method, a salesperson receives a fixed amount of money for work during a specified time. The salesperson is assured of a steady income and can develop a sense of loyalty to customers. The company also has more control over the salesperson. Because income does not depend directly on results, the company can ask the salesperson to do things in the best interest of the company, even if those activities may not lead to immediate sales. Straight salary, however, provides little financial incentive for salespeople to sell more. For example, in Exhibit 16.2, the salesperson receives $3,500 per month no matter how much is sold.

Straight salary plans are used when sales require long periods of negotiation, when a team of salespeople is involved and individual results cannot be measured, or when other aspects of the marketing mix (such as advertising) are more important than the salesperson's efforts in generating sales (as in trade selling of consumer products). Most sales trainees also receive a straight salary.

A **straight commission** plan pays a certain amount per sale and includes a base and a rate but not a salary. The **commission base,** the item from which commission is determined, is often unit sales, dollar sales, or gross margin.

Many companies offer incentives, such as special awards, bonuses, and other rewards, for outstanding sales performance.

Exhibit 16.2
How Different Types of
Compensation Plans Pay

				Amount Paid to Salesperson		
Month	Sales Revenue	Straight Salary	Straight Commission*	Combination†	Point Plan‡
January	$50,000 6 copiers 10 faxes	$3,500	$5,000	$1,500 (salary) 3,000 (commission) 4,500 (total)	$3,800
February	$60,000 6 copiers 15 faxes	3,500	6,000	1,500 (salary) 3,600 (commission) 5,100 (total)	4,800
March	$20,000 2 copiers 5 faxes	3,500	2,000	1,500 (salary) 1,200 (commission) 2,700 (total)	1,600

*Commission plan pays 10 percent of sales revenue.
†Commission portion pays 6 percent of sales revenue.
‡Copiers are worth three points, faxes are worth two, and each point is worth $100 in commission.
Note: These commission rates are used only to illustrate how compensation schemes work. Point plans, for example, do not necessarily always yield the lowest compensation.

Exhibit 16.3
An Example of a Draw
Compensation Plan

Month	Draw	Commission Earned	Payment to Salesperson	Balance Owed to Company
January	$3,000	$0	$3,000	$3,000
February	3,000	5,000	3,000	1,000
March	3,000	4,500	3,500	

The **commission rate,** which determines the amount paid, is expressed as a percentage of the base (such as 10 percent of sales or 8 percent of gross margin) or as a dollar amount (like $100 per sale). Exhibit 16.2 illustrates two straight commission plans: One pays 10 percent of sales revenue, and the other is a point plan that pays $100 per point (using the copier and fax example we discussed previously).

Commission plans often include a draw. A **draw** is money paid to the salesperson against future commissions—in essence a loan that guarantees a stable cash flow. For example, in Exhibit 16.3 the salesperson receives a draw of $3,000 per month. No commissions were earned during January, but the salesperson still received $3,000. In February the rep earned $5,000, but $2,000 went to pay back some of the draw from January, and the rep received only $3,000. In March the rep earned $4,500, of which $1,000 finished paying off the balance from January. Thus the rep was given $1,500 in March.

Straight commission plans have the advantage of tying the salesperson's compensation directly to performance, thus providing more financial incentive for the salesperson to work hard. However, salespeople on straight commission have little company loyalty and certainly are less willing to perform activities, such as paperwork, that do not directly lead to sales. Xerox experimented with such a plan but found that customer service suffered, as did company loyalty among salespeople.

Companies that do not emphasize service to customers or do not anticipate long-term customer relationships (like a company selling kitchen appliances directly to consumers) typically use commission plans. Such plans are also used when the sales force includes many part-timers because part-timers can earn more when their pay is tied to their performance. Also, part-timers may need the extra motivation straight commission can provide.

Under a bonus plan, salespeople receive a lump-sum payment for a certain level of performance over a specified time. Bonuses resemble commissions, but the amount paid depends on total performance, not on each individual sale. Bonuses, awarded monthly, quarterly, or annually, are always used with salary and/or commissions in **combination plans.** Combination plans, also called salary-plus-commission plans, provide salary and commission and offer the greatest flexibility for motivating and controlling the activities of salespeople. The plans can incorporate the advantages and avoid the disadvantages of using any of the basic plans alone.

The main disadvantage of combination plans lies in their complexity. Salespeople confused by this complexity could unknowingly perform the wrong activities, or sales managers could unintentionally design a program that rewards the wrong activities. Using the earlier office equipment example, if faxes and copiers were worth the same commission (for example, $100 per sale), the salesperson would sell whatever was easiest to sell. If faxes were easier to sell than copiers, the firm may make less money because salespeople would expend all of their effort selling a lower-profit product unless the volume sold made up for the lower margin. Even then, however, the firm may be stuck with a warehouse of unsold copiers.

thinking **it** through	As a buyer, under which plan would you prefer your salesperson to work? Which would you prefer if you were a salesperson? What conflicts might occur between buyer and seller because of the type of compensation plan?

FIELD SALES MANAGERS

Salespeople report directly not to a sales executive but to a **field sales manager.** Field sales managers hire salespeople, evaluate their performance, train them, and perform other important tasks. Salespeople find it useful to partner with their managers because the managers often represent the salespeople to other parts of the organization. Also, the salesperson often has to sell the manager first on any new idea before the idea can be pitched to others in management. Building a partnering relationship with managers can go a long way toward getting ideas accepted.[15]

Evaluating Performance

Field sales managers are responsible for evaluating the performance of their salespeople. The easiest method of evaluating performance is to simply add up the amount of sales that the salesperson makes. But sales managers must also rate their salespeople's customer service level, product knowledge, and other, less tangible qualities. Some companies, such as Federal Express, use customer satisfaction surveys to evaluate salespeople. In other companies the manager rates each salesperson, using evaluation forms that list the desired aspects. (An example of an evaluation form appears in Exhibit 16.4.) Such evaluations help managers determine training needs, promotions, and pay raises.

The records and reports salespeople submit also play an important role in communicating their activities to the sales manager. The manager uses these reports to evaluate performance in a manner similar to the way the salesperson would. But these written reports are not enough; sales managers should also make calls with salespeople to directly observe their performance. These observations can be

Exhibit 16.4
Behavioral Observation Scale (BOS)

	Almost Never						Almost Always
1. Checks deliveries to see whether they have arrived on time.	1	2	3	4	5	6	7
2. Files sales reports on time.	1	2	3	4	5	6	7
3. Uses promotional brochures and correspondence with potential accounts.	1	2	3	4	5	6	7
4. Monitors competitors' activities.	1	2	3	4	5	6	7
5. Brushes up on selling techniques.	1	2	3	4	5	6	7
6. Reads marketing research reports.	1	2	3	4	5	6	7
7. Prospects for new accounts.	1	2	3	4	5	6	7
8. Makes service calls.	1	2	3	4	5	6	7
9. Answers customer inquiries when they occur.	1	2	3	4	5	6	7

the basis for recommendations for improving individual performance or for commending outstanding performance. Other information, such as customer response to a new strategy, can be gained by making calls. This information should be shared with upper management to improve strategies.

Training

The sales manager trains new hires and provides refresher training for experienced salespeople. To determine what refresher training they need, managers often use information gathered while observing salespeople making sales calls. Content of training for new salespeople may be determined by a sales executive, but the field sales manager is often responsible for carrying out the training.

Most experienced salespeople welcome training when they perceive that it will improve their sales. Unfortunately salespeople often view training as an inconvenience that takes away from precious selling time. Dave Stein argues, though, that basic sales training is just that—basic—and if you want to sell to higher levels of the organization, if you want to work on bigger deals, and if you want to make more money, advanced skills are needed. Unfortunately he cites one study showing that less than half of companies surveyed offer any training, and of those, only half offer sales training. Thus, in some organizations, salespeople have to find advanced training on their own.[16] You should continue to welcome training, no matter how successful you are. It always offers the opportunity to improve your performance, or at least achieve the same level with less effort. Also, as you will see in Chapter 17, continuing to learn is important to the salesperson who is part of a learning organization.

Professional salespeople constantly need to upgrade their skills; here a group at InFocus Systems is reviewing a role play sales call.

MANAGING ETHICS IN SALES

Salespeople, particularly those within certain industries, have earned a reputation that is unfavorable. Most salespeople, though, want to act ethically. Because we have emphasized throughout this book methods of selling that help people solve problems and satisfy needs, we believe it is important to understand what companies do to encourage ethical behavior and how salespeople should work with their sales management partners to choose ethical options. First we discuss the sales executive's role in making ethics policy. Then we cover the roles of the field sales manager and the salesperson in implementing that policy.

ETHICS AND THE SALES EXECUTIVE

As mentioned earlier, sales executives should strive to create an ethical culture. While part of a sales executive's job is to determine corporate policy concerning what is considered ethical and what is not and how unethical behavior will be investigated and punished, it is also important that the sales executive support positive behaviors.[17] In addition, the sales executive must ensure that other policies, such as the performance measurement and compensation policies, support the ethics of the organization. Performance measurement and compensation policies that reward only outcomes may inadvertently encourage salespeople to act unethically because of pressure to achieve and a culture supporting the credo "the end justifies the means." But when behavioral performance measurement systems are in place, the compensation system can reward those who do things the right way. In addition, research shows that closer relationships with ethical managers support ethical behavior.[18] Although unethical behaviors may result in short-term gain (and therefore may accidentally be rewarded in an outcome-only compensation scheme), they can have serious long-term effects, such as loss of customers, unhappy salespeople who quit, and other negative outcomes.[19]

Sales executives must therefore develop a culture that creates behavioral norms regarding how things should be done and what behaviors will not be tolerated. Such a culture can be enhanced through the development of formal policy, training courses in ethics, ethics review boards, and an open-door policy. **Open-door policies** are general management techniques that allow subordinates to bypass immediate managers and take concerns straight to upper management when the subordinates perceive a lack of support from the immediate manager. Open-door policies enhance an ethical culture because salespeople can feel free to discuss troublesome issues that involve their managers with someone in a position to respond. Two versions are **ethics review boards** and ethics officers, both providing expert advice to salespeople who are unsure of the ethical consequences of an action. Ethics review boards may consist of experts inside and outside the company who are responsible for reviewing ethics policies, investigating allegations of unethical behavior, and acting as a sounding board for employees.

Salespeople also have the right to expect ethical treatment from their company. Fair treatment concerning compensation, promotion policies, territory allocation, and other actions should be delivered. Compensation is probably the area with the most common concerns, although problems can arise in all areas. Compensation problems can include slow payment, hidden caps, or compensation plan changes after the sale.

For example, IBM published a brochure for its salespeople that said that there was no **cap**, or limit, on earnings. Yet the brochure also had, in bold letters, the statement that IBM had the right to modify the program—even after the sale—until the commission was paid. When a salesperson sold one major account $24 million worth of software, the company changed his commission plan so he received less than $500,000 instead of the $2.6 million he expected. The salesperson filed suit, but IBM won in part because of the modification statement in the letter.[20] IBM had every legal right to take the action it did, and caps are not unethical; what was questionable was that the salesperson was not made aware of the cap prior to making the sale.

thinking **it** through Should schools have ethics review boards? What advantages would such boards have for the student? For the teacher? Would salespeople reap the same types of benefits if their companies had ethics review boards?

ETHICS AND THE FIELD SALES MANAGER

Salespeople often ask managers for direction on how to handle ethical problems, and the sales manager is usually the first person to investigate complaints of unethical behavior. Field sales managers can provide a role model for salespeople by demonstrating ethical behavior in role plays during training or when conducting sales calls in the field. Sales managers should also avoid teaching high-pressure techniques and manipulative methods of selling.

RESPONDING TO UNETHICAL REQUESTS

Salespeople may find themselves facing a sales manager who encourages them to engage in unethical behavior. When that situation occurs, a salesperson has several ways to avoid engaging in such behavior. Perhaps the most obvious option is to find another job, but that is not always the best solution. If the organizational culture supports the unethical request, however, finding another job may be the only choice. Exhibit 16.5 lists choices available to the salesperson.

Another way to handle unethical requests is to blow the whistle, or report the behavior, if the salesperson has adequate evidence (if adequate evidence is not available, sometimes simply threatening to blow the whistle may work). If this course of action is followed, the salesperson must be ready to accept a perception of disloyalty, retaliation by the manager, or other consequences. However, if senior management is sincere in efforts to promote ethical behavior, steps should be taken to minimize those negative outcomes. If an open-door policy or an ethics review board exists, the salesperson can take the concern to higher levels for review. For example, the salesperson could say, "I'm not sure that is appropriate. I'd like to get the opinion of the ethics review board." If the action is unethical, the sales manager may back down at that point. It is also possible that the manager will try to coerce the salesperson into not applying to the ethics review board; if that is the case, another course of action may prove to be a better choice.

Another strategy is to negotiate an alternative. This response requires the salesperson to identify an alternative course of action with a high probability of success. For example, if a sales manager tells the salesperson to offer a prospect a bribe, the salesperson should be prepared to prove that a price reduction would be just as effective. A similar tactic is simply to ignore the request. The salesperson may say to the manager that the request was carried out, when in fact it was not; the potential problem with this approach is that the salesperson has admitted to carrying out an unethical act (even though she or he did not), which can lead to future problems. Finally, the salesperson can simply deny the request. Denial can be a dangerous action in that it opens the salesperson to possible retaliation, particularly retaliation that is not obviously linked to the denial, such as denying access to training or reducing the size of the salesperson's territory.

Exhibit 16.5
Strategies for Handling Unethical Requests from a Manager

- Leave the organization or ask for a transfer.
- Negotiate an alternative course of action.
- Blow the whistle, internally or externally.
- Threaten to blow the whistle.
- Appeal to a higher authority, such as an ethics officer or ethics review board or a senior executive if ethics offices do not exist.
- Agree to the demand but fail to carry it out.
- Refuse to comply with the request.
- Ignore the request.

thinking it through

Is it ethical to lie to your manager and say that you will engage in the unethical behavior that your manager demanded when you know you won't? Is all fair when you are combating a request to engage in unethical behavior?

The salesperson's choice of action will depend on how much proof is available, what alternative actions to the unethical action exist, and the type of relationship with the manager. Other factors to consider include the ethical climate of the organization and whether an open-door policy exists. The salesperson is always in control of his or her behavior and should never rationalize a behavior by placing responsibility on the sales manager.

SALESPEOPLE AS PARTNERS

Many types of salespeople exist, including telemarketing representatives, field salespeople, product specialists, and account specialists. Often there is some overlap in responsibilities; when overlap occurs, companies should have policies that facilitate serving the customer.

GEOGRAPHIC SALESPEOPLE

Most sales departments are organized geographically. A **geographic salesperson** is assigned a specific geographic territory in which to sell the company's products and services. Companies often combine geographic territories into larger branches, zones, or regions. For example, Eli Lilly has geographic regions that include 50 or more salespeople. Each Lilly salesperson has responsibility for a specific geographic area. For example, one rep may call on physicians in a portion of Dallas, using zip code boundaries to determine the territory; that rep may have all physicians in zip codes 75212, 75213, 75218, 75239, 75240, and 75252. Geographic salespeople may also work with account managers, product specialists, inside salespeople, and other members of the company's sales team.

ACCOUNT SALESPEOPLE

Companies may organize salespeople by account in several ways. The most extreme example is to give a salesperson the responsibility to sell to only one company but at every location of that company in the country or the world. In another common form of specialization, some salespeople develop new accounts while others maintain existing accounts. Developing new accounts requires skills different from maintaining an already sold account. For example, Holland 1916 recently reorganized around these lines. The decision was based on a desire to focus on larger accounts that could grow, recognizing that growing these accounts might require a different skill set than was needed to acquire the accounts. As a result of this thinking, Jim Humrichouse, CEO, developed a list of larger accounts with potential for more growth (recall the sales effort allocation grid from the last chapter—these would be high opportunity/strong position current accounts), then assigned these to reps with a track record of success in growing current customers. He then hired new salespeople to take over those reps' geographic territories and tasked them with new account acquisition.[21]

Similar customers often have similar needs, whereas different types of customers may have very different needs for the same product. In such cases salespeople may specialize in calling on only one or a few customer types, although they sell the same products. NCR has different sales forces for calling on manufacturing companies, retailers, and financial companies. Andritz, an international heavy machinery company, has salespeople who sell only to paper producers and other salespeople who sell only to wastewater treatment plants, even though the same product is being sold. Some Procter & Gamble salespeople call on central buying offices for grocery store chains; others call on food wholesalers.

Companies also divide their customers on the basis of size. Large customers, sometimes called **key accounts,** may have a salesperson assigned only to that account; in some cases a small sales force is assigned to one large account. In some firms one company executive coordinates all the salespeople who call on an account throughout the nation or the world. These executives are called **national account managers (NAMs)** or **strategic account managers (SAMs).** These account managers are more than salespeople; they are business executives.

Strategic account managers sometimes manage large teams of salespeople. Account strategy for a global account may be determined by this strategic account manager, who has to rely on local salespeople to implement the strategy at the local level. For example, Hershey's has an account rep that calls on Walmart in Bentonville, Arkansas, but local salespeople work with individual stores and store managers. The local geographic rep's responsibility may involve coordinating delivery with the local customer. This coordination may also require customer training on the product (if the product is a machine or some other system) or working with a local store manager to set up displays, plan inventories, and so on. Local reps should also look for sales opportunities in the customer's location and provide this information to the SAM. They often become the eyes and ears of the SAM and provide early notice of opportunities or threats in the account, just as a service rep does for the geographic rep. SAMs often report directly to the vice president of sales or to a director of global sales, as illustrated in Exhibit 16.6, but work with geographic reps.

As described in Chapter 6, a **house account** is handled by a sales or marketing executive in addition to that executive's regular duties, and no commission is paid on any sales from that account. House accounts are often key accounts, but not all key accounts are house accounts. The main difference is that house accounts have no "true" salesperson. Walmart has negotiated to be a house account with some suppliers with the expectation that those suppliers will pass on to Walmart what they do not have to pay in commission or salary. General Dynamics attempted the same strategy when buying, but abandoned the plan upon realizing that lower costs also meant reduced service.

Somewhat different is the mega-account strategy used at Motorola. The top 20 international accounts are actually managed by Motorola's CEO, who

Exhibit 16.6
SAMs in the Sales Force

Although SAMs and geographic salespeople have different immediate managers, they still work together. SAMs coordinate the efforts of geographic reps within local buying offices of global accounts.

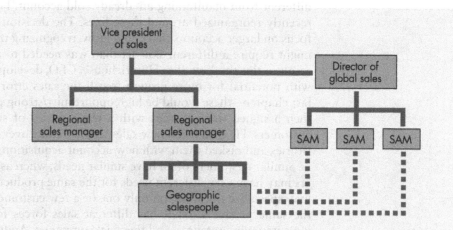

From the BUYER'S SEAT

SELLING IN MY COMPANY

By Anonymous

As marketing manager of a *Fortune* 500 company, I'm tasked with analyzing customer data to find new markets and new ways to generate revenue. I have to think about how to generate new sales from existing customers, and that means I need the right tools to understand my market and convince them to make additional purchases.

At the same time, however, I have to convince my management to spend the money to get the right tools. Currently we're in the midst of some major changes in how we seek to understand our customers, and these changes will require an investment of a million dollars or more for the right set of tools.

The process of selling my management on the need for these tools has been a long process, and it's not over yet. Among some of the leadership, the belief is that marketing doesn't influence demand—if people want our service, they will purchase it whether we market to them or not. So if I sell my new tools on the premise that these tools will help us convince people to buy more, I'll lose the sale based on my premise. Although I have a solid understanding of how these tools will help, not all of the leadership team does. Part of my job, then, is educating within the people I report to on how this will all work.

The primary tool we need is called Speed-Trap, a software product that provides detailed data about our customers' Web site activities. To complicate matters, we would also need to enhance our services from Teradata, the company that provides us with data warehousing services.

Most of the time, a presales group from a company like Teradata or Speed-Trap is responsible for teaching someone how to change the business. They have to create internal champions by selling them on the vision and

educating them on the need and process for change. Usually they look for a vice president, not just a marketing manager. But Speed-Trap recognized that I already knew what they could do, that I didn't need their education as much as I needed their support, and they supported me in my internal selling. We had biweekly calls to discuss how to move this along, some pricing and configuration conversations, and some presentation conversations; and we jointly planned a presentation to the leadership team. I gave Speed-Trap cases to configure their presentation within the context of our business problems. The day before the big presentation, we met and made sure that everything was aligned properly.

In addition, while we needed Teradata people there to answer any questions about interfaces and implementation, this wasn't their sale. True, they have a product and services that we will need to buy in order to make this work, but the big decision for my management team is the Speed-Trap purchase. I had to make sure that Teradata understood their role and participated appropriately.

The big meeting lasted all day. At the end of it, not only did my company's leadership team understand and appreciate the need for Speed-Trap, they also recognized that they needed someone who understood the business model around the Speed-Trap implementation. That led to a promotion for me.

Still, I'm not done yet. The next question is how will we pay for this? Remember, it costs more than a million dollars. So now I'm working on the business case, documenting how Speed-Trap will save money as well as generate new revenue. Saving money is a little easier to document; increasing revenue requires some things to happen that I don't have complete control over. But I'm working on it!

Source: Personal interview; anonymous by request.

works directly with the CEO in each account. These accounts are a form of house account, but the CEO has sales responsibility and sales goals to achieve.

PRODUCT SPECIALISTS

When companies have diverse products, their salespeople often specialize by types of products. Johnson & Johnson, which sells baby products, has two specialized sales forces: the disposable products sales force and the toiletries sales force. Hewlett-Packard has separate sales forces that specialize in selling computers, electronic test instruments, electronic components, medical test equipment, or analytical test equipment. Each sales force has its own regional, district, and area sales managers. Insuror's of Texas has salespeople who specialize in auto insurance, others who specialize in homeowner's insurance, and still others who specialize in medical and disability insurance. However, all of Insuror's salespeople operate under the same sales management structure. Regardless of the management structure, sometimes the technical knowledge requirements are so great that organizing territories by product makes sense.

In addition to having management responsibilities similar to those for geographic reps, product salespeople must coordinate their activities with those of salespeople from other divisions. Success can be greater for all involved when leads and customer information are shared. For example, a Hewlett-Packard test instrument salesperson may have a customer who is also a prospect for electronic components. Sharing that information with the electronic components rep can help build a relationship that can pay off with leads for test instruments.

INSIDE VERSUS OUTSIDE

Our discussion to this point has focused on outside salespeople, called **field salespeople**—that is, salespeople who sell at the customer's location. **Inside salespeople** (first identified in Chapter 1) sell at their own company's location. Inside salespeople may handle walk-in customers or work entirely over the telephone and Internet, or they may handle both duties. For example, a plumbing supply distributor may sell entirely to plumbers and employ inside salespeople who sell to those plumbers who come into the distributorship to buy products.

As we discussed in Chapter 6, the job of some inside salespeople is to provide leads for field salespeople. Other types of inside salespeople include account managers, field support reps, and customer service reps. An inside salesperson who is an account manager has the same responsibilities and duties as a field salesperson except that all business is conducted over the phone. Jean Heger, vice president of business development for Rail Europe, began her career in inside sales, where she managed relationships with tour and travel organizers.

A **field support rep** is a telemarketer who works with field salespeople and does more than prospect for leads. For example, field support reps at e-Rewards (you will meet one of the salespeople for this marketing research company in the next chapter) write proposals and price jobs, work directly with vendors to ensure satisfactory project completion, and interact with clients when needed. We discuss these representatives further when we address team selling strategies shortly.

Customer service reps (CSRs) are inbound salespeople who handle customer concerns. **Inbound** means they respond to telephone calls placed by customers, rather than **outbound**, which means the telemarketer makes the phone call (prospectors, account managers, and field support telemarketers are outbound reps). For example, if you call the 800 telephone number on the back of a tube of Crest toothpaste, you will speak with an inbound customer service rep. Many companies are now using customer service reps to identify cross-selling and up-selling opportunities, either by sending leads to field salespeople or closing the sales themselves. SuddenLink Communications, for example, has implemented a predictive model system that uses data from the CRM system to identify potential offers for customers who call about service. The customer service reps then make the sales pitch. Because the offers are more likely to be relevant to the buyer than a generic offer, customers don't seem to mind. In fact, they seem to like the approach—sales have increased over 20 percent since the launch of this system.[22]

Many companies use teams to work with large accounts. There may be members of management, finance, manufacturing, and engineering on the account team.

SALES TEAMS

A growing number of companies are adopting a team approach to sales.[23] This concept is being used by companies that recognize they can best build partnerships by empowering one person, the account manager, to represent the organization. In **team selling** a group of salespeople support a single account. Each person on the team brings a different area of expertise or handles different responsibilities. As you see in Exhibit 16.7, each specialist can be called on to team up with the account managers.

Before adopting team selling, companies may have had one salesperson for each product line. Xerox, for example, once had separate copier, supplies, fax machine, printer, computer workstation, and communication network salespeople all calling on the same buyer. These reps would pass in customers' lobbies without recognizing one another. Customers grew tired of seeing as many as six salespeople from Xerox. Now one account manager calls on the buyer and brings in product specialists as needed.

Xerox uses permanent teams, whereas Teradata forms teams as needed. The data warehousing company will create a team that might include an expert in the vertical market in which the customer operates, a group of finance experts who can help develop the right financial measures for the decision, software engineers who make sure the Teradata product will work with the systems the customer already has in place, and the account manager.

In an extension of team selling, **multilevel selling,** members at various levels of the sales organization call on their counterparts in the buying organization. (As charted in Exhibit 16.8, for example, the vice president of sales calls on the vice president of purchasing.) Multilevel selling can take place without a formal multilevel sales team if the account representative requests upper-level

Exhibit 16.7
Team Selling Organization

In team selling, product specialists work with account managers, who have total account responsibility. Product specialists are responsible for sales and service of only a limited portion of the product line and may work with several account managers.

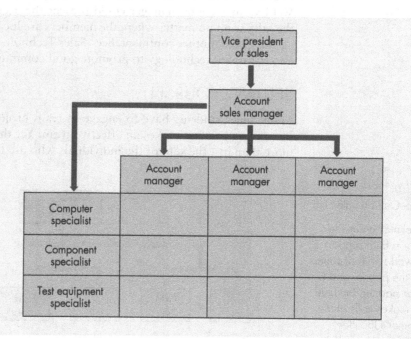

Exhibit 16.8
Forming Sales Teams for
Multilevel Selling

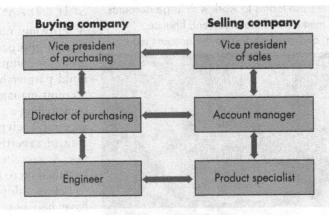

management's involvement in the sale. For example, you may ask your company's vice president of sales to call on the vice president of operations at a prospect's company to secure top-level support for your proposal.

Another type of sales team is made up of the field rep and the field support rep (see Exhibit 16.9). Some companies use one telemarketer for each field salesperson, whereas other companies have several salespeople working with a telemarketer. The telemarketer performs as many selling tasks as possible over the telephone. But when a sales call is needed at the customer's location, the field support rep makes the appointment for the field rep. Such is the case with IBM.com, a division of IBM that provides software and technology consulting. Good communication and joint planning are necessary to avoid overbooking the field rep, as well as to prevent duplication of effort.

Technology has played a key role in promoting good communication and joint planning. Companies can use CRM systems, for example, to give every member of the sales team access to all of the same customer records. This access means everyone knows what sales calls are planned and what happens as a function of the call. Another form of technology, represented by services like WebEx, enables someone to deliver a PowerPoint presentation to people scattered all over the world. Using WebEx, an account manager could present the account strategy, for example, to the sales team no matter where the members are located or present a proposal to a customer on another continent. See "Sales Technology 16.1" for additional insight into the use of technology to promote good communication and joint planning.

SELLING YOURSELF

Many times students have to engage in team projects, sometimes without much instruction in what makes an effective team. Yet the quality of the team is much more than just the sum of the individuals who are team members. Just as in team

Exhibit 16.9
Inside–Outside Sales Team

Sometimes an inside rep or a field support rep works with accounts over the phone, and his or her partner, the field rep, makes calls at the customer's location.

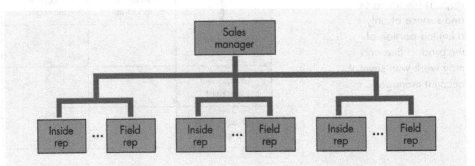

SALES Technology

MAKING THE MOST OF SALES TECHNOLOGY

A common response when times get tough is to try to make the most of what you have. Companies aren't likely to spend a lot on new technologies, particularly if they think there are gains to be had with what's already on hand. And sometimes what you have on hand is what you sell.

Cisco, for example, manufactures and sells Internet technology. Susan Denny, sales manager for Cisco, says the recession forced Cisco to look for ways to improve salesperson productivity. "We immediately implemented a hiring freeze and a travel freeze, so we had to find ways to do more with less." Cisco turned to its own products and services, and began implementing virtual training and virtual meetings. Cisco, for example, owns WebEx, a service that enables online meetings. Combining voice with visual presentation, participants around the world can log in and participate in a meeting that includes telephone conversations, instant messaging, PowerPoint, and other visual media.

Jeffrey Bailey, sales manager for Oracle, says his organization is similar. Oracle provides CRM software among its many offerings. Making the most of that software was one of its strategies. "We knew we had great solutions that our customers were using, and it was time we used them, too. A key factor for us was the need to collaborate across sales teams. We have so many products that require sales specialists—no one account manager can know or do it all. So using our technology enabled identification of more sales opportunities, as well as better collaboration once an opportunity was identified."

Mac MacIntosh, a noted B2B marketing consultant, agrees and suggests that salespeople can make these systems significantly more powerful simply by entering the right data. Here are some of the questions he recommends:

- When customers buy, are they solving technical problems or business problems?
- Who drives the decision? Who else is involved? Who should be involved but isn't?

MacIntosh says that the answers are already known to most salespeople, but the data aren't in the CRM database. As a result, marketing programs that could drive more leads to the salespeople are less effective.

Coca-Cola Bottling Co. Consolidated couldn't turn to its own products to improve sales force efficiency, so it turned to Microsoft. Using collaboration tools like Microsoft SharePoint, the company rolled out mobile devices that equip salespeople to take orders, conduct surveys, and communicate with the distribution sales team. "The biggest efficiency the technology has brought is more time out in the field doing core selling," says Onyeka Nchege, vice president of information systems. Bill Elmore, president and chief operating officer, also believes that the collaboration across distribution and sales was another major point of efficiency.

In each of these situations, the key has been to increase sales productivity through collaborative technology. Now that the recession seems to be easing, though, there's no going back. Says Nchege, "The organization is ready to take advantage and leverage some of the technologies that are coming ahead."

Sources: Susan Denny and Jeffrey Bailey, personal interview; M.H. "Mac" MacIntosh, "For the Win," *Print Professional* 48, no. 3 (March 2010), p. 18; Elizabeth Fuhrman, "Bottler of the Year: Coca-Cola Bottling Co. Consolidated," *Beverage Industry* 101, no. 1 (January 2010), pp. 30–35.

selling, each member of the team has to understand what the overall objective is, what each individual's role is, and what activities have to be undertaken when. But simply understanding what to do is a small part of making the team successful. More importantly, each individual has to perform and complete each task on time.

In addition, each class has a compensation plan—how grades are distributed. Sometimes the grades are team-based, just as in sales. Sometimes grades are entirely individual, and sometimes the overall grade is a function of both team and individual evaluations. But other motivations can entice students to learn. Recognition, the opportunity to work on real business problems, recognition of the relevance of the material being covered, and even monetary awards in competitions such as the National Collegiate Sales Competition can motivate different students to different levels of effort.

As you think about the courses you are taking, consider how you are compensated. Does the official compensation plan (grades, recognition, or the like) meet your motivational needs? In a group project, are your group members' needs being met? And are they living up to their responsibilities? These are real questions that plague professionals, whether they be salespeople or sales managers. Understanding how these questions apply to you now will help you select the right job later, as well as help you perform to your goals now.

SUMMARY

Successful salespeople manage resources and build internal partnerships with people in order entry, credit, billing, and shipping, as well as sales and marketing. These partnerships allow salespeople to keep the promises they make to customers when someone else must carry out those promises.

Salespeople in learning organizations also have a responsibility to carry the voice of the customer to other areas of the organization. Successful learning organizations are more adept at adapting to changing customer needs and developing successful products when salespeople fulfill their role of speaking for the customer.

In the sales organization salespeople work with and for a sales executive and a field sales manager. The sales executive determines policy and maintains financial control over the sales organization. Salespeople participate in the development of forecasts that the sales executive uses in the planning process.

Another policy decision involves the method of compensation for the sales force. The four basic methods are straight salary, straight commission, bonus, and a combination plan. Straight commission plans provide strong financial incentives for salespeople but give the company little control over their activities. Salary plans give greater control to the company but offer less incentive for salespeople to work hard.

Sales executives are also responsible for creating a culture that supports ethical activities. Policies (such as open-door policies) can encourage salespeople to act ethically. Ethical review boards are also useful in reviewing ethics policies, investigating potential ethics violations, and counseling salespeople who have concerns about the ethics of possible actions. Sometimes, however, salespeople face unethical requests from their managers. If that occurs, salespeople can choose from several courses of actions, such as blowing the whistle or appealing to an ethics review board.

Partnerships must be built within the sales force too. Some examples include team selling with product specialists, inside and outside teams, and multilevel selling.

KEY TERMS

activity quota 444
bonus 445
bottom-up forecasting 443
cap 449
combination plans 447
commission 445
commission base 445
commission rate 446

customer service rep (CSR) 454
draw 446
ethics review board 449
field sales manager 447
field salespeople 454
field support rep 454
geographic salesperson 451
gross margin quota 444

ETHICS PROBLEMS

1. It took you four months to find a job, and you were almost out of money, when you finally landed your position. Today your boss asked you to do something you think is unethical, but she assures you that it is normal for this industry. You aren't sure what the corporate culture is yet because you are new at the company. How do you respond?

2. Your company pays straight commission based on gross margin, and you have some ability to determine the price, thereby influencing gross margin. The product is standard, and changes are not made to it when it is sold. What should determine how much you charge someone?

QUESTIONS AND PROBLEMS

1. In Dave Brock's essay, "Building Partnerships 16.1," he describes a very poor sales effort. What was the problem? What should the rep have done? Who has the responsibility for creating the materials you use as a salesperson? If you are in a company with poor support materials, what should you do?

2. A company that rents office equipment to businesses pays its salespeople a commission equal to the first month's rent. However, if the customer cancels or fails to pay its bills, the commission is taken back, even if the customer cancels 10 months later. Is this policy fair? Why or why not? Why would the company have this plan?

3. Look at the opening profile (Lillie Sanchez) and "From the Buyer's Seat 16.1" (Teradata and Speed-Trap). Draw or describe the relationships that each must develop in their business, and discuss how they are similar or different, and why.

4. What is the role of the geographic salesperson in a national or strategic account? Assume that you are a NAM. What would you do to ensure the support of geographic reps? How would

that support differ if you were a product specialist and worked in a team situation, with different NAMs on different accounts? As a product specialist, how would you get the support of the account manager?

5. Consider your own experience in group work at school. What makes groups effective? How can you translate what you have learned about group work into working as part of a sales team? Reread "Sales Technology 16.1." What do you think are the characteristics of effective sales teams that have to operate virtually? Could you use any technology tools to collaborate in school work groups more effectively?

6. Some companies are using contact management software to observe salespeople's activities and to supervise salespeople more closely. Some salespeople, though, are not supervised closely—as long as they close enough sales, the company is satisfied. To what extent should salespeople be allowed to manage themselves? What risks do you take as a sales manager when you allow self-management among salespeople? How can you minimize those risks?

7. A sales manager gets one too many complaints about pushy salespeople, poor follow-up after the sale, and a lack of customer care and wonders if the compensation plan is to blame. What can a manager do with compensation to promote greater customer service? Are there other ways to motivate good customer service?

8. Many wise people say to worry about the things you can control and not to worry about the things you can't control. What does that mean for a salesperson, when so many promises a salesperson makes are actually fulfilled by someone else?

9. An experienced salesperson argues against salaries: "I don't like subsidizing poor performers. If you paid us straight commission, we'd

know who could make it and who couldn't. Sure, it may take a while to get rid of the deadwood; but after that, sales would skyrocket!" Explain why you agree or disagree with this statement.

10. In "From the Buyer's Seat 16.1" a former student describes the situation and the people involved in one purchase. Create a flowchart based on the information provided, and determine who was involved when, from both sides. Could this process have been managed more efficiently? If you were the Speed-Trap representative, what would you do now? How would your answer differ if you were the account manager for Teradata with sales responsibility for this customer?

CASE PROBLEMS

case 16.1

Flow Master Controls

Flow Master Controls, a manufacturer of heating and air conditioning control systems, has the following compensation program. Reps are paid a $2,500 draw per month, with straight commission paid on a point system and a bonus based on quota performance. The Digital Master, Flow Master's newest product, does much the same thing as the older Flow Master but is 30 percent faster and has greater accuracy. The point system is shown in Table 1.

Table 1

Product	Points/Sale	Quota
Digital Master	50	4 (units per month)
Flow Master	40	5
Hydrameter	35	6
Quadrameter	25	8
Triplex Scanner	5	45

Reps are paid $5 per point, or $5,165 plus a bonus of $500, if they sell quota for each product, for a total of $5,675. The total number of points to reach each month is 1,035, but reps have to reach quota for each product to get the bonus. Tables 2–4 show the performance of the district.

Table 2

Product	Quota	Number Sold
Digital Master	40	22
Flow Master	50	78
Hydrameter	60	63
Quadrameter	80	82
Triplex Scanner	450	479

Table 3

Name	Digital Master	Flow Master	Hydrameter	Quadrameter	Triplex Scanner	Total Points
McMahon	3	11	7	9	52	1,320
Davis	5	6	7	9	53	1,255
Foreman	2	9	7	11	46	1,210
Wu	4	8	6	8	48	1,160
Sanchez	3	8	7	6	48	1,105
Gruber	2	8	6	7	48	1,045
Sakamoto	1	8	6	8	48	1,020
Flora	1	7	7	8	47	1,010
Ricks	1	7	5	8	45	930
Dixon	0	6	5	8	44	835
Total	22	78	63	82	479	

Table 4
Total Sales Calls

Sales Call	Digital Master	Flow Master	Hydrameter	Quadrameter	Triplex Scanner	Total Calls
Quota	20	20	10	10	10	70
Foreman	28	16	11	9	10	75
Gruber	24	24	8	8	7	71
District average	27.2	18.6	9.5	10.4	9.7	75.4

Questions

1. Evaluate the district's sales performance. Draw conclusions ("Where are we doing well? Doing poorly?"), but don't fix anything yet. Justify your conclusions.
2. Compare the performance of Foreman and Gruber. What are some possible explanations for the poor Digital Master sales?
3. The VP of sales says the problem is the compensation plan. How would you fix it?
4. The company is planning to create a new position called product specialist. This salesperson will work with territory salespeople and will have a sales quota for Digital Master only. The product specialist salesperson will work with one sales team (8 to 12 salespeople), and once a territory rep has identified a Digital Master prospect, the rep will bring in the product specialist. How should the compensation plan be adjusted? Why?
5. The VP of sales managed to get the product specialist idea approved by the CEO, even though the CEO argued that the salespeople were just too lazy to make the effort to sell the Digital Master. "Lower the compensation on it to the territory reps, and everyone will sell the Flow Master at its lower price," the CEO says. "The best way to get more Digital Master sales is to cut compensation on the Flow Master to 20 points." What do you think should be done? Why?

case 16.2

IKOH Office

Karen Kennedy looked up, surprised to see her manager standing next to her. She had just hung up the phone after talking with Miranda in the Credit Department. "Um, did I get a little too loud, Rick?" she asked her manager.

"Why don't you come in my office and let's talk over what just happened," he replied, grimly.

"Great," she thought to herself. "First, the Kansas Hospital Resources order gets delayed to the point where they want to cancel it, then Credit wants me to get another form filled out, and now, the boss wants to talk over what just happened. Well, what just happened was I lost my temper, but they deserved it!" She sat down across the desk from Rick in his office, as he looked at her expectantly.

"I got a call this morning from Kansas Hospital Resources; you know, that's the 10-machine order I took two weeks ago." Rick nodded, so Karen continued. "They were upset because nothing has been delivered yet, but I had told them lead times were only a week. Which is what I was told."

"Yes, they are a week. Why hasn't this shipped?" he asked.

"That's what I wanted to know. So I called Frank and asked him." Frank Mangione is head of the warehouse in St. Louis that serves all of Kansas, Missouri, and a few other areas. "Frank said the order was a credit hold. What you heard was my conversation with Miranda in Credit. She tells me that it's on hold because a signature is missing on one of the forms. What gets me is no one called or e-mailed me about it. They let it sit, and I had to call and ask them. Rick, I'm tired of our Credit Department being a Sales Prevention Department. It's as if they do everything they can to screw us up. Now KHR is threatening to cancel the order if I can't get them a machine by Friday, but I've got to call them and say we missed a signature line and it will be a week after that before I can get them their first machine! Does IKOH want me to sell or what?"

Rick sat silently for a moment, then began to speak in a lower voice, trying to lower the tension in the room. But he knew she wouldn't like what he had to say. "Sounds like you have a problem to me."

Karen protested, "I have a problem? No, IKOH has a problem. It's just like trying to get paid. I can't get them to pay the right commission. And service. Don't get me started on our so-called service department! They never seem to want to fix my customers' machines!"

Rick said quietly, "Listen, we have 12 reps here in the Kansas City office. Of the 12, I have only one that keeps having problems with people in corporate or at the distribution center or with the service department. So I've got two questions for you. How are you going to handle KHR? And how are you going to fix your problems with everyone else?"

Questions

1. Answer Rick's questions as if you were Karen. To help you with your answer, consider that she and the service reps are in Kansas City, distribution is in St. Louis, and the corporate office (where credit, payroll, and other such functions are located) is in San Francisco. Regarding KHR, would it matter to your answer if this were a new customer versus a long-time customer? Why or why not, and if so, how?

2. What should or could Rick do to help Karen? Assume her sales performance is good, and he doesn't consider firing her an option.

ROLE PLAY CASE

You've just gotten back from KB Homes, one of the fastest-growing home builders in the United States. The KB Homes sales leadership team is considering NetSuite for all of their salespeople, and they've raised a number of questions that you need to get answered. If successful, this sale could be as big as 1,000 units. But they want to know several things:

1. Can you create a kiosk that will allow customers who visit KB's model homes to input their own data directly into a file that will load with NetSuite?
2. The buying center wants a license that includes all upgrades for three years.
3. They want permission to send a rep to your corporate headquarters to make a presentation to all the NetSuite employees about KB Homes. Employees who work in the field will be mailed a DVD presentation about KB Homes.

Each student will take turns playing the salesperson. The first question has to be addressed by the chief engineer. The second has to be addressed by the legal department. The final question has to be solved by the chief operations officer. If there are three people in a group, take turns observing. Your instructor will provide you with sheets for your role as one of the other NetSuite managers.

ADDITIONAL REFERENCES

Avlonitis, George J., and Nikolas G. Panagopoulos. "Exploring the Influence of Sales Management Practices on the Industrial Salesperson: A Multisource Hierarchical Linear Modeling Approach." *Journal of Business Research* 60, no. 7 (2007), pp. 765–77.

Brehmer, Per-Olof, and Jakob Rehme. "Proactive and Reactive: Drivers for Key Account Management Programmes." *European Journal of Marketing* 43, no. 7–8 (2009), pp. 961–84.

Guenzi, Paolo, Catherine Pardo, and Laurent Georges. "Relational Selling Strategy and Key Account Managers Relational Behaviors: An Exploratory Study." *Industrial Marketing Management* 36, no. 1 (2007), pp. 121–34.

Guenzi, Paolo, Laurent Georges, and Catherine Pardo. "The Impact of Strategic Account Managers' Behaviors on Relational Outcomes: An Empirical Study." *Industrial Marketing Management* 38, no. (2009), pp. 300–12.

Jones, Eli, Lawrence B. Chonko, Deva Rangarajan, and James Roberts. "The Role of Overload on Job Attitudes, Turnover Intentions, and Salesperson Performance." *Journal of Business Research* 60, no. 7 (2007), pp. 663–78.

Joshi, Ashwin W. "Salesperson Influence on Product Development: Insights from a Study of Small Manufacturing Organizations." *Journal of Marketing* 74, no. 1 (January 2010), pp. 94–108.

Judson, Kimberly, Denise D. Schoenbachler, Geoffrey L. Gordon, Rick E. Ridnour, and Dan C. Weilbaker. "The New Product Development Process: Let the Voice of the Salesperson Be Heard." *Journal of Product and Brand Management* 15, no. 3 (2007), pp. 194–210.

Liu, Sandra S., and Lucette B. Comer. "Salespeople as Information Gatherers: Associated Success Factors." *Industrial Marketing Management* 36, no. 5 (2007), pp. 565–80.

Paparoidamis, Nicholas G., and Paolo Guenzi. "An Empirical Investigation into the Impact of Relationship Selling and LMX on Salespeople's Behaviours and Sales Effectiveness." *European Journal of Marketing* 43, no. 7–8 (2009), p. 1053.

Pappas, James M., Karen E. Flaherty, and C. Shane Hunt. "The Joint Influence of Control Strategies and Market Turbulence on Strategic Performance in Sales-Driven Organizations." *Journal of Behavior and Applied Management* 8, no. 2 (2007), pp. 141–64.

Rouziès, Dominique, Anne T. Coughlan, Erin Anderson, and Dawn Iacobucci. "Determinants of Pay Levels and Structures in Sales Organizations." *Journal of Marketing* 73, no. 6 (November 2009), pp. 92–104.

Smith, Brent, Trina Larsen, and Bert Rosenbloom. "Understanding Cultural Frames in the Multicultural Sales Organization: Prospects and Problems for the Sales Manager." *Journal of Transnational Management* 14, no. 4 (October 2009), pp. 277–92.

Steward, Michelle D., Michael D. Hutt, Beth A. Walker, and Ajith Kumar. "Role Identity and Attributions of High-Performing Salespeople." *The Journal of Business & Industrial Marketing* 24, no. 7, pp. 463–76.

Vilela, Belen Bande, Jose Antonio Varela Gonzalez, Pilar Fernandez Ferrin, and M. Luisa del Rio Araujo. "Impression Management Tactics and Affective Context: Influence on Sales Performance Appraisal." *European Journal of Marketing* 41, no. 5–6 (2007), pp. 624–39.

The Partnership Process

PART 2

chapter **10**

RESPONDING TO OBJECTIONS

SOME QUESTIONS ANSWERED IN THIS CHAPTER ARE

- How should salespeople sell value and build relationships when responding to objections?
- When do buyers object?
- What objections can be expected?
- Which methods are effective when responding to objections?
- How do you deal with tough customers?

PROFILE

PROFILE My name is Rachel Gober, and I graduated from Texas State University in December 2008 with a bachelor's degree in marketing. I was honored to participate at the National Collegiate Sales Competition in 2007, where our sales team was privileged to be led by the one and only Mrs. Vicki West.

The National Collegiate Sales Competition is actually where I was recruited by Standard Register, a company that specializes in document management systems and services for the health care, industrial manufacturing, financial services, government, retail, and transportation industries.

During my experience here so far, I have found three keys to helpfully respond to objections: (1) anticipate objections and prepare your response, (2) reduce objections from the beginning by helping the buyer to trust you, and (3) ask questions and listen to the answers.

In sales, you are going to get objections from prospects at every stage in the sales cycle, so you might as well be ready for them. When I first started making cold calls, I had a list of typical objections that our reps hear, and wrote out responses to each of them. I kept this sheet in front of me every day when I was on the phone until I felt comfortable with them. It may sound corny, but some buyers use objections just to make you nervous or to get you off the phone or out of their office, so it is better to be prepared than to be left stuttering and mumbling. For example, this is typical: Prospect's objection: "What are you trying to sell me?" My response: "At this point I'm not trying to sell anything. I don't know enough about your current process to recommend a solution, so right now I would just like to set an appointment with you to learn more about it."

Once I set the appointment, I try to find ways to help the buyer trust me. This often reduces objections. For example, buyers will object when they think you are DUMB, which means that the salesperson Doesn't Understand My Business. Many times, at my initial meetings with prospects, I will explain to them the DUMB acronym, and ask them questions about their business so they know I am not trying to sell them something; rather I am trying to learn more about them so that I can put together a custom solution that best fits their needs.

It is important to let buyers know that you are on their side, and you understand where they are coming from. For example, a common objection is "We are happy the way we are currently doing things." By asking simple questions like "How's that working for you?" or "That's great, I'm glad you have a system that works for you, but what could make it better?" you will typically uncover areas for improvement that your product or service might be able to help with.

I think of objections as an opportunity to build relationships with my customers, gain knowledge about their business, and learn how to sell to them.

Visit our Web site at
www.standardregister.com.

THE GOAL IS TO BUILD RELATIONSHIPS AND SELL VALUE

An **objection** is a concern or a question raised by the buyer. Salespeople should do everything they can to encourage buyers to voice concerns or questions. The worst type of objection is the one the buyer refuses to disclose because a hidden objection cannot be dealt with. Many sales have been lost because salespeople didn't find out the objections or didn't helpfully respond to them.

Salespeople should keep in mind that the goal with regard to objections is the same as with every other part of the sales call: to sell real value to the buyer. Having a positive attitude about objections is paramount in this regard. Proper attitude is shown by answering sincerely, refraining from arguing or contradicting, and welcoming—even inviting—objections. Objections should be expected and never taken personally.

Simply pretending to be empathetic is useless; buyers can easily see through such pretense. Also, once the buyer gets the idea that the salesperson is talking for effect, regaining that buyer's confidence and respect will be almost impossible. Empathy shows as much in the tone of voice and facial expressions as in the actual words spoken.

The greatest evidence of sincerity comes from the salesperson's actions. One successful advertising agency owner states, "I have always tried to sit on the same side of the table as my clients, to see problems through their eyes." Buyers want valid objections to be treated seriously; they want their ideas to be respected, not belittled. They look for empathetic understanding of their problems. Real objections are logical to the prospect regardless of how irrational they may appear to the salesperson. Salespeople must assume the attitude of helper, counselor, and advisor and act accordingly. To do so, they must treat the prospect as a friend, not a foe. In fact, buyers will feel more comfortable about raising objections and will be much more honest the more they trust the salesperson, the better the rapport, and the stronger the partnering relationship.

The reality is that salespeople run into more rejection in a day than most people have to absorb in weeks or months. Because of the emotional strain, many see selling as a tough way to make a living. However, salespeople must remember that objections present sales opportunities. People who object have at least some level of interest in what the salesperson is saying. Further, objections provide feedback about what is really on the prospect's mind. Only when this openness exists can a true partnering relationship form. To capitalize on these opportunities, salespeople must show that they welcome any and all objections. Salespeople have to make the prospect believe they are sincerely glad the objection has been raised. This attitude shows in remarks such as the following:

I can see just what you mean. I'd probably feel the same way.

That's a great question!

I'm glad you mentioned that, Mr. Atkinson.

If I were purchasing this product, I'd want an answer to that same question.

Maintaining a positive attitude toward objections is paramount. As one international sales consultant put it, "Studies show that prospective clients hate fighting—they don't want you arguing and working to overcome their concerns; they want you to listen to their problems, understand the impact of those issues, and then offer to help, if you are able. That's a world away from the combative old-style approach to selling."[1]

WHEN DO BUYERS RAISE OBJECTIONS?

Salespeople can expect to hear objections at any time during the buyer–seller relationship (see Chapter 3 for a review of the buying process). Objections are raised when the salesperson attempts to secure an appointment, during the approach, during the presentation, when the salesperson attempts to obtain commitment, and during the after-sale follow-up. Objections can also be made during formal negotiation sessions (see Chapter 12).

SETTING UP AN INITIAL APPOINTMENT

Prospects may object to setting the appointment times or dates that salespeople request to introduce the product. This type of objection happens especially when products, services, or concepts are unfamiliar to the buyer. For example, a commercial benefits salesperson for Coast Dental might hear the buyer make the following statement when asked to meet and learn more about a cafeteria-style benefits package: "No, I don't need to see you. I've not heard many good things about the use of cafeteria-style packages for dental products. Most employees just get confused!"

THE PRESENTATION

Buyers can offer objections during the beginning of the presentation (see Chapter 8). They may not like or believe the salesperson's attention-getting opening statement. They may not wish to engage in small talk or may not agree with statements made by the seller attempting to build rapport. Buyers may object to the salesperson's stated goals for the meeting.

Objections often come up to points made in the presentation. For example, a computer disaster recovery salesperson for Rackspace Hosting might hear this objection: "We've never lost a lot of computer data files before! Why should I pay so much money for a service I may never use?"

Such objections usually show the prospect's interest in the topic; thus they can actually be desirable. Compared to a prospect who just says, "No thanks," and never raises his or her concerns, selling is easier when buyers voice their concerns because the salesperson knows where the buyers stand and that they are paying attention.

ATTEMPTING TO OBTAIN COMMITMENT

Objections may be voiced when the salesperson attempts to obtain commitment. For example, an AK Steel salesperson who has just asked the buyer's permission to talk to the buyer's chief engineer may hear this objection: "No, I don't want you talking to our engineers. My job is to keep vendors from bugging our employees."

Skill in uncovering and responding to objections is very important at this stage of the sales call. Also, knowing the objections that are likely to occur helps the salesperson prepare supporting documentation (letters of reference, copies of studies, and so on).

Salespeople who hear many objections at this point in the sales call probably need to further develop their skills. An excessive number of objections while obtaining commitment may indicate a poor job of needs identification and the omission of significant selling points in the presentation. It may also reveal ineffective probing during the presentation to see whether the buyer understands or has any questions about what is being discussed.

AFTER THE SALE

Even buyers who have agreed to purchase the product or service can still raise objections. During the installation, for example, the buyer may raise concerns about the time it is taking to install the equipment, the quality of the product or service, the customer service department's lack of friendliness, or the credit department's refusal to grant the terms the salesperson promised. To develop long-term relationships and partnerships with buyers, salespeople must carefully respond to these objections. After-sale service is more fully discussed in Chapter 14.

COMMON OBJECTIONS

Prospects raise many types of objections. Although listing every objection is impossible, this section attempts to outline the most common buyer objections.[2]

It should be noted that some buyers like to raise objections just to watch salespeople squirm uncomfortably. (Fortunately, most buyers aren't like that!) Seasoned buyers, especially, sometimes like to make life difficult for sellers—particularly for young, nervous sellers. For example, Peggy, a manufacturer's salesperson for Walker Muffler, used to call on a large auto parts store in an attempt to have the store carry her line of mufflers. Jackie, the store's buyer, gave Peggy a tough time on her first two calls. At the end of her second call, Peggy was so frustrated with the way she was being treated that she decided never to call there again. However, as she was walking out of the store, she ran into a Goodyear rep who also called on Jackie to sell belts and hoses. Because the two salespeople were on somewhat friendly terms, Peggy admitted her frustrations to the Goodyear rep. He replied, "Oh, that's just the way Jackie operates. On the third call he is always a nice guy. Just wait and see." Sure enough, Peggy's next call on Jackie was not only pleasant but also productive! Buyers like Jackie usually just want to see the sales rep work hard for the order.

The following sections examine the five major types of objections (objections related to needs, product, source, price, and time), which are summarized in Exhibit 10.1, as well as several other objections that salespeople sometimes hear.

OBJECTIONS RELATED TO NEEDS

I Do Not Need the Product or Service

A prospect may validly state that the company has no need for what the salesperson is selling. A manufacturer that operates on a small scale, for example, may have no use for expensive machinery designed to handle large volumes of work. Similarly, a salesperson who is selling an accounts receivable collection service will find that a retailer that sells for cash does not require a collection service.

Salespeople may encounter such objections as "My business is different" or "I have no use for your service." These objections, when made by an accurately qualified buyer, show that the buyer is not convinced that a need exists. This problem could have been prevented with better implication and need payoff questions (see Chapter 8).

If the salesperson cannot establish a need in the buyer's mind, that buyer can logically be expected to object. In **pioneer selling**—selling a new and different product, service, or idea—the salesperson has more difficulty establishing a need in the buyer's mind. For example, salespeople for Alken often hear "I don't think we need it" when the buyer is asked to carry a line of biodegradable citrus degreasers.

Exhibit 10.1

Five Major Types of Objections

Objections Related to Needs
I do not need the product or service.
I've never done it that way before.

Objections Related to the Product
I don't like the product or service features.
I don't understand.
I need more information.

Objections Related to the Source
I don't like your company.
I don't like you.

Objections Related to the Price
I have no money.
The value does not exceed the cost.

Objections Related to Time
I'm just not interested today.
I need time to think about it.

I've Never Done It That Way Before

Most human beings are creatures of habit. Once they develop a routine or establish a custom, they tend to resist change. Fear or ignorance may be the basis for not wanting to try anything new or different. The buyer's natural tendency to resist buying a new product or changing from a satisfactory brand to a new one can be found behind many objections.

Habits and customs also help to insulate the prospect from certain risks to some degree. For example, suppose you are selling a new line of marine engines to Newton, a newly promoted assistant buyer. If Jane, the previous assistant buyer and now the senior buyer, bought your competitor's product, Newton would appear to take less risk by continuing to buy from your competitor. If Newton buys from you, Jane may think, "I've been doing business with the other firm for 15 years. Now, Newton, you come in here and tell me I've been doing it wrong all these years? I'm not sure you're going to be a good assistant buyer."

OBJECTIONS RELATED TO THE PRODUCT

I Don't Like the Product or Service Features

Often the product or service has features that do not satisfy the buyer. At other times the prospect will request features currently not available. Customers may say things like these: It doesn't taste good to me! I was looking for a lighter shade of red. It took a month for us to receive our last order.

I Don't Understand

Sometimes objections arise because customers do not understand the salesperson's presentation. Because these objections may never be verbalized, the seller must carefully observe the buyer's nonverbal cues. (See Chapter 4 for a discussion of nonverbal communication.) Misunderstandings frequently occur with customers who are unfamiliar with technical terms, unaware of the unique capabilities of a product, or uncertain about benefits arising from services provided with the product, such as warranties. Unfortunately buyers often will not admit that they do not understand something.

This buyer doesn't understand what the seller is saying.

For example, when desktop publishing programs were introduced for personal computers, a salesperson for an IBM distributor gave a presentation to a very busy plant manager of a consumer products firm. The new software would allow the manager to create and produce the plant's monthly newsletter to plant employees in-house instead of sending the work out to be typeset and printed. The manager, however, did not understand the new product's concept. He thought that the software would create the newsletter but that the firm would still have to send the work out to be typeset and printed. However, he did not want to appear ignorant and simply told the salesperson that he was not interested. The rep never knew that the manager simply had not understood the product until later, when the manager bought a competitor's desktop publishing program.

I Need More Information

Some buyers offer objections in an attempt to get more information. They may have already decided that they want the product or service but wish to fortify themselves with logical reasons they can use to justify the purchase to others. Also, the salesperson may not have provided enough credible proof about a particular benefit.

Conflict may also exist in the buyer's mind. One conflict could be a struggle taking place between the dictates of emotion and reason. Or the buyer may be concerned about the risk, and the seller hasn't sufficiently sold value. The buyer may be trying to decide between two competitive products or between buying and not buying. Whatever the struggle, buyers who object to get more information are usually interested, and the possibility of obtaining commitment is good.

OBJECTIONS RELATED TO THE SOURCE

I Don't Like Your Company

Most buyers, especially industrial buyers, are interested in the sales representative's company because the buyer is put at risk if the seller's firm is not financially sound, cannot continually produce the product, and so forth. These buyers need to be satisfied with the selling company's financial standing, personnel, and business policies. Buyers may ask questions such as these: How do I know you'll be in business next year? Your company isn't very well known, is it? Why does your company have a bad image in the industry?

Of course buyers who don't want to be rude may not actually voice these concerns. But unvoiced questions about the sales rep's company may affect their decisions and the long-term partnerships the sales rep is trying to establish.

I Don't Like You

Sometimes a salesperson's personality clashes with a prospect's. Effective salespeople know they must do everything possible to adjust their manner to please the prospect. At times, however, doing business with some people appears impossible.

Prospects may object to a presentation or an appointment because they have taken a dislike to the salesperson or because they feel they cannot trust the salesperson. Candid prospects may say, "You seem too young to be selling these. You've never worked in my industry, so how can you be trained to know what I need?" More commonly, the prospect shields the real reason and says, "We don't need any."

In some situations, the buyer may honestly have difficulty dealing with a particular salesperson. If the concern is real (not just an excuse), the seller's firm sometimes institutes a **turnover (TO)**, which simply means the account is given to a different salesperson. Unfortunately, TOs occasionally occur because the buyer has gender, racial, or other prejudices or because the salesperson is failing to practice adaptive selling behaviors.

thinking it through

Assume that you have worked as a salesperson for an industrial chemical firm for six months. You have attended a two-week basic selling skills course but have not yet attended any product knowledge training classes. You are making a sales call with your sales manager. The buyer says, "Gee, you look too young to be selling chemicals. Do you have a chemistry degree?" Before you get a chance to respond, your manager says, "Oh, he [meaning you] has already completed our one-month intensive product knowledge course. I guarantee he knows it all!" What would you say or do? What would you do if the buyer later asked you a technical question?

OBJECTIONS RELATED TO THE PRICE

I Have No Money

Companies that lack the resources to buy the product may have been misclassified as prospects. As indicated in Chapter 6, the ability to pay is an important factor in lead qualification. An incomplete or poor job of qualifying may cause this objection to arise.

When leads say they cannot afford a product, they may have a valid objection. If so, the salesperson should not waste time; new prospects should be contacted.

The Value Does Not Exceed the Cost

Most buyers must sacrifice something (called *opportunity costs*—see Chapter 9) to buy a product. The money spent for the product is not available for other things. When we buy as individuals, the choice may be between the down payment on a new car and a vacation trip; for businesses, it may be between expanding the plant and distributing a dividend to stockholders.

Buyers usually object until they are sure that the value of the product or service being acquired more than offsets the sacrifice. Exhibit 10.2 illustrates this concept. The question of value received often underlies customers' objections.

Whatever the price of a product or service, somebody will object that it is too high or out of line with the competition. Here are some other common price objections: I can beat your price on these items. We can't make a reasonable profit if we have to pay that much for the merchandise. I'm going to wait for prices to come down.

Although objections about price occur more often than any other kind of objection, they may be just masks to hide the real reason for the buyer's reluctance. (A more complete discussion of dealing with price objections appears later in this chapter.) Implicit in many price objections is the notion of product or service quality. Thus the buyer who states that your price is too high may actually be thinking, "The quality is too low for such a high price."

Exhibit 10.2
Value: The Relationship between Costs and Benefits

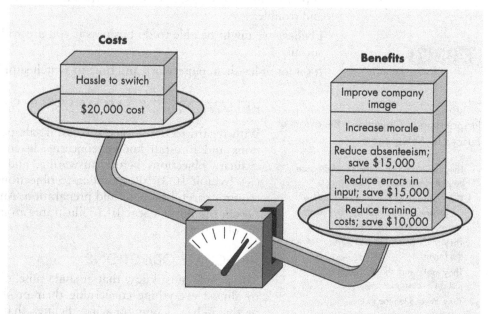

Note: If costs outweigh benefits, the decision will be not to buy. If benefits outweigh costs, the decision will be to buy.

OBJECTIONS RELATED TO TIME

I'm Just Not Interested Today

Some prospects voice objections simply to dismiss the salesperson. The prospect may not have enough time to devote to the interview, may not be interested in the particular product or service, may not be in the mood to listen, or may have decided because of some unhappy experiences not to face further unpleasant interviews.

These objections occur when salespeople are cold calling (see Chapter 6) or trying to make an appointment. Particularly aggressive, rude, impolite, or pesky salespeople can expect prospects to use numerous excuses to keep from listening to a presentation.

I Need Time to Think about It

Buyers often object to making a decision "now." Many, in fact, believe that postponing an action is an effective way to say no. Salespeople can expect to hear objections such as the following, especially from analyticals and amiables (see Chapter 5): I haven't made up my mind. I'd like to talk it over with my partner. Just leave me your literature; I'll study it and then let you know what we decide.

OTHER OBJECTIONS

Listing every possible objection that could occur under any situation would be impossible. However, following are a number of additional objections that salespeople often hear:

We have no room for your line.

There is no demand for your product.

Sorry, but I just don't do business with people of [your gender or your race or your ethnicity or your sexual preference or your religion, and so forth].

I've heard from my friends that your insurance company isn't the best one to use.

Sure, we can do business. But I need a little kickback to make it worth my time and trouble.

I believe we might be able to do business if you are willing to start seeing me socially.

It's a lot of hassle in paperwork and time to switch suppliers.

Exhibit 10.3

Responding to Objections: Behaviors of Successful Salespeople

They anticipate objections and prepare helpful responses.

They address known problems before the prospect does; that is, they forestall known concerns.

They relax and listen and never interrupt the buyer.

They make sure that the objection is not just an excuse.

They always tell the truth.

BEHAVIORS OF SUCCESSFUL SALESPEOPLE

With regard to objections, successful salespeople anticipate objections and forestall known concerns, listen without interrupting, evaluate objections before answering, and always tell the truth (see Exhibit 10.3).[3] Responding to objections in a helpful manner requires careful thought and preparation. And for what it's worth, "From the Buyer's Seat 10.1" illustrates an ineffective way to handle objections.

ANTICIPATE OBJECTIONS

Salespeople must know that at some time, objections will be made to almost everything concerning their products, their companies, or themselves. Common sense dictates that they prepare helpful,

From the BUYER'S SEAT

THIS IS NOT HOW TO HANDLE OBJECTIONS

We've all read about the failures of the mortgage industry and the massive impact that legal and moral lapses there had on the economies of the world. Salespeople, at least some of them, are partly to blame for the mess we are in.

Mortgage wholesalers (who work for banks and other types of money lenders) buy loan applications from independent mortgage brokers and then turn these applications into actual loans. Mortgage wholesalers package a group of such loans into securities and sell the securities in the marketplace. The more loans the mortgage wholesalers could get from brokers, the more the lenders could sell on the marketplace.

Obviously there were many mortgage wholesalers out there, and brokers could easily come up with objections and reasons for going with a different wholesaler. In essence, their objection was "I can get a better deal elsewhere!" The solution? Mortgage wholesalers often hired attractive saleswomen to woo brokers (the brokers were often young and predominantly male) to use the services of their firms.

Evan Stone, the president of a mortgage brokerage company in California, says "minimally trained and minimally dressed" female salespeople would regularly visit his office, wearing unusually short shirts. On these visits the brokers were being encouraged to party at a local steak house with the saleswoman. One mortgage wholesaler even offered to fly Evan to Chicago to "have a good time."

Having the saleswomen attempt to use sexual favors to generate business was a turnoff for Evan. He declined all offers of sexual favors. If the saleswomen were trying to build strong business relationships with Evan in that manner, they failed miserably.

Source: Mara Der Hovanesian, "Sex, Lies, and Mortgage Deals," *BusinessWeek*, November 24, 2008, pp. 71–74.

honest answers to objections that are certain to be raised (probably 80 percent or more can be anticipated) because few salespeople can answer objections effectively on the spur of the moment.

Many companies draw up lists of common objections and helpful answers and encourage salespeople to become familiar with these lists. Most firms also videotape practice role plays to help salespeople become more proficient in anticipating objections and responding effectively in each situation. Successful sales representatives may keep a notebook and record new objections they encounter. For those objections you can't think of an answer to, you might want to use technology, as "Sales Technology 10.1" describes.

FORESTALL KNOWN CONCERNS

Good salespeople, after a period of experience and training, know that certain features of their products or services are vulnerable, are likely to be misunderstood, or are materially different from competitors' products. The salesperson may have products with limited features, may have to quote a price that seems high, may be unable to offer cash discounts, may have no service representatives in the immediate area, or may represent a new company in the field.

In these situations, salespeople often forestall the objection. To **forestall** is to prevent by doing something ahead of time. In selling, this means salespeople raise objections before buyers have a chance to raise them. For example, one salesperson forestalled a concern about the different "feel" of a split computer keyboard

SALES Technology

10.1

USE TECHNOLOGY TO PREPARE FOR OBJECTIONS

Let's say you're preparing for an upcoming sales call. True to this chapter's suggestion, you decide to list all possible objections that you think can arise. As you do so, you realize that a few of them are tough ones, and you don't know how to answer them. What do you do?

Of course you can talk to your sales manager or other salespeople at your company and see if they have dealt with those issues before. If you're in field selling however, and not physically close to these people on a daily basis, you might use e-mail or texting to get some feedback from them.

But are you constrained to just those people? No. If you have a Twitter account, it's easy to tweet the gist of your objection and ask anyone out there who reads your tweet to supply some feedback. People on Twitter especially like to answer questions instead of just reading what others are doing.

If your question is too long and will take more than the 140 characters that Twitter allows, you can post your question on a blog and then point people on Twitter to that blog. But that raises a new problem: Some blog URLs are just too long to fit on a tweet. Solution? Go to http://tinyurl.com/ to transfer your long URL into a short one that will easily fit on Twitter.

Speaking of blogs, that's another source for finding potential answers to your objection lists. There are many available where you read what others say about objections. On many you can post comments or questions. A few to consider are the following:

http://www.topsalesblog.com/

http://jigsawsworld.typepad.com/garthsworld/

http://heavyhittersales.typepad.com/
heavy_hitter_sales_sales_/

http://sellingsherpa.typepad.com/
the_selling_sherpas_blog/

www.salessensesolutions.com

http://salesforceone.typepad.com/salesforceone/

No doubt, blogs come and go. You may want to visit http://www.blogs.com/topten/10-popular-sales-blogs/ to find the top 10 blogs for salespeople.

You can also pose a question on your LinkedIn account and have your contacts provide suggestions. Or you can join one of the many sales-related groups on LinkedIn and ask the group the question. There are even several LinkedIn groups by this textbook's authors you may want to use. One is called Selling Partners.

(the ones that are split down the middle to relieve stress and strain on the hands and wrists):

> I know you'll find the feel to be different from your old keyboard. You're going to like that, though, because your hands won't get as tired. In almost every split keyboard I've sold, typists have taken only one day to get accustomed to the new feel, and then they swear that they would never go back to their old-fashioned keyboards again!

A salesperson might bring up a potential price problem by saying, "You know, other buyers have been concerned that this product is expensive. Well, let me show you how little it will really cost you to get the best."

Some salespeople do such a good job of forestalling that buyers change their minds without ever going on record as objecting to the feature and then having to reverse themselves.[4] Buyers are more willing to change their thinking when they do not feel constrained to defend a position they have already stated. Although not all objections can be preempted, the major ones can be spotted and forestalled during the presentation. Forestalling can be even more important in written proposals (see Chapter 9) because immediate feedback between buyer and seller is not possible. Such forestalled objections can be addressed throughout the proposal. For example, on the page describing delivery terms, the seller could insert a paragraph that begins this way: "You may be wondering how we can promise an eight-day delivery even though we have such a small production capacity. Actually, we are able to . . . because. . . ." Another option for forestalling objections in written proposals is to have a separate page or section titled something like "Concerns You May Have with This Proposal." The section could then list the potential concerns and provide responses to them.

This seller is listening carefully.

RELAX AND LISTEN—DO NOT INTERRUPT

When responding to an objection, listen first and then answer the objection. Allow the prospect to state a position completely. A wise man said, "He that answereth a matter before he heareth it, it is folly and shame unto him."[5]

Do not interrupt with an answer, even if the objection to be stated is already apparent to you. Listen as though you have never heard that objection before.

Unfortunately too many salespeople conduct conversations somewhat like the following:

SALESPERSON: Mr. Clark, from a survey of your operations, I'm convinced you're now spending more money repairing your own motors than you would by having us do the job for you—and really do it right!

CUSTOMER: We're probably doing it fine right now. Now, I'm sure your repair service is good, but you don't have to be exactly an electrical genius to be able to . . .

SALESPERSON: Hang on! It isn't a matter of anyone being a genius. It's a matter of having a heavy investment in special motor repair equipment and supplies like vacuum impregnating tanks and lathes for banding armatures, boring bearings, and turning new shafts.

CUSTOMER: Yeah I know all that, but you missed my point. See, what I'm driving at . . .

SALESPERSON: I know what you're driving at, but you're wrong! You forget that even if your own workers are smart cookies, they just can't do high-quality work without a lot of special equipment.

CUSTOMER: But you still don't get my point! The maintenance workers that we now have doing motor repair work . . .

SALESPERSON: Could more profitably spend their time on plant troubleshooting! Right?

CUSTOMER: That isn't what I was going to say! I was trying to say that between their troubleshooting jobs, instead of just sitting around and shooting the bull . . .

SALESPERSON: Now wait a minute, Mr. Clark. If you think that a good motor rewinding job can be done in someone's spare time, you're wrong!

Obviously attitudes and interruptions like these are likely to bring the interview to a quick end.

Salespeople should plan to relax as buyers offer objections. It's even OK to plan on using humor in your answers to objections. For example, if the buyer objects to the standard payments and asks how low your company could go, you could respond as follows: "Well, if I could get the bank to send you money each month, would you buy it?"

After laughing, the seller could talk about the various payment options. Using humor, as in this example, may help defuse the nervousness that both buyer and seller are feeling during this part of the process. For more insight into the use of humor, see Chapter 4.

What if the buyer asks a question for which you've already covered the material? Don't say, "I've already covered that!" Instead let the buyer finish asking the question and then answer the question with enthusiasm.

EVALUATE OBJECTIONS

To truly sell value and establish a relationship, the seller must evaluate objections before answering. Objections may be classified as unsatisfied needs (that is, real objections) or excuses. **Excuses** are concerns expressed by the buyer that mask the buyer's true objections. Thus the comment "I can't afford it now" would simply be an excuse if the buyer honestly could afford it now but did not want to buy for some other reason.

A buyer seldom says, "I don't have any reason. I just don't want to buy." More commonly the buyer gives a reason that appears at first to be a real objection but is really an excuse: "I don't have the money" or "I can't use your product." The tone of voice or the nature of the reason may provide evidence that the prospect is not offering a sincere objection.

Salespeople need to develop skill in evaluating objections. No exact formula has been devised to separate excuses from real objections. Sometimes it is best to follow up with a question:

> BUYER: I just wish your company sold the full range of insurance products, you know, things like variable annuities.
>
> SELLER: If we did offer variable annuities, would you be interested in having all of your insurance needs met by me?

If the buyer says yes, you know the concern is real. If the buyer says no, you know the buyer is just offering the objection about annuities as an excuse.

Circumstances can also provide a clue to whether an objection is a valid concern. In cold calling, when the prospect says, "I'm sorry, I don't have any money," the salesperson may conclude that the prospect does not want to hear the presentation. However, the same reason offered after a complete presentation has been made and data on the prospect have been gathered through observation and questioning may be valid. Salespeople must rely on observation, questioning, knowledge about why people buy (see Chapter 3), and experience to determine the validity of reasons offered for objections.

One study asked executives how often salespeople offer price discounts when in fact price wasn't the issue. The answer was an astounding 70–100 percent of the time.[6] The moral: Discover the true objection before offering what you think is a solution.

ALWAYS TELL THE TRUTH

In dealing with prospects and customers, truthfulness is an absolute necessity for dignity, confidence, and relationship development. Recall that our purpose is not to manipulate but to persuade, when appropriate, so the buyer can make the most effective decision. Lying and deception are not part of a successful long-term relationship. Over time it will be hard to remember which lie you told to which customer. Salespeople should avoid even white lies and half-truths when they answer objections.

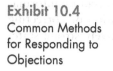

Salespeople who tell lies, even small ones, need to recognize they have a problem and then find ways to change. One way to avoid lies is to spend more time gaining knowledge about their products and the products of their competitors. Sellers who do so aren't as tempted to lie to cover up the fact that they don't know some information requested by the prospect. Sellers also should commit to tell the truth, even if competitors don't follow suit. It is simply the right thing to do.

EFFECTIVE RESPONSE METHODS

Any discussion of specific methods for responding to objections needs to emphasize that no perfect method exists for answering all objections completely. Some prospects, no matter what you do, will never believe their objections have been adequately addressed.

In some instances, spending a lot of time trying to convince the prospect may not be wise. For example, when an industrial recycling salesperson contacts a prospect who says, "I don't believe in recycling," the salesperson may better spend available time calling on some of the vast number of people who do.

This section describes seven common methods for responding to objections. As Exhibit 10.4 indicates, the first two, direct denial and indirect denial, are used only when the prospect makes an untrue statement. The next five methods—compensation, referral, revisiting, acknowledgment, and postponement—are useful when the buyer raises a valid point or offers an opinion.

Before using the methods described in this section, salespeople almost always need to probe to help the prospect clarify concerns and to make sure they understand the objection. This method is often called the **probing method**. If the prospect says, "Your service is not too good," the salesperson can probe by saying, "I'm not sure I understand," or by asking a question. For example, the seller could ask one or more of the following: Not too good? What do you mean by not too good? Exactly what service are you referring to? Is service very important to you? Can you explain what you mean?

Exhibit 10.4
Common Methods for Responding to Objections

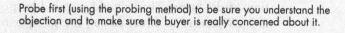

Probe first (using the probing method) to be sure you understand the objection and to make sure the buyer is really concerned about it.

If the buyer makes a statement that is factually not true, use → Direct denial
Indirect denial

If the buyer raises a valid concern or offers an opinion, use → Compensation
Referral
Revisit
Acknowledge
Postpone

While this probing is usually verbal, it can also include nonverbal probing. For example, Professor Donoho at Northern Arizona University teaches a method called the **friendly silent questioning stare (FSQS)** to encourage buyers to elaborate or explain more fully what their concerns are.

Many serious blunders have occurred because a salesperson did not understand a question, answered the wrong question, or failed to answer an objection fully. For example, a sales training manager was listening to a representative for a consulting firm talk about her services. At one point in the conversation, the manager asked, "Has anyone in our industry, the electrical products industry specifically, ever used this training package before?" The consultant answered, "Sure, we have sold this package to several firms. Why, just last week I received a nice letter from Colgate that had nothing but good things to say. . . ." The manager did not buy the training package; he figured that if the consultant did not even know how to listen, the sales training package she was selling could not be very good either. (Chapter 4 provides many helpful suggestions regarding the art of questioning and probing.)

A salesperson who doesn't know the answer to the buyer's objection might say, "I don't know the answer to that question. But I'll find out and get the answer to you." The seller should paraphrase the question, write it down (this step helps jog the seller's memory as well as demonstrate to the buyer that the seller really intends to follow up), gather the information, and follow up quickly and exactly as promised. If you call the customer with the information and he or she is not available, leave the information on voice mail and then call later to verify that the prospect got the information. And don't forget that it is your responsibility to know most facts, so be prepared the next time for similar and additional questions and concerns. You can be sure your competitor is going to try to have complete answers ready.

Remember that sometimes it is in the salesperson's best interest to walk away from a prospect's business. And it is not necessary to resolve all objections in those situations, as "Building Partnerships 10.1" describes.

thinking **it** through

How can the use of technology (such as databases, computers, and communication technology) help prevent a seller from having to answer, "I don't know the answer to that question. But I'll find out and call you with the information as soon as I can get it"?

DIRECT DENIAL

At times salespeople face objections based on incomplete or inaccurate information of the buyer. They should respond by providing information or correcting facts. When using **direct denial**, the salesperson makes a relatively strong statement to indicate the error the prospect has made. For example:

BUYER: I am not interested in hearing about your guidance systems. Your firm was one of the companies recently indicted for fraud, conspiracy, and price fixing by a federal grand jury. I don't want to do business with such a firm.

SALESPERSON: I'm not sure where you heard that, but it simply is not true. Our firm has never been involved in such activity, and our record is clean. If you would care to tell me the source of your information, I'm sure we can clear this up. Maybe you're confusing us with another firm.

BUILDING Partnerships

10.1

YES, YOU CAN REFUSE TO DO BUSINESS WITH A PROSPECT

Occasionally, but not often, when an objection arises, it is best for the salesperson to make a decision not to do business with the prospect. That's not because the salesperson doesn't like the question or takes offense at how it was phrased, but because in raising the objection, along with other cues and information, the prospect is revealing that she will not be a good customer.

This is counter to what many salespeople have been taught. As one expert, Jason Compton, noted, "Salespeople are trained to accommodate, entice, and overcome objections, not to raise their own. As organizations take an increasingly long-term view of their sales relationships, however, it is clear that the right decision for some sales opportunities is simply to walk away from the customer who will not be part of a healthy, profitable relationship for years to come." Martha Rogers, cofounder of Peppers & Rogers Group, agrees: "Customers have a right to say, 'This is not a good deal,' and merchants have that same right."

For one property management group, Home America Property Management, the use of "no" when dealing with potential customers is a daily occurrence. The firm has found that refusing to do business with customers who are

not going to be profitable is one of the key ways in which it can maintain a strong presence in its marketplace while maximizing long-term profitability.

One small publisher decided not to do business with one of the largest distributors in the country because that distributor kept raising objections and making demands that were not profitable for the publisher to meet. Less than six months later, that distributor called back asking to do business with the publisher; this time it agreed to follow the publisher's methods rather than push for its own demands. Why the change? The distributor realized that the publisher was the only one that could supply the books, and it had no choice other than doing business with the publisher on its terms.

Remember that satisfied customers are going to be one of your best sources of new prospects. Imagine what would happen if you allowed people to be your customers (when you should have said "no" instead) and then they were dissatisfied and gave your company a bad reputation.

Sources: Jason Compton, "The Power of No," *1to1media*, March/April 2008, pp. 40–41; http://creditmanagementassociation.org; personal experience.

No one likes to be told that he or she is wrong, so direct denial must be used with caution. It is appropriate only when the objection is blatantly inaccurate and potentially devastating to the presentation. The salesperson must also possess facts to back up such a denial. Direct denial should never be used if the prospect is merely stating an opinion or if the objection is true. For example, direct denial would be inappropriate to this objection: "I don't like the feel of simulated leather products." Direct denial should be avoided even for a false statement if the objection is of little importance to the buyer. An indirect denial would be more appropriate in that case.

INDIRECT DENIAL

In the **indirect denial method**, the salesperson denies the objection but attempts to soften the response. The salesperson takes the edge off the response by agreeing with the prospect that the objection is an important one. Prospects expect salespeople to disagree; instead, a salesperson who recognizes the sincerity of the objection will carefully respect the prospect's view. This approach avoids a direct contradiction and confrontation. To begin an answer, a salesperson would do well to agree with the prospect, but only to the extent that the agreement does not weaken the validity of the salesperson's later denial. For example:

BUYER: Your machines break down more often than those of most of your major competitors.

SALESPERSON: I can see why you might feel that way. Just 10 years ago that statement would have been right on target. However, things have changed with our new quality assurance program. In fact, just last year Syncos Ratings, a well-respected independent evaluator of quality in our industry, rated us as number one for fewest breakdowns.

The important features of indirect denial are that salespeople recognize the position of the customer who makes the objection and then continue by introducing substantial evidence. The beginning statement should always be true and assure the prospect that the question is a good one. Examples of such statements follow:

With the market the way it is today, I can certainly see why you're concerned about that.

I'll bet 90 percent of the people I call on voice the same concern.

That's really an excellent question, and it allows me to clear up a misconception that perhaps I've given you.

Indirect denial should never be used if the prospect has raised a valid point or is merely expressing an opinion. It can be used for all personality types and is especially effective for amiables and analyticals because they like less assertive salespeople.

COMPENSATION METHOD

Every product has some advantages and some disadvantages compared to competing products. Also, an absolutely perfect product or service has never been developed; the firm always has to make cost–benefit decisions about what features to include.

Buyers note these trade-offs and often object because the salesperson's product is less than perfect. The wise salesperson will admit that such objections are valid and then proceed to show any compensating advantages. This approach is called the **compensation method** of responding to objections. Here is an example:

PROSPECT: This machine has only four filling nozzles. Your competitor's has six nozzles.

SALESPERSON: You're absolutely right. It has only four nozzles, but it costs $4,000 less than the competitor's models, and you said you needed a model that is priced in the lower range. Also, our nozzles are designed for easy maintenance. You have to remove only four screws to get to the filter screens. Most other models have at least 10 screws. Fewer screws will reduce downtime considerably, which is something else you said you were very concerned about.

The compensation method is an explicit use of the multiattribute model discussed in Chapter 3. A low score on one attribute can be compensated for by a high score on another attribute. In fact, the compensation method is often referred to as the **superior benefit method** because the benefit of one attribute overcomes a concern about a less important attribute. The method can be effective for many objections and concerns. It seems most appropriate for analyticals, who are accustomed to conducting trade-off analyses. However, it is useful for all other personality types as well.

Of course the buyer may not value the compensating advantages. The buyer may really need the features at issue (perhaps the machine must have six nozzles to work with another piece of the prospect's equipment). In such cases salespeople can recommend a different product (from their own line, if available, or from a competitor) or search for other prospects.

Another time that the compensation method may be used is when the prospect says, "I'm just going to think about it. I'll be in touch with you later." The seller can show how acting today more than compensates for the "pain" of making a decision today. These reasons usually include explaining the hidden costs of delaying the decision (it will go off sale, you will be saving money over your current system each month that you have our proposed system, our product may be out of stock when you need it, summer is a particularly good time to install a new system, or the like).

A buyer may question the credibility and knowledge of a salesperson. In this situation the salesperson can use the referral method to help resolve those concerns.

REFERRAL METHOD

When buyers' objections reflect their own attitudes or opinions, the salesperson can show how others held similar views before trying the product or service. In this method, called the **referral method** or the **feel–felt–found method**, the salesperson goes on to relate that others actually found their initial opinions to be unfounded after they tried the product:

PROSPECT: I don't think my customers will want to buy a DVD player with all these fancy features.

SALESPERSON: I can certainly see how you feel. Bob Scott, down the road in Houston, felt the same way when I first proposed that he sell these. However, after he agreed to display them next to his current DVD line, he found that his customers were very interested. In fact, he called me four days later to order more.

Those who teach this as the feel–felt–found method highlight the importance of the proper sequence, as well as the person or people identified in each stage. The sequence should be as follows: I can see how you feel . . . others felt the same way . . . yet they found. . . . Inexperienced salespeople often mix up the order or the parties identified (for example, by saying ". . . yet you will find").

Proof of the salesperson's assertion in the form of a testimonial letter strengthens the method; in fact, some trainers refer to this approach as the **third-party-testimony method**. If a letter is not available, the salesperson might be able to supply the name and phone number of the third party. The salesperson should always secure the third party's permission first, however. (See Chapter 9 for suggestions about testimonials and references.)

Although the referral method can be used for all personality types, it seems most appropriate for expressives and amiables. Both types tend to care about what other people think and are doing.

REVISIT METHOD

When using the **revisit method** (also called the **boomerang method**) of responding to objections, the salesperson turns the objection into a reason for buying the product or service. This method can be used in many situations (when making an appointment, during the presentation, when attempting to secure commitment, and in postsale situations):

> BUYER: I don't think these would sell in my gun shop. They're really drab looking.
>
> SALESPERSON: It's interesting that you mention that. In fact, their drab color is probably their best selling point and the reason you should carry them. You see, when a hunter is in the field, the last thing she wants to do is attract attention to herself. Thanks to the finish we use on this gear . . .

The revisit method requires care. It can appear very pushy and "salesy." This method does have useful applications, however. Often the product or service is actually designed to save the buyer substantial amounts of time or money. If the buyer objects to spending either the time to listen or the money, the revisit method may be a powerful tool to help the buyer see the benefit of investing these resources.

This method works with most personality types. Drivers may require the revisit method more often than other buyers because drivers tend to erect time constraints and other barriers and are less willing to listen to just any salesperson's presentation.

ACKNOWLEDGE METHOD

At times the buyer voices opinions or concerns more to vent frustration than anything else. When this occurs, the best strategy may be to use the **acknowledge method,** also called the **pass-up method.** Simply let the buyer talk, acknowledge that you heard the concern, pause, and then move on to another topic.

> BUYER: Hey, you use Tiger Woods in your commercials, don't you? Sure you do. Now I want to tell you that I don't like what he stands for! Kids today need a role model they can look up to. What happened to the kind of role models we used to have?
>
> SALESPERSON: I certainly understand your concern. I remember my dad talking about some of his role models and the respect he had for them. [*Pause*] What were we talking about? Oh, yes, I was telling you about the coupon drop we are planning.

In this example the salesperson used the acknowledge method because the buyer apparently was just blowing off steam. A buyer who really wanted some response from the salesperson would have used the salesperson's pause to ask a direct question (Can't you change your commercials?) or make a statement (I refuse to do business with companies that use stars like Tiger Woods in their commercials!).

In reality a salesperson often can do little about some prospects' opinions. What are the chances that this salesperson's firm will pull a $5 million ad campaign because one buyer objects? It is doubtful that a firm would take such action unless the buyer had tremendous power in the relationship.

Sometimes the salesperson can use the acknowledge method by simply agreeing with the prospect and then moving on, which suggests to the buyer that the concern really should not be much of an issue. For example:

> BUYER: You want $25 for this little plastic bottle?!
>
> SELLER: Uh-huh. That's what they cost . . . [*Pause*] Now do you see the switch on this side? It's used if you ever need to . . .

The acknowledge method should not be used if the objection raised is factually false. Also, it should not be used if the salesperson, through probing, could help clarify the buyer's thinking on the topic. Experience is the key to making such a determination. In general, though, the acknowledge method should be used sparingly.

POSTPONE METHOD

In the early part of a sales interview, the prospect may raise objections that the salesperson would prefer to answer later in the presentation, after discovering the prospect's needs. Using the **postpone method,** the salesperson would ask permission to answer the question at a later time:

> BUYER [*very early in the call*]: How much does the brass engraving equipment cost?
>
> SALESPERSON: If you don't mind, I would prefer to answer that question in a few minutes. I really can't tell you how much it will cost until I learn more about your engraving needs and know what kinds of features you are looking for.

The prospect will seldom refuse the request if the sales representative appears to be acting in good faith. The sales representative then proceeds with the presentation until the point at which the objection can best be answered.

Some objections are best answered when they occur; others can be responded to most effectively by delaying the answer. Experience should guide the sales representative. The salesperson should take care not to treat an objection lightly or let it appear that he or she does not want to answer the question. Another danger in postponing is that the buyer will be unable to focus on what the salesperson is saying until the concern is addressed. On the other hand, the salesperson is responsible for helping the buyer to critically evaluate the solution offered, and often the buyer can process information effectively only after learning preliminary facts.

Salespeople make the most use of the postponement method when a price objection occurs early in the presentation. However, this method can be used for almost any type of objection or question. For example, postponing discussions about guarantees, delivery schedules, implementation time frames, and certain unique product features until later in the presentation is often preferable.

What if the buyer is convinced that he or she needs the answer right now? Then the salesperson should answer the objection now. Salespeople usually have more to lose by demanding that the buyer wait for information than by simply providing the answer when the buyer strongly requests it. For example:

> PROSPECT: What are the delivery schedules for this new product?
>
> SALESPERSON: I would really prefer to discuss that after we talk about our unique production process and extensive quality control measures.
>
> PROSPECT: No, I want to know now!
>
> SALESPERSON: Well, keep in mind that my later discussion about the production process will shed new light on the topic. We anticipate a four- to five-month delivery time after the contract reaches our corporate headquarters.

USING THE METHODS

The seven methods just discussed appear in sales training courses across all industries and geographic boundaries. To help you more easily distinguish the

Exhibit 10.5
Responding to Objections: Using Each Method

Objection: Your product's quality is too low.

Responses*

Direct denial: That simply is not true. Our product has been rated as the highest in the industry for the last three years.

Indirect denial: I can certainly see why you would be concerned about quality. Actually, though, our product quality has been rated as the highest in the industry for the last three years.

Compensation: I agree that our quality is not as high as that of some of our competitors. However, it was designed that way for consumers who are looking for a lower-priced alternative, perhaps just to use in a weekend cottage. So you see, our somewhat lower quality is actually offset by our much lower price.

Referral: I can certainly understand how you feel. Mortimer Jiggs felt the same way before he bought the product. But after using it, he found that the quality was actually equal to that of other products.

Revisit: The fact that the quality is lower than in other products is probably the very reason you should buy it. You said that some of your customers are looking for a low-priced product to buy for their grandchildren. This product fills that need.

Acknowledge: I understand your concern. You know, one of the things I always look for is how a product's quality stacks up against its cost. [Pause] Now, we were talking about . . .

Postpone: That's an interesting point. Before discussing it fully, I would like to cover just two things that I think will help you better understand the product from a different perspective. OK?

*These are not necessarily good answers to the stated objection. Also, the choice of method would depend on whether the objection is factual. Thus the replies given in this table are designed simply to differentiate the various methods.

---

differences among the various methods, Exhibit 10.5 provides an example of the use of each method for the objection, "Your product's quality is too low."

Salespeople often combine methods when answering an objection. For example, a price objection may initially be postponed and then be discussed later using the compensation method. At other times several methods can be used in one answer. Here is an example:

> BUYER: I don't think this product will last as long as some of the other, more expensive competitive products.
>
> SALESPERSON: That's probably the very reason you should buy it [*revisit method*]. It may not last quite as long, but it is less than half the cost of competitive products [*compensation method*]. I can certainly understand your concern, though. You know, Mark Hancock felt the way you do. He was concerned about the product's life. But after he used our product for one year, he found that its life expectancy didn't create any problems for his production staff [*referral method*].

Sometimes the buyer will ask multiple questions at once—for example, "How much did you spend on R&D last year, what percentage of your revenue does that represent, and what is your R&D model going forward?" What is a seller to do? Remembering the questions so they don't get lost, the salesperson answers them one by one.

Before moving on with the presentation, the salesperson needs to make sure that the buyer agrees that all objections have been completely answered. Without this commitment, the salesperson does not

Make sure the buyer agrees before moving on.

know whether the buyer understands the answer or whether the buyer's concerns have been fully addressed. To achieve this commitment, the salesperson can use one or more of the following types of phrases: Did I answer your question? Does that make sense? Do you see why that issue is not as important as you originally thought? Did that resolve your concern?

OBJECTIONS WHEN SELLING TO A GROUP OF BUYERS

Selling to a group of buyers (see Chapter 8) requires some extra care. If one person offers an objection, the seller should try to get a sense of whether other buyers share the concern. At times it may make sense to throw the issue back to the group. For example, if a buyer says that the people in his or her department won't attend the type of training sessions being proposed, the seller might respond as follows: Does anyone else have that same problem in their department? You all know your organizational climate better than I do. Have any of you found a way to deal with that issue that you would like to share with us? Any response from the seller should usually be directed to all buyers, not just the one who asked the question. After responding, the seller needs to make sure that all buyers are satisfied with the answer before moving on.

THE PRICE OBJECTION

Price is the perhaps the most frequently mentioned obstacle to obtaining commitment. In fact, about 20 percent of buyers are thought to buy purely on the basis of price (which means that a full 80 percent buy for reasons other than price). As a result, all salespeople need to prepare for price objections. This section relates the concepts covered in this chapter to this common objection.

Price is still an issue even between partnering firms. One leading firm in its industry has estimated that only 3 percent of its orders are sold at list price; the rest are price-discounted.[7]

Unfortunately the first response of many salespeople to a price objection is to lower the price. Inexperienced salespeople, desiring to gain business, often quote the lowest possible price as quickly as possible. They forget that for a mutually beneficial long-term relationship to exist, their firm must make a fair profit. Also, by cutting prices the firm has to sell more to maintain profit margins, as Exhibit 10.6 clearly illustrates.[8]

When faced with a price objection, salespeople should ensure that they have up-to-date information, establish the value of the product, and use communication tools effectively.

USE UP-TO-DATE INFORMATION

Successful salespeople make sure they have the most current pricing information available to them. They know not only their prices but competitors' prices as well. Firms are helping salespeople in this regard. For example, many firms have developed intranet sites for their salespeople. If a salesperson finds that the company's price points are a little higher than the competition, the salesperson can use the intranet site to look for some sales or trade-in program that she or he can leverage to get the deal. It is important for sellers to have correct pricing facts.

ESTABLISH THE VALUE

The product's value must be established before the salesperson spends time discussing price. The value expected determines the price a prospect is willing to pay. Unless the salesperson can build value to exceed the price asked, a sale will not occur.[9] As a rule, value cannot be established during the early stages of the presentation.

Exhibit 10.6
Look before You Cut
Prices! You Must Sell
More to Break Even

Cut Price	Present Gross Profit					
	5.0%	10.0%	15.0%	20.0%	25.0%	30.0%
1%	25.0	11.1	7.1	5.3	4.2	3.4
2	66.6	25.0	15.4	11.1	8.7	7.1
3	150.0	42.8	25.0	17.6	13.6	11.1
4	400.0	66.6	36.4	25.0	19.0	15.4
5	—	100.0	50.0	33.3	25.0	20.0
6	—	150.0	66.7	42.9	31.6	25.0
7	—	233.3	87.5	53.8	38.9	30.4
8	—	400.0	114.3	66.7	47.1	36.4
9	—	1,000.0	150.0	81.8	56.3	42.9
10	—	—	200.0	100.0	66.7	50.0
11	—	—	275.0	122.2	78.6	57.9
12	—	—	400.0	150.0	92.3	66.7
13	—	—	650.0	185.7	108.3	76.5
14	—	—	1,400.0	233.3	127.3	87.5
15	—	—	—	300.0	150.0	100.0
16	—	—	—	400.0	177.8	114.3
17	—	—	—	566.7	212.5	130.8
18	—	—	—	900.0	257.1	150.0
19	—	—	—	1,900.0	316.7	172.7
20	—	—	—	—	400.0	200.0
21	—	—	—	—	525.0	233.3
22	—	—	—	—	733.3	275.0
23	—	—	—	—	1,115.0	328.6
24	—	—	—	—	2,400.0	400.0
25	—	—	—	—	—	500.0

A business truism says that you can cut, cut, cut until you cut yourself out of business. This can certainly apply to cutting prices in an effort to increase profits. The two don't necessarily go together. For example, select the gross profit being earned at present from those shown at the top of the chart. Follow the left column down until you line up with the proposed price cut. The intersected figure represents the percentage of increase in unit sales required to earn the same gross profit realized before the price cut. Obviously it helps to know this figure so you don't end up with a lot of work for nothing.

See for yourself: Assume that your present gross margin is 25 percent and that you cut your selling price 10 percent. Locate the 25 percent column under Present Gross Profit. Now follow the column down until you line up with the 10 percent cut in selling price in column 1. You will need to sell 66.7 percent more units to earn the same margin dollars as at the previous price.

Price objections are best handled with a two-step approach. First, the salesperson should try to look at the objection from the customer's viewpoint, asking questions to clarify the customer's perspective: "Too high in what respect, Mr. Jones? Could you tell me how much we are out of line? We are usually quite competitive on this model, so I am surprised you find our price high. . . . Are the other quotes you have for the same size engine?"

After learning more about the customer's perspective, the next step is to sell value and quality rather than price (see Chapter 9 for a full discussion of the customer value proposition). Most customers prefer to buy less expensive products if they believe they will receive the same benefits. However, many customers will pay more for higher quality when the quality benefits and features are pointed out to them. Many high-quality products appear similar to lower-quality products; thus salespeople need to emphasize the features that justify a difference.

For example, a Premier Industrial salesperson who sells industrial fasteners and supplies may hear this objection: "That bolt costs $750! I could buy it elsewhere for $75." The salesperson should reply, "Yes, but that bolt is inside your most important piece of production equipment. Let's say you buy that $75 bolt. How much employee time and production downtime would it take to disassemble the machine again and replace that one bolt?" The salesperson can then engage in a complete cost–benefit analysis (see Chapter 9) to solidify the point.

A supplier of integrated circuits (ICs) was competing with another company whose price was 10 cents less. The buyer asked for a price concession, noting that the competitor's product was obviously less expensive. Unbeknownst to the supplier, however, the buyer had already examined the value propositions of the two companies and determined that the higher-priced one was actually worth 12 cents more than the less expensive one, due to services offered. Thus, in reality, the buyer had already realized that the higher-priced one was actually less expensive in terms of value (12 cents more in value minus the 10 cents higher in price = 2 cents higher in value per IC). The higher-priced supplier caved in and gave the buyer a 10 cent reduction in price, costing his firm $500,000 (5 million units at 10 cents each) in potential profits! And the sad fact is that the buyer was already planning on going with the higher-priced supplier.[10]

Intangible features can also provide value that offsets price. Some of these features are services, company reputation, and the salesperson:

- Good service in the form of faster deliveries, technical advice, and field assistance is but one of the many intangibles that can spell value, savings, and profits to a customer. For example, one company cut its prices in response to buyers' demands. However, the company later found that what the customers really wanted was technical support. As the company cut its prices, it had only reinforced its image as low-priced with little technical support.

- For a customer tempted to buy on price alone, salespeople can emphasize the importance of having a thoroughly reliable source of supply: the salesperson's company. It has been demonstrated time and again that quality is measured by the reputation of the company behind it.

- Customers value sales representatives who go out of their way to help with problems and promotions—salespeople who keep their word and follow through when they start something. These services are very valuable to customers.

USE COMMUNICATION TOOLS EFFECTIVELY

One pharmaceutical salesperson often hears that her company's drug for migraines is too expensive. Her response is to paint a word picture:[11]

DOCTOR: How much does this product cost?

SALESPERSON: It costs about $45. . . . There are 15 doses per bottle, so it ends up about $3 per dose.

DOCTOR: That's too much money!

SALESPERSON: Consider your patients who have to lie in the dark because their headaches are so bad they can't see straight, can't think straight, and are nauseated by migraine pain. A price of $3 is really inexpensive to relieve these patients' pain, wouldn't you agree?

Just telling customers about quality and value is not enough; they must be shown. Top salespeople use the communication tools discussed in Chapter 9 to describe more clearly the quality and value of their products. This process includes activities such as demonstrating the product, showing test results and quality control procedures, using case histories, and offering testimonials.

DEALING WITH TOUGH CUSTOMERS

Sellers need to maintain the positive attitude discussed earlier, even with rude, hard-to-get-along-with prospects. It's not easy, and it's not fun.[12]

Salespeople must learn to deal with tough prospects and customers.

Sellers need to realize that we all have bad days. Maybe the buyer is having one. If the rudeness is quite blatant and the seller believes that this behavior is just due to the timing of the visit, the seller might say, "I'm sensing that this might not be the best time to talk. Should we reschedule for another time?"

If the buyer continues to communicate aggressively, being downright rude, you probably need to call attention to the fact.[13] After all, to develop a long-term win–win relationship and partnership, you both need to be on the same footing. Perhaps saying something like this will clear the air: "I'm sorry, Joe. I don't know quite how to say this. But it seems to me that you wish to argue more than learn about my products. I'll gladly continue if you think we can both approach this problem with professionalism and courtesy." By doing so, you are asserting yourself and confronting the issue head-on. At the same time, you are avoiding an emotional reaction of anger. Of course it is important to keep in mind the various personalities that buyers can have (see Chapter 5) and the adjustments suggested for each.

Also remember that the buyer's culture often dictates how he or she will respond to a seller. For example, Germans are known as being thorough, systematic, and well prepared, but they are also rather dogmatic and thus lack flexibility and the desire to compromise. As a result, sellers not accustomed to such a culture could have difficulty dealing with a German prospect who raises a price objection in a strong tone of voice.

Believe it or not, some of the toughest customers aren't those who are noisy and boisterous. Rather, they are often the passive ones, the quiet ones—the ones

Believe it or not, the hardest prospects can be the quiet ones.

who don't object, don't question, and don't buy. What should a seller do? Be open, direct, and honest. Stop talking. Ask questions. Try your best to get the buyer involved. Establish trust so the buyer can feel confident enough to ask questions. If the buyer is still quiet, use a trial close. If this doesn't result in gaining commitment, ask the prospect what he or she would like to do at this point.

SELLING YOURSELF

You will be doing a lot of selling in the next couple of years, from trying to get a job out of college, to getting promotions and raises. You may be selling township leaders on the need to enact new rules that are consistent with your views and may be trying to convince your neighbors to keep their dogs on their own property.

In all of those situations, you can expect that objections are going to arise. The best thing you can do is to prepare for those objections. Make a list of every possible objection or question that someone can raise and then write down what you consider to be a healthy, helpful response. Some responses are going to require you to do more homework, like preparing visuals and graphs, researching what others have done, and analyzing the costs and benefits of going with other approaches. So do your homework well, and give a polished, well-reasoned presentation of your idea.

Sometimes it is best to just forestall known concerns. For example, maybe you've never had a sales job in your life. Don't wait for the interviewer to raise that concern (or worse yet, never raise it, but be thinking it all the time). Instead, raise the issue yourself: "As you can see, I've never held a sales job before. But let me tell you why I think you should still strongly consider me for this sales position. If you look at my résumé you'll see. . . ."

Remember to probe to make sure you know what the other party is objecting to; then provide a clear, unemotional response that addresses those concerns. And don't forget to always probe after you've addressed the objection to make sure your response resolved the concern. In many situations the other party will never tell you that you didn't answer a question unless you ask.

If other parties go off the deep end and start shouting or being overly aggressive, don't go there with them. Bring them back to reasoning and logical discussion. Even if you can't convince them, you will impress others who might be observing the situation. And you will be developing skills in how best to deal with life's toughest situations.

SUMMARY

Responding to objections is a vital part of a salesperson's responsibility. Objections may be offered at any time during the relationship between buyer and salesperson. They are to be expected, even welcomed, and they must be handled with skill and empathy.

Successful salespeople carefully prepare effective responses to buyers' concerns. Salespeople need to develop a positive attitude, commit to always telling the truth, refrain from interrupting, anticipate and forestall known objections, and learn how to evaluate objections.

Buyers object for many reasons. They may have no money, or they may not need the product. They may need more information or misunderstand some information already offered. They may be accustomed to another product, may not think the value exceeds the cost, or may not like the product's features. They may want to get rid of the salesperson or may not trust the salesperson or his or her company. They may want time to think or may object for many other reasons.

Effective methods of responding to objections are available, and their success has been proved. Methods exist both for concerns that are not true and for objections that either are true or are only the buyer's opinion. Sensitivity in choosing the right method is vital. Salespeople need to develop skill in responding to price objections and in dealing with tough customers. Nothing will substitute for developing skill in these areas.

KEY TERMS

ETHICS PROBLEMS

1. A prospect has just raised an objection about the price of your service, which is commercial carpet cleaning. You know that the service you are selling usually goes on sale a couple of times each year, but you're not sure when the next time will be. It could be as soon as a few weeks. Should you tell the buyer about the possible lower price?

2. One student in a selling class once said, "Why are we learning these objection-handling methods? These techniques are just to help us manipulate our buyers!" How would you respond?

QUESTIONS AND PROBLEMS

1. Categorize each of the following responses into the five basic types of objections. Then illustrate one way to handle each:
   a. After a sales presentation, the lawyer says, "You've made some good points, but your competitor's product can do just about everything yours can do."
   b. After the salesperson answers an objection, the prospect remarks, "I guess your product is all right, but as I told you when you walked in, things are going pretty well for us right now without your product."
   c. After a thorough presentation, the prospect answers, "Whew, that's a lot of money!"
   d. The customer says, "I can buy that online for a lot less than what you're selling it for."

2. Betty Hadaldo spent considerable time working with a prospective buyer. She thought a good order would be forthcoming on her next call. A portion of her conversation with the buyer went as follows:

   BUYER: You know, I like what I hear about your concrete pumping service. But how can I be sure it will be available on the days that we need it for our next project?

   BETTY: We've never had any real complaints before. I'm pretty sure they will be easily available.

   BUYER: You are sure of that?

   BETTY: Well, I've never heard of any problems that I can remember.

   BUYER: [appearing unconvinced and looking at some papers on his desk without glancing up]: I'll let you know later what I plan to do. Thanks for dropping by.

   How can you improve on Betty's answer to the buyer's concern?

3. Describe the differences between postponing an objection and forestalling an objection. Then provide a clear example of appropriate postponing for this objection: "This iPod is way too expensive. I can buy MP3 players much cheaper than buying your iPod!"

4. Occasionally a buyer will offer several objections at one time. How would you respond if a buyer made the following comments without pausing? "Say, how long does it take your lab to get the results back to us? And what if we need same-day service sometime? Are your technicians certified? That's important, you know!"

5. In "Building Partnerships 10.1" you learned that it is OK to walk away from some prospects and just say "no" to their requests. Make a list of rules you could follow that indicate when it might be appropriate to walk away from a prospect, assuming you are a salesperson.

6. Choose a restaurant in your town. Assume that you work at that restaurant and are planning to make calls to campus club organizations. Assume that the restaurant has a private meeting room available that will seat 25 people. Your objective is to have officers of the clubs schedule their meetings at the restaurant.
   a. Make a list of objections you may expect to encounter.
   b. What can you do to meet these objections effectively? List the answers you would propose, and label the methods used.

7. In "From the Buyer's Seat 10.1" you read about ways that salespeople inappropriately handled the "I can get a better deal somewhere else" objection. How would you respond if you were a salesperson who heard that objection if you knew how other mortgage wholesalers were handling the situation (by offering special favors)?

8. You have been describing to a retail security officer and his boss a new security camera that your firm just introduced. The camera has tracking features that make it easier for security officers to review tapes. The security officer says, "I would really like that!" The boss says, "Well, if it's what you think we need, OK. How much does it cost?" At your reply, "This one is $2,498," the boss exclaims, "For that little thing?" What should you say or do?

9. For each of the following objections, provide answers that clearly demonstrate the direct denial and indirect denial methods. Assume each objection is not true:
   a. My obstetric patients will never need that service.
   b. The cost of replacing the filter will be more than just buying a new unit.
   c. I heard that the paint used in manufacturing your unit can cause cancer.
   d. I can buy this cheaper online.

10. For each of the following objections, provide answers that clearly demonstrate the compensation method and referral method. Assume all the objections are either true or are the prospect's opinion:
    a. Your repossession service costs a lot of money!
    b. I don't think our customers will like the new beverage you're selling.
    c. Your diesel mechanics aren't certified by the ATSG.
    d. My customers have never asked for this brand of dishwasher.

CASE PROBLEMS

case 10.1

BrainScope (Part B)

An estimated 1.6 million to 3.8 million sports-related traumatic brain injuries (TBIs) occur each year. Yet all too often, when a person gets hurt in sports, the team doctor asks a few questions and, assuming there are no major concerns, sends the player right back into the game. However, studies show that if a player gets another concussion before the brain has healed, there is a much greater chance of long-term brain damage.

The problem is that there isn't an MRI machine at the sidelines. But that may change if the BrainScope company has its way. It will be introducing a new product that will gauge how serious a concussion is. The tool is small enough and inexpensive enough for all teams to have one on their sidelines.

The feedback from the BrainScope is a meter that shows if brain activity is anywhere near the danger zone. The system does this by picking up brain signals and comparing them to 15,000 scans in its database. The database was created based on scans performed at New York University's Brain Research Lab.

Some doctors claim the technology isn't cutting-edge. Originally developed in the 1930s, the technology uses qEEG (quantitative electroencephalograms).

However, the developers of the BrainScope claim that their new device was developed with the advice of 30 leading brain experts.

According to the company's Web site, "BrainScope's novel application of advanced mathematics and miniaturized hardware is designed to bridge the limitations of traditional EEG tools (bulky, expensive, need expert data interpretation) to provide easy-to-use, noninvasive, timely, frontline tools that can assist with an initial assessment of brain function as well as provide adjunctive assessment across the brain care path."

The BrainScope could also be used at hospitals as emergency room testing devices to see if a patient has a real problem and thus needs to have more sophisticated testing done. The company is currently focusing its efforts on military settings. For example, the U.S. Army can deploy the device in combat situations. This would be very helpful to assess soldiers who were nearby when a roadside bomb exploded.

In August 2009 BrainScope's ZOOM-100DC brain electrical activity data collection system was cleared for marketing by the U.S. Food and Drug Administration.

Assume you are selling the new ZOOM-100DC to a team trainer/physician for a local football or hockey team. Assume the tool will sell for $495.00 and comes with a four-year guarantee.

Questions

1. What objections could the buyer raise? (Use any assumptions necessary to develop this list.)
2. Provide a response to each objection you listed in Question 1 (make any assumptions necessary to create your responses). Include the name of the method you recommend for each objection.

case **10.2**

Bally Total Fitness
Concepts

Prestwick is a large multinational corporation that manufactures and sells furniture and kitchen and bath fixtures; it also has a group of 20 luxury resort destinations in France and Germany. Thanks to rapid expansion, Prestwick has been able to offer many benefits to its corporate headquarters employees, including a fitness center with a full-size gym. However, over the years, the size of the firm at corporate headquarters has grown tremendously (from 1,500 to over 2,500 employees), resulting in the fitness center becoming more and more crowded. On many days, employees can't get on a treadmill or find room to work out because of the large number of employees trying to use the facility. Currently Prestwick is managing the fitness center itself, staffing it with a small group of employees who oversee the operations there.

Amanda Hightower is a salesperson for Bally Total Fitness Concepts. Bally works with firms like Prestwick and designs and outfits new and remodeled fitness centers. Amanda was called by Jerry Mays, an assistant in the HR department, who told her that Prestwick could really use a larger and more comprehensive facility. However, Jerry asked that his name not be used when Amanda called on the firm.

Amanda made an appointment to meet with Barb Granroth, vice president of human resources for Prestwick, to discuss Prestwick's current fitness center and how Bally could improve it. Specifically, Amanda is planning to discuss creating a larger fitness center with new equipment. Amanda also intends to suggest that the larger and remodeled facility be managed and staffed by Bally personnel.

Questions

1. List objections you think might occur during this first meeting with Barb. Make any assumptions necessary to develop this list.

2. Describe how you would respond to each objection listed in Question 1. Be sure to label the methods. Make any assumptions necessary to create your responses.

ROLE PLAY CASE

Today you will repeat your role play presentation from Chapter 9. (If you have not done role plays before, you will need to review the information about the various role play customers that can be found at the end of Chapter 3. If you didn't do the role play for Chapter 9, you will need to review that material also, which can be found at the end of Chapter 9.) When you act as the observer today, you should identify what objection-handling method the seller used and if it was done effectively. The professor will give you a sheet to use as a buyer, listing objections for you to use during the role play. When you sell, try to use a variety of objection-handling methods.

Note: For background information about these role plays, please see page 27.

To the instructor: Additional information needed to complete the role play is available in the Instructor's Manual.

ADDITIONAL REFERENCES

Bud, Peter Paul. *How to Be a Best Seller: 18 Simple and Proven Steps You Must Know to Succeed.* Lulu, 2009.

Compton, Jason. "The Power of No." *1to1media,* March/April 2008, pp. 40–41.

McGaulley, Michael. *How to Sell Face-to-Face Survival Guide.* ChamplainHouseMedia, 2010.

Mulvey, Richard. *Handling Objections/Closing the Sale.* Perception Business Skills, 2010.

Reilly, Tom. *Crush Price Objections: Sales Tactics for Holding Your Ground and Protecting Your Profit.* McGraw-Hill, 2010.

Shaltz, Gerry. *The DNA of Selling: What You Won't Learn in Business School.* iUniverse, 2009.

Taylor, Charles R., Kyung Hoon Kim, Eunju Ko, Myung Hwan Park, Dong Ryul Kim, and Hak Il Moon. "Does Having a Market Orientation Lead to Higher Levels of Relationship Commitment and Business Performance? Evidence from the Korean Robotics Industry." *Industrial Marketing Management* 37, no. 7 (October 2008), pp. 825–32.